THE BOOK OF HOAXES

THE BOOK OF HOAXES

An A–Z of Famous Fakes, Frauds and Cons

Stuart Gordon

HEADLINE

First published in 1995
by HEADLINE BOOK PUBLISHING

10 9 8 7 6 5 4 3 2 1

British Library Cataloguing in Publication Data

Gordon, Stuart
Book of Hoaxes
I. Title
001.95

ISBN 0-7472-1203-1

Typeset by
Letterpart Limited, Reigate, Surrey

Printed and bound in Great Britain by
Mackays of Chatham PLC, Chatham, Kent

HEADLINE BOOK PUBLISHING
A division of Hodder Headline PLC
338 Euston Road
London NW1 3BH

Contents

Dedication

This book's for Jenny and Skye and Steve at Penwaun,
for the three-month party and much good friendship;
It's for Lorraine my editor at Headline,
whose good humour and patience have been a life-saver;
Also it's very much for Cliff, who put up with me,
and gave me the space to write this book –
And particularly it's for Beth, who knows why . . .

Acknowledgements

My thanks are due to Cliff Johnson for contributing the piece on the **Presidential Nuclear Launch Authority** Cold War hoax.

Introduction

Human trickery and human credulity have always gone hand in hand. 'There's one born every minute' and 'Never give a sucker an even break' have been the watchwords and war cries of tricksters, hoaxers, pranksters and impostors and, at the lower end of the scale, conmen, fraudsters, swindlers, liars and cheats since the dawn of time. And with so many of us endlessly unsure what's actually real or not (and frequently preferring what's not), every society from Sumeria to today's era of virtual reality has offered innumerable opportunities for games of chance and illusion, innocent or otherwise. 'Illusion is the first of all pleasures', declared Voltaire, and maybe so, but precisely because of it two millennia ago the Romans asserted a commercial principle as true now as then: *Caveat emptor* – 'Let the buyer beware'. Then again, the Sufi poet Jalaluddin Rumi (1207–73) once reminded the world that: 'Counterfeiters exist only because there is true gold.'

Nothing is sure. Ambiguity and change underlie our every certainty. The sense of a cosmic joke is ancient – either that the world itself is an illusion (as in Buddhist belief) due to our own inability to see straight, or (dualist belief) that it's a hoax, ruled by a false god, not the true creator. The Bible, the world's most popular book, kicks off with a hoax of stunning proportions. The first thing Yahweh tells Adam and Eve is that if they eat of the fruit of the Tree of the Knowledge of Good and Evil, they will die. But the Serpent proves God a liar, and for so upsetting the applecart is ever after damned – as a liar. But even as the Gates of Eden slammed shut on monotheistic Judaea, elsewhere mythical tricksters were on the rampage – gods and goddesses hoaxing each other and shapeshifting to seduce mortals; mortals tricking the gods to steal fire; sly pranksters like Coyote, Raven, Renard the Fox and Mr Spider all on the prowl looking for the new mark, the next easy chicken – and so of course in time to the image of that old serpent, Satan himself, forever trying to cheat not-so-good-but-not-so-bad folks out of their immortal souls.

A sense of hoax, of contradiction, pervades human life. But what *is* a hoax? The *Oxford English Dictionary* defines it as 'a humorous or mischievous deception with which the credulity of the victim is imposed upon'. The word may be a contraction of 'hocus-pocus', in turn derived from *hoc corpus est* (a corruption of *hoc est enim corpus meum*), a phrase defining the point in the Catholic Mass when the bread turns into the body of Christ – a Protestant implication that transubstantiation is a lie, hocus-pocus, a delusion, a hoax.

So, hoaxing is about persuading another that what isn't, is, or vice versa. At its best it may be a prank, a practical joke committed to fool pompous officialdom, like **Cole**'s Bunga-Bunga hoax of 1910, or today to manipulate the media to make a point – American Alan **Abel**'s SINA scam, or Joey **Skaggs**'s 'Cathouse for Dogs' (which almost got him killed by outraged animal-lovers; pranksters take risks).

Pranks may be nasty or just plain silly, but there's rarely criminal intent in them. Typically they're meant to open people's eyes, get a laugh, or just draw attention to the prankster. When Cole dressed up as an Abyssinian prince and was officially piped aboard HMS *Dreadnought*, all Europe rocked with laughter. There was no criminal intent, he didn't steal anything – though doubtless the Admirals of the Fleet wanted to string him up for making such public idiots of them.

Pranks may often be less comic than cruel, yet they're preferable to frauds and cons designed to fleece suckers for private gain. But there you go. Such scams are as old as the hills. Check Genesis 27 for the tale of how Rebecca hoaxes blind Isaac her husband into blessing not Esau but Jacob. Indeed, the most holy institutions (if institutions can be holy) have never been averse to forgery for gain. For six centuries popes of Rome used the fake **Donation of Constantine** to support their claim to power. Glastonbury Abbey became the richest in England when tourist-pilgrims started flocking in to see the grave of King **Arthur** the monks said they'd found in their grounds. As for Turin's famous **Shroud**, that seems to have originated in a penniless widow's need for cash.

Today, despite new scams like **computer fraud** and **Hollywood** illusions, most frauds are just variations on ancient ways to part fools from their money, legally or illegally. Some display panache but many, however carefully planned and executed, are boringly motivated, and as such excluded here. But those with flair, like **Furguson** selling Nelson's Column and Buckingham Palace to tourists; **Lustig** conning Al Capone and getting away with it, and the incredible Sir Francis Drake scam pulled in the 1920s by Oscar Merril **Hartzell**, making him two million dollars before his luck ran out – they're all here.

Revenge as well as profit is often a motive, especially among art fakers like **de Hory**, **Hebborn** and **Keating**, despising the 'experts' they fool by feeding new Chagalls and Rembrandts on to the market. The best-known forger, Dutchman Han **Van Meegeren**, painted fake Vermeers so convincing that, arrested as a Nazi collaborator in 1945 for having sold one to Luftwaffe chief Hermann Göring, to save his neck he had to paint a new 'Vermeer' to prove the others were fake too.

In cases like this, as with the amazing impostures of men like **Demara** (who, masquerading as a naval surgeon, successfully operated under battle conditions without any medical training at all), few can conceal a sneaking admiration for the hoaxer. We all like seeing 'experts' brought down a peg or two, and often the victims of such hoaxes are only too glad to keep quiet, and refuse to press charges, so that men like Van Meegeren and Demara, no matter how outrageous their scams, rarely stay in jail long even when caught. And why they do it and what's psychologically wrong with them often seems much less interesting than their incredible persistence in pretending to be who they're not, and their success in fooling others with the pretence.

Women are less prominent in the field of hoax and fraud, *pace* Marthe **Hanau** and one or two others; imposture is more to their taste, as in the cases of 'James **Barry**', Princess **Caraboo** and Sarah **Wilson**. Most of us like to dress up and pretend to be someone else at some time or another, and even if there aren't as many fake princes and princesses about as there used to be, still, those who pull it off, like Cole or Stanley **Weyman**, always get more laughs than condemnation.

Likewise largely inoffensive are literary hoaxers, few of whom end up behind bars, though they may suffer public ridicule, as **Ireland**, **Macpherson**, and **Psalmanazar** found out two hundred years ago, or end up on the run, like the creator of Baron von Munchausen, Rudolf Eric **Raspe**. Today hoaxes like those of **Castaneda** or **Rampa** can prove highly lucrative for the author, with sales actually increasing once the scam is revealed. And even when, as with **Irving** or **Kujau**, the hoaxer goes to jail, he's rarely there for long. As with art experts, when publishers are fooled nobody is really upset. After all, as the French publisher Gaston Gallimard remarked, 'No one is more dishonest than authors – except publishers.'

Another kind of literary scam is pulled not so much for profit as to satirise best-sellers, as with Mike **McGrady**'s *Naked Came the Stranger* (1966), a joke at the expense of the steamy bonkbusters by Jacqueline Susann and Harold Robbins; or simply for fun, as with *The Cruise of the Kawa*, the fake travel book by 'Walter E. Traprock'.

As for real explorers and adventurers, fake claims are legion. The North Pole in particular seems to attract fraud. **Byrd**'s claim to have flown over it in 1926 was as false as **Peary**'s claim to have walked to it in 1909. Peary's claim remains widely regarded as genuine, but it seems almost certain that, though he got within a hundred miles of his goal, he never made it all the way. Yet his vanity and the years of struggle he'd invested in the attempt led him to insist that he had. Even more extraordinary, Frederick **Cook**, having faked a claim to have climbed Alaska's Mount McKinley in 1906, then faked a *second* claim; that he'd reached the North Pole, in 1909. Neither claim was believed, yet he maintained the pretence up to his dying day – as doubtless will Cesare **Maestri**, who still insists that in 1959 he climbed the Patagonian peak, Cerro Torre. On the other hand, the Scot James **Bruce**, derided in

England for claiming to have discovered the source of the Blue Nile, had in fact done so.

Morally more complex are scientific frauds to prove (or disprove) pet theories. Often it can be hard to tell if the hoax is deliberate, the result of self-deception, or (as in the tragedy of Austrian biologist Paul **Kammerer**) if the seeming hoaxer has been set up by a secret enemy. More clearly deliberate (and thus criminal) are the frauds by men like British psychologist Sir Cyril **Burt**, or the Soviet geneticist **Lysenko** – and it may come as a shock to some to learn that even **Newton** cooked data to support his theories. In addition, the academic world is beset by fake professors – men like Marvin **Hewitt**, who never had any of the degrees he claimed, and (yet again) the extraordinary Ferdinand Waldo **Demara**.

Another hoax-beset area is that benighted field, the paranormal. Yet, though it's as easy as falling off a log to discover and expose spurious cases of **levitation**, **psychic surgery**, ESP, contact with the dead via **mediums** and so on, it remains impossible to prove *all* such cases fake. Indeed, debunkers like Harry **Houdini** have been caught rigging evidence to disprove seemingly genuine phenomena. Hoaxers hoaxing hoaxers? Well, why not? It's all part of the Hall of Mirrors.

More dangerous are political or spiritual 'Big Lies' in which common prejudices are exploited to justify pogroms or persecutions. Take **anti-Semitic hoaxes**. The 'blood libel' (that Jews kidnapped and killed Christian infants in order to drink their blood) was as eagerly believed by medieval anti-Semites as the fake *Protocols of the Elders of Zion* were recently believed by Hitler and other Jew-haters to prove that an 'International Jewish Conspiracy' aimed to conquer the world. The result? Six million dead Jews.

Cult belief systems are especially hard to prove fake. For a start, it can be hard to tell how far their originators believe their own ravings. L. Ron **Hubbard** almost certainly didn't, but how about the **end-of-the-world scams** of fanatics like Jim Jones, David Koresh, David **Berg**, or the Russian leaders of the apocalyptic new **White Brotherhood of Kiev**? Do they really believe in the imminent end of the world, or is it just a scam to gain power over others? Did **Rajneesh** really believe he was God, or was it just a convenient way to collect a hundred Rolls-Royces? Such charismatic conmen typically offer the devotee false security in return for total obedience – and in these days of failing traditions, many will cling to whatever straw offers comfort, even if sceptics see only fraud, disinformation and psychological manipulation. And as for established beliefs, are they exempt? Modern research into **Christianity**'s roots suggests more than a little humbug in the transformation of a messianic, apocalyptic Judaic cult into the late Roman Empire's state religion. But how to untangle it? After all, 'History is the lie commonly agreed upon', and we all know **Richard III** was a hunchback – **Shakespeare** says so.

As complex is the murky area of 'False Memory Syndrome'; of past-life memories and the growing number of people who claim to recall being 'abducted' into UFOs. All too often such 'memories' are drawn out by faulty techniques of hypnotic regression that involve leading questions. Appropriate answers are taken as literally true. In such cases, all involved in the 'hoax' may not realise they conspire unconsciously to validate a false set of beliefs. They hoax themselves. As for the odd world of UFOlogy, in which nothing is as it seems, it's riddled with theories of conspiracy and deception, as with the Roswell Incident or the Gulf Breeze case. It becomes hard, if not impossible, to know who is fooling who; whether the reported phenomena have any objective reality, or if they originate purely in the imagination.

What is clear is that human beings have an inbuilt need to believe in something, even in a lie, and that this need makes most of us suckers at one time of our life or another. Nothing is ever as it seems, and so the world remains a riddling playground of opportunity for pranksters, hoaxers and fakers. 'Nothing is true,' said Hassan ibn Sabbah, 'The Old Man of the Mountains' (1054–1124). 'All is permitted.' Then again, maybe he didn't say it. So be warned. Few if any of the stories herein are reliable, though almost all are adapted from other books presenting them as the facts about fakery. There may even be a few of the author's own hoaxes – *fake* stories about non-existent hoaxes. How can you be sure? One tale included – derived from other recent accounts – concerns the Tasaday, an allegedly Stone Age tribe 'discovered' in 1971 amid the shrinking depths of rainforest in the Philippines. These accounts say that the Tasaday have been clearly revealed as a hoax pulled by a Filipino government minister who, bribing two local tribes to run about naked, brought in the Western media and made a packet. The Tasaday themselves had admitted the hoax!

Yet only last night I was watching a PBS TV documentary, *The Lost Tribe*, which asserts that the Tasaday are *not* a hoax – but neither are they 'Stone Age'. It now seems likely that about a century ago this tribe, originally part of another larger local tribe, fled into the jungle to avoid slavers, stayed there, and were only recently rediscovered when the rainforest was logged out. Maybe.

There's only one solution, and the Romans knew it all along.

'*Caveat emptor*', meaning: 'LET THE BUYER BEWARE.'

And thus, the motto of this, *The Book of Hoaxes* . . .

How to Use This Book

The system of cross-referencing in *The Book of Hoaxes* works as follows:

1. Bracketed references in ***BOLD ITALIC*** alongside the title of each entry refer to a specific general category of hoaxes (i.e., ***ART FORGERIES, PRANKS***, etc.) as headlined in the Concordance at the back of the book, under which headline all other entries relating to that specific area will be found listed alphabetically.

2. Bracketed references alongside the title of each entry in **BOLD** script alone (i.e., *See* **LUSTIG, 'Count' Victor**) refer to other related entries in the main body of the text.

3. References to other related entries in each entry's text are set **bold**, but in lower case, (i.e., Joey **Skaggs**).

Note on Sources

In referencing the sources used for each entry I have drawn so frequently on certain authors and texts that it becomes a waste of space to cite them in full time and time again. So instead I cite them in brief, e.g., Yapp, *op. cit.*, p.–, and list all such texts here below:

Blundell, Nigel, *The World's Greatest Crooks and Conmen*, Octopus Books, London 1982.

Clark, David, *Vanished! Mysterious Disappearances*, Michael O'Mara Books, London 1990.

Goldberg, M. Hirsch, *The Book of Lies*, Quill/William Morrow, New York 1990.

Kohn, Alexander, *False Prophets*, Basil Blackwell Ltd., Oxford 1986.

Larsen, Egon, *The Deceivers*, John Baker, London 1966.

Lindskoog, Kathryn, *Fakes, Frauds and Other Malarkey*, Zondervan, Grand Rapids, Michigan 1993.

Madison, Joyce, *Great Hoaxes, Swindles, Scandals, Cons, Stings, and Scams*, Signet Books, New York 1992.

McCormick, Donald, *Taken For a Ride*, Harwood-Smart, Blandford 1976.

Newnham, Richard, *The Guinness Book of Fakes, Frauds, and Forgeries*, Guinness Publishing, Enfield, Middlesex 1991.

Randi, James, *Flim-Flam!*, Prometheus Books, Buffalo, New York 1986.

Roberts, David, *Great Exploration Hoaxes*, Sierra Club, San Francisco 1982.

Stephen, Sir Leslie and Lee, Sir Sidney, *Dictionary of National Biography*, Oxford University Press, Oxford 1938 (1917).

Vale, V., and Juno, Andrea (eds), *Pranks!*, Re/Search #11, San Francisco 1987.

Wilson, Colin and Wilson, Damon, *Unsolved Mysteries Past and Present*, Headline, London 1993.

Yapp, Nick, *Hoaxers and Their Victims*, Robson Books, London 1992.

Other texts used are cited in full below each entry. Where there is no citation, the entry is based on two or more of the sources as given above, and is thus regarded as a story in common circulation not requiring specific reference.

The 'Ten Commandments for Conmen'

1. Patient listening, not fast talk, gets the conman his coups.
2. Never look bored.
3. Wait for the victim to reveal any political opinions, then agree with them.
4. Wait for the victim to reveal any religious opinions, then agree with them.
5. Hint at sex talk, but drop it if the victim shows no interest.
6. Never mention illness, unless a special concern is shown.
7. Never fish for personal details (they'll spill them all soon enough).
8. Never boast. Just let your importance be quietly obvious.
9. Never be untidy.
10. Never get drunk.

These helpful rules for successful swindling were devised and proposed by 'Count' Victor **Lustig** (1890–1947: 'the Man who Conned Capone', 'the Man who Sold the Eiffel Tower'; 'the best distributor of counterfeit money who ever lived'; etc., etc.). But would-be conmen please note: the Count died while serving a twenty-year jail sentence. Eleven of those years he spent in Alcatraz – not exactly a holiday camp. (See pages 186–9.)

A

'People will swallow anything at all,
provided you give it to them with a serious
demeanor.'

(Alan Abel, American prankster)

ABDUCTIONS (*See* **UFO ABDUCTIONS**)

ABEL, Alan (contemporary) (*MEDIA HOAXES*)
Perhaps the most prolific hoaxer in the USA today (though Joey **Skaggs**
runs him close), musician and comedian Alan Abel believes that laughter
is healthy; that most of us have an endless appetite for practical jokes,
and that 'People will swallow anything at all, providing you give it to
them with a serious demeanor.' Distinguishing between the unaccept-
able hoax (crazy thought, serious action, like planting a bomb on a plane
while masquerading as a baggage handler) and the acceptable variety
(serious thought, crazy action), he says 'improvisation is what life's
about'. Delighting in manipulating the media, which, he says, 'lies and
lies and lies', he adds 'On a slow news day I like to jump in and create
some havoc in between the axe murders and the hostage-taking'.
    Abel is famed for promoting the Society for Indecency to Naked
Animals (SINA); for his 1967 invention of the Topless String Quartet
('France's first gift to America since the Statue of Liberty'); for
perpetrating the (illusory) World Sex Olympics; and for running 'Yetta
Bronstein', an invented Jewish grandmother (his wife Jeanne), for the
presidency. His movie, *Is There Sex After Death?*, the *New York Times*
called 'The only really funny movie since Woody Allen's *Bananas*.' His
books include *Don't Get Mad, Get Even; How to Thrive on Rejection* and
The Great American Hoax (*Yours for Decency* in the UK).
    The SINA hoax dates from 1959. Stuck in a traffic jam beside a field
where two horses were copulating, the obvious embarrassment of other
motorists led Abel to write a satirical short story which he turned into 'a

living social satire, an allegory cloaked with the absurd purpose of putting panties on pets, half-slips on cows, and Bermuda shorts on horses'.[2] Inventing G. Clifford Prout Jr, the crank creator of the Society for Indecency to Naked Animals, he hired jobless actor Buck Henry to impersonate Prout. Telling NBC that Prout (said to have inherited $400,000 from his father) planned to build the society's membership before going nationwide with membership drives and publicity campaigns, Abel soon realised how easy it is to get publicity. In May 1959 Prout appeared on NBC's *Today* TV show to demand that all animals over four inches high be clothed for decency's sake. So few people realised it was a put-on that Abel hired pickets to march past the White House and engaged a full-time telephone answering service on MOrality-1-1963. SINA even managed to get a giant pâpier-maché horse removed from the New York office in Northwest Orient Airlines when Prout complained that even a naked *model* horse was offensive. His complaint about the RCA Victor dog 'Nipper' (as seen on HMV record labels) was less successful, but SINA continued to prosper, Prout visiting zoos and farms while Abel organised parades featuring the SINA Marching Band. Not even the awful cacophony produced by the band members, playing in whatever key suited them, stopped onlookers applauding in the belief that SINA was a genuinely worthy moral crusade. But then it got out of control. The Inland Revenue Service wrote demanding back taxes on the money Prout had supposedly inherited from his father. Dissatisfied with the written replies, they visited SINA's New York office and found it to be a broom closet acting as a reception point for the thousands of letters sent by supporters. They threatened prosecution but, realising it was a hoax and not wishing to seem stupid or humourless, left Abel and Prout alone. Yet by now the end was nigh. Buck Henry gained a part in a TV soap opera and, becoming well known, was identified as Prout and gave no more interviews as head of SINA. Even so, years later many people still believed that SINA had been genuine and that animals should be clothed for decency's sake.

Quite different (at least in its attitude to nudity, animal or human) was Abel's 1967 promotion of the Topless String Quartet from France. In a press release announcing their arrival in the USA he explained that Madeleine Boucher, Michelle André, Maria Tonchet and Gretchen Gansebrust (a cellist and three violinists) played topless so as to produce pure and 'unhampered' tones. Hiring four models for a photo session at which they appeared in white formal skirts, he sent the photos to leading newspapers and magazines. The hoax took off. Hundreds of people wanted autographed photographs, agents wanted to promote recitals, and Frank Sinatra wanted the Quartet to record for his Reprise label.

In 1964, bored by the presidential campaign which Lyndon Johnson ran away with, and with the press hungry for small-time candidates, on a radio phone-in programme he introduced 'Yetta Bronstein', the archetypal

Jewish grandmother. Demanding the issue of postage stamps portraying Jane Fonda nude to help the US Post Office raise money and to please folk 'who can't afford *Playboy*', Yetta was an instant hit in New York. Handbills appeared: 'VOTE FOR YETTA AND WATCH THINGS GET BETTER'. Though failing in her campaign, Yetta was so popular that in 1968 Abel revived her for the New York mayoral campaign under the banner 'NEW YORK NEEDS A MOTHER'.

Later capers relying on human naivity and on the low level of media information include his impersonation (swathed in bandages) of reclusive billionaire Howard Hughes (*see* **Irving**); the production during the Watergate scandal of 1973 of a fake 'Deep Throat' (anonymous source of the information leading to **Nixon**'s downfall); and the organisation in 1985 of an audience 'faint-in' at a live broadcast of the *Phil Donahue Show* after one of Donahue's assistants asked him for a good media stunt to improve the show's ratings. Seven or eight people pretended to faint: Donahue, attributing their collapse to an outbreak of Legionnaire's Disease, cleared the studio and finished the show without an audience. ENTIRE STUDIO AUDIENCE FLEE DONAHUE SHOW! the headlines screamed. Said at first to be furious to learn it had all been a hoax, Donahue was much happier when his ratings did in fact improve as a result of the publicity.

Then there was the marriage of former Ugandan dictator Idi Amin to an 18-year-old white woman, ostensibly so that Amin could gain US citizenship. Raising $8,000 from eight businessmen and persuading a friend in South Africa to wire the American media about the event, Abel found an Amin lookalike, put him in a tan uniform jingling with medals, hired an actress and uniformed Pinkerton guards, and staged a wedding at New York's Hotel Plaza. Over a hundred and fifty reporters showed up. The wedding, in a suite decorated with a huge Ugandan flag, was a riot. The 'judge' was drunk, and amid the ceremony the 'bride' began complaining that $50,000 wasn't nearly enough for the assignment. The State Department and FBI both arrived to interview Amin, but the guards wouldn't let them, at which point Abel and his co-conspirators revealed the hoax.

Abel continues to outrage some and amuse others, as when he got his own obituary into the *New York Times*. Visiting 'Sundance' – actor Robert Redford's ski lodge in Utah – he checked in and next day failed to return. His skis were found arranged in the form of a cross in a snowbank. Taking the bus back to New York, he lay low for a week, greatly admiring the *Times* write-up about his career before emerging to say that 'Reports of my demise have been greatly exaggerated.' Meanwhile, thousands of letters had poured in to his 'widow', not all sympathetic. Upon his resurrection, he sent all concerned a certificate saying they'd achieved 6.7 on the Richter Scale for Emotional

Upheaval – but some of his friends were so angry they never spoke to him again.

'When I *really* go next time,' he says, 'nobody will believe it, so I'll become immortal – I figure *this* is the way to achieve immortality.'

Is this why he does it?

Deriding the media as hungry and ruthless, he says 'they deserve to be pricked once in a while', adding that his aim 'is to just shake people up – give them a verbal or visual kick in the intellect, so they are able to suddenly stop and look at themselves and laugh more, and to participate in life rather than be just passive bystanders'.[3]

1. Vale and Juno (eds), *op. cit.*, pp.103–7.
2. *Yours for Decency*, Alan Abel, Elk Books, London 1966.
3. *op. cit.* note 1, p.107.

ABNAGALE, Frank (20th century) (*IMPOSTORS*)
Variously a bogus airline pilot, paediatrician, graduate of Harvard Law School and sociology teacher, in his autobiography *Catch Me If You Can*[1] this enterprising impostor says of himself that: 'I was simply a poseur and swindler of astonishing ability.' Maybe so, but his ability was not so astonishing that it kept him out of trouble: he wrote his life-story in a prison cell, from which he was released after serving four years of a twelve-year sentence. As with many another criminal hoaxer, his chief victim was ultimately himself. 'I stole every nickel and blew most of it on gourmet food and luxurious living,' he wrote, having spent his entire adult lifetime to date hoaxing and donning false identities. 'I never felt I was a criminal.' But prison must have taught him something, because once released he got an honest job for the first time in his life, reportedly going into the crime prevention business and making himself a fortune . . . a case of 'Set a thief to catch a thief'.

1. Quoted in Yapp, *op. cit.*, p.11.

ABOMINABLE SNOWMAN (*See* **YETI**)

ABYSSINIA, Emperor of (*See* **COLE, Horace**)

ADAMS, Clarence (19th century) (*CONMEN*)
The career of this unique nineteenth-century American conman culminated in persuading his fellow citizens that he was dead. A wealthy lover of books on crime and the occult, he collected such books and selected them for the public library of Chester in Windsor County, New England. Though outwardly energetic and involved in local politics, at home in his farmhouse on the edge of Chester he spent hours browsing in his private library, inhabiting the dream-worlds created

by Poe, Hoffmann, Wilkie Collins and Robert Louis Stevenson. The latter's 1886 novel *Dr Jekyll and Mr Hyde* – the terrifying tale of a split-minded doctor, kind and decent by day, a murderous monster by night – so influenced him that he decided to create a double life that would fool all who thought they knew him.

So, while presiding over committee meetings and acting as a welfare officer by day, by night he became a thief. He had no family, and his housekeeper was an old woman who asked no questions. During the next sixteen years he planned and executed a brilliant set of burglaries, almost all by night, plundering a wide range of goods from neighbours, factories and warehouses. He enjoyed publicly criticising the baffled police for their ineptitude, advancing his own theories as to the type of criminal they should be seeking. Arrests of known burglars were made, but the crimes continued, and it was not until 1902 that the truth emerged. A doctor, summoned urgently to Adams' house, found him badly wounded. The wound had been caused by a spring-gun set at a local mill: Adams could not deny his involvement, traces of his blood having been found at the mill.

Even when facing sentence he gave nothing away. 'It has all been a great adventure and I have had a lot of enjoyment out of it,' he declared. 'Being a burglar has kept me mentally alert all these years and I have proved to myself that, if studied properly, like a professional, it can be carried out despite all the police in the world. But I never did this for money, only for the sheer fun of it.'

Sent to the State Prison at Windsor for ten years, he was a model inmate, running the library and schooling other prisoners. Meanwhile he prepared his biggest con of all; one planned long before his arrest, and on the assumption that sooner or later he would be caught. He knew there would be no life for him in Chester after his release. The only way out was to 'die', then adopt a new identity. To this end he had studied hypnosis and, specifically, self-induced hypnosis, so that, by the time he went to jail, he could induce a state of suspended animation virtually indistinguishable from death.

Likewise, before he was jailed, he prepared outside help. He had used professional burglars in various raids in and about Chester and, remembering the old saw about honour between thieves, managed to smuggle several thousands of dollars with him into prison, where his main confederate was a convict who had been a doctor.

His planning was immaculate. Though summer was a more comfortable time to be interred for a night in a cemetery vault, his scheme demanded that he fake his death during winter. His will, which named the person who would collect his body from the prison, also named the cemetery – a remote site called Cavendish. It had the specific advantage that, during winter months when the ground was too hard to dig, coffins awaiting burial were left in the vault until spring, when the ground was softer.

On the anniversary of George Washington's birthday in February 1904 he 'fell ill' and was admitted to the prison hospital. On 26 February his tame convict doctor declared him dead, signing a death certificate stating that Adams had died of pneumonia. The prison governor inspected the 'corpse' and was duly fooled, whereupon William Dunn – the man named in Adams' will – arrived with a wool-lined coffin that had hidden air-holes. Adams was removed in it; the coffin was locked in the vault; and later that night his helpers arrived to take him to a distant town. Adopting a disguise, he crossed the Canadian border.

Some months later a local man returning to Chester claimed to have seen the 'dead man' alive in Nova Scotia. Still in the vault, the coffin was opened to reveal a body so decomposed that firm identification was impossible. A post mortem would have revealed the truth, but the authorities were satisfied and the coffin was later buried, the body in it. Yet during the following year there were so many other reports that Adams was still alive that an official inquiry was demanded, but resisted: rumour had it that Adams himself retained sufficient local power to have stopped it. At any rate, it seems likely that he had originated the stories of his survival, being unable to resist letting the good folk of Chester know how he had hoaxed them – an understandable touch of vanity.

Despite rumours that he had gone to Mexico, he was never heard of again – save once in 1911 when Chester's public librarian received a postcard from Paris. Posted on 26 February, the anniversary of Adams' 'death', in printed letters it declared: 'In memory of Clarence Adams, the immortal joker. R.I.P.'[1]

1. McCormick, *op. cit.*, pp.127–34.

ADAMSKI, George (1891–1965) (*UFO HOAXES*)

The modern UFO cult began on 24 June 1947 when businessman Kenneth Arnold saw nine shining discs weaving between the mountains while flying his private plane near Mount Rainier in Washington State. Five years later, Californian mystic George Adamski became the first American to claim contact with extraterrestrial beings. In his book *Flying Saucers Have Landed* he later wrote: 'It was about 12.30 in the noon hour of Thursday, 20th November, 1952, that I first made personal contact with a man from another world. He came to Earth in his space craft, a flying saucer. He called it a Scout Ship.'[1]

This encounter allegedly occurred at Desert Center, some way outside Los Angeles. Adamski claimed to have been directed there telepathically by the aliens. Along with six friends (including occult theorist George Hunt Williamson), he saw the bell-like 'scout ship' appear overhead then land nearby. A blond-haired entity emerged to tell Adamski by signs and telepathy that its race feared to land in populous areas but came to warn against human misuse of atomic power. This became a stock-in-trade of many later contactee tales: it is, presumably, to Adamski's credit that he came up with it first (though such warnings were common enough in science fiction tales even then).

His best-selling book was just what millions of anxious people wanted to read as the Cold War developed. Our space brothers would save us from ourselves! Adamski was quick to capitalise. His next volume, *Inside the Space Ships* (1955), told how his new friends took him to UFO bases amid mountains, rivers and cities – on the far side of the moon. This was published four years before the first photos of the moon's dark side showed it to be as sterile as the side facing Earth. But by then Adamski had made his fortune. In any case it hardly mattered to his fans what science proved or disproved.[2]

An odd coda to his saga was reported in England. On 24 April 1965 Mr E.A. Bryant, walking near Scoriton in Devon, allegedly saw a UFO land nearby. Three figures in 'diving gear' emerged. One said his name was 'Yamski', and that it was a pity 'Des' or 'Les' wasn't there to understand the visitation. Did Bryant know that Adamski, who had collaborated with Desmond Leslie on his first bestseller, had died the day before?

How far do folk telling such tales believe in them? Why disbelieve them?

As for Adamski, did he believe he'd been to the moon?

1. *Flying Saucers Have Landed*, George Adamski and Desmond Leslie, T. Werner Laurie, London 1953.
2. *Inside the Space Ships*, George Adamski, Abelard-Schuman, New York 1955.

AESOP (*LITERARY HOAXES*)
As fabulous as his famous *Fables* (the world's longest-running bestseller after Homer), in which moral lessons are presented by talking, humanised animals, this legendary Greek author almost certainly never lived. The name 'Aesop' was used as a sort of literary umbrella or convenience; a name under which fables collected from all over the classical world were published. Perhaps the first reference to 'Aesop's Fables' dates from *c*.450 BC, when the Greek historian Herodotus says they were penned a century earlier by a slave of this name. Herodotus is said to be the 'Father of History', but remember: *caveat emptor*. An Egyptian biography of the first century AD (probably following Herodotus) describes Aesop as a slave on the isle of Samos who, freed by his master, served King Lycurgus of Babylon as a riddle-solver before returning to Greece to die at Delphi. The Roman author Plutarch describes Aesop as an adviser to the wealthy Lydian king Croesus (d. 546 BC).

So the main accounts all place Aesop in the sixth century BC. But the consensus of modern opinion is that he never lived at all. The first known collection of the *Fables* was by Demetrius Philareus in the fourth century BC, but this version had vanished by AD 800. The enduring version, treating the fables consecutively and so influencing all later editions, was collated in Rome in the first century AD by an author called Phaedrus.

Phaedrus's Fables? Doesn't sound right, somehow . . . let's stick with *Aesop*.

AETHERIUS SOCIETY (*PARANORMAL HOAXES, UFO HOAXES*)

Among the more bizarre organisations springing from the UFO enthusiasms of the 1950s, this cult was founded in 1954 by British occultist George King (1919–). Alone in his West London flat one day, it seems he heard a disembodied voice cry out: 'Prepare yourself! You are to become the voice of Interplanetary Parliament.' A week later an Indian swami 'walked straight through' the locked door and laid down the rules for the Aetherius Society. Soon King, claiming to be guided by notable discarnate spirits like the nineteenth-century psychic researcher Sir Oliver Lodge, not only received telepathic news from the depths of 'etheric space', but visited Venus and Mars. He engaged in a space battle forty million miles from Earth, and later publicised trance messages from such entities as Mars Sector Six, the Master Aetherius, and Jesus Christ – said currently to be resident on or near Venus.

Despite or because of such claims, the society still thrives, concentrating on the 'task' imposed by the Interplanetary Parliament via King's mediumship. This task is to store up, via the extraterrestrial entities, 'spiritual energy' in 'spiritual batteries' located in high places, this energy to be released to prevent sickness and suffering the whole world round. Society members have undertaken dangerous pilgrimages up high mountains including Kilimanjaro in Tanzania to fulfil their mission as communicated by King.

Is King a deliberate hoaxer? As with many other gurus of far-out cults, it's hard to tell. He's not a Jim **Jones** or David **Koresh**, or even a **Rajneesh**. No deadly scandals are associated with the Aetherius Society. The worst that might be said of it is that it constitutes a self-deluding belief system. But then, some might say that *all* belief systems are self-deluding, and so who's the first glasshouse-dweller to throw a stone?

AFGHAN PRINCESS (*See* **WEYMAN, Stanley**)

AFRICAN HEIR SCAM (*See* **BLAY-MIEZEH, John Ackah**)

ALCHEMY (*HISTORICAL HOAXES*, *see also* TAUSEND, Franz)
Folk long dreamed that lead or other base metals may be turned into
gold by the art or pseudo-science called alchemy and that, by similar
transformative magical arts, the elixir of life said to confer immortality
might be manufactured. Such dreams have led to many a successful
scam . . . and not only in the remote medieval past.

First things first. Originating in ancient China and in Alexandria's
Neo-platonic schools, 'alchemy' comes from the ancient name for Egypt,
Khem, meaning 'black earth'. Alchemy is thus 'the Art of the Black
Land'. Traditionally, there were two kinds of alchemist. Pragmatists
laboured for years in smoky laboratories, laying the basis of modern
chemistry. Theorists, scorned in the sixteenth century by Paracelsus
(1493–1541) for 'carrying golden mountains in their heads before they
had put their hands to the fire',[1] dreamed and philosophised about
finding the magical transformative ingredient, the so-called 'Philosopher's Stone'.

Were they all charlatans? The original Graeco–Roman alchemists
aimed to imitate gold by producing yellow alloys of base metals, by using
impure gold, or by colouring metals and alloys. Egyptian recipes for
colouring glass and glazing pottery indicate an advanced technology.
Zosimos (third century AD), the first known writer on chemistry,
thought gold might be produced from base metal. Later, during the
European Dark Ages, Arab chemists like Geber (eighth century) developed the practical processes of distillation, sublimation and calcination.
Geber regarded patience and perseverance as the alchemist's chief
qualities, and also encouraged a belief that the key to transmuting base
metal lay in the combining sulphur and mercury. It sounded good.

The mystique thus developed was boosted by the rediscovery in
medieval Europe of works attributed to the legendary Hermes Trismeg-
istus ('Thrice-Great Hermes'). First mentioned in *De Mineralibus*,
attributed to Albertus Magnus (1206–80), the legend of Hermes (a
mythic Egyptian magus said to have lived three generations after Moses)
took off in the fifteenth century when the Italian scholar Marsilio Ficino
translated the *Pimander* and the *Asclepius*, ancient texts which, though
then ascribed to Hermes, in fact originate in early Christian Gnostic
mystery teachings. But whatever their origin, their mystic appeal to a
lost Golden Age legitimised the idea that gold might be made out of lead.

Soon alchemists all over Europe were working their scam behind a
barrage of pseudo-mystical profundity: a quest leading to Renaissance
pranks like the **Rosicrucian** furore. With Europe in turmoil in the
1620s, it was widely believed that an **Invisible College** of alchemical
adepts ruled behind the scenes, making deals with Satan and owning
purses that never emptied. This profitable mystique endured until
proto-scientists like Sir Robert Boyle in his *The Sceptical Chymist* (1661)
at last demolished the dream, even as the Jesuit Father Anathasius

Kircher (in *The Subterranean World*), himself long a diligent alchemist, denounced his brothers as 'a congregation of knaves and impostors'.[2] Kircher sounds like yet another disappointed man of a sort found all too often in the history of science. (*See* **Kammerer** for the tale of William Bateson, a dedicated Darwinian only after he failed to find evidence for the opposing Lamarckian view.)

Yet for at least a century afterwards there were not only many alchemists at work, but plenty of suckers to keep them happy. Wild tales persisted, typically relying on the supposed authority of the rich, royal, famous or seemingly knowledgeable to validate the impossible – that lead might be turned into gold. Some examples:

Helvetius, the seventeenth-century doctor to the Dutch Prince of Orange and himself at first a sceptic, tells (in *Of A Transmutation*) how a stranger showed him three sulphur-coloured lumps of stone, claiming these to be the fabled Philosopher's Stone. Stealing a fragment, Helvetius heated it in a crucible with six grams of old lead. What came out was said by a goldsmith to be pure gold. The philosopher Spinoza attested to the reality of the transmutation. Helvetius was widely thought above suspicion. If he was conned, nobody knew how – then or now.

The Scot Alexander Seton travelled Europe with a lemon-yellow powder. With it he and others made gold, before witnesses. The Elector of Saxony demanded the secret. Refusing it, Seton was tortured and jailed. A student, Sendivogius, helped him escape. When Seton died soon afterwards, Sendivogius got the powder – but not the secret, because, claimed occultist Lewis Spence, 'it was impossible to [Seton] as an adept to reveal the terms of the awful mystery'.[3] Well, maybe. It's a good martyr-tale.

Others said that the Swedish emperor Gustavus Adolphus (d.1636) had transmuted quicksilver into pure gold, courtesy of a certain merchant of Lubeck, who had died with a fortune of one million seven hundred thousand crowns. Many things were said. Rumour flourished. Europe was full of mysterious mages able to impart (for a price) the secret of the Philosopher's Stone. Many such charlatans were patronised by the wealthy. Among them was the Frenchman Jean Delisle, confidently said by the evidently broadminded cleric M. de Cerisy to be able to turn 'lead into gold, and iron into silver, by merely heating these metals red-hot, and pouring upon them in that state some oil and powder he is possessed of; so that it would not be impossible for any man to make a million a day, if he had sufficient of this wondrous mixture'.[4]

Delisle's fame so spread that he was invited to Paris, to the court of Louis XIV, but the invitation embarrassed him. He continually refused, saying he had not enough powder. In 1711 he was arrested and carted off to the Bastille to prove himself or rot in jail forever. En route his guards, believing he had the Stone, tried to rob and murder him. The plan backfired: he was only wounded. In his Bastille dungeon he was visited by his protector, the Bishop of Senes, and promised his freedom if he could transmute lead into gold before the king. Unable to do so, he died, still in jail, aged just forty-one.

In England in 1782 James Price invited to his Surrey house several distinguished men, who saw him turn mercury into silver by heating it with a white powder, and into gold by means of a red powder. Asked to produce more powder, Price said that the effort would damage his health (implying, for believers, that the process is psychic, not 'merely' chemical). Breaking down amid the subsequent controversy, he killed himself by drinking cyanide before three members of the Royal Society sent to study his controversial claims. A faker found out? There's no sure proof either way.

Alchemical tricks were outlined in a paper read in April 1722, at a sitting of the Royal Academy of Science in Paris, by M. Geoffrey, a sceptic. He described how fakers might use a double-bottomed crucible, the lower surface of iron and copper, the upper of wax, painted to resemble the lower. Between these surfaces they put gold or silver dust. It was not surprising when, on heating their lead, they found a lump of gold or silver at the bottom of the pot. Some used hollow wands filled with gold or silver dust and stoppered with wax or butter to stir the boiling metal amid elaborate distracting ceremonies. Or they drilled holes in lumps of lead, in which they poured molten gold; or, producing nails made half of gold and half of iron, pretended they had transmuted the precious half from iron by dipping it in strong alcohol. Everywhere there were coins in circulation, half gold and half silver, made by fakers who, after their first or second successful 'experiment', had promptly disappeared. So what's new? Yet the fantasy persisted. Pseudo-aristocratic charlatans such as **Saint-Germain** made their way by claiming that they knew the ultimate secret of eternal youth, vitality and wealth – and that if you sign on their dotted line, you too will never have to worry again. Sounds familiar?

Even so – and here is the *caveat* to make rationalists shudder – 'Counterfeiters exist only because there is true gold' (Jalaluddin Rumi: 1207–73).

1. *The Alchemists*, Ronald Pearsall, Weidenfeld & Nicolson, London 1976, p.85.
2. *Extraordinary Popular Delusions and the Madness of Crowds*, Charles Mackay (1841), Farrar, Straus and Giroux, New York, p.213.
3. *The Occult*, Colin Wilson, Grafton, London 1989, pp.317ff.
4. *op. cit.*, note 2, p.217.

ALFONSO, Barry (contemporary) (*See also* **TELEPHONE HOAXES**)
Contemporary US journalist and songwriter who, beginning in San Diego in the mid-1970s alongside fellow prank-activist Boyd **Rice**, has

since also run a separate career as a dedicated media-prankster, exploring the possibilities for distortion and manipulation offered by the media, and specialising as a 'telephone research psychologist'.

'When I was about ten, I would go into stores and stand in the window like I was a mannequin holding an invisible vacuum cleaner. People would stop and look. That was a joke, but it was also getting a hold on the handles of reality and making the store your own little playhouse . . . and why not?'

Barry is dedicated to making good prank telephone calls. 'You're playing a little game in which the other person can beat you, and if the other person hangs up early, you've lost.' But why? What's the motivation? Barry explains. 'What we're up to is the alchemy of thought. What you think about anything defines how you perceive it, and how you perceive it defines what your experience of it will be. Alter the thought and you've also altered perception and experience.'[1]

1. Vale and Juno (eds.), *op. cit.*, p.208ff.

ALIEN ANIMALS (*See CONCORDANCE*)

ALIENS AMONG US (*See* UFO ABDUCTIONS)

AMITYVILLE GHOST SCAM (*PARANORMAL HOAXES*)

One of the more successful 'true ghost' book/movie tie-ins of recent years concerns events allegedly occurring in a house in Amityville, New York, after one Ronald DeFeo killed his parents and his brothers and sisters there in 1974. A year later George and Kathy Lutz and their two boys moved into the house, to be harassed by nasty phenomena including strange music and green slime. Doors and windows were invisibly damaged; odd hoof tracks appeared in the snow round the house. Several times they called the police for help, and a priest called in to bless the house heard a voice tell him to 'Get out!' Not surprisingly, they moved. Jay Anson, a scriptwriter who had worked on *The Exorcist*, wrote up their tale as *The Amityville Horror*. It was a big hit. In the movie that followed, new events were added, like an axe attack on Kathy Lutz.

It was all a scam. Researchers found out that the priest had never been to the house, the police denied they had ever been called out, the doors and windows were in good repair, and weather records showed there had been no snow on the ground when the hoofprints supposedly appeared. Eventually Ronald DeFeo's lawyer admitted that he had concocted the idea of the haunted house with George Lutz, a confidence trickster, and then got Jay Anson to write the story. Their motive? Simple. M-O-N-E-Y!

ANASTASIA (*See* **ANDERSON, Anna**)

ANDERSON, Anna (d.1984) (*IMPOSTORS*)
An enduring mystery concerns the fate of the Russian Czar Nicholas II, his wife Alexandra, his son Alexei, and his four daughters – Olga, Tatiana, Marie, and (b.1901) Anastasia. Imprisoned for over a year first by the provisional government and then by the Bolsheviks during the Russian Revolution, it is said they were shot and bayoneted to death in a basement late on 16 July 1918 at Ekaterinburg in Siberia. Five of their servants also died. Recent DNA tests at Aldermaston in England have 'proved virtually beyond doubt' that five of the nine skeletons found in a burial pit nearby in 1991 were those of the Czar, his wife, and three of their children.[1]

Yet rumours have persisted ever since 1918 that one or more of the royal family escaped – in particular, the youngest daughter, Anastasia. The bones of three children in the grave have been confirmed as belonging to the Czar's daughters – but *which* three? Science cannot tell. Likewise, the body of Alexei vanished, leading many impostors to step forward. None were convincing, and all are now dead. The one nagging doubt remains in regard to the claim made by 'Anna Anderson', a claim in which she persisted for over sixty years until her death in 1984 in Charlottesville, Virginia, that she was the real Anastasia.

'Anna Anderson' first turned up in Berlin in 1920. Saved by police from a suicide attempt, she spent two years in the Dalldorf asylum and on release let herself be identified as Anastasia. Denying the accepted account of the massacre at Ekaterinburg, she said she'd been rescued by a man she later married and borne a son; that her husband had died amid street fighting in Bucharest, and that she had escaped to Germany in search of her mother's relatives. This account emerged some months after another inmate at the asylum identified her not as Anastasia but Tatiana, the Czar's second daughter. Leaving the asylum for the home of a Russian monarchist in exile, Anna spent more periods in hospital, but persisted in her claim. She couldn't prove she was Anastasia, but nobody could prove she wasn't. The Czar's sister, Olga, eventually said: 'Not my niece', but remained uncertain all her life. A former maid of honour, sent by the Czar's mother to inspect Anna, at first denied her but later became an enthusiastic supporter. And though (why?) she refused to speak Russian and seemed ignorant of everyday Russian life, she knew details of events unlikely to be known by an impostor, like a peace-making bid which had secretly taken Anastasia's German uncle Ernest to St Petersburg in the First World War. Ernest, Grand Duke of Hesse, never forgave Anna for knowing about this: it was the last thing he wanted publicised.

In 1928, while Anna was being feted in the USA, a dozen Romanovs issued a document denying her claim. In retaliation Anna incorporated herself as 'Grandanor', or the Grand Duchess Anastasia of the Romanovs, registered in February 1929. When in 1933 certificates of inheritance were issued to the Czar's surviving relatives, she disputed the claim on one certificate that Anastasia had died. There was, after all, a massive fortune in foreign investments. Up to forty million pounds sterling had been deposited by the royal family in London banks. The subsequent legal action brought by Anna against the one named relative – Barbara, Duchess of Mecklenburg, chosen to represent all the certificate holders – ran for over thirty years. Anna never got a penny out of it.

Remaining in Germany, after 1946 she lived a hermit's existence in the Black Forest. In 1968 she moved to America, settling at Charlottesville, Virginia, and marrying John Manahan, a retired history professor. Though still prey to nervous illness, she relaxed at last, calling her story that 'nonsense'. Typically, when in February 1984 she died *The Times*, announcing the death of Mrs Anna Anderson Manahan, mistakenly printed the photo of another woman, an actress with almost the same name . . .[2]

A lock of Anna Anderson's hair was sent to the Aldermaston scientists who did the DNA tests on the skeletons found in the Ekaterinburg grave. The results of their tests tend strongly to deny the assertion that Anna and Anastasia were one and the same, but many questions remain unanswered.

1. Article in the *Guardian*, London, 10 July 1993.
2. Newnham, *op. cit.*, pp.214–16.

ANGLO-TEXAN FRIENDSHIP SOCIETY (*See* **GREENE, Graham**)

ANTI-SEMITIC HOAXES (*See also* **CHRISTIANITY**)
Anti-Semitism, or the irrational hatred and demonisation of Jews, has persisted for at least a thousand years, giving rise to cruel hoaxes designed to justify the hatred. A Jew (Hebrew *Yehudi*) is a member of *Judah*, meaning of the tribe of Judah, originally one of twelve Hebrew tribes claiming the Promised Land. After the Israelite exile in Babylon ended in 538 BC, the term 'Yehudi' was used of all adherents of Judaism. Following continual uprisings against Roman rule (from the revolt of the Maccabees, *c.*167 BC, to that of Simeon bar Kochba in AD 132), the Jews were enslaved and dispersed. After the Emperor Constantine (AD 279–337) embraced **Christianity** as Rome's religion, the sole civil rights Jews had were to become Christians . . . or to lend money at interest (usury: a Deadly Sin). As usurers, the despised but useful Jews spread through Europe. But, prohibited by Judaic law from marrying non-Jews, and as crusading hysteria seized the continent after AD 1096,

increasingly they became the butt of fantastic prejudices, like the belief that Antichrist would be a Jew of the tribe of Dan, or that Christ-denying Jews habitually slaughtered Christian children to obtain blood for use in Passover rites. This cruel deception, the so-called 'blood libel', originates with 'Hugh of Lincoln' in England in 1255: soon it was used to justify atrocity. Jews under torture vainly pointed out that they could not consume blood in any form, but they could not halt the spread of popular belief in the 'demonic' Jew.

In 1290 they were expelled from England, in 1395 from France, and in 1492 from Spain. Forced into ghettoes throughout northern Europe, they were blamed for the Black Death which decimated populations between 1348 and 1350. They were said to have poisoned the wells. In 1349 the folk of Brussels, Frankfurt, Mainz and Cologne killed every Jew they found, 'because they thought to please God in that way'.[1]

Modern times have seen the myth of the demonic Jew at its most rabid. In 1903 in Russia appeared a fraudulent text: *The Protocols of the Elders of Zion*, apparently proof of an 'international Jewish conspiracy' for world conquest, said to have been issued by the Judaic Congress at Basle in 1897. It purported to represent how the Jews would use the arts, the press, and modern socialist movements to undermine Christianity and the nation state, so establishing a Jewish world empire. The (probably Russian) author remains unknown, but the text plagiarises a French political pamphlet of 1864 attacking the Emperor Napoleon III. Nothing in the original attack mentions Jews or Judaism.

Promoted by the Czar's secret police, who wanted to foment anti-Semitism, this masterpiece of rabid sleaze was dismissed by the Czar as a 'vile' hoax, but after the 1917 Revolution it became hugely influential, being eagerly believed by anti-Semites throughout the world. In 1919 the White Russian army slaughtered some 60,000 Jews, blaming them for the Revolution; the American car manufacturer Henry Ford supported the campaign so vehemently that the Nazi leader Adolf Hitler was later pleased to keep a photograph of Ford on his desk, and as late as 1921 the London *Times* called the *Protocols* genuine.

In *Mein Kampf* (another fraud: he wrote little of it), Hitler used the *Protocols* to justify his hatred of the Jews (he may himself have had Jewish blood). On seizing power in Germany in 1933 he began a pogrom leading to the 'Final Solution': the attempt to exterminate all Jews. Some six million Jews died, many in the gas chambers of Auschwitz and Belsen. A further cruel irony is that even today there are right-wingers, like the British neo-Nazi historian David Irving, who claim that this massacre, the Holocaust, never occurred. It is all, apparently, a Jewish hoax . . .

There is no stopping such hateful deceptions. In the USA, the names of George Washington and Benjamin Franklin have been scurrilously attached to recent false anti-Semitic texts. Washington's oft-quoted warning, calling the Jews 'pests . . . and the greatest enemies we have to the happiness of America', is an edited and altered version of his attack on currency speculators. As for the 'Benjamin Franklin Prophecy', warning that if the Jews are not excluded from the USA, then: 'in less than 200 years they will dominate and devour the land and change our form of government', this forgery first appeared in William Dudley Pelley's pro-Nazi news-sheet, *Liberation*, in North Carolina. Pelley said he found it in the Constitutional Convention Diary of Charles Cotesworth Pinckney. In fact, nobody should be surprised to learn, there is no such document.[2]

None of which is to claim that the Jews are any better than anyone else. But nor, by and large, are they any worse.

1. *The Pursuit of the Millennium*, Norman Cohn, Paladin, London 1970, p.139.
2. Lindskoog, *op. cit.*, pp.245–6.

APRIL FOOL'S DAY HOAXES (*MEDIA HOAXES*)

'April 1 is the day on which we are reminded of what we are on the other 364,' said Mark Twain. Also known as All Fool's Day, ancient European custom has it that on 1 April people can play outrageous pranks on each other. In England, the victim is called an April Fool, in France an April Fish, and in Scotland an April Gowk, meaning a cuckoo. The origin of the day lies in 1564, when France adopted the reformed calendar of Charles IX, shifting the New Year from 1 April to 1 January. Those continuing to celebrate the New Year on 1 April became known as April Fools, and so the custom was launched.

April Fool's Day hoaxes have always been good for a laugh. In 1860 important Londoners received formal invitations reading: 'Tower of London. Admit Bearer and Friend to view the annual Ceremony of Washing the White Lions on Sunday, April 1. Admittance Only at White Gate.' Those turning up learned to their chagrin that there is no White Gate at the Tower of London, and that the White Lions were as little in evidence as their Ceremonial Washing.

In 1966, fronting the BBC's TV news programme *Panorama*, commentator Richard Dimbleby, renowned for his grave integrity, presented a documentary on spaghetti farming on the Swiss-Italian border. 'Many of you, I'm sure,' he asserted in his orotund, reliable tones, 'will have seen pictures of the vast spaghetti plantations in the Po Valley.' He went on to speak of the spaghetti weevil, and explained why spaghetti grows in such uniform lengths . . . and since few in Britain could imagine Richard Dimbleby telling a lie (or even possessing a sense of humour), enormous numbers of people believed every word of it.[1]

This spoof travelled well. Over the Atlantic four years later, on NBC's *Huntley-Brinkley* programme, the well-respected commentator John

Chancellor reported on 1970's fine pickle crop, showing the viewers an excellent specimen of a dill pickle tree on the 'Dimbleby Pickle Farm'. Few in America having heard of Richard Dimbleby, as many fell for it in the USA as in Britain.

In 1985, American humorist George Plimpton published, in the 1 April edition of *Sports Illustrated*, an article about 'Sidd' (Siddhartha) Finch, a young Englishman who had studied mind control in a Tibetan retreat, learned to pitch a baseball at 168mph with perfect accuracy, mastered the French horn, and was testing for the New York Mets. Plimpton began: 'He's a pitcher, part yogi and part recluse. Impressively liberated from our opulent life-style, Sidd's deciding about yoga – and his future in baseball.' In the first letters of these words smart readers picked up the hidden message: 'Happy April Fool's Day: ah, fib.' Many wrote in, delighted by the trick, but about forty cancelled their subscriptions.[2]

In London on 1 April 1979 a Capital Radio broadcast claimed that Britain was out of clock synchronisation with other countries due to continual changing back and forth between British Summer Time since 1945. Britain now being forty-eight hours ahead of the rest of the world, the Government had decided to cancel 5 and 12 April. The studio was promptly swamped by anxious callers believing every word of it, including a man due to sell his house on one of the cancelled days. Well, it was on the radio, wasn't it?

On 1 April 1990 the popular British Sunday tabloid *News of the World* ran a story claiming that the French and English halves of the new Channel Tunnel, then in construction, wouldn't meet in the middle. Why? Because the French had used metres but the British had used yards. The two halves would miss by fourteen feet! This delightful possibility, fortunately or not, has not materialised. As of late 1993, Britain is now firmly connected to mainland Europe by what is known as the *Chunnel*.

1. Yapp, *op. cit.*, pp. 24–5.
2. Lindskoog, *op. cit.*, p. 21.

ARIGÓ (*See* **PSYCHIC SURGERY**)

ARIS, Rutherford (1929–) (*LITERARY HOAXES*)
Professor Rutherford Aris, a respected chemical engineer, was already listed in the American edition of *Who's Who* when the compilers, writing to ask for further details, wrote to him as 'Aris Rutherford'. Aris seized his opportunity, writing back that 'Aris Rutherford' had been born in a Scots whisky distillery, worked as a whisky consultant, and that his hobby was drinking whisky. *Who's Who* printed it all without question.

ARNOLD AND SLACK (19th century) (*CONMEN*)
One summer day in 1872 two veteran prospectors, Philip Arnold and John Slack, handed a teller in San Francisco's Bank of California a drawstring sack, asking him to look after it while they went and got drunk. Peeking into it after they left, what he saw sent him straight to his boss, the banker William Ralston. Opening the sack, Ralston saw a fortune in uncut diamonds. It took him three days to find the prospectors and sober them up. They admitted finding a diamond field 'bigger than Kimberley', but they didn't own the site and wouldn't tell him where it was. If he wanted to invest, they would appreciate it, but anyone inspecting their find had to make the journey to the site blindfold. Ralston agreed, sending mining engineer David Colston along with them. Three weeks later, an ecstatic Colston was back, with a fistful of diamonds. It was all true!

Paying Arnold and Slack $50,000 apiece, Ralston put aside another $300,000 for their use, promising a further $350,000 when the field started to produce. Other famous contributors included Baron Anthony de Rothschild, editor Horace Greeley, and Charles Lewis Tiffany, the jeweller. Ralston now sent in another inspection party, again blindfold and led by Arnold and Slack. The trek from the train depot at Rawlings in Wyoming was long, and the land was wild, yet when the blindfolds were lifted – Ralston's men saw ant hills shimmering with diamond dust, and rubies casually scattered across the range.

Deciding to dump Arnold and Slack and threatening them with complex lawsuits, Ralston got them to accept $700,000 as their share. Seemingly fooled, they took the money and ran. Meanwhile, with the diamond lode a worldwide sensation, a doubting geologist, E.W. Emmonds, tracked down the site. The first thing he noted was that it lay only a few miles from the rail station at Rawlings. The blindfold party had been led round in circles. Further inspection showed that the 'ant hills' were man-made; the first diamond he picked up bore the marks of a lapidary tool. He wired San Francisco with the bad news that the field had been 'salted'. Within hours, his syndicate in ruins, Ralston realised just who was the real sucker. It turned out that Arnold and Slack had been to Europe before setting up the con, spending their life savings of $35,000 on the jewels they later scattered.

They were never prosecuted. Slack went who knew where, Arnold to Kentucky, where he founded a bank. As for Ralston, he went bankrupt in 1875.[1]

1. Blundell, *op. cit.*, pp.183–4.

ARNSTEIN, Nicky (*See* **LUSTIG, 'Count' Victor**)

ART FORGERS (*See CONCORDANCE*)

ARTHUR'S GRAVE (*HISTORICAL HOAXES*)

Hoaxing for profit was never limited to the secular classes. Many so-called 'men of God' have always been among the most active hoaxers, especially those claiming a hot-line to the Almighty. Particularly inventive were medieval monks and churchmen, forever trying to boost the revenue of their abbey or diocese by claiming to possess a piece of the True Cross, or the bones of popular saints, or whatever other relics might attract pilgrims.

One such hoax was perpetrated by the monks of Glastonbury Abbey in England. By *c.*1150 encouraging the rumour that the Holy Grail, supposedly brought to Glastonbury by Joseph of Arimathea after Christ's death, was lodged (invisibly) in their Chalice Well, in 1191 they claimed to have found in their grounds the grave of the mystic King Arthur and his queen, Guinevere. So Glastonbury became England's premier medieval tourist site.

Some background: Arthur, said to have held invading Saxons at bay in the sixth century, was a legendary figure throughout cultured Europe at the time, thanks to Geoffrey of Monmouth's bestselling *The History of the Kings of Britain* (1135). Yet that Arthur had actually lived was not in doubt: Nennius, a ninth-century Welsh monk, had read in the Welsh 'Easter Annals' how Arthur had defeated the Saxons at Badon Hill in the year 518, then died fighting his son Modred at the Battle of Camlann in 539. So it may or may not have been true, as the monks later claimed, that in 1184 King Henry II had told their abbot how a Welsh bard had said that Arthur lay buried sixteen feet deep between two pyramids in the grounds of Glastonbury Abbey. Nor perhaps is it coincidence that the tale surfaced only after the Abbey burned almost to the ground on 25 May 1184.

Amid rebuilding, a dying monk's last wish in 1191 was to be buried at a spot where two crosses stood on tapering (pyramidical) marble pillars. Perhaps recalling the prophecy, the gravediggers dug below the usual depth, and at seven feet found a stone slab. On its underside was a lead cross inscribed: *Hic jacet sepultus inclytus Rex Artorius in insula Avalonia* ('Here lies buried the renowned King Arthur in the isle of Avalon'). Glastonbury, once a marsh-bound isle, was also known as *Ynys Avallon*, 'Isle of Apples'. An association with the legendary Avalon was convenient, to say the least.

Digging on, at sixteen feet they uncovered a large oak coffin, in it the skeleton of a huge man, his skull smashed by heavy blows. A lock of yellow hair that fell apart when touched belonged to a smaller skeleton. So they claimed. Gerald the Welshman, one of the era's more reliable chroniclers, asserts a year later that he saw the skeletons, and that the inscription on the lead cross also mentioned 'Queen Wenneveria'. No doubt he did. But that doesn't prove that either the inscription or the skeletons were 'Arthurian'.

The skeletons vanished, but the cross was in circulation for centuries. In 1607 the antiquarian William Camden published a picture of it, with Arthur spelled *Arturius*. In 1962 the archaeologist Dr Ralegh Radford, excavating the site, proved that the monks had indeed dug down to sixteen feet. Why would they have done that unless there had been truth to the tale, or unless they had believed that there was?

Modern opinion is that the monks were fakers. Oxford linguist James Hudson claims that the style of Latin in the inscription betrays the cross as a twelfth-century fraud, as far removed from sixth-century Latin as modern English is from Shakespeare's. Moreover, Arthur's were not the only famous bones conveniently found after the fire. The monks also claimed to have disinterred St Patrick, the sixth-century scholar Gildas, and even Archbishop Dunstan – buried peacefully at Canterbury for over two centuries. It seems likely that they discovered an unmarked grave and made up the rest. In any case, the public loved it, and Glastonbury was soon the richest abbey in England.[1]

1. *King Arthur: The True Story*, Graham Phillips and Martin Keatman, Arrow, London 1993, pp.16–18.

AZEFF, Ievno (1869–1918) (*IMPOSTORS*)

Posing as a revolutionary while working as a Russian police informer, organising assassinations of leading politicians to trap the plotters into arrest and execution, Ievno Azeff is one of the few double-agents nobody ever completely unmasked. 'So skilfully did he conceal his tracks,' writes British historian Graham Stephenson, 'that it is impossible to say which side he mainly betrayed.'[1]

The son of a Jewish tailor, Azeff was born at Kyskovo in Russia's Grodnensky province. Working in Rostov as a reporter, he befriended a revolutionary group. Fleeing charges of theft, he joined the Russian Democratic Group in exile in Karlsruhe, Germany. Hard up, in 1893 he betrayed this group to the Czarist secret police, the Ochrana, and within a year was at work as one of their foreign agents. Posing as a terrorist extremist, he became a prominent revolutionary. In 1899 the Ochrana doubled his salary and promised him safe employment as an electrical engineer if he returned to Russia. From Moscow he established links with other revolutionaries, betrayed an illegal print shop in Tomsk, had terrorist leaders arrested, and then got himself elected leader of the entire organisation.

By 1900 his information enabled the Ochrana to penetrate the innermost circles of the Social Revolutionaries' movement. He also told the police about a special revolutionary squad, the 'Battle Organisation', its aim the assassination of leading statesmen, even as he urged the 'Battle Organisation' to act. In April 1902 Sipyagin, Minister of the Interior, was assassinated. Insisting that the top men in the movement, whose names he had already betrayed, be left at large in case suspicion fall on him, his tactic was to safeguard all his revolutionary supporters while eliminating enemies by betraying them. The revolutionaries were happy with him, but the Ochrana had doubts. Even while negotiating a price to betray G.A. Gershuni, head of the 'Battle Organisation', he plotted with Gershuni to murder Bogdanovitch, Governor of Ufa. Gershuni went to Ufa, Bogdanovitch died, and when Gershuni was arrested, Azeff became head of the 'Battle Organisation'.

Next he organised the death of Plehve, the new and even more hated Minister of the Interior, doing so even while eliminating a rival group also planning to murder Plehve. His failure to tip off the Ochrana about Plehve's death in a bomb blast on 18 July 1904 made the police suspicious. Then the Grand Duke Sergei Alexandrovitch was murdered. Count Witte, then the Prime Minister, later stated his belief that Azeff was responsible for this death too. The revolutionary L.P. Menstchikoff infiltrated the Ochrana to learn that Azeff was a police agent even as the Ochrana doubled his pay, perhaps to lull him into a sense of false security. Yet still he rode the tide. Menstchikoff's report was disbelieved: Azeff retired temporarily to a life of luxury on the Italian Riviera. But the easy life was not for him. Recalled to tackle new terrorist groups, he threw himself back into the double-sided fray. Yet his luck was running out. 'Tried' by his comrades for libelling Azeff, the academic revolutionary V.L. Burtsev, instructed to shoot himself, saved his skin by revealing facts about Azeff learned from a former Ochrana chief.

Even with the net tightening Azeff thought himself safe, having told each side that to some extent he worked for the other, always convincing each side that the other had been double-crossed. To restore revolutionary confidence in him he planned even more daring coups, including the assassination of the Czar. Going to Glasgow where a new Russian cruiser, the *Rurik*, was being built, he recruited a sailor, Avdeyev, to kill the Czar. Giving the man a revolver and detailed instructions, he got Avdeyev to write him a letter explaining his motives. This would be published after the assassination. Azeff then went to his Paris apartment to await the telegram saying the Czar was dead. He could then produce Avdeyev's letter to prove his impeccable revolutionary credentials. But the assassination never happened. Fleeing revolutionary cross-examination, Azeff disappeared to Germany with his mistress. Heads rolled in the Ochrana and, with his erstwhile comrades also after him, Azeff kept moving, changing his name and hotels. In 1914 the German secret police, learning his true identity, arrested him and jailed him as a revolutionary. Released in 1917, he died in Berlin on 24 April 1918, of natural causes . . . in itself a considerable miracle.

1. Quoted in McCormick, *op. cit.*, p.136.

B

'Help Fight Truth Decay.'

(sign in Baltimore City Police Department)

BACH, Charlotte (*See* **KAROLY, Hadju**)

BACKHOUSE, Sir Edmund (1873–1944) (*FRAUD*)
Charming black sheep of a rich English family, as an Oxford student Sir
Edmund Trelawney Backhouse ran up debts of £23,000, bought jewels
on credit for actresses, and in 1895 was declared a bankrupt. Yet he had
a flair for learning languages. Learning Russian and Japanese, in 1898 he
found himself in Peking and soon mastered Chinese. Hired to teach
English at the new university, he proceeded to become a highly
successful conman.

When Clydeside shipbuilders John Brown & Co. hired him to secure
contracts with the Chinese navy and he was fired from his government
contract, Backhouse persuaded the shipbuilders to trust him and carry
on paying his (huge) expense account. The orders, he said, would just
roll in. No ships were ever built. The non-existent navy became a great
joke in Peking. Next he showed his versatility by forging the diary of a
Chinese aristocrat who'd lived through the Boxer Rebellion. In 1910,
pretending he'd found the diary in 1900, he used it as the basis of his
popular *China Under the Empress Dowager*, co-written with London
Times journalist J.O.P. Bland. The fraud went undetected for years.

His main success was as an antiquarian. Amid the revolutionary chaos
of 1913 he sent to Oxford twenty-nine crates containing over 27,000
manuscripts, possibly stolen. To avoid transportation costs he donated
them to the Bodleian Library, which paid the charges. With his
reputation as a collector secure, librarians paid him handsomely to
extend the collection. Over-valuing whatever he found, he accepted
honorary doctorates from London and Oxford, and became so respected
that even when the Bodleian realised that some of its purchases were

forgeries, it decided that Backhouse had been tricked by the wily Chinese.

He arranged in 1915 with the British government to buy 30,000 Chinese rifles left over from the Russo-Japanese war, shipping them down the Yangtse to Shanghai then to British Hong Kong, and by summer 1915 he was promising 100,000 rifles and three million rounds of ammunition. The fortune the British paid to the Chinese government to maintain secrecy was wasted: the deal existed only in Backhouse's imagination. In 1916 he swindled the American Bank Note Company of New York by promoting a non-existent deal to print 650 million Chinese treasury notes, took money for a phoney plot to steal the late Empress's decorated pearl jacket, and thereafter indulged in one fraud after another. His embarrassed victims all kept quiet: he was never exposed, but went on playing the role of the quiet, humble orientalist with long white beard and white silk robe. In his old age in Peking he wrote his memoirs, claiming that in 1904 he'd had an affair with the Empress Dowager, then 69 years old. In 1973 historian Sir Hugh Trevor-Roper (*see* **Hitler Diaries**) found the memoirs to be lurid pornographic fantasy. Yet at the Bodleian a marble tablet of this engaging fraud still commemorates him as one of the Library's greatest benefactors.

BACON, Francis (*See* **SHAKESPEARE, William**)

BAKKER, Jim and Tammy Faye (*See* **TELEVANGELISTS**)

BALFOUR, Jabez (1842–1909) (*FRAUD*)
Justice of the Peace, Mayor of Croydon, and Member of Parliament for Burnley, this pillar of Victorian society made a fortune persuading the English to invest in fraudulent companies. Inventing the snowball technique by which one company finances another, the Liberator Building Society (1868) was the first of many companies, with the London and General Bank (1882) established to process the dubious cheques flowing between them. 'A man of business turned squire', with 'an air of genial ruffianism about him . . . and an open joviality', this merciless City bully kept his investors happy by paying eight per cent interest annually on their savings. So long as new money flowed in he was safe, and there was no hint of scandal – but neither were there any real company profits.

He foresaw the end. When in 1892 the Liberator crashed, the financial world was stunned, but Balfour had already salted away a fortune. Waiting long enough to be re-elected to Parliament, boasting that he expected high office in Gladstone's government, suddenly he fled to Argentina, 'the one country with any pretence of civilisation where a criminal can live without fear of extradition'.[1] Recognised in the Chilean town of Salta three years later and extradited after a long struggle, he was sentenced at the Old Bailey to fourteen years in jail for fraud. 'You will never be able to shut out the cry of the widows and orphans you have ruined,' declared the judge, Mr Justice Bruce.

Serving his time, he was planning to return to business when he died of a heart attack. Few mourned him.

1. Westminster Popular No. 5, *The Story of the Liberator Crash*, London 1896 (quoted in Yapp, *op. cit.*, p.44).

BALMORI, Don Carlos (*See* **JURADO, Concepción**)

BALSAMO, Guiseppe (*See* **CAGLIOSTRO**)

BARRY, James (?1799–1865) (*IMPOSTORS*)
Joining the British army as a surgeon in 1816 and showing gallantry in campaigns about the world, Dr James Barry ultimately attained the rank of Inspector General of Hospitals in Canada. Nothing would have been odd about this but for the fact, revealed only on the death-bed, that 'he' was not a man but a woman.

Her identity is unknown. Arriving in London from Ireland in 1805 as a nameless, fatherless child, she may have been a niece of artist James Barry, but concealed whatever she knew of her ancestry, even calling her mother 'my aunt'. Wishing to study, as girls could not then enter higher education, she enrolled at Edinburgh University's medical school – as a boy. Aided by the rich Beaufort family (the Dukes of Somerset), the imposture succeeded, though fellow students noted that she was nervous in rough areas, refused to box, and often kept her arms folded over her chest. Graduating young, she worked in London as a pupil dresser to a top surgeon, then joined the army aged fourteen. Again the Beaufort connection helped. Posted to South Africa as personal physician to Lord Charles Somerset, Governor of the Cape, she began an odd relationship with him.

Rumour linked them and queried her gender from the start but, despite her slight figure and dyed hair, Barry played her role with style. A noted duellist, she fought for a leper colony to be built, for lunatics to be regarded as sick people, and reformed and improved hospital conditions and diet. High-minded and outspoken, when in 1825 she would not let a drunken sailor on a prison charge be declared mad she was summoned to explain herself but refused. Lord Charles annulled the civil sentence imposed on her, but she persisted with the case and was demoted, only to re-establish her reputation by saving a patient, Mrs Munnik, who seemed to be dying in labour. Barry had only read about the Caesarean operation, but carried it out successfully: both mother and daughter survived.

She was always making enemies. In Corfu during the Crimean war she verbally attacked to her face the soldier's nurse Florence Nightingale, who later wrote of her that: 'she was the most hardened creature I ever met throughout the army'.

Despite gossip that in Mauritius she had borne Somerset's child, her true sex seems only to have emerged once in her lifetime, when in the 1840s she fell ill and went to sleep uncovered. Awakening, she found two 'brother' officers at her bedside and swore them to secrecy. Yet tales must have persisted. On her final posting as Inspector General of Hospitals in Canada, she wore a silk bow on her uniform frock coat, long white gloves, and elegant patent leather boots. It seems likely that her true sex was common knowledge in the army and, when in 1865 she died in London, an army surgeon-major who had known her for years certified her death without mentioning her sex. It was left to Sophie Bishop, the Irishwoman who laid out the body, to declare that: 'The devil a General – it's a woman.' Noting stretch marks, she added: 'And a woman that has had a child.'[1] Failing to secure a bribe from the army agents to keep quiet, she gave the story to a Dublin newspaper. Asked why he hadn't mentioned Dr Barry's sex in his death certificate, the surgeon-major said he didn't consider it his business.

Barry, who left no record as to why she maintained this astonishing imposture so long, is commemorated today by the Barry Room at the Royal Army Medical College in Chelsea – the only part of the college where visiting women may remain unaccompanied.

1. Newnham, *op. cit.*, pp.197–9.

BARUCH, Hugo (1907–?) (*CONMEN, LITERARY HOAXES*)
Best known as 'Jack Bilbo,' this son of a rich German father and an English mother terrorised Scheveningen in Holland with his childhood gang before being sent to a boarding school, where later he claimed he had bullied his way to the top. Basically an adventurer-playboy with literary aspirations, an early visit to the USA soon saw him back in Germany, producing the *American Express Revue*, a show that failed when his leading lady, jealous of another woman, tried to poison him. Undeterred, in his early twenties he decided precociously that:

'It's stupid to try and work against the law. It doesn't pay. It's much better to bring off criminal transactions *with* the consent of the law . . . to be a banker and spread about false news, to corrupt the Press, and under cover of false information to put inflated dividends in one's pocket. That's merely called intelligent speculation.'[1]

His early attempts to put this philosophy into practice were not a success. First he toured Weimar Germany with his magic carpet trick. Possessing two genuine handmade Persian carpets of real value, he convinced pawnbrokers he had an entire store of such items, then pawned cheap imitations. Buying a carpet for one hundred marks and pawning it for two hundred against a supposed value of four hundred, he did well – until the law caught up with him. He later claimed that in jail he dominated the warders, writing their letters for them, and that, transferred to a lunatic asylum, he lectured the staff on 'The Place of Psychology in the Modern Prison System'. Whether any of this is true, the style is plain – that of the invincible egoist, in love with his own cleverness.

Released when the case collapsed, for the first time in twelve years he met his father, who claimed to have sold Ferdinand of Bulgaria's crown jewels for 100,000 marks. Moving on, at last he got his break, persuading the editor of the *Münchener Illustrierte Presse* to commission him as 'Jack Bilbo' to write *Carrying a Gun for Al Capone* (1930). This dramatic account of Chicago gangsterism, allegedly by one of Capone's mob, made 'Bilbo' famous. This burly thick-necked man who had never even been to Chicago posed for publicity shots in trenchcoat and hat with brim pulled down, pistol in his hand. When in 1934 he admitted the hoax, saying he had never carried a gun in his life, nobody wanted to know. The fantasy was much preferable, and for years to come he played it up to the hilt. None of his entertaining tales of his doings in the 1930s are reliable.

Wealthy now (the book was in print for years), Jack Bilbo drove to Monte Carlo, where a Russian, Gorguloff, asked for his help in assassinating the French President, Daumier. Declining, Bilbo returned to Berlin: Daumier duly died. Bilbo later claimed he had warned the French police but was ignored; that the Nazis warned him to keep quiet about Gorguloff; and that attempts were made to kill him. True? There is no way to tell.

In Paris he worked as a journalist, then 'quit the civilised world'. He opened a bar in Majorca then with his English girlfriend, Billi, moved to Sitges on the Costa Brava. Here, opening a new bar, he served his famous 'Knockout' (one part each of gin, absinthe, vodka and kummel) and entertained celebrities like Douglas Fairbanks and English author G.K. Chesterton, who in his autobiography described Bilbo as an 'authentic American gangster who had actually written a book of confessions about his own organised robbery and racketeering'.[2]

Next, he later claimed, he went to smuggle gold for the Ethiopians in their war against Italy. In Marseilles he met Father Philip, the tramps' padre, a conman specialising in faking road accidents, then, with a mysterious unnamed pilot and a man named John Brook went to Genoa, Athens, Cairo and the Sudan. Amid a forced landing in the desert, the intrepid adventurers were attacked by 'wild tribesmen'. In Ethiopia, Brook and the pilot were arrested by the Italians: Bilbo obtained Italian uniforms and they escaped. In Addis Ababa, received by the King of Ethiopia (he doesn't name Haile Selassie), he learned that the pilot was to take over the Ethiopian Air Force, and that John Brook was to manage the National Bank. 'I suddenly stopped being astonished,' he wrote, tongue doubtless firmly in cheek. 'Things like this are always happening to me.'

Further adventures in the Spanish Civil War brought him, Billi and his daughter to London in 1939. Exhibiting paintings, he was identified by *Time* magazine as a famous Chicago mobster, while a London newspaper said he'd killed at least a dozen people. Writing many more books as Bilbo, after the Second World War he became known as a sculptor and broadcaster. Sailing round the world in 1949 in a motor launch, the *Bambula*, when he returned he executed a huge sculpture, *Life*, 'symbolising the Women of England beaten to a kneeling position by the Blitz, but getting up more powerfully every time.'

One of the more attractive hoaxers, Hugo Baruch alias Jack Bilbo got what he wanted – to become (like Baron von **Münchausen**) the successful author of outrageous tales about his own life which almost everyone wanted to believe.

1. *I Can't Escape Adventure*, Jack Bilbo, Cresset Press, London 1937, p.32 (quoted in Yapp, *op. cit.*, p.84).
2. *Autobiography*, G.K. Chesterton, Hutchinson, London 1936, pp.315–16.

BATHTUB HOAX, The (*MEDIA HOAXES*)

The hoaxer's nightmare: a hoax you start but can't stop. On 28 December 1917 renowned American journalist H.L. Mencken published in the New York *Evening Mail* an article called 'The Neglected Anniversary'. In it, tongue-in-cheek, he regretted that nobody had noticed the passing of: 'the seventy-fifth anniversary of the introduction of the bathtub into these states'. Deadpan, he described how the first tub had been set up in Cincinnati by Adam Thompson, a cotton and grain dealer who had got into the unusual habit of bathing while visiting England. It was there, Mencken continued, that in 1828 a Lord John Russell had introduced a small tub – 'little more than a glorified dishpan' – and that by 1835 Russell had become so obsessed with bathing that he 'was said to be the only man in England who had yet come to doing it every day'.

Thompson decided, Mencken went on, to improve the English tub by enlarging it to hold an adult, and by feeding it via pipes bringing water from a central reservoir. So in 1842 he had constructed a tub of Nicaragua mahogany, seven feet long by four wide, that weighed 'about 1,750 pounds'. Early on 20 December 1842 he took a cold bath, then in the afternoon a warm one. On Christmas Day, four of his party guests 'risked plunges into it'. Despite medical opposition, the new invention spread rapidly. By 1850 nearly a thousand tubs were in use in New York. In 1851 the tub's respectability was assured when President Millard Fillmore had one installed in the White House. By 1860 every hotel in New York had a bathtub; some even two or three; in 1862 bathing was introduced to the army, and in 1870 a Philadelphia prison received its first tub.

'One is astonished,' Mencken concluded, 'to find that so little of it [the history of the bathtub] has been recorded.'

Soon he was horrified to see his 'tissue of absurdities' reprinted as fact in learned periodicals. Readers wrote requesting more information. Some even offered corroboration of his 'facts'. On 23 May 1926, nearly nine years later, he published a retraction of the original article, noting how his 'preposterous "facts" ' had taken on a reality of their own. They had been recited by quacks, by doctors, by Congressmen, in England and in Europe. They were appearing as fact in standard works of reference. 'Today, I believe,' he wrote, 'they are as accepted as gospel everywhere on earth. To question them becomes as hazardous as to question the Norman Invasion.' And he added: 'It is out of such frauds, I believe, that most of the so-called knowledge of humanity flows.'

This retraction was printed by nearly thirty American newspapers, including the *Boston Herald*, which published it under the headline: 'The American public will swallow anything.' Three weeks later, on the front page of its editorial section, the same newspaper reprinted Mencken's original fake story – but as a straight news article. Whether or not this was a deliberate prank by the editorial staff is not known.[1]

1. Goldberg *op. cit.*, pp.207–10.

BEGELMAN, David (contemporary) (***FRAUD***, *see also*
HOLLYWOOD HOAXES)
Who says crime doesn't pay? David Begelman, president of Columbia pictures, embezzled his own company in the 1980s by making out cheques for $10,000 to movie stars, forging the star's name, then cashing them. By Hollywood standards these were paltry sums. The swindle only came to light when actor Cliff Robertson, asked by the Inland Revenue Service why he hadn't declared $10,000 'paid' to him by Columbia pictures in a year when he hadn't worked for the studio, asked Columbia's accountants for the cancelled cheque. When he saw it he pointed out that the signature was forged. Begelman's 'creative book-keeping' came to light. Robertson went public. 'We're trying to stop a corruption that has become malignant in our industry and grown every year,' he said on the *Phil Donahue Show* – and didn't land another major role for years.

As for Begelman . . . Tinseltown couldn't afford to martyr him. Tried for grand felony theft, which should have carried a stiff jail sentence, he was fined $5,000 and sentenced to three years probation doing public service. A year later, after producing a film on the dangers of the drug PCP, his conviction was reduced from felony to misdemeanour by Judge Thomas C. Murphy, who had originally sentenced him. Revoking the remaining two years probation, Murphy declared that this pillar of the Hollywood community 'can go forward without the stigma of probation'.

So he did. To the horror of Robertson and others, Begelman was restored as head of Columbia, and a year later named President of Metro-Goldwyn-Mayer. BEGELMAN'S BACK AND MGM'S GOT HIM, ran a headline in the *Los Angeles Herald-Examiner*.

Enough said.[1]

1. Madison, *op. cit.*, pp.44–7.

BELANEY, Archibald (1888–1938) (*IMPOSTORS, LITERARY HOAXES*, *see also* **CARTER, Asa**; **DAVISON, Linda**; **JAMES, Will**)
Allegedly born in Mexico in 1888 to a Scotsman and his Apache wife just back from touring England with Buffalo Bill Cody and his Wild West Show, and later famed as Grey Owl ('The first Indian who really looked like an Indian'), Archibald Belaney was the greatest of several modern fakers to profit from the romantic image of Native Americans.

Son of a notorious local rake and the thirteen-year-old sister-in-law his father had married after the first wife died suspiciously, he was raised by maiden aunts in Hastings, England. With his father paid by the family to stay abroad, he attended the local grammar school but didn't fit in. He was always camping, tracking, living out his fantasy that he was really a North American Indian. He even began dyeing his skin dark, so that in 1906 his doubtless despairing relatives gave in and paid his way to Canada.

From Toronto he made his way into the forests of the interior, where he met the Ojibway tribe. He stayed with them, marrying a girl called Angele. Little emerged about his life in that period, but when the First World War broke out he enlisted as a private in the Canadian army. Wounded in Flanders in 1916, he found himself convalescing in Hastings Military Hospital. Renewing a childhood friendship with a local girl, Florence Holmes, he married her, but two years later left her and returned to the Ojibway.

Back in Canada he was horrified to see how the old ways were being destroyed so fast. Mines, railroads, and timber mills were everywhere. He went west to the land of the Iroquois, there marrying Gertrude Bernard who, adopting the Iroquois name of Anahareo, persuaded him to see how even traditional cultures were out of step with nature, and that hunting and trapping threatened wildlife.

At last Belaney found himself – as someone else. Adopting his Ojibway name of Wa-Sha-Quon-Asin, meaning 'He-Who-Flies-By-Night', duly simplified to 'Grey Owl', he began to write. His first book, *Men of the Last Frontier* (1931), was followed by *Pilgrims of the Wild*. And though the Ojibway and other Canadian woodsmen knew he was a fake, by 1930, when interviewed by writer Lloyd Roberts, Archibald Belaney had all but vanished. As Roberts enthused: 'the stamp of his fierce Apache ancestors showed in his tall, gaunt physique, his angular features, his keen eyes, even in his two braids dangling down from his fringed buckskin shirt'. So, before a delighted public, emerged the man allegedly born in Mexico in 1888 and adopted by the Ojibway, the backwoods trapper and guide who had fought in France then returned to nature with his beloved Iroquois wife. Falling in love with some orphaned baby beavers, he now devoted his life to animals. And this part was real enough. Public talks on nature boosted his income, and when in 1935 his publisher persuaded him to tour England, Grey Owl was a sensation.

Giving two hundred lectures in four months to over a quarter of a million people, with *Pilgrims* reprinted nine times in thirteen months, at Buckingham Palace he made a dramatic entry in fringed buckskins with wampum belt and sheathed knife, upstaging King George by announcing: 'I come in peace, brother.' He lectured in Hastings, asking if there were any Belaneys in the audience, and was recognised by Mary McCormick, who had grown up next door to the owl-hooting boy. Booked to speak on BBC Radio *Children's Hour*, he refused to delete a passage from his talk urging children to reject blood sports, and the show was cancelled. Rich and famous, he returned to Canada, where he wrote on until his premature death in April 1938.

The hoax promptly exploded, 'GREY OWL HAD COCKNEY ACCENT AND FOUR WIVES', ran one incorrect headline. And, yes, he was a bigamist, but impostor, charlatan, fake? If so, he was consistent throughout his life. He had always wanted to be an Indian, he lived the life he espoused, his hoax was well meant, and his conservationist work admirable. Probably he was a much greater man as the fake 'Grey Owl' than he could ever have been as the genuine but plain Archibald Belaney.

BERAHA, José (*See* **COUNTERFEITERS**)

BERG, David (1919–) (*FAKE MESSIAHS*)
Among the most lurid of the new religious cults emerging since the 1960s, the Children of God (later the Family of Love) was founded in southern California by David Brandt Berg, alias 'Moses' or 'Mo'. Originally a minister in the conservative Christian and Missionary Alliance Church, his mother (an evangelist who claimed to receive revelations about the future) alerted him to the growing numbers of young people living the 'turn on, tune in, and drop out' hippie life in Huntington Beach. Already critical of established faith, Berg went among them preaching worldly withdrawal and total commitment to the 'Jesus Revolution'. Abandoning drugs, his early followers called themselves 'Teens for Christ'.

His behaviour soon grew bizarre. In 1969, receiving a revelation that earthquake threatened California (so what's new?), he moved his fifty followers to Tucson, Arizona. Dividing into four teams, they preached the Jesus Revolution across America. Ordaining these first followers as bishops, elders and deacons, Berg told them of new revelations he had received. One, 'Old Church, New Church', justified his adultery with his secretary. Rather than end the liaison, he declared that his wife and mistress were models of the Old and New Church respectively. As God had abandoned the old church for the new, so Berg had turned from his wife Sarah to another woman. Acceptance of this arrant self-inflation by his followers led to an emphasis (justified as revolutionary Christian love) on group sex. Denouncing America as the Great Whore, Berg led his disciples to Washington and other cities where, wearing red sackcloth, they mourned the death of the God-forsaking USA. Adopting the name a reporter had given them, 'Children of God', they began calling Berg 'Moses', and in February 1970 settled on evangelist Fred Jordan's Soul Clinic ranch by Thurber, Texas.

Meanwhile angry parents losing children to the cult formed FREECOG (Parents Committee to Free Our Sons and Daughters from the Children of God'). Alleging brainwashing by drugs and hypnosis, they began physically kidnapping group members (their children) and 'deprogramming' them. Hostile publicity followed lurid accounts by ex-members of the cult's orgiastic lifestyle and subjugation of women. The cult dispersed after Jordan evicted it from the Soul Clinic, and Berg fled the USA, though not before (tax-exempt status being denied the Children of God due to the bad publicity) he had set up a second corporation (Youth for Truth, Inc.) to receive any financial assets.

Increasingly reclusive, communicating with his followers (now several thousands strong) from secret European locations via his 'Mo letters', Berg's megalomania increased. His warnings about the dangers of the approaching Comet Kohoutek (a damp squib on arrival in 1973) persuaded many followers to join him in Europe, where increasingly their ideas were moulded by the prophecies he received, supposedly from discarnate spirits with little or no Christian connection. Claiming to fulfil specific biblical prophecies, also the authority to teach new truth, in a Mo Letter of early 1974 Berg ordered the cult's women to use their sexual allure as 'flirty fishers' ('Hookers for Jesus') to seduce new members. After initial indoctrination as 'babes', these recruits became 'brothers' and 'sisters'. With nearly 10,000 members in Europe and Latin America, paedophilia, incest and even rape were encouraged (as witnessed by Berg's abandoned wife Sarah, and later by his daughter, Deborah Davis) – excesses toned down only after the spread of VD in the cult, later by the spread of AIDS in the wider community, and also after the 1978 mass cyanide suicide (alleged) in Guyana by 900 members of the People's Temple, the dupes of Jim **Jones**.

Renaming the cult the Family of Love, Berg (a prime example of a fake messiah corrupting others to justify his own lusts) continued to direct his fading empire from a suburban estate in London, though little more was heard of his now dispersed followers.[1]

1. *Encyclopedic Handbook of Cults*, J. Gordon Melton, Garland, New York 1986, pp.154–8.

BERKELEY, Humphry (20th century) (*PRANKS*)
In 1948 Humphry Berkeley, an undergraduate at Cambridge's Pembroke College, played a prank exposing the gullibility of supposedly intelligent men. Inventing Selhurst – an ancient college with 175 imaginary male boarders sited near Petworth in Sussex – he had letterhead stationery printed for Selhurst's equally imaginary headmaster, H. Rochester Sneath. Sneath began writing to prominent men, including the headmasters of England's most famous schools. On 15 March he wrote asking Marlborough's headmaster: 'how you managed to engineer a visit recently from the King and the Queen', as he desired such a visit for Selhurst's approaching tercentenary. Marlborough's headmaster, F.M. Heywood, replied huffily, saying he had not 'engineered' the royal visit. A week later he got another letter from Sneath, warning him not to hire a (fictional) French teacher, Agincourt, who in his one term at Selhurst had been seen climbing a tree naked by night, and who had thrown a flowerpot at the wife of the Chairman of the Board of Governors. When Heywood replied that Agincourt had not applied for a job, Sneath wrote back saying that Agincourt was now a waiter in a Greek restaurant in Soho. Adding that: 'Incidentally, I dined with the Lord Chancellor last night, and he spoke of you to me in the highest possible terms', Sneath now asked Heywood the name of his private detective, also asking him to recommend a good nursery maid. Tiring of the dour Heywood, he played other fish too. He offered Sir Giles Gilbert Scott, then rebuilding the Houses of Parliament, the chance to design a new House at Selhurst. He wrote to George Bernard Shaw, claiming that the late Mrs Shaw had Selhurst connections, inviting the aged playwright to speak at Selhurst's anniversary celebrations. Shaw declined, as did Sir Adrian Boult, invited to conduct the Selhurst School Orchestra in the first performance of the 'Selhurst Symphony'.

Asking Stowe's headmaster for advice on how to give his pupils sex education, Sneath told Rugby's headmaster that homosexuality among his pupils was: 'harmless . . . in most cases a transitory phase', suggested to Ampleforth's head arranging an art exhibition to tour South America, and thanked Blundell's for an imaginary invitation to preach there.

Of the thirty or so recipients of these absurd letters, only two saw through them. Berkeley's downfall came from his 13 April letter to the *Daily Worker*, bemoaning (at the peak of the Cold War) the difficulty in establishing compulsory Russian at his school. He couldn't even get hold of textbooks. Requesting an interview, the magazine *News Review* was not put off when Sneath's imaginary secretary Penelope Pox-Rhyddene explained that Sneath was ill and could communicate only by letter. Learning that Selhurst School did not exist, a reporter tracked down Berkeley at Cambridge and exposed his hoax in a 29 April article, 'Death of Rochester Sneath'.

The English establishment was not amused. Sent down for two years amid the subsequent pompous outcry, Berkeley later graduated to become a Member of Parliament, suggesting (what a relief!) that at least some politicians have a sense of humour.[1]

1. *The Life and Death of Rochester Sneath*, Humphry Berkeley, Davis-Poynter, London 1974.

BERMUDA TRIANGLE, The (*PARANORMAL HOAXES*)

Perhaps less hoax than folk-myth, in the 1970s this western Atlantic area between Bermuda, Puerto Rico and Florida was famed for the many ships and planes said to have been lost in it, leaving no wreckage or survivors. It was said such losses were preceded by garbled radio reports, strange fogs, electronic failures, and other oddities. Coastguard insistence that unexplained losses were due to heavy traffic, sudden violent storms and the capacity of the Gulf Stream to carry disabled ships rapidly off course was ignored amid a fever of popular speculation. Occultists and UFOlogists theorised that an unknown force (electromagnetic?) destroyed the lost vessels, or translated them into other dimensions, or even that the derangement was caused by submarine crystal generators left by Atlanteans ten millennia ago. Official denials, of course, proved a cover-up, of ignorance or complicity.

The myth began on 5 December 1945 when Training Flight 19 of five US Navy Grumman TBM-3 torpedo-bombers from Fort Lauderdale was lost after odd radio calls were received from the flight leader: 'We seem to be off course. We cannot see land. We don't know which way is west. Everything is wrong . . . even the ocean doesn't look as it should.' Fading inter-flight messages suggested magnetic compasses and gyros in the planes 'going crazy'. A thirteen-man Martin Mariner went out and was also lost. A vast search found nothing. 'They vanished as completely as if they had flown to Mars,' a Naval Board member allegedly said. In fact the authenticity of this statement is as dubious as that of the Flight 19 radio calls, which originate in a 1962 magazine article. It didn't matter. The mystery grew with each succeeding 'unexplained' loss. In 1964 author Vincent Gaddis coined the name 'Bermuda Triangle'. Novels, movies, even a board-game came out. Milked for all it was worth, the mystery was enlarged via fake data, hyperbole, and plain invention by authors like Charles Berlitz in his influential 1974 bestseller.[1]

Consider the 1924 case of the Japanese freighter *Raifaku Maru*. Its last radio call, said to be: 'Danger like dagger now', was actually logged as: 'Now very danger . . .' And though the barque *Freya* was found abandoned in October 1902, it was in the Pacific, not the Atlantic. Other Bermuda Triangle 'losses' offered as such occurred as far away as the coasts of Ireland and Portugal. As for Eastern Airlines Flight 401, which Berlitz claims 'suffered a loss by disintegration' (implying a sudden mysterious mid-air break-up), what happened is that the plane, flying at night with autopilot off, lost altitude without the pilots noticing and flew into the ground – and in the Florida Everglades, not in the sea at all![2]

There *have* been losses in this perilous area, but evidence of distortion in most loss reports is plain. Flight 19 involved an inexperienced crew, rough weather, poor radio conditions, and a flight leader uncorrected when off course. Running out of fuel amid a storm, the planes ditched in heavy seas that tore them apart. Forty-six years later, the wreckage of Flight 19 was located on the sea-bed (an identification since disputed). Maybe there are electromagnetic anomalies in the region – but more to the point are the imaginative anomalies in the human mind, and the way that popular belief can be led by the nose to create a bandwagon which, despite total lack of evidence, makes some people wealthy while entertaining others with a fantastic tale.

1. *The Bermuda Triangle*, Charles Berlitz, Granada, London 1975.
2. Randi, *op. cit.*, p.46.

BETTELHEIM, Bruno (1903–90) (*SCIENTIFIC SCAMS*)
Surviving a Nazi concentration camp during the Second World War, this Jewish-born scholar emigrated to the USA, developed a reputation for profound psychiatric insight, and in time became an authority on childhood autism.

In 1976 (the year Sir Cyril **Burt**'s frauds were exposed), and by now the Director of Chicago's Orthogenic School for emotionally disturbed children, he published what at first appeared to be a seminal work, entitled *The Uses of Enchantment: The Meaning and Importance of Fairy Tales*.

Claiming to have tapped the authentic original versions of the tales he psychoanalysed, and assuming the existence of an archetypal folk wisdom in their detail, his case was not improved by his reliance on the scholarship of those recently exposed fakers, the **Brothers Grimm**. Even so, no scandal would have attached itself to his name – had his opinions been his own.

But after his death it emerged that *The Uses of Enchantment* had largely been copied from *A Psychiatric Study of Fairy Tales*, a book published in 1963. With stunning academic gall, Bettelheim had discussed the same tales not only in the same order but, for the most part, in the same words. It was, said a whistle-blowing professor of anthropology from the University of California's Berkeley campus: 'not just a matter of occasional borrowing of random passages, but a wholesale borrowing of key ideas'.

Of course, given the laws of libel, it is always much safer to attack a revered expert *post mortem*. Yet not only Bettelheim's academic honesty but the rest of his reputation crashed after his death, when it emerged that in life he had been less than the kindly war-wounded sage he'd appeared to be.

Adults who'd been in his Orthogenic School, fearing to speak out during his lifetime, now said he'd often diagnosed normal children as disturbed so that later he could claim to have cured them. Persuading desperate parents that autism was due to bad mothering, he had accepted large sums of money to offer help he could not give. Nonetheless, and despite evidence that he had been an impulsive child-abuser, he had never been exposed.

'He will not be missed,' said Bernard Rimland, an expert on autism.[1]

1. Lindskoog, *op. cit.*, pp. 170–1.

BIDLO, Michael (contemporary) (*ART FORGERS, PRANKS*)
Proponent of 'plagiarism as art', this contemporary New York artist has produced many famous paintings. Problem is, they were all made famous by other painters. Bidlo's imitations infuriate critics, and the critics infuriate him. He asserts that: 'Most people only "know" art through the eyes of critics . . . who are tied up in cliques and political grudges. It all gets me very mad.' Imitating Andy Warhol's soup cans and Marilyn Monroe silk-screens, filling a room with pseudo-Brancusi heads, or hiring three models to stand stock-still before his recreation of Picasso's *Les Demoiselles d'Avignon* for five hours straight, his work is not so much hoax as implication that the entire art world, with its intellectual fads and inflated prices for dead artists, is itself a hoax – which may well be why so many art critics (not always renowned for seeing through fakes) loathe him.[1]

1. Vale and Juno (eds), *op. cit.*, pp.54–9.

BILBO, Jack (*See* **BARUCH, Hugo**)

BLACK, Charles (*See* **COUNTERFEITERS**)

'BLACK RADIO' (*See* **HOAXES IN WARFARE**)

BLAY-MIEZEH, John Ackah (contemporary) (*IMPOSTORS*)

This sweet-talking Ghanaian, passing himself off as the royal heir to a snowballing $27 billion trust fund tied up at home, took many wealthy Americans for a ride. Seeking loans to aid his fight to acquire what he said was rightfully his, in return he offered interest of up to 1,000 per cent. It is said that in Philadelphia alone he scooped up to $18 million, and that between 1972 and 1986 he and his US 'agent', Robert Ellis, took in sums close to a billion dollars. Though continually called a fraud by the media, for years he lived in luxury while raking it in. Yet when he went back to Ghana to monitor the 'trust fund', he was arrested and condemned to death. Maybe his visit was stimulated by his imminent arrest in America: his partner Ellis remains (1994) imprisoned for fraud and grand theft.

His flirtation with Death Row didn't last long. Aided by rich friends, soon he was living the high life in London, prising more cash out of wealthy idiots. By all accounts he continues to live the opulent life of one who knows that the biggest lie is also the best.[1]

1. Madison, *op. cit.*, pp.133–5.

BLOOD LIBEL (*See* **ANTI-SEMITIC HOAXES**)

BLOXHAM, Arnall (*See* **PAST-LIFE MEMORIES**)

'BODYGUARD OF LIES' (*See* **HOAXES IN WARFARE**)

BOTTOMLEY, Horatio (1860–1933) (*CONMEN*, *see also* **TOPLIS, Percy**)

As unsavoury as Jabez **Balfour**, this son of London's East End was orphaned aged five. Intelligent and self-confident, from the start he sought wealth, fame, women and power. Bored with honest work as a solicitor's clerk then as a shorthand writer in the Law Courts, he turned to fraud. Launching a publishing company, he bought other properties including a printing works in Devon for over £200,000, then sold them to the publishing company for £325,000. Tried for fraud, he defended himself so well that the trial judge, acquitting him, suggested he should be a lawyer – so much for judicial discretion. Making a fortune promoting Australian gold mines, between 1895 and 1905 he promoted over fifty companies with a total capital of over £20 million.

His technique was to start a company, declare high dividends so the shares would rocket, then sell at the inflated price. With the company sinking he would create a new company to buy up the lame duck with new funds offered by eager shareholders. He did well for himself. With a country estate in Sussex, a flat in London's Pall Mall, and a villa in the

South of France, he ran racehorses and a stable of mistresses. Founding the ugly jingoistic magazine *John Bull* in 1906, his fake patriotism was rewarded by his election as Liberal MP for South Hackney in London. Though forced to resign from Parliament in 1912 due to a bankruptcy case, when war broke out in 1914 he established himself as 'the Tommies' Friend' and 'The Hater of the Hun'. He even had the nerve to charge £50 a time making recruitment speeches to get young men to join the army. In 1915 he all but ruined the pacifist leader of the Labour Party, Ramsay MacDonald, calling him (in *John Bull*): 'Traitor, Coward, Cur', and 'the illegitimate son of a Scotch servant girl.' Nothing was too low for the well-named Bottomley.

Oddly, in 1917 he was at the British army base camp at Etaples near Boulogne when mutiny led by deserter Percy Toplis erupted. It was to Bottomley that Toplis made his demand that army pay be improved before the mutineers returned to their posts.

Re-elected to Parliament in 1918, a year later he went too far. The government had issued Victory Bonds with a face value of £5. Investors could buy them at a discount, but working people could not afford them. Posing as the little man's friend, Bottomley launched his Victory Bond Club. People could invest as little or as much as they wanted; the club would buy the bonds for them. Of the estimated half-million pounds that flowed into the club in six months, Bottomley took a third for himself. Accused of fraud by a former partner, he found himself and his empire under investigation. Prosecuted in 1922 for fraud, this time his silver tongue was useless. Sentenced to seven years in prison, he boasted that fifty thousand ex-Servicemen would march on Westminster in his support. They didn't. Released on licence in 1926, he tried but failed to restore his former lifestyle, and died in poverty in 1933. There's some justice after all.

BOWER, Doug (*See* **CROP CIRCLES**)

BRINKLEY, 'Doc' John (1885–1942) (*SCIENTIFIC SCAMS*)
From time immemorial impotent men have sought rejuvenation via implantation of sexual organs or by taking testicular extracts. Early in the twentieth century the Russian Serge-Samuel Voronoff was using testicular slice grafts in experiments on rams, and at San Quentin prison Leo Stanley made the first transplant operation on human testicles. Further pioneer research was undertaken by two doctors in Chicago; and by 1920 people spoke knowledgeably of the 'monkey gland' treatment. By then 'Doc' John Brinkley had already concluded that goats' glands offered a more promising area for profitable development.

Growing up in rural north Carolina, Brinkley spared no effort to gain educational qualifications, in 1915 gaining an arts degree from a 'diploma mill' in St Louis despite never studying there. Bribing the registrar to backdate the award by two years, he persuaded the Eclectic Medical University of Kansas to put his St Louis degree towards its diploma. Licensed to practise in Kansas, in October 1917 he settled in rural Milford. His medical knowledge was sound, and he opened a pharmacy that stocked useful drugs. He could have been content with being a useful citizen. But he was ambitious, and soon after his arrival at Milford did his first graft, using a goat as donor. A year later the patient, impotent for sixteen years, fathered a baby which he and his wife called Billy.

Brinkley was sensible. The testicles of goats (less prone to diseases like TB and VD) are small, can be implanted whole, are easy to obtain in the Mid-West, and symbolise sexual prowess. Soon his business thrived. Paying $750 for the standard goat implant, or $2,000 if the testes came from a human donor, patients in on a Monday were usually out by Friday. The effect of the implantation, if any, was psychological – the human body's immune system ensures that any animal tissue grafted in will soon be rejected. Yet soon the 'Doc' had hired most of Milford's two hundred citizens to run his mail-order scheme, and by 1923 his radio station daily solicited anxious men. Up to 2,000 letters a day went out to prospective clients. Slaughterhouses were full of doomed goats. He became well known. Questions were asked. His claims and qualifications were doubted by a local newspaper, the *Kansas City Star*, then by the journal of the American Medical Association. In 1929 the Kansas board of medical registration and examination took him to court. The case opened in July 1930. Brinkley played the man of the people, and medical opinion was on his side, but his qualifications were clearly fake. He lost his licence, but that autumn ran as a popular 'write-in' candidate for state governor. He lost only because 50,000 votes were spoiled, and thereafter continued in medicine and broadcasting, first in Texas, then in Arkansas. Still making over a million dollars a year, in 1936 he rented one of his three yachts to the Duke of Windsor and Wallis Simpson for their honeymoon.

At last in 1938 he sued the American Medical Association for calling him a quack, came off worst, then declined into obscurity, dying of a heart attack. Same old story.[1]

1. Newnham, *op. cit.*, pp.59–61.

BROCKWAY, William (*See* COUNTERFEITERS)

BRUCE, James (1731–94) (*EXPLORATION HOAXES*)
It is rare in this survey to find a man who did all he claimed, only to be accused of fraud. Such a man was the Scot James Bruce. Perhaps the

greatest African explorer of the eighteenth century, in 1769 he disappeared into Northeast Africa, then four years later reappeared at Marseilles, claiming to have found the source of the Blue Nile. His exotic tales made him a celebrity, but he died derided as a fake, his reputation in eclipse for years.

In part this is because he was a Scot, and his critics were English; in part because then there were so many travel hoaxes and hoaxers that nobody knew what to believe, and in part because, like many explorers, he had a difficult personality. Tall, imposing, loud and energetic, he lost his mother aged two, and was sickly into early adulthood – which also fits the pattern of many solo explorers.

Well-educated but directionless, aged twenty-two he fell in love with Adriana Allen, daughter of a rich wine merchant. In October 1754, three months pregnant and after less than a year of marriage, she died of tuberculosis.

Bruce spent the next four years studying languages and travelling Europe. Learning Arabic, he encountered the Ethiopian studies of the German scholar Job Ludolf. Back in Scotland, he retired early to manage his estate, but in 1762 was persuaded by Lord Halifax to go to North Africa to draw the ancient Roman ruins for King George III's collection.

It was twelve years before he returned. Enduring disease, shipwreck and local hostility, adding medicine and astronomy to his skills, he developed an obsessive will, and in 1769 – increasingly seized by the mystery of Ethiopia, unvisited by any European since Poncet in 1699 – reached Massawa on the Red Sea coast, intending to find the source of the Nile. To do so he endured such hardships and witnessed so many outlandish events – like men cutting steaks from a living cow – that his account (*Travels to Discover the Source of the Nile*, 1790) only stimulated further disbelief.

Traversing deserts and mountains to the inland fortress of Gondar, he reached the source of the Blue Nile while serving as a general in the Ethiopian civil war. Ingratiating himself with both sides, he saved his own life by saving the lives of the sons of Ozoro Esther, wife of rebel leader Ras Michael, when he cured them of smallpox. Virtually imprisoned in Gondar for a year and a half, at last he escaped north into Egypt. It took him eleven months to reach Aswan. On the twenty-day trek between Berber and Aswan some of his men and all his camels died. Abandoning his drawings and writings, he reached safety. Returning for his records, to his 'unspeakable satisfaction' he found them untouched.

Reaching Marseilles in March 1773, he was lionised in France and Italy, but on his return to London in June 1774 was derided by Samuel Johnson and James Boswell among others. Taciturn and rude, he was regarded as a curiosity, and soon his account met with open disbelief.

Far from endorsing the popular image of Rousseau's 'Noble Savage', he described a barbarous, treacherous and debauched land. Nobody wanted to believe it. Retiring to Scotland and withdrawing from society, his long-awaited memoirs appeared at last in 1790. It was an overnight bestseller, but the London critics scorned it. The worst insult came when a new supplement appeared to the adventures of the popular fictional hero Baron von **Münchausen**, dedicated to Bruce and based directly on his Ethiopian travels.

In April 1794, helping an old lady down his staircase, he slipped and fell the length of the steps. Crushed by his own enormous bulk, by morning he was dead.

He died believing that his daughter (he had remarried): 'would live to see the truth of all I have written completely and decisively confirmed'. She did.[1]

1. Roberts, *op. cit.*, pp.57–77.

BRUSSELS MARATHON (*FRAUD*)

When in September 1991 the Algerian runner Abbes Tehami finished far ahead of the field in the Brussels Marathon, spectators noted that he seemed to have grown bigger during the race, and that his moustache had vanished. It emerged that his coach had run the first ten miles before swapping his running vest with Tehami, who had been hiding behind a tree. Tehami was disqualified. 'In my time I have not come across such an incident in an international race,' said a senior IAAF official, who obviously had forgotten or never heard of Rosie Ruiz, a runner who similarly tried to fake victory, in the 1980 Boston Marathon. In the publicity over her deception, which unravelled when videotapes showed her failing to pass checkpoints, the *Boston Globe* revived the tale of an English Channel swimming hoax from the 1920s. Like Ruiz, a woman who had ridden in a boat most of the way then claimed a record had wilted under hostile questioning.

Commenting on these last two cases, author David Roberts remarks that women seem less able or willing than men to perpetrate and carry through hoaxes; that they lack 'that dogged, secretive fanaticism that allowed [a hoaxer like] Frederick **Cook** to insist up to his dying days that he had been wronged . . .'[1]

Can feminists accept this no doubt politically incorrect suggestion that women may inherently be more honest than men?

1. Roberts, *op. cit.*, p.176.

BUFFALO CHAINSAW HOAX (*See* HOFFMAN, Abbie)

'BUNGA BUNGA' (*See* COLE, Horace de Vere)

BURT, Sir Cyril (1883–1971) (*SCIENTIFIC SCAMS*)
Widely considered the most prestigious and powerful psychologist of his day, Sir Cyril Burt held the chair of psychology at London's University College from 1932 to 1950, was knighted by King George VI, and received many academic awards. Much of his career, beginning with an Oxford scholarship from his home in rural Warwickshire, was based on statistical studies of the intelligence of identical twins, purporting to prove poverty due to the inferior intelligence of the working classes – a theory found acceptable by conservatives for social if not for scientific reasons. At any rate, his reputation led the British government to seek his advice in the 1940s in setting up a three-tier school system segregating students on the basis of the 'Eleven Plus' – an IQ test taken at the age of eleven.

Yet, though a dazzling public speaker of enormous charm, not everyone was sure he could be trusted. Late in life he seemed to undergo a change of character. Faking letters to his own journal, playing down colleagues in favour of himself and his own conclusions, he edited genuine papers in a way that often outraged their authors. 'I don't believe a word the old rogue says,' remarked the famous geneticist L.S. Penrose after a speech by Burt at a London symposium in 1960, 'but, by God, I admire the way he says it.'

When Burt died aged 88 in 1971, tributes flooded in – for a while.

A year after his death, Princeton psychologist Leon Kamin found major flaws in his statistics. In three different studies of different numbers of identical twins, Burt had (incredibly) reported the same statistical correlation of IQ scores to the third decimal point. Similar flaws in his work dated back as far as 1909. Many were reluctant to face the implications, saying if Burt had truly faked his data he would have made a better job of it.

Then in 1976 the *Sunday Times* reported the shocking news that Burt's two field investigators and co-authors of his studies, Margaret Howard and J. Conway, had never existed. These two experts, who had often praised Burt in their reviews and attacked his enemies, were pseudonyms for Burt himself. It became clear that Burt had systematically lied and falsified data throughout his professional career. Given that much of his 'research' had grave social implications concerning the assumed inheritance of intelligence, the fraud he perpetrated was vicious. Ordinary conmen indulge ordinary greed: men like Burt, **Bettelheim** and **Lysenko**, who use their prestige and the trust invested in them to falsify data supporting continuing social inequities or spurious political theories, are perhaps more iniquitous. Then again: to err is human, to forgive, divine.

Despite the evidence, it took the British Psychological Society another six years to acknowledge Burt as a faker. 'Burt's crime is the very plausibility of his fiction, which was manufactured to feed his, and our prejudices,' accurately wrote R. Estling in the *New Scientist* for 17 June 1982, perhaps not without a trace of shamefacedness.[1]

1. Kohn, *op. cit.*, pp.52–7.

BYRD, Admiral Richard E. (1888–1957) (*EXPLORATION HOAXES*)

Another man driven to claim what he never achieved, when what he did achieve was enough. In 1926 Commander Richard E. Byrd had been retired from the US Navy for ten years due to a bad leg. Learning to fly in Florida, he had hired a young mechanic, Floyd Bennett, as his official pilot. Though a superb airman, Bennett was in awe of his employer, and it may be that deference arising from that awe persuaded Byrd to pretend to the world that he truly had made the trans-polar flight he genuinely attempted, even though Bennett, not he, was the pilot.

Efforts to reach the North Pole had already generated hoaxes. **Cook**'s reputation had been ruined, and **Peary**, though credited with the feat in 1909, remains doubted by many. Only the Norwegian Roald Amundsen, who had reached the South Pole in 1911, remains regarded as undoubtedly honest. Amundsen had already tried to fly to the North Pole in 1925, but one of the engines on his Dornier-Wal amphibious plane had failed just 156 miles short and the effort had been abandoned. He had not pretended otherwise. In April 1926 he was ready to try again, in a dirigible piloted by the Italian Umberto Nobile.

On 29 April his party was already at King's Bay, Spitzbergen, when Byrd's fifty-strong American expedition arrived on a steamship. On board it was a Dutch tri-motor Fokker, the *Josephine Ford*. Amundsen learned that Byrd also planned to fly to the Pole.

Byrd had been to Greenland a year before with Donald MacMillan, a veteran of Peary's 1909 expedition. That expedition, like this, had been sponsored by the National Geographic Society. Byrd, who was well connected, also had the financial support of the millionaires John D. Rockefeller, J. Vincent Astor and Edsel Ford. A race was in the offing, but Amundsen was magnanimous, even offering Byrd the help of an additional pilot, Bernt Balchen. Byrd, anxious to get going, declined all assistance, and on 9 May 1926, after two test flights, with Byrd as navigator and Bennett as pilot, the *Josephine Ford* took off. Byrd told reporters he expected the round-trip flight to take about twenty hours, and he had, he estimated, enough fuel to last for a twenty-four-hour flight.

Less than sixteen hours later the Fokker returned to King's Bay. Byrd claimed the crown, and nobody, least of all Amundsen, accused him of fakery, though the *Josephine Ford* was leaking oil from the right engine.

Two days later Amundsen's dirigible the *Norge* took off. On 12 May it passed directly over the North Pole and on 14 May landed at Teller in Alaska. Meanwhile Byrd had scooped the fame. Reaching London on 27 May, he was lionised. Yet doubts began to emerge. Norwegian and Italian journalists, championing their own crew, publicly denied that Byrd could have made the round trip so quickly. Byrd said he would submit his proofs to the National Geographic Society, once back in America.

In New York he was mobbed as a national hero. There was a ticker-tape parade up Broadway. President Coolidge gave him the National Geographic Society's Hubbard Gold Medal. Bennett, who seemed subdued, was ignored . . . and said nothing. Answering his European doubters, Byrd said his unprecedented speed was due to a helpful tailwind all the way north which, when they reached the Pole, had promptly changed direction and swept them all the way south again. Nothing could be proved against him. Bennett, who kept quiet, caught influenza in Labrador in 1928 and died before medicine could reach him.

'One thing I want you to promise me, Bernt,' he said to the pilot Bernt Balchen, among the last to see him alive. 'No matter what happens, you fly to the South Pole with Byrd.' Which Balchen duly did.

Byrd was a hero all his life, and though his achievement was doubted by polar explorers, no gossip surfaced. But after Byrd's death in 1957 Balchen, writing his own memoirs in *Come North With Me*, set the record straight. He told how, in a Chicago hotel in 1927, Bennett had uneasily admitted to him that the *Josephine Ford* had got nowhere near the Pole. He also claimed that, on the Atlantic and South Pole flights he had piloted for Byrd, the hero (supposedly the navigator) had not taken one single sextant reading. So not even the South Pole flight could be verified. Moreover, on one flight in Antarctica Byrd had got so drunk on cognac he had to be carried from the plane when it landed.

E.P. Dutton & Co. had printed 4,000 copies of *Come North With Me* when the pressure began. Lawyers representing Byrd threatened Balchen with libel, slander, and defamation of character suits, even though Balchen had characterised Byrd as a great man who had 'dreamed a big dream'. They talked of having him deported back to Sweden, even though he was now an American citizen. Dutton gave way, printing a censored second edition. Balchen had little option but to acquiesce. Yet after his death in 1971, Random House and author Richard Montague revealed the censorship, bravely reviving Balchen's original passages which showed Byrd in such a poor light.

The controversy continues. Many refuse to disbelieve Byrd's claims – but all the evidence suggests that he and Bennett got nowhere near the North Pole, and that Amundsen and Nobile were the first. Yet not even

Amundsen and Nobile actually *stood* on the Pole. So, assuming that Peary as well as Cook lied about reaching the Pole, the first men actually to stand there were four members of the crew of a ski-equipped American C-47 which landed on 3 May 1953. What were their names? Who knows? The exploring world then was more concerned with the conquest of Everest.[1]

1. Roberts, *op. cit.*, pp.126–35.

C

'In wartime, truth is so precious that she should always be attended by a bodyguard of lies.'

(attributed to Winston S. Churchill; in fact a Russian proverb quoted to Churchill by Stalin)

CABOT, Sebastian (*c.*1475–1557) (*EXPLORATION HOAXES*)
A voyage vital to English claims in North America was made from Bristol in 1508 by Venetian mariner Sebastian Cabot. With 300 men in two ships he crossed the Atlantic, visited the Newfoundland Banks which his father John had found in 1497 on the first English New World expedition, then pushed on northeast up the Labrador coast to the ice-clogged Hudson Strait to enter Hudson Bay a century before Hudson 'discovered' it. Turning south, he explored the eastern seaboard to the tip of Florida, before returning to England in April 1509 to find his patron King Henry VII replaced by King Henry VIII.

So history claims. But this epic voyage may have been a fake.

An accomplished hoaxer, Sebastian Cabot won success in both England and Spain as an expert in northern navigations by convincing folk he owned secret geographical lore. He so downplayed his father's achievements that by 1550 John Cabot's name was all but forgotten. In 1512, four years after the supposed 1508 voyage, he entered Spanish service and next worked for the English in 1548. The first English source for the 1508 voyage is in 1555, when one Richard Evans recorded skimpy details of it from the old man's lips. Otherwise the sole references to it consist of fragmentary, mutually contradictory accounts in Latin, Italian, Spanish, French and Portuguese, nearly all third or fourth hand. The nearest thing to evidence by Cabot himself appears in a 1556 volume of navigations of the Venetian Ramusio, printing the summary of a letter he claimed Cabot had sent him.

Modern doubt was first thrown on Sebastian's voyage in 1897 by the Frenchman Henry Harrisse as England celebrated the four-hundredth anniversary of John Cabot's discovery of the American mainland (Columbus only reached the West Indies in his early voyages). Harrisse concluded, with much evidence, that only Cabot's own 'vainglorious and erratic' boasts suggested that the expedition had ever happened.

For example, when Cabot, then in Spanish service, visited England in 1521 and agreed with Henry VIII to lead a major English expedition of discovery, the king ordered London's twelve great livery companies to contribute. But the Drapers objected, stating that: 'Sebastyan, as we say here, was never in that land hym self, all if he makes reporte of many thinges as he hath hard [heard] his Father and other men speke in tymes past.' London's merchants knew Sebastian Cabot was a fraud who (as history suggests) spent his life playing Venice against England and Spain (and who got away with it).[1]

The arguments pro and con may never be resolved. But worth noting is that the English king allegedly patronising the 1508 expedition was Henry VII, a hoaxer himself. He had seized the throne in 1485 despite lack of proper claim by blackening the name of his predecessor whose downfall he engineered – **Richard III**, alias 'Crookback Dick', the vile hunchback who murdered the Princes in the Tower to seize power. Many still suspect that this image of Richard was Henry Tudor's propaganda, designed to support his own shaky position. Such a wily man would have been quite capable of agreeing to a fake expedition, acceptance of which would only improve English claims in America.

1. Roberts, *op. cit.*, pp.1–15.

CAGLIOSTRO, Count Alessandro Di (1743?–95?) (*IMPOSTORS*)
Either the 'King of Liars' (Carlyle) or 'One of the great occult figures of all time' (Lewis Spence), Cagliostro was a remarkable man. 'While not actually handsome,' wrote a hostile witness, the Baroness D'Oberkirch, 'his face was the most remarkable I have ever seen. His eyes were . . . indescribable – all fire and yet all ice.'

Born Guiseppe Balsamo to a poor Sicilian family, his death in an Inquisition prison only increased the legend of this adventurer who lived all his life by his wits. He began by stealing from the church poor box and his uncle's savings to escape Sicily, was rejected as a novitiate monk for blasphemy, roamed in Egypt with the Greek alchemist Altotas, then settled to a lucrative criminal life in Rome. Forging banknotes and peddling aphrodisiacs, he insinuated himself into high society by marrying a beautiful fourteen-year-old slum girl, Lorenza Feliciani, when twenty-six. The bait to lure rich victims into Balsamo's clutches, she helped him to the heights of fame – then sent him tumbling down again.

Soon after their marriage in France they met Casanova, who thought them persons of rank. In London he worked as a painter but was jailed for debt. When a benefactor, M. Duplessis, seduced Lorenza, in outrage he applied for royal redress, and Lorenza spent a year in jail. Apparently she forgave him and on her release they returned to Italy, Balsamo now the Marchese Pellegrini. He pulled off spectacular confidence tricks – until in Palermo a goldsmith he'd swindled had him thrown in jail. It was time for a change. So in 1776, now calling himself Count Cagliostro and Lorenza the Countess Serafina (stolen, he said, from an oriental harem), he returned to London – and discovered Freemasonry.

The rage to join this mysterious, semi-occult order had consumed Europe's rich merchant classes. It was tailor-made for Cagliostro. Inventing 'the Egyptian rite', claiming powers of second sight and clairvoyance, as Grand Master of his London lodge he began a triumphant tour of Europe. Celebrated everywhere, he lost no opportunity to exercise his powers. In Leipzig he declared that if the local lodge failed to adopt the Egyptian rite, its master would feel the hand of God within the month. Soon the master, Scieffort, killed himself. In the Baltic state of Courland, the nobles wanted to crown him king. He took Paris and Moscow by storm, everywhere recruiting followers, often by occult fraud. Using young boys or girls he called *colombes* ('doves') to scry the future for him by gazing into bowls of clear water, at least twice he had to brazen his way out when the *colombe* said it was all a fake. About then he met that other great faker, **Saint-Germain**.

On 19 September 1780, with liveried servants on black horses preceding him, he entered Strasbourg in his black coach. Now claiming to have been born before the Flood, to have talked with Moses and to have studied under Socrates, and to have drunk wine at the wedding feast in Cana, he dated his letters 550 BC. Taking a room in a poor quarter of the city he distributed alms and snubbed those who called him a fake. To the philosopher Lavater he said: 'If your science is greater than mine, you have no need of my acquaintance; if mine is the greater, I have no need of yours.' Likewise he insulted the Cardinal de Rohan, an intimate of French Queen Marie Antoinette.

Both Lavater and de Rohan became his disciples. Yet here lay his downfall. Driven on to Paris by the hostility of local doctors, he and Lorenza got involved in de Rohan's plot to gain the Queen's love via the infamous Diamond Necklace Affair. Thrown into the Bastille, they were exonerated at their trial, but his craven behaviour and Lorenza's admissions under interrogation of the tricks of his trade made him a laughing stock.

Expelled from France, they wandered Europe, increasingly shunned, and in 1789 made the mistake of returning to Rome. Creating a new Egyptian Rite Masonic Lodge to revive his fortunes, in 1791 (denounced by Lorenza to save her own skin) he was seized by the papal police and condemned to death as a heretic. The Pope commuted the sentence to life imprisonment, but it was in the dungeons of the Castel San Leo that he died, probably strangled, on 26 August 1795, a year after Lorenza's death in a nunnery. He was not so immortal after all.

CAMPBELL, Ken (contemporary) (*PRANKS*)

Already known in Britain for the gargantuan thirty-hour production by his Science Fiction Theatre of Liverpool of the cult *Illuminatus!* trilogy (itself a through-the-looking-glass maze of hoaxes) by Robert Shea and Robert Anton Wilson, in 1980 director and TV actor Ken Campbell pulled off an ambitious spoof – the fake creation of the Royal Dickens Company. It began when, at a Royal Shakespeare Company production of the Dickens novel *Nicholas Nickleby*, a friend in the cast told him that director Trevor Nunn had encouraged the company to adopt the style of *The Ken Campbell Road Show* in their approach to the play. The connection escaped him, but his visit stimulated the hoax.

Preparing headed writing paper perfectly duplicating Royal Shakespeare Company notepaper, save that 'Dickens' replaced 'Shakespeare' and 'RSC' became 'RDC', and having learned that Trevor Nunn signed his letters, 'Love Trev', Campbell wrote letters to dozens of theatrical luminaries. Writing as Nunn, he explained that *Nicholas Nickleby* 'has been such a real joy to cast, staff and audience that we have decided to turn to Dickens as our main source of inspiration'.

Thus declaring the shocking news that the RSC was about to abandon the Bard, and suggesting that the next production should be *Sketches by Boz*, *Bleak House*, or *The Pickwick Papers*, he ended each letter with an individually tailored invitation. To director Lindsay Anderson he suggested *The Old Curiosity Shop* as a project; Max Stafford Clark was offered *Barnaby Rudge*, and Arts Minister Norman St John Stevas was told that the first RDC production would be *Little Dorrit*. To back this up he had the Aldwych Theatre covered in RSC-style RDC posters giving advance notice of the *Little Dorrit* production.

Trevor Nunn, suspecting an inside job, called in the Special Branch. 'It is deeply embarrassing,' he reportedly said as the media gleefully played up the hoax, 'a lot of people have written to me refusing, or, even more embarrassing, accepting the offers.'

Some months later a researcher for the BBC TV programme *Newsnight* phoned Campbell, accusing him of being a hoaxer. Campbell came clean, making his confession on *Newsnight*, and the affair ended without recriminations.[1]

1. Yapp, *op. cit.*, pp.182–3.

'CARABOO' (18th century) (*IMPOSTORS*)

In April 1817 a penniless, bewildered young woman turned up in the village of Almondsbury, Gloucestershire, not far from the port of Bristol. She spoke an unknown foreign tongue, gave no name, and seemed lost. Local magistrate Samuel Worrall gave her shelter, but she would eat only food she prepared herself, insisted on sleeping on the floor, and kept doing an odd one-legged hopping dance. All she would say, over and over again, was 'Caraboo! Caraboo!' When they asked in sign language if this was her name, she nodded. The mystery deepened until, some weeks later, a young man turned up. Claiming to be Martin Eynesso from Portugal, he said he'd travelled in the East and could understand her. Interpreting for her, he said she was indeed Caraboo, from Javasu near Sumatra, and that Malay pirates had seized her and sold her into slavery. Bought by the captain of a ship sailing to England via the Cape of Good Hope, in Bristol she had jumped overboard and swum ashore, so reaching Almondsbury lost and confused.

Caraboo became a nine-days'-wonder, but was soon identified by a Mrs Neale, her former Bristol landlady, as Mary Willcocks (or Baker), daughter of a Devon cobbler. Escaping her stern father aged fifteen, passing from one brief job to another, in 1813 (she claimed) she had mistaken a brothel as a convent, where a man who had travelled in the Far East gave her the basis of her deception. Inventing the act to escape poverty and get into a wealthy household, she had persuaded Eynesso to become her accomplice.

Confronted by Mrs Neale, she confessed. She could have been jailed, but public sympathy gave her the money to go to America and start a new life. Seven years later she was back in Bristol, exhibiting herself as Princess Caraboo for a shilling a peep. She ended her days selling leaches to folk avoiding doctors' bills by bleeding themselves.[1]

1. Blundell, *op. cit.*, pp.70–2.

CARDIFF GIANT, The (*See also* **FOSSIL FORGERIES**)
Those fooled by Piltdown Man and other fake fossils or skeletons planted in the ground and then dug up as genuinely antique by hoaxers might have done well to recall the case of the Cardiff Giant, 'discovered' in 1869 on a farm near Cardiff, New York State. Dug up by well-diggers, this twelve-foot-tall stone giant became a sensation. Thousands came to gawk at it. Four local doctors declared it to be a petrified body, a fifth said it was a 300-year-old statue. Other experts thought it an ancient Phoenician idol (supporting their theory that Phoenicians had reached America), or a long-dead American Indian prophet. The director of New York State Museum was as baffled as philosopher Ralph Waldo Emerson.

The truth was less weird. Prankster George Hull, a relative of the farmer who had found the giant, had spent a small fortune buying gypsum from Iowa, hiring a sculptor from Chicago, and arranging the giant's transportation to and burial on the New York farm, where it lay for a year before being discovered.

Hull refused to sell his giant to the showman Phineas T. Barnum, so Barnum paid a sculptor to make a copy, then exhibited it as the original. Hull took his giant to New York to display it, only to find that Barnum had beat him to it with his hoax of a hoax. Hull's comments are not recorded, but the original Cardiff Giant remains on view at the Farmer's Museum in Cooperstown, New York.[1]

1. Lindskoog, *op. cit.*, pp.162–3.

CARTER, Asa (*LITERARY HOAXES*; *see* **DAVISON, Linda)**

CASTANEDA, Carlos (1925–) (*LITERARY HOAXES*)
One of the most inadvertently lucrative literary hoaxes of the twentieth century, with over four million copies of over half a dozen books sold to date and all still in print, and with the author (now a famous if enigmatic 'New Age' cult figure) still in possession of his doctorate from the University of California at Los Angeles.

Born in the Peruvian city of Cajamarca in 1925, son of a prosperous jewellery store owner, Carlos Cesar Aranha Castaneda grew up as a teller of tall tales. In 1951 he left his wife and child in Lima and moved to the USA. Studying creative writing at Los Angeles City College, in 1959 he enrolled at the University of California at Los Angeles (UCLA), where in 1962 the Anthropology Department funded his field work. Specialising in ethnobotany (the study of psychotropic plants), some years later he presented his doctoral thesis. Published in 1968 as *The Teachings of Don Juan: A Yaqui Way of Knowledge*, this and its sequels purport to recount his experiments with Yaqui Indian religion, magic, and hallucinogenic drugs under the tutelage of Don Juan Matus, an aged desert shaman.

Claiming to have been born in Brazil in 1935 as the nephew of Oswaldo Aranha, President of the UN General Assembly and Brazilian ambassador to the USA, he said he had graduated from Hollywood High School, studied art in Italy, and in the summer of 1960 had travelled to the Sonora Desert in northwest Mexico to collect information on medicinal plants used by the Yaqui Indians. So he had met Don Juan who, taking a liking to him, admitted to being a *brujo* (shaman) instructed by a *diablero*, an evil sorcerer able to shapeshift. Accepting Carlos as his apprentice in 1961, Don Juan had introduced him to another sorcerer, Don Genaro Flores. These two old men taught him how to 'stop the world' and perceive non-ordinary reality, aided by psychotropic drugs like peyote, datura, and the *Psilocybe mexicana* mushroom.

Extraordinary magical adventures ensued. One book followed another. For the third, *Journey to Ixtlan* (1973), Castaneda gained his Ph.D. By now he was world-famous, with millions of fans buying each new, more incredible account as it appeared. Questions began to be asked. It emerged that only he had ever met 'Don Juan', 'Don Genaro' or any of the other weird characters in his books; that he had no corroborating tape-recordings, photographs, or any other evidence at all. In his nine years of alleged field research he learned nothing of the region's plants or animals, or even the Indian names for them. Presenting himself as the dull, reluctant pupil of a magus as romantically potent as Merlin, he claimed to have transcribed Don Juan's Spanish monologues verbatim and at lightning speed; to have climbed unclimbable trees and stalked unstalkable animals. He had hiked for hours in burning desert heat and been drenched by warm winter rains in a desert where winter rains are freezing. Plainly, he knew nothing at all about the Yaqui people. In fact, he had done all his 'field work' in the UCLA library.

As with those who a decade earlier had thrilled to the imaginary Tibetan marvels of Lobsang **Rampa**, none of this mattered to his fans. He had done his magical homework. His myth-making power counted more than the academic truth. And he changed with the times. When hallucinogens were in fashion, Don Juan used them to propel his clumsy pupil into the spirit-world. In later books, with hallucinogenic drugs now widely decried in the world at large, Don Juan explains that they are no longer needed: Carlos the eternal pupil now no longer needs such props, his magical will is enough.

The real mystery remains how Castaneda's examiners were not only fooled to begin with but apparently continued to be fooled. After all, the enigmatic Castaneda himself has continually warned interviewers that nothing he says can be trusted.

In *Castaneda's Journey* (1976) and *The Don Juan Papers* (1980), literary sleuth Richard De Mille reveals that UCLA's Professor Goldschmidt, ranking anthropologist on the editorial committee of the University of California Press which published Castaneda's first book, saw to it that Castaneda was taken seriously to begin with. It was his laudatory foreword to *The Teachings of Don Juan* which encouraged, among others, an eminent reviewer in the *American Anthropologist* to state that the book: 'should attain a solid place in the literature of both hallucinogenic drugs and the field behaviour of anthropologists'. In 1978, faced by massive evidence of fraud, Goldschmidt insisted on behalf of his colleagues that: 'We possess no information whatever that would support the charges which have been made . . . I am not going to say *mea culpa*.'

How can this be? De Mille suspects that a group of UCLA dissidents arranged publication of Castaneda's first book as a joke aimed at their opponents but when it became a bestseller they could neither repudiate it nor admit to their prank. Either way they'd lose. They could only stonewall, thumbing their noses at the critics by awarding Carlos his doctorate. So Castaneda has continued on his merry way, producing yet more chapters in his saga, which endures due to the fact that, hoax or not, it is wonderfully inventive, apparently profound, and never less than colourful. It continues to appeal to millions who long to believe in the imaginative fairyland of marvels he presents. It is yet another case of a hoax outstripping its creator(s) and getting out of control to take on a life of its own.

But is Castaneda complaining?[1,2]

1. *The Teachings of Don Juan: A Yaqui Way of Knowledge* (et. seq.), Carlos Castaneda, University of California Press, Los Angeles 1968.
2. *Castaneda's Journey*, Richard De Mille, Capra Press, Santa Barbara 1978.

'CATHOUSE FOR DOGS' (*See* SKAGGS, Joey)

CATHOUSE RANCH, The (*PRANKS*)

In 1875 newspaper editor Willis B. Powell of Lacon, Illinois, induced Associated Press to offer newspapers across the USA a prospectus offering a foolproof way to get rich almost overnight with minimum effort or overhead. This 'glorious opportunity' involved investor support for a company proposing to pioneer a 'cat ranch'. With the initial 100,000 cats each giving birth to twelve kittens a year, so multiplying rapidly; with each cat's skin when ready for market worth thirty cents; and with one hundred men skinning five thousand cats a day, the prospectus concluded that there would be a net daily profit of $10,000. As for how to feed the cats – well, how about a rat ranch next door?

Beginning with a million rats, and as rats breed twelve times faster than cats, then soon there would be four times as many rats to feed as cats waiting to eat them. The solution? Simple! Feed the rats the carcasses of the skinned cats! With cats feeding rats, and rats cats, the prospectus insisted, each cat skin would cost virtually nothing to produce!

How many eager entrepreneurs believed this one? Who would fall for such a scam these days? Anyone who did would get skinned alive by rat and cat lovers!

CAZAZZA, Monte (contemporary) (*PRANKS*, see also 'DISGRUNTLED EMPLOYEE' SCAMS)

Maybe this California-based avant-gardist has the answer.

'A prank,' he says, 'can be a multi-functional tool like a hammer – you can hit somebody over the head with it, or pound nails with it. Pranks are techniques to change life with; they're based on principles that are not widely known or recognised.'

Living in London Cazazza experimented – on himself – with ultra-low frequency sounds that made people sick. This was too indiscriminate. Later in Oakland (California) at night he'd play out into the street on a big sound system the sound-effects record of a car crash. He'd watch the neighbourhood lights come on, and people running out on the street to see the wreck that wasn't there.

He sees this as sleight-of-hand, as misdirection: making something that isn't seem to be what it is. The British press in particular, he says, is good at this – whipping up false furores that sell papers, fabricating sensational stories, and working with the police – as when in the sixties the Rolling Stones were busted for drugs. Did reporters from all major papers just *happen* to be there? Businessmen, he says, are always pulling pranks, 'wheedling money out of banks and other businessmen on various pretexts, pretending they have what they don't have'. As for those who want to have fun at work, he suggests that secretaries are particularly well placed to cause office turmoil, and that you can always change a Yes to a No and a No to a Yes – 'people who work in **computers** do that all the time. Even computers do it to themselves!'

Another Cazazza prank? Dress up mannequins as bag ladies or winos, place in them cassette recorders playing six-second loops of people muttering to themselves, and leave them in the streets. Then watch and laugh as people, thinking them real: 'go up to them and try to mug them or something'. Or drop a mumbling doll in a municipal trashcan or dustbin, bury it in rubbish, and watch folk try to dig out the lost child.

Thanks a lot, Monte! We really need it.[1]

1. Vale and Juno, *op. cit.*, pp.72–4.

CELESTIAL BED, The (*SCIENTIFIC SCAMS*)

Remembered for its connection with Lady Hamilton, mistress of English naval hero Admiral Lord Nelson, this invigorating couch was invented by 'Dr Graham', a shadowy Scot who in London *c.* 1780 set up 'The Temple of Health', an establishment of dubious virtue maintained both in Pall Mall and in the Adelphi. Liveried footmen outside the door enticed passers-by into the opulently erotic interior. Stained glass overlooked satin sofas; the reinvigorating power of the Celestial Bed (also known as the Electro-Magnetic Bed) itself was supported by a range of other quack cures like 'earth baths' and 'Divine Balm'. Aided by the lovely Emma Lyon, later Lady Hamilton, the good Dr Graham enticed wealthy hedonists to part with their cash. 'To spend a single night in the bed costs as much as one hundred pounds,' notes 'Trojan', a pseudony-mous columnist of the time, 'but there are other electric-magnetic beds for which the charge is only half as much. The doctor says that he has spent some sixty thousand on the construction of the Celestial Bed and that if any woman sleeps in it she is guaranteed to have a beautiful child.'

'Trojan' and other commentators fail to explain if the 'guarantee' involved a visit by the Holy Ghost (Graham called the bed the 'Holy of Holies', or 'the Throne of Supreme Grace'), or a visit by Graham himself, or if the male clients brought the would-be mothers with them.

Either way, it is clear that Graham knew about **Mesmer**, and that his favourite clients were those with health worries, sexual or otherwise. Supported on six solid glass legs, the bed with its drapings, sheets and pillows was doused in perfumes 'guaranteed to arouse in anyone the most dormant feelings of passion and the most fervent sentiments'. To further such arousal, little electrical shocks and shivers kept penetrating the mattress while a 'self-playing organ' (with Emma at the keys?) provided the romantic muzak.

It sounds like Graham (who died in 1794 after his business failed, the 'Celestial Bed' being sold at public auction) was born two centuries too soon.[1]

1.   McCormick, *op. cit.*, pp.63–8.

CHANNELLING (*See* MEDIUMS)

CHATTERTON, Thomas (1752–80) (*LITERARY HOAXES*)
'The greatest genius that England has produced since the days of Shakespeare'? None of the praise Chatterton received did him any good – it all came after his tragically early death. Born the posthumous son of a lay clerk of Bristol, his mother thought him an idiot until one day aged six he saw her tear up an old French musical folio, 'fell in love' with the illuminated capitals, and thereafter read anything he could find. Already writing poetry and studying medieval scripts, aged ten he came across old documents his father had removed from the church of St Mary Redcliffe, and in 1764 wrote a poem, 'Elinoure and Juga', in medieval script on a discoloured piece of manuscript. Adopting obsolete spelling and words, his success in selling forged pedigrees, coats of arms, and 'ancient poems' to local antiquarians encouraged him, aged just thirteen, to invent the 'Rowley Romance'.

His father's documents had mentioned William Canynge, Lord Mayor of Bristol (d.1474), and Canynge's friend, the merchant Thomas Rowley. Turning Rowley into a monkish editor, Chatterton began forging medieval poetry which, extolling Bristol at the expense of 'cowarde Londonne', soon proved locally popular. His output increased even after he went to work in 1767 copying precedents for a Bristol lawyer. In 1768, when a new footbridge over the Severn was opened, a local newspaper published an account of a mayor first crossing the old bridge in 1248. Appearing at the newspaper office, Chatterton said he'd copied it from a parchment removed by his father from St Mary Redcliffe. Yet at the same time he showed at least two friends, John Rudhall and Edward Gardner, how he had forged it. Chatterton, Gardner later said, would: 'rub a parchment in several places in streaks with yellow ochre, then rub it several times on the ground, which was dirty, and afterwards crumple it in his hand, saying "That was the way to antiquate it" '.[1]

A set of Rowley poems he'd given the antiquarian George Catcott was praised by author Horace Walpole even as the youth admitted to his mother and sister that he'd written 'Goddwyn', 'The Parliament of Sprites', and other fakes to prove both his scholarship and his poetic *élan*. Writing to Walpole in March 1769, he enclosed new Rowley poems and Rowley's *A History of English Painters*. Walpole, whose own first novel, *The Castle of Otranto* (1764), had been offered as his translation of a sixteenth-century Italian romance, was enthusiastic – at least until Chatterton, encouraged, now introduced himself as the son of a poor widow with a taste for more elegant studies. Accepting the judgement of friends that the Rowley poems were fake, Walpole distanced himself. The boy was, after all, of the lower classes.

Embittered, Chatterton considered suicide, and when his employer John Lambert found on his desk 'The last Will and Testament of me, Thomas Chatterton of Bristol', he was fired. Rejecting Bristol, in April 1770 he left for London. Renting an attic in Brooke Street, Holborn, for months he hardly ate or slept while furiously producing a torrent of squibs, tales, songs, and new Rowley poems like 'An Excelente Balade of Charitie'. Though published in various journals, he was paid a pittance, and his Rowley work was rejected. By now desperate and literally starving, he refused charity and, on 25 August 1774, was found dead, surrounded by torn-up manuscripts, an almost empty phial of arsenic in his hand.

Reviled as a forger, he was also posthumously praised on his own merits. 'I do not believe there ever existed so masterly a genius,' declared Hugh Walpole, and Doctor Johnson called him: 'the most extraordinary young man' he had encountered. Catcott the antiquarian spoke of his 'hawk's eye' through which 'one could see his soul'; while the anatomist Barrett: 'had never seen such eyes, fire rolling at the bottom of them', and said he had often disagreed with Chatterton simply: 'to see how wonderfully his eye would strike fire, kindle, and blaze up'.[2]

Would his fate had been different had he not been born in poverty in a time when the poor were despised as such? Who can tell? It was a brief, frustrating, yet potent blaze of a life: his early death remains among the tragedies of English literature.

1. Quoted in Yapp, *op. cit.*, p.148.
2. Stephen and Lee, *op. cit.*

'CHERN, Mr' (*See* **SIX S JOB**)

CHEVALIER D'EON (*See* **D'EON DE BEAUMONT**)

CHIAPPINI, Stella (1773–1843) (*IMPOSTORS*)
Some people are just never satisfied. Born in the Tuscan village of Modigliana young Stella Chiappini was just starting out on the stage in

Florence in 1786 when she caught the roving eye of Lord Newborough, a fifty-year-old English widower with land in Wales. Despite protesting that she'd rather be a nun and seemingly much against her will, she married him. In 1792, still liking him no better, she moved with him to Wales, learned she was required to extend the family line, and efficiently bore two boys within a year. When Newborough died in 1807 she was quick to marry a Russian baron and extend *his* family line, and that might have been the end of it – but in 1821 she got an extraordinary letter from her father. On his death bed, he confessed that: 'The day when you were born to a person I must not name and who has already passed away, a boy was born to me. I was asked to make an exchange, and in view of my financial circumstances at the time I fell in with the repeated requests, to some advantage. So it was that I adopted you as my daughter just as my son was adopted by the other party.

'I see that heaven has made good my shortcomings by raising you to a better position than that of your real father, even though he was of almost similar rank. This affords me some peace of mind as I end my life.'

Stella went straight to Modigliana. Who knew about her birth half a century earlier? She learned that in April 1773 a French couple, the Count and Countess de Joinville, had reached the inn in an urgent state, the very pregnant lady giving birth only hours later – to a girl. The disappointed husband, who required a male heir, had struck an immediate deal with the Chiappinis, to whom that day had been born a son, exchanged for cash.

She tracked the Joinvilles to a ruined castle in Champagne. They were extinct, but the ducal house of Orléans now used the name. She advertised for information and in 1823 learned that a Count de Joinville had been held on Church orders at Brisinghella, just twelve kilometres from Modigliana, in April 1773. Applying to ecclesiastical court for her baptismal certificate to be changed, in May 1824 she gained the ruling that there had been a substitution. She was now officially Stella de Joinville. But who exactly was the boy with whom she'd been swapped? She sought, and found him in Louis-Philippe of Orléans.

This identification was optimistic. Louis-Philippe would soon be King of France. Yet Stella had a case. Born in 1773, his father, the 'revolutionary duke' Egalité, was dead – guillotined despite voting for Louis XVI's execution in 1793. His mother Adélaide had been among France's richest women when they had married. Also, one of Egalité's titles in their marriage contract was 'Comte de Joinville'. Stella visited the Orléans palace with her Russian son and they both agreed how much a portrait of Louis-Philippe looked like father Chiappini. Stella was sure! Now calling herself 'Marie Etoile d'Orléans', and with her family wishing she'd drop it, she was championed by supporters of the Elder Bourbon royal line. Regarding the Orléans family as usurpers, they were happy to embarrass them by endorsing her claim, legitimate or not.

'The revolutionary usurper of rights which henceforth he cannot keep without guilt', she called Louis-Philippe, and the controversy continued throughout the century: in 1889 Bourbonists staged a play, *Maria Stella, or the Last of the Orléans*. But by then her case had fallen apart. It had soon become clear to everyone but possibly herself that neither Egalité nor Adélaide could have visited Italy secretly in April 1773. Their diaries for that month had survived, every day crammed with public appearances in France. As for Louis-Philippe, his birth in Paris in October 1773 (not April), had been witnessed by at least five people, and baptism had taken place on the spot. Nor was there reason for a substitution. Four more children had followed Louis-Philippe, two of them boys.

Stella Newborough alias de Joinville alias Chiappini had most likely been born into the minor nobility. The title de Joinville was used by at least one other family at the time. But it seemed not to count with her that she had already by luck attained high social status, marrying first an English then a Russian aristocrat.

A mere aristocrat? She wanted to be *royal*.

There's no pleasing some folk.[1]

1. Newnham, *op. cit.*, pp.199–202.

CHILDREN OF GOD (*See* BERG, David)

CHORLEY, Dave (*See* CROP CIRCLES)

CHRISTIANITY (*HISTORICAL HOAXES*)

Virgin birth? Resurrection from the dead? Bodily ascension into heaven? Is it still controversial to suggest that such dogmas (never asserted by the first Christians) are part and parcel of what may be one of the most profoundly influential hoaxes ever perpetrated? For increasingly it looks as if early Christianity was a militant, messianic Judaic cult with little or no resemblance to the supernatural myth of Jesus later constructed out of it.

The evidence that explodes the myth is recently found. Texts buried for safety at the start of the Christian era have emerged again. First, in 1945 a cache of Gnostic texts was found at Nag Hammadi in Egypt. Named from the Greek word *gnosis*, 'knowledge', the Gnostics were not one cult but many among the ferment of different interpretations, sects and beliefs characterising Christianity throughout the Roman Empire about a century after the new religion's first appearance. But characterising most if not all of the Gnostic cults (which drew on older traditions) was a reliance on personal revelation, rejection of the single authority of the patriarchal Church, and acknowledgement of the equality of women.

Their individualism and the increasing organisation of the Church of St Peter meant that by the end of the second century AD most Gnostic sects were destroyed or in hiding. One such group hid the Nag Hammadi texts, published in 1978 as *The Nag Hammadi Library*.

Some, like the 'Gospel of Philip', 'Thunder, Perfect Mind' and 'Pistis Sophia', are very revealing. They reject dogmas like the Resurrection, gnostically seen as spiritual, not physical. Perhaps most revealing of all is their presentation of a Jesus remote from the asexual figure of the official Four Gospels in the New Testament. This Jesus is married to Mary Magdalene, the disciple he loves the most. In the 'Apocalypse of Peter', this Jesus says of orthodox Christians that: 'They will cleave to the name of a dead man, thinking that they will become pure. But they will become greatly defiled and they will fall into a name of error and into the hand of an evil, cunning man and a manifold dogma, and they will be ruled heretically . . .'[1]

And who was this 'evil, cunning man'? More answers began to emerge with a second vital find, made in 1947 in caves honeycombing cliffs at Qumrun by the Dead Sea near Jerusalem. Leather scrolls wrapped in decaying linen in earthenware jars recorded fragmentary texts by the Essenes, a radical first-century Judaic cult. Early translations suggested a challenge to orthodox Holy Writ. The Vatican moved fast to establish a monopoly, entrusting most of the scrolls to a group of Catholic scholars under Fathers Roland de Vaux and Josef Milik. For forty years this 'international team' published precisely nothing. In 1992 his academic outrage led American scholar Robert Eisenmann to publish his own (pirated) translation and interpretation of fifty of the withheld texts.[2]

He and others now offer a view of early Christianity so radical as to suggest another religion altogether. Even if claims that 'Jesus' was the codename for a psychedelic mushroom (Allegro[3]); or that he was a woman, not a man (Harris[4]); or that he was the sacrificial died-and-reborn corn-god (like Tammuz or Osiris) of an ancient fertility religion (Smith[5]), seem too bizarre, serious questions now beg to be answered. What was early Christianity? Who was the *real* Jesus? And how was the new religion moulded into the dogmatic form which, with variations, has survived two millennia?

The new evidence suggests a picture like this. Roman-held Judaea during the reign of Tiberius (AD 14–37) was an uneasy land. Since the Revolt of the Maccabees (*c*.167 BC) had driven out the Greeks there had been sporadic rebellion against their successors the Romans, but without luck. The Messiah, a prophesied priest-king who would drive out the enemy and establish Yahweh's kingdom on earth, was daily expected by stern sects like the Essenes. Once, before the Babylonish captivity six centuries before, at any time there had been *two* messiahs: king and high priest.

The Hebrew term *māshīahh* refers to the unction of a king or high priest; just as the Greek word *Christos* refers to the unction of an initiate of the Mysteries. Under Hellenic, then Roman occupation, there had been no messiahs or christs. Then arose an Essene leader, Jesus (*Yeshua*, a common Aramaic name), accepted by his followers as being of the royal line of David. The Essenes acknowledged him as the Messiah, but other Jews did not. He would have to prove himself by fulfilling scriptural prophecy. The Essenes, conventionally viewed as peaceful mystics, were more likely a wing of the Zealots, who were Judaic freedom fighters of the time.

The editors of the Four Gospels did not quite hide this connection. Hints abound. Of Christ's disciples, 'Simon Zelotes' is Simon the Zealot, while 'Iscariot' implies the *sicarius*, a dagger used by the Zealots for assassinations. Christ's title, 'the Nazarene', may refer not to a village, Nazareth, but to the Nazareans, a branch of the Essenes.[6]

The scrolls mention two individuals: the 'Teacher of Righteousness', and 'The Liar' or 'Wicked Priest'. Identifications vary. Baigent and Leigh claim that Jesus was the former and St Paul the latter: see below.[7] Thiering's interpretation, claiming that Hebrew texts used a technique called *pesher*, whereby hidden meanings lie within specific words in the surface text, views Jesus as the 'Wicked Priest', seen as such by orthodox Judaism for preaching to uninitiated Gentiles.[8] In the tale of how he turned water into wine at Cana, 'wine' means the initiated, 'water' the uninitiated. Additionally, the marriage was his – to Mary Magdalene, the 'disciple he loved the most'.

As for the crucifixion, it was symbolically conducted at Qumrun (Thiering), or physically carried out to fulfil Old Testament prophecies to the letter, Jesus being drugged (sop of wine) and later revived (Lemesurier). Muslim belief is that not Jesus but another man died on the cross. The Gospel account is odd: victims of crucifixion typically lingered for days, but Jesus dies rapidly, and is removed as rapidly.

Increasingly we see not the celibate 'gentle Jesus, meek and mild' of orthodoxy, but a man both more prosaic and believable, one outstanding enough to encourage perhaps the most successful hoax in history. Which brings us to St Paul, a most suspicious character.

Born at Tarsus in Cilicia, his father a Jewish citizen of Rome, he received the tribal name *Saul*, also the Roman name *Paul*. The unknown author of Acts tells how he persecuted Christians before undergoing a sudden conversion en route to Damascus. Now preaching Jesus as Son of God, his former victims doubt his good faith. A surprise? In AD 43 the Jerusalem Christians, under James (brother of Jesus) accuse him of denying Judaic law. Why? Because already he mythologises Jesus as a died-and-reborn god, and speaks of virgin birth, miracles, resurrection, and original sin – all contrary to Judaism. Fleeing, he preaches to Jews and Gentiles abroad. Writing to his congregations (AD 50–58), he attacks the apostles James and Peter, who knew Jesus (as he never did), insisting that *he is not a liar* (which means, many say, he is: remember Richard **Nixon**'s *I am not a crook!*). His return to Jerusalem in AD 58 causes a riot (Acts xxi: 28): the Roman army saves him from being lynched by angry Jews, perhaps Zealots. Again, why? Removed safely by the Romans to Caesarea he demands to be heard in Rome, where in AD 60 he is imprisoned and later tried. He may or may not have been martyred in Nero's reign.

Why did the Romans rescue a man glorifying a 'criminal' they had executed? Why did the Jews hate him? Is Paul the 'Liar' of the Dead Sea Scrolls, the outsider who, admitted to the community of the 'Teacher of Righteousness', 'flouted the Law' and deceived people with false tales? Was he an opportunist, not to be trusted? Perhaps. After all, it was his version of 'Christianity' that prevailed. Developing and inflating a supernaturalism based on earlier (still competing) cults, and spreading that hatred of 'many foolish women' (as he calls them) which later envelops the masculine Church, his influence was such (meaning that many agreed with him) that by *c.*AD 180 Bishop Clement of Alexandria orders the suppression of those parts of the original Gospel of Mark encouraging Gnostic and female influence. Meaning that Clement, deliberately censoring the past, knows that power not *truth* is at stake, however justified. By then the war is a purely political struggle, though cloaked in theology.[9]

The Church has always been a bastion of masculine authority. The figures of Mary, mother of Jesus, and Mary the Magdalene suffered massive distortion in the process of initial deception – as did that of Jesus himself. Jesus is said to be asexual and celibate; a misogynist who refers only twice to his mother, and then as 'woman'. There is a mystery here too. In Mark vi: 3 Jesus is called 'son of Mary', not 'son of Joseph', which in Semitic usage implies doubt as to the father's identity. But Mark, the first Gospel, never even mentions the virgin birth. The implication is that Jesus was not Joseph's son, that his birth was irregular, and that the myth of virgin birth was invented to cover up an embarrassment (while usefully agreeing with earlier pagan myths, as of the birth of Egyptian Horus).

As for the Magdalene, she remains the most ambiguous figure of all – save in the Nag Hammadi texts. The *Gospel of Mary* portrays her as the one disciple who strengthens the other (male) disciples after Jesus has left them, and as the only one who knows his final words. When the men react with hostility and disbelief, Levi reminds them that Jesus made her worthy, knows her well, and loved her more than any of the others.[10]

One of history's great hoaxes? Certainly there was a vast distortion of the original events, with Paul in the middle. Persecutor of a messianic Jewish cult, he reinterpreted, hijacked, and sold it to a wider audience. What a scam! Some say Christianity is more accurately named *Paulianity*

– not the first, by no means the last, but perhaps the most audacious holy hoax of all time.

1. *The Nag Hammadi Library*, ed. James M. Robinson, Harper & Row, New York 1981, p.341.
2. *The Dead Sea Scrolls Uncovered*, Robert Eisenmann and Michael Wise, Element Books, Shaftesbury 1992.
3. *The Sacred Mushroom and the Cross*, John M. Allegro, Abacus, London 1970.
4. *The Sacred Virgin and the Holy Whore*, Anthony Harris, Sphere, London 1988.
5. *Jesus the Magician*, Morton Smith, Aquarian Press, Wellingborough 1985.
6. *The Armageddon Script*, Peter Lemesurier, Element Books, Shaftesbury 1981, p.92.
7. *The Dead Sea Scrolls Deception*, Michael Baigent and Richard Leigh, Corgi, London 1992.
8. *Jesus the Man*, Barbara Thiering, Corgi, London 1993.
9. *The Secret Gospel*, Morton Smith, Aquarian, Wellingborough 1985.
10. *op. cit.*, pp.471–4.

COLE, Horace (20th century) (*IMPOSTORS, PRANKS*)
In February 1910 HMS *Dreadnought*, iron-clad pride of the British Navy, was at anchor in Weymouth Bay, Dorset, when Vice-Admiral Sir William May, Commander-in-Chief Home Fleet, received a telegram from Sir Arthur Hardinge of the Foreign Office. It warned of an imminent visit by the Emperor of Abyssinia and his entourage. There was barely time to organise taxis and roll out the red carpet at Weymouth railway station before the dignitaries arrived, accompanied by an interpreter and a Foreign Office official. With protocol strictly observed by officers in full dress uniform, they were piped on board the *Dreadnought*. The flag run up and national anthem played were Zanzibar's, due to naval ignorance of Abyssinia. The exotically robed visitors did not object, but admired all they saw, shouting 'Bunga-bunga!' in approval when guns were fired in salute (some accounts say no guns were fired, and that 'Bunga-bunga' was a later journalistic invention). All in all, the visit was a great success, though the visitors refused lunch and, with no prayer mats available for their evening devotions, left somewhat rapidly. At Weymouth Station, they tipped the sailors, embarked on the train, and on the way back to London insisted that the waiters serving dinner wear white gloves, which meant holding up the train at Reading while an attendant went to buy them.

A few days later the *Daily Mirror* revealed the visit as a hoax engineered by high society dilettantes and directed by man-about-town William Horace de Vere Cole. It was Cole who, determined to be known as a great practical joker, leaked the story. The British naval high command became the laughing stock of Europe. Sir William May was pursued through Weymouth by urchins shouting 'Bunga-bunga'. There were endless music hall 'Bunga-bunga' jokes. Questions were asked in Parliament. Crimes had been committed, like sending a telegram under a false name. The whole affair slid out of proportion. By now several of the hoaxers wished they'd never become involved.

As it was, it had been so hastily planned and executed it was a wonder it worked. The conspirators were Cole, his friends Adrian Stephen, Anthony Buxton, Guy Ridley, Duncan Grant, and Stephen's cousin Virginia, later novelist Virginia Woolf. The intention was to prank the pompous and authoritarian British Navy. With visiting cards printed in Swahili, wearing rented costumes and false beards, made up by Sarah Bernhardt's make-up man while an accomplice sent the telegram to Sir William May, they had embarked for Weymouth. Only Cole was optimistic. The others wondered what they'd got themselves into. Their disguises were absurd; their preparation virtually nil. They'd survived the full-scale reception, but as they reached the *Dreadnought* rain had begun to fall; their make-up had begun running; Duncan Grant's moustache began slipping down his face. But Cole, supporting Buxton in the latter's role as the 'Emperor', had got them below decks. They'd refused lunch, being unsure what food their unknown religion allowed them, and fearing more make-up trouble. And when the chief staff officer, appalled by the interpreter's heavy German accent, had begun to suspect that they were spies, Cole had swept his party ashore under the pretext of 'sunset prayers'. He alone had suffered not a moment's doubt.

No action was taken, and the furore died down, but Cole alone was delighted. The others were sick of it. Virginia Woolf, in it for the fun of it, felt she had learned how silly men can be, and later used the hoax in a 1921 short story, 'The Society'.

COLLIER, John Payne (1789–1883) (*LITERARY HOAXES*)
The plays and reputation of **Shakespeare** (himself involved in a hoax?) have always attracted hoaxers, like William Henry **Ireland** (1777–1835), who passed off his own work as newly discovered plays by the Bard, and John Payne Collier. A journalist fascinated by the Tudor era, and especially by Shakespeare himself, in 1831 this scholar published to general critical acclaim his *History of English Dramatic Poetry and Annals of the Stage*. What nobody realised at the time was that this affable man could not resist forging his sources. One such forgery involved a request from the Lord Chamberlain's Players to renovate the Blackfriars Theatre and continue acting there. Dated 1596, and with Shakespeare's name listed as fifth of the signatories, this made it by seven years the oldest such document to carry Shakespeare's name, thus an important find.

With his reputation secure, Collier gained access to Sir Francis

Egerton's extensive library at Bridgwater House in London, and in 1835 published *New Facts Regarding the Life of Shakespeare*. This again was full of forgeries which, neatly reinforcing each other, included 'evidence' that *Othello* had been performed before Queen Elizabeth in 1602, and the 'discovery' of an original ballad that, he claimed, may have inspired *The Tempest*.

In 1840 Collier launched a Shakespeare Society, which in 1844 published his 'Life of Shakespeare' – again, full of clever flim-flam that nobody spotted – yet. Elected vice-president of the Society of Antiquaries and granted a civil list pension in 1850, he remained secure until Joseph Hunter of the Public Records Office began to doubt the language, dates, and age of the paper of the Bridgwater House finds. Though muted in his criticism, Hunter was soon joined by another critic, J.O. Halliwell, who openly asserted that all these 'finds' had been forged by the same person.

But Collier continued to forge ahead, in 1852 announcing the most momentous find yet – a copy of the second folio Shakespeare (1632) bought, he said, for thirty shillings from the bookseller John Rodd before the latter's death in 1849. Stained by tobacco and wine, and annotated in a seventeenth-century hand which had made numerous changes in punctuation, text, and stage directions, on its cover was written 'Tho. Perkins his Booke'. An actor called Perkins was known to have worked with the playwright Marlowe's company in Shakespeare's lifetime. Collier published this text as the original version used by Shakespeare, only to find his word doubted by the anonymous author of *Literary Cookery* (1855). He sued, but the inconclusive hearing did his reputation no good. Still insisting it was genuine, he gave the Perkins text to the Duke of Devonshire's library. But when in 1859 Devonshire's heir donated the original to the British Museum, Sir Frederick Madden proved that pencil writing lay under the ink of the alterations, and that the ink was coloured water.

Further critical research called into question all Collier's finds from Bridgwater House on, though whether he was the victim of fraud or its perpetrator was not pursued. Collier went on writing, but there were no more 'discoveries'. The tragedy is that, though much of his work was of real value, thereafter, all of it was tainted and suspect. Why he acted as he did, nobody knows, for in all other respects he was known and admired as a genial and kind-hearted man. Perhaps there's a devil in all of us that longs to make fools of others, though only some of us try to get away with it.[1]

1. Stephen and Lee, *op. cit.*

COLUMBUS, Christopher (1451–1506) (*EXPLORATION HOAXES*)
Hoaxes always flavoured the European discovery of America. Even the name 'America' comes from an explorer who faked the voyage he

claimed (*see* **Vespucci**). And though the Italian Christopher Columbus is widely credited with the first American landfall, in 1492, he landed in the West Indies, not on the mainland. So, despite claims of prior New World landings by Phoenicians, Irish St Brendan, Leif Erickson, Prince Madoc of Wales, Prince Henry Sinclair of Orkney and so on, it seems likely that John Cabot was the first to reach the mainland in 1497. As for Columbus, idealised for centuries, he has even been credited with discovering that the world is round. Truly, 'History is the lie commonly agreed upon'. And Columbus' fame has inspired numerous forgeries. One parchment, bought by a lawyer in Mexico City in 1876, was legible though soaked in brine and crusted with sand and shells. It was written not in Italian or Spanish but German, 'Columbus' explaining that this was so that his crew members couldn't read it.

Oddly, on his epochal 1492 voyage, he *had* tried to con his crew. To sustain their courage he kept two logs of the expedition's sailing distance, recording in the log he showed them a false figure for the distance sailed each day. His son Ferdinand says he comforted his men 'with great promises of lands and riches', and that, 'To sustain their hope and dispel their fears of a long voyage, he decided to reckon less leagues than they actually made, telling them they had covered only fifteen leagues that day when they had actually covered eighteen. He did this that they might not think themselves so great a distance from Spain as they really were, but for himself he kept a secret accurate reckoning.'

The ruse worked – just. Faced by mutiny, he extracted from the crew an agreement to sail on for another three days. Land was sighted with one day to go.

Even odder, his biographer Samuel Eliot Morison has shown that, due to errors in his calculations, his false log was more accurate than the one he kept for himself. And when at last land was sighted, Columbus played another trick. An annuity of 10,000 maravedis had been promised to the first man to sight land. The sailor who first spotted land demanded his prize, but Columbus said he had made the first sighting earlier that evening. He later demanded, and was given, the reward money.[1]

1. Goldberg, *op. cit.*, pp.44–5.

COMPUTER FRAUD (*FRAUD*)

Who can do without computers these days? More to the point, how many of us *understand* them? Even the managers of vast corporations annually generating billions in turnover are rarely computer-literate. They rely on programmers. And with computer systems only as smart or honest as their operators, it's no surprise that computer fraud is now the fastest-growing, most profitable area of financial crime.

How many such frauds occur is unknown, but probably no more than ten per cent of such crimes (even if discovered or reported: companies are typically too embarrassed or fearful of losing their reputation to admit their losses) lead to prosecution. But in Britain alone over fifty Scotland Yard detectives work full-time on at least £100 million worth of such frauds, while American computer crooks reportedly enjoy the fruits of a $150,000 million-a-year growth industry. All such crime requires is knowledge and enterprise, and the cases that follow are only the tip of the iceberg, consisting of those found out, like the American bank employee who added ten cents to every customer service charge of less than ten dollars, and a dollar on those of over ten dollars. Crediting the difference to an account he opened for himself under the unlikely name of Zzwicke, he'd have got away with it but his bank decided, as a promotional stunt, to make gifts to the first and last names on their alphabetical list of clients.

Another ambitious US bank employee shaved ten cents off every account, added his gains to the last account on the books, and opened an account under an assumed name also beginning with 'Z'. A real Mr Zydel (his name even further down the alphabet) opened an account. When his balance kept inexplicably growing, the honest Mr Zydel rang the bank, and so the fraud was revealed.

In Minneapolis, a bank clerk ordered the computer to ignore all cheques drawn on his own account; a scam revealed only when the computer broke down and the bank had to revert to old-fashioned human accounting. In Washington, a tax clerk programmed an Internal Revenue Service computer to list all unclaimed refunds and had these sent to his relatives. Stanley Rifkin, programmer at a Los Angeles bank, memorised the day's codes in the bank's wire room and transferred $10 million to his own account, to be caught only when an accomplice confided in a man who turned out to be an FBI agent. Another sly customer opened an account in a Washington bank, so obtaining personalised deposit slips. He knew the bank's computer recognised not the signatures on the slips but the magnetic ink symbols printed on them. Leaving slips from his own pay-in book among those put on the counters for customers forgetting their own deposit books, in three days he scooped $100,000, withdrew his balance, and vanished.

Many such frauds are so complex that they come to light only if the swindler slips up. Between 1979 and 1981 L. Benjamin Lewis, operations manager at a branch of Wells Fargo in Los Angeles, embezzled $21.3 million from customers by 'electronic kiting'. Pretending to make a deposit at one branch, he'd credit it to another account at a different branch. The inter-branch settlement system would throw up this deposit after five working days. From a terminal which issued the required documentation, Lewis would create a new transaction to cover the first one. As his pyramid grew, he had to transfer ever-larger credits. The snag was that the programme triggered an automatic review of any transaction involving any sum above six figures. To avoid this, he had to create twenty-five new accounts and increase the number of his smaller transactions. This required so much work that at length, exhausted, he made a clerical error and was caught. He got six years.

Similarly betrayed by exhaustion was accountant Eldon Royce, who between 1963 and 1969 embezzled a million dollars out of a fruit and vegetables wholesale company by inflating the costs of produce bought, then crediting seventeen dummy companies with the difference between inflated costs and those entered in the ledger. His programme showed him how much could be taken from specific accounts without being detected by audit, tailoring his inflation to stay within the percentage of stock known to shrink. Eventually, though, he grew careless, and was detected and jailed.

But maybe the most successful scam arose when a London-based chemical combine decided to control the accounting for its three major divisions through a central computer system. Learning through it that one division was selling to another at the full market price, though the buying department should have been claiming a forty per cent discount for bulk purchases, the chief programmer and the head of the buying department set up a fictitious subsidiary. This bought all the chemicals at full discount and on extended credit terms. They then resold to the parent company at full price and on terms of immediate payment. Making a profit of £150,000 in two years, and supplying fifty outside companies too, by the time the scheme was unmasked it was undercutting the combine so effectively that the perpetrators were not only not prosecuted, but were hired as fee-earning consultants to advise on how to run the once-fraudulent operation.

The computerisation of credit means that much of what we call 'money' no longer exists in any solid form, but only as constantly altering electronic data, easily subject to manipulation. Given such a situation, how can any of us be sure what's going on?[1,2]

1. Newnham, *op. cit.*, pp.104–5.
2. Blundell, *op. cit.*, pp.122–5.

CONAN DOYLE, Sir Arthur (1859–1930) (*See also* **FOSSIL FORGERIES**)
The famous author of the Sherlock Holmes novels also pursued a parallel career as a spiritualist and occultist. In these areas his track record was not so successful. Famously fooled by the **Cottingley Fairies** hoax, and insisting that renowned escapologist Harry **Houdini**, while also 'the greatest physical **medium** of modern times', was also a faker of evidence against mediums like Margery Crandon, by the end of his life he was widely regarded as gullible. Yet, as outlined in 'The Perpetrator at Piltdown' (an article in *Science 83*), it may be that he, not Charles **Dawson**, was behind the great Piltdown Man hoax.

A retired medical doctor who loved jokes, Conan Doyle was expert in anatomy, interested in evolution and palaeontology, found dinosaur fossils near his house, and in 1912 (the year Piltdown Man's discovery was announced), published *The Lost World*, a fantasy in which brave Professor Challenger (his photo at the start of the tale was of Conan Doyle in disguise) discovers an Amazonian plateau where dinosaurs and ape men survive. Just seven miles from his house, he often visited the Piltdown gravel pit to watch Dawson and **Woodward** dig, and encouraged them when they made their find. Moreover, he had easy access to the materials used in the hoax: an old human skull, an orang-utan jaw, a fossilised hippo tooth and other items. The proof is only circumstantial, but – who knows?

A coda to the tale of the Conan Doyle family as hoaxers is that in 1912 Sir Arthur bought from one of his admirers a Sherlock Holmes story, 'The Man Who Was Wanted', thinking he might use it someday. In 1942 his son Adrian found it in a trunk and, pretending it was in his father's handwriting, sold it to magazines in Britain and the USA. Whether or not he really believed it was by his father is unknown but, when the real author of the tale wrote to him to set the record straight, Adrian sued him for slander. Luckily, the author had kept letters from Sir Arthur recording the transaction.[1]

1. Lindskoog, *op. cit.*, pp.159–61.

CONMEN (*See CONCORDANCE*)

COOK, Florence (*See MEDIUMS*)

COOK, Frederick (1865–1940) (*EXPLORATION HOAXES*)
Surviving the debunking of his claim in September 1906 to have climbed Mt McKinley in Alaska, North America's highest mountain at 20,300 feet, three years later this enterprising faker emerged from the Arctic claiming that with two Eskimo companions he had reached the North Pole. Nobody believed that either yet, though spending the last thirty years of his life (five of them in a federal penitentiary for oil-land fraud) derided by all, even on his death bed in 1940 he still protested his innocence, lawsuits pending against those who called him a liar, as he certainly was.

Cook is the classic case of the loner so driven by personal demons he has to claim more than he achieves. Losing his father at five, embarrassed all his life by a lisp, his failure as a Manhattan doctor then the death in childbirth of his wife and the infant not surprisingly drove him into the wilderness. Though resourceful and brave, he was not highly intelligent. 'I think he would face death and disaster without a word,' remarks his 1903 colleague Robert Dunn in *The Shameless Diary of An*

Explorer (1907), 'but through the insensitiveness of age and too much experience, rather than by true courage. I cannot believe he has imagination; of a leader's qualities he has not shown one.' Clearly not a friend, in his 1956 autobiography *World Alive* Dunn describes Cook as 'dumb, with a bovine face, straight pale hair and a walrus moustache, milk-blue eyes, a set smile, and a slight lisp . . . He made desultory decisions, seemed indifferent, yet his confident, pompous solemnity killed criticism.'

Contradictions abounded in Cook. Norwegian explorer Roald Amundsen, his own reputation untarnished, called him 'the finest traveller I ever saw' – yet Cook did not even know how to use a theodolite. And when he claimed his ascent of Mount McKinley with Edward Barrill (who remained ambiguous about the whole affair), he was clumsy enough to offer in evidence a 'summit' photograph revealing the tips of two neighbouring peaks behind and above it. From it his 'Mount McKinley' was later identified as a minor peak barely 6,000 feet high.

Why did he do it? A social death wish? A desperate need for self-exaltation? By all other standards his 1906 expedition was a success. He'd penetrated a hitherto inaccessible region, and explored and mapped it – a great achievement. But it wasn't enough for him.

Journalist W.T. Stead met Cook in Copenhagen in 1909 after the alleged, already controversial polar journey and noted that: 'He does not strike us as a man, but rather as a child – a naive, inexperienced child, who sorely needed someone to look after him, and tell him what he ought to do in his own interest.' Noting Cook's inability to make up his mind about anything, Stead remarks: 'If he had been as indecisive and changeable in the Arctic regions he would never have got anywhere, and certainly could never have got home.' Stead, who later died on the *Titanic* despite warnings not to take that fatal trip, concluded: 'He is not, I should say, an imaginative man.'

One gets the idea that Cook courted a martyrdom that only he and his persistent supporters saw as such. **Peary** and **Byrd** may have been liars too, but their claims were accepted. Cook was not so smart. Naively unable (or secretly unwilling) to cover his false tracks, he was found out, not once but twice. One recent favourable biographer claims that Cook was 'not simply one of the greater victims in America's history, but the all-time champion'. Maybe. But if so, he was the victim not of sceptical opinion but of his own confused and self-torturing personality.[1]

1. Roberts, *op. cit.*, pp.88–105.

COOKE, Janet (contemporary) (*LITERARY HOAXES*)
In 1981 this ambitious young *Washington Post* reporter received a Pulitzer Prize for her articles about a homeless drug-addicted waif

willing to do anything for a fix. Photos of the child tugged at America's heartstrings. Her story was printed and reprinted round the world. Later printed around the world was the fact that it was a lie. Yes, she had found squalor and addiction on the streets, but the individual child she evoked did not exist. The boy was a composite of many such tales. Janet Cooke lost the Pulitzer Prize, her job, and her reputation as a result of stretching the truth too far.

COSMIC JOKER, The (*See also* INTRODUCTION)

Is existence itself a hoax? Is all we see delusion? Gnostics, Manichaeans, and other early sects persecuted by the Church always thought this, asserting that the world was created by a false god, Jehovah, who'd stolen the light of the original creation and conned humanity ever since. This belief got a lot of them burned at the stake or otherwise corrected. Yet Buddhism suggests the same: all phenomenal experience belongs to the realm of Maya, delusion: we are here on earth to reject false appearance and attain Nirvana.

Nirvana, like heaven (*see* **Hell**) may sound beside the point, but the idea that we are the playthings of some cosmic prankster persists, not least because life so often seems to be a bad joke. Take the case of General Sedgewick, who during an American Civil war siege encouraged his troops by raising his head over the parapet and shouting: 'They couldn't hit an elephant at this dist—' Famous last words. Or the shoplifter in Barnsley, Yorkshire, who learned too late that the store he hit was holding a meeting for store detectives. Or the 1911 English murder case where the three men hanged for killing Sir Edmundbury Godfrey at Greenberry Hill were named Green, Berry and Hill.

The iconoclastic American author Charles Hoy Fort (1874–1932) spent his life chronicling such lunacies and coincidences. He concluded that the human race belongs to a childishly cruel celestial joker who just likes to play with us.

Or do we hoax ourselves unconsciously? *Nessiteras rhombopteryx*, the Latin name given by respected British naturalist Sir Peter Scott to the **Loch Ness Monster** (in which it seems he believed), is a perfect anagram of 'monster hoax by Sir Peter S.'

COTTINGLEY FAIRIES (*PARANORMAL HOAXES*)

Ruining Sir Arthur **Conan Doyle**'s reputation, this hoax or invention originated in the imagination of two girls. 'Elsie and I are very friendly with the beck [stream] fairies', eleven-year-old Frances Griffiths wrote on the back of a snapshot sent to a friend in South Africa, where she'd lived before her family moved to Yorkshire in England. 'It is funny I never used to see them in Africa. It must be too hot for them there.'

Taken in July 1917 and developed by cousin Elsie's father, the snapshot showed Frances, chin in hand, with four butterfly-winged little dark-haired sprites dancing on a bush before her. The image was vague: Arthur Wright made light of it. But a month later when Elsie photographed Frances under oak trees with a little winged gnome dancing before her, he was angry. With his wife Polly he searched the girls' bedroom, but found no cut-outs to explain the pictures. Both girls insisted that there really *were* fairies at the bottom of the garden, but Arthur knew kids: the camera was confiscated.

But Polly was occultly inclined. In 1919 she heard a lecturer at the Theosophical Society of Bradford say that fairies are elemental spirits as seen by clairvoyants. Soon her daughter's 'fairy photographs' were in the hands of Arthur Gardner, President of the London branch of the Theosophical Society. Though suspicious, he sought expert advice. This suggested that the (now sharpened) photographs were genuine.

Sir Arthur Conan Doyle, preparing an article on fairies for the *Strand* magazine, asked to see them. Going to Cottingley, Gardner gave the girls cameras and sealed filmplates. Their new fairy photographs convinced both Gardner and Conan Doyle, whose *Strand* article about them caused many to doubt his sanity. 'For the true explanation of these photographs what is wanted is not a knowledge of occult phenomena but a knowledge of children,' declared *Truth* magazine on 5 January 1921, while Arthur Wright was sad that the great Sir Arthur had been: 'bamboozled by our Elsie, and her at the bottom of her class'. Conan Doyle now sent clairvoyant Geoffrey Hodson to Cottingley. Talking to the girls, he claimed he had seen fairy forms, but there were no new photos. Tired of it all, Elsie and Frances later said they'd told Hodson whatever he wanted to hear. Photographs of gnomes and sprites were off their agenda by 1922, when Conan Doyle published his widely derided *The Coming of the Fairies*.

In 1966 *Daily Express* journalist Peter Chambers found Elsie back in Yorkshire after years in India. She called the fairies 'figments of my imagination', but denied faking the photos. Interviewed in 1971 by *Nationwide*, a BBC TV news programme, both cousins remained evasive. In 1976 local folklorist Joe Cooper persuaded them to appear on TV. Still denying fakery, when asked why she had never tried to grab the fairies, Frances said: 'You couldn't. It's like grabbing for a ghost or something.'

Which is true of many an occult hoax. Now you see it, now you don't. And is it a good idea to take childish imagination at face value? Take modern cases of alleged satanic child abuse. In the USA and elsewhere some parents, teachers, and child-care assistants have been jailed (*see* **False Memory Syndrome**) solely on 'evidence' coaxed from frightened or vengeful children by zealots with predetermined agendas and belief-systems.

They might do better to remember the Cottingley case. Unless there really *were* fairies at the bottom of the garden.

COUNTERFEITERS (*FRAUD*)

Counterfeiters have been busy ever since coins were coined and value assigned to gems and other rare items useful in barter or exchange. Once the scam was **alchemical**; involving the alleged transformation of lead into gold. And though cheques and promissory notes had been in use for centuries, it was only with the introduction of the standardised bank note from the eighteenth century on that modern counterfeiting began.

The first rogue to use recognisably modern methods was William Brockway (1822–1920). His forgeries were so good the US Treasury was sure that he had duplicates of the original printing plates. Born an orphan named Spencer and fostered, he had no formal education, but sat in on Yale classes in electro-chemistry and law. At that time bank notes were printed locally. An official guarded the plates and paper. Keen to advance himself, Brockway began by distracting the official of a New Haven bank while its $5 bill was being printed. Slipping through the press a sheet of soft, thin lead, he gained front and back impressions good enough to make and pass off a thousand bills. Setting himself up in Philadelphia, he married, passing himself off as a stockbroker. In 1860 he hired British engraver, William Smith. Working by day for a New York bank, Smith's counterfeits were flawless. In 1865 he produced his masterpiece: a Union government $1,000 interest-bearing bill. This aroused the suspicion of William P. Wood, head of the newly formed Secret Service and himself hardly honest. Brockway, now in partnership with landowner James B. Doyle, was hauled in. The Treasury, sure the bill was duplicated from its own plates, offered a reward for information. Wanting it for himself, Wood pressurised Brockway to hand over the (non-existent) plates – but Brockway held out until four years later Wood lost his job.

His luck ran out in 1880. Unhappy with their marriage, his wife went to a lawyer even as Smith finished forging a $1,000 coupon bond to be redeemed in 1881. The lawyer suggested to his friend, Secret Service Agent Drummond, that Brockway had been at large long enough, so Drummond had him watched. One day the agents saw Brockway (who enjoyed fishing) meet Doyle in a boat off the south shore of Brooklyn. They followed Doyle to a house which belonged, they learned, to a note engraver named Smith. When Doyle left the house and boarded the Chicago train he was detained. On him were found 204 coupon bonds – again, such fine counterfeits the Treasury doubted they were forgeries.

Arrested, Brockway again made a deal, surrendering plates, paper, and counterfeit notes. He went free but, though in court he lied his face off for Doyle, in 1882 his partner went down for twelve years. Caught in 1883 forging railway bonds, Brockway got five years in Sing Sing. Out after three, he went on faking it until, betrayed by an engraver 'turned' by the Secret Service, he got a further ten years. Seen buying tracing paper in a store in 1905 and taken in, he was released next day on account of his age. He was eighty-three years old and still at it. A man with a mission![1]

The finest dollar forgeries ever originated in Britain. Totalling $4.9 million in 'funny money' when seized in 1979 by Scotland Yard, in court a US Treasury official called these fake $20 and $50 bills so good they made the hair stand up on the back of his neck. In the dock were Charles Black (b.1929) and Brian Katin (b.1939). They got seven and three years respectively. A jobless printer's employee on meeting Black at a printing trade show in 1975, Katin was a perfectionist. The forgery of perfect bills became the great challenge of his life. Working with offset litho in a secret room at the back of the garage of his bungalow on the Sussex coast by Bognor Regis, and supplied with photographic plates by Black, Katin had laboured for eight months over the colour mixture of the inks before getting it right. In addition, magnetic inks were needed for the serial numbers and filigree patterns on the note faces. Katin achieved embossing by handpressing against an incised brass block. Photographed onto a 100 per cent rag quality paper meeting the required flexibility standards, with a final glycerine texturing applied, the notes were at last ready – but so, by then, was the law. The haul was seized before the counterfeiters had distributed more than a fraction of it. The distributors were never caught.

Those working to suppress counterfeits have a hard time inventing unreproducible new features in bank notes. Laser colour photocopiers are now outwitted by patterns of concentric circles that blur when copied. Yet costly new features like holographic 'latent images' and magnetic safeguards mean that only high-value bank notes can recoup the investment. The Bank of England claims that their next £5 note is unaffordable.[2]

José Beraha (b.1907) tried a different angle. Born in Skopje of a Sephardic Jewish family from Spain, when the Nazis seized Yugoslavia in 1943 he fled to Italy with two nephews, the only other survivors of his family. He was resourceful. Moving in 1946 to Milan, where he married, he sought to free his export ventures from post-war Europe's money controls. The British sovereign, though no longer legal tender in Britain, was then thought the safest of trade currencies. Beraha learned that, though customers paid up to $20 per sovereign, the coin's metal value was only $9. He went into business. With Milanese engineer Guiseppe Bernardi in charge of production, he paid his manager a fee of $68 per kilo of gold made into sovereigns while developing a global network of sales agents. His coins, each containing 124.64 grains of gold instead of the 123.67 specified, were in fact superior to the original sovereign. The sovereign had not been legal tender in Britain since 1931, when Britain had left the gold standard. Creating no debt in the UK Treasury, he was producing a coin of greater gold content than the original. How could he be prosecuted?

Making a fortune, in 1951 he moved to Switzerland, but British pressure led Italian police to raid his mint and arrest its management team. Extradited on counterfeiting charges, he sent a lawyer to London with only sovereigns for out-of-pocket expenses. Nobody would take them. The Treasury advised him to sell them in a coin shop for their metal content. Impressed by this demonstration, in 1952 his Swiss judges dropped the case. A year later an Italian court returned the ingot gold and equipment seized in the raid on Bernardi's team. So he proved that not every form of counterfeiting is necessarily illegal.[3]

A hoax closer to wrecking the British economy emerged soon after the German surrender in 1945, when a lorryload of forged Bank of England notes worth £21 million was seized by US counter-espionage officers near the Swiss border. It was what was left of Operation Bernhard, named after its director, Major Bernhard Kruger, and the brainchild of Gestapo chief Heinrich Himmler. The aim had been to break the British economy. With engravers and printers recruited from concentration camps, plates were made and Bank of England notes forged to the value of about £140 million.

Sent out in batches of £100,000, these notes were distributed by Gestapo agents in Zurich, Lisbon, Stockholm and other neutral cities before reaching London. The British realised they were up against the German government only when a German spy was caught in Edinburgh carrying the perfect forgeries. With the Allies closing in, Kruger persuaded Himmler to move the operation to the Alps, to provide escaping Nazis with forged money and documents. In the last days of the war the plates were destroyed, but not the notes. It was this final hoard that was intercepted in the lorry, en route to be buried for later recovery. As for Kruger, his forged notes stood him in good stead. He was never found.

Then there is Arthur Virgilio Alves Reis (1896–1955), a Portuguese colonial official who began by forging a diploma from the non-existent 'Oxford University Polytechnic'. This got him a job as an engineer in Angola. In need of cash after a minor fraud landed him in Lisbon jail for two months, in 1924 he learned that some of the Bank of Portugal's notes were printed by the British firm of Waterlow and Sons, and that the Bank had no way to check for duplicate notes. Choosing three confederates – Karel Marang, a Dutch merchant; José Bandeira, brother of the Portuguese Minister to the Hague; and the German businessman Gustav Hennies, he put his scheme to work. Marang and Bandeira began as dupes. Telling them he had authority to arrange a loan for Angola, he showed them a contract bearing the forged signatures of the High Commissioner of Angola and the Portuguese Minister of Finance. Taking the contract to London, Marang told Sir William Waterlow that the print-run of notes had to be kept secret for political reasons. Waterlow required authorisation from the Governor of the Bank of

Portugal. This soon arrived, also contracts signed by prominent Portuguese bankers and the High Commissioner of Angola – all forged by Reis. The letter from the 'Governor' said that the notes, to be circulated only in Angola, could be printed on the same plates with the same serial numbers as a previous issue. To avoid confusion, the Bank of Angola would overprint 'Angola' on them.

Marang, also Consul-General of Persia at the Hague, had diplomatic immunity, and thus easily carried the notes through Lisbon customs. Opening accounts at branches of big banks, and later withdrawing from other branches, Reis exchanged the fake notes for foreign currency and blocks of industrial shares, and became so rich he opened his own bank – the Bank of Angola and Metropole. But with 200,000 perfect but fake 500 Escudo (each worth about £5) flooding the country, suspicions grew. The notes passed all tests, but when Bank of Portugal inspectors raided the Bank of Angola and Metropole, they found new notes with the same serial numbers as some already in circulation. Arrested, Reis forged documents implying that the Governor of the Bank of Portugal and some of his directors were responsible for the fraud. For five years these delayed his trial, but in May 1930 on his own confession he was found guilty and jailed for twenty years. Bandeira also got twenty years; Hennies died in Germany in 1936; and Marang, tried in the Hague, was jailed for eleven months for receiving stolen property.

Released in 1945 and denied entry to Brazil, Reis died in 1955, so poor he was buried in a bedsheet so his son could inherit his only suit. I hate to draw a moral, but . . .

1. Newnham, *op. cit.*, pp.99–100.
2. *ibid.*, pp.108–9.
3. *ibid.*, pp.100–106.

CROISET, Gerard (1909–80) (*PARANORMAL HOAXES*)
This famous Dutch 'psychic detective' reputedly used telepathy and psychometry to locate hundreds of missing people, dead and alive. His reputation rested on claims by parapsychologist Wilhelm Tenhaeff (d.1981) to have documented his work accurately over many years. But Tenhaeff embellished and manipulated the data; a process abetted by the popular press. When in 1979 Croiset tried to help to uncover the notorious 'Yorkshire Ripper' sex-killer, *Sun* reporter Derek Shuff made the claim that Croiset's: 'most famous case was to describe the killer of a young Dutch girl found dead beside her bicycle'. But in fact in this case (Wierden 1946) the girl had not in fact been killed; and Wierden's chief of police had long since debunked Dutch press accounts claiming that Croiset had solved it.

Croiset was also said to demonstrate precognition in 'chair tests' by which he tried to describe a person who at a specific future time would sit in a specified chair. Despite a few hits, the evidence is dubious. Tenhaeff suppressed misses, invented hits, and ignored procedural errors. None of it proves Croiset a fraud. But many of his alleged successes simply did not occur; while other 'predictions' relied not on ESP but on the interpretation of available information.[1]

1. 'Croiset: double Dutch?', Piet Hein Hobens, *The Unexplained*, Orbis partwork, London 1983, pp.2630–33.

CROP CIRCLES (*PARANORMAL HOAXES*)

Seemingly as mysterious, though more creative and much less destructive than the cattle mutilations in the USA during the 1970s, this phenomenon first made news in August 1980 when a tourist walking above the Vale of Pewsey in southern England saw, swirled with inexplicable precision into a cornfield below, three oddly perfect circles. A report in the *Wiltshire Times* gained the attention of local **UFO**logists. Finding no evidence of hoaxing or alien intervention, and wondering if the circles were caused by a meteorological abnormality like a whirlwind, they contacted meteorologist Terence Meaden – and so began one of the most entertaining, creative, and longest-running 'silly season' media stories of the 1980s.[1]

By summer 1982, new circles were appearing all over southern England. Typically, these were 'singletons' (on their own). As the phenomenon (and media interest) developed, more complex formations began to appear – not only groups of related circles but, by 1989, complex 'pictograms' – key-forms, Celtic crosses, and images drawn from modern fractal geometry.

In the early days, when the formations were relatively simple, two main theories of causation emerged. Meaden argued that a rare species of atmospheric vortex was creating localised whirlwinds that swirled circles into the corn. As the formations (and reports) grew more complex, he posited what he called a 'plasma vortex'; a theory later taken up and developed by Yoshihiko Ohtsuki of Tokyo's Waseda University.

More popular with the media were the wilder theories generated by New Age enthusiasts, occultists and UFOlogists who, as each new summer saw ever more circles appear, flocked to sites like the Devil's Punchbowl near Winchester, or ancient megalithic sites like Avebury. Here, experiencing 'higher vibrations' and setting up all-night watches to try and catch the 'Circlemakers' at it, such mystics concluded that alien intervention was obviously responsible! UFOs had caused the circles, or the 'collective unconscious', or even Gaia, the mythical Earth-Mother who, distressed by humanity's lack of reverence to Her, was warning us all to mend our ways!

This sensationalist position was advanced particularly by researchers Pat Delgado and Colin Andrews, whose *Circular Evidence* became a bestseller in 1989. Suggesting that the circles favoured specific sites year after year, they invoked various odd events as 'evidence'. Why, for example, above a circle at Winterbourne Stoke in Wiltshire, had a Harrier jump jet pilot mysteriously ejected (to his death), leaving his plane to fly on and crash in the Irish Sea? Why, when Andrews took home soil samples from one circle, did a burglar alarm in a hut where he put the sample keep going off at 4.15 a.m? Why did his dog, taken against its will to the centre of another circle, begin to vomit? Obvious! The 'Circlemakers' were responsible!²

Of course, they agreed, *some* hoaxers were afoot. This was well known. In one case, the *Daily Mirror* paid a farming family named Shepherd to fake a five-circle complex. This they did by entering the field on stilts (to leave no footprints), before trampling out a circle with their feet. Even so, true believers (while deploring such crass commercialism) noted that the edges of the circles were uncharacteristically rough and imprecise.

Yet other researchers also noted how dogs reacted to *genuine* circles, as if sensing the alien energies, while many others reported seeing strange lights hovering by night over fields where circles later appeared, or heard high-pitched hummings, or noises like electrical static. Believers made much of reports such as how, on 16 June 1991, as a 75 foot-wide circle appeared on Bolberry Down near Salcombe in Devon, ham radio operator Lew Dilling had heard odd high-pitched blips and clicks when tuned into a regular frequency.

'The signals were so powerful,' he said, 'that you could hear them in the background of Radio Moscow and Voice of America – and they would normally swamp everything.' Meanwhile the owner of the local pub had reportedly learned of the circle only after his dog went berserk, tearing up the carpet.³

Even so, by then it had become obvious to all not totally infatuated with a need to believe in alien intervention that the phenomenon showed disturbing signs of purely *human* origin. Not only did it evolve rapidly from simple circles, to complex circles, and then to 'pictograms' and even 'insectograms', but the 'Circlemakers' confounded every new 'reasonable' theory by producing these new formations (exploding each new theory) with uncanny immediacy. When Meaden pointed out that so far all the swirling had been clockwise, an anti-clockwise circle immediately appeared. When it was suggested that hoaxers were using helicopters, a new circle appeared directly under a powerline.

Yet the 'alien intervention' theories of Delgado and Andrews (who by now had shrugged off Meaden's boring 'scientific' ideas), rode high until, in July 1990, in a field near Alton Barnes, appeared the most spectacular pictogram yet. The 400-feet spread featured not only five circles but amazing new shapes, including a dumb-bell and a skeleton key. The media (and crop-watchers) so invaded the instantly famous site that farmer Tim Carson made £5,000, charging £1 a head for admission. All serious cerealogists (or cereologists: the spelling kept changing) were convinced that this was the major circle so far. Meaden thought it proved his theory of a plasma vortex. Delgado and Andrews were confident that their own more *outré* theories were about to be proved. With the media panting, they set up 'Operation Blackbird'. This crop-watch would, the world was assured, capture on film the mysterious agents behind the crop circle phenomenon – which made it all the more disconcerting when, at the centre of a newly swirled crop circle, the intrepid investigators found not evidence of the alien Circlemakers, but six 'Zodiac' board games, left as a signature (it later emerged) by a Bristol-based hoaxer who called himself 'Merlin'.

HOAXERS RUN RINGS ROUND CIRCLE OF EXPERTS was a typical headline. A year later, in September 1991, the dwindling band of true believers was further embarrassed when two pranksters in their sixties, Dave Chorley and Doug Bower, revealed that they'd been making circles since 1978 even while pretending to be dedicated cerealogists. Their preferred technique was the 'stalk-stomper'; a plank held beneath one foot by a loop of rope. To the despair of Delgado, Andrews, and other enthusiasts, they demonstrated on TV how they'd done it. Other techniques they employed included signalling by torch so as to space quintuplet satellite circles, and a cap-mounted wire sighting device for accurately forming pictogram avenues and sidebars.

Later it emerged that up to a dozen groups had busily been hoaxing circles and pictograms throughout England since the mid 1980s, their motives and methods various. These groups included 'Merlin' (alias George Vernon) and his followers (motive: to enchant the world); the Northamptonshire-based 'Bill Bailey Gang' (motive: pride in artistic achievement); the 'Wessex Skeptics' who, using garden rollers and cardboard mats, wished to prove all circles man-made; and the 'United Bureau of Investigation', a group of Wiltshire-based garden-rollers whose main motive was, apparently, not only to hasten the apocalypse and establish contact with aliens but to find something to do at night after quaffing a few pints of cider.[4]

Yet the crop circle hoax is one of the better of recent years. Little damage was done, and many of the circles and the later, more complex, forms were beautiful! They were works of art not only in themselves but in the way that their midnight makers had stolen into the rich, private cornlands of Middle England to set out shapes that (for a time) fooled many!

Garden rollers, wooden planks set underfoot, strange signs stamped in the fields by night – what's wrong with that? Believe what you want; but isn't it reassuring when we find out that we are so inventive? Art takes many forms, and maybe the best are those which aren't even seen as such at first. Who needs alien intelligence, when we have our own?

1. *Round in Circles*, Jim Schnabel, Hamish Hamilton, London 1993.
2. *Circular Evidence*, Pat Delgado and Colin Andrews, Bloomsbury, London 1989.
3. *Unsolved Mysteries*, Colin and Damon Wilson, Headline, London 1993.
4. 'Pick of the Crops', Jim Schnabel, *Fortean Times* No. 69, London 1993.

CROWHURST, Donald (1932–69) (*EXPLORATION HOAXES*)
The sad tale of an ill-planned voyage that ended in hoax and death. Born in British India in 1932, a mother's boy dressed as a girl until he was eight whose drunkard father died when he was sixteen, Donald Crowhurst grew up self-critical and self-destructive. Involved in more than his share of serious car crashes and forced to resign from both the RAF and the army for riotous behaviour, married in 1958, he drifted through various jobs in electronics. In 1967, now a father of four and a keen amateur sailor, he set up a business manufacturing navigation equipment. It didn't do well. Ever more moody and introverted, his sense of invincibility frustrated by the low key of his life, in May that year lone sailor Francis Chichester returned to Plymouth after a one-stop circumnavigation.

Crowhurst's fate was shaped. Telling a friend that for four years he'd wanted to make the first *non*-stop solo circumnavigation, he wrote to the Town Clerk of Greenwich, where Chichester's yacht *Gypsy Moth* was laid up, requesting loan of the boat for a year. The letter went unanswered. But on 17 March 1968 the *Sunday Times* announced it was sponsoring a round-the-world solo yacht race. There would be a 'Golden Globe' trophy for the first boat home; a prize of £5,000 for the fastest circumnavigation. Competitors could start between 1 June and 31 October 1968. Crowhurst, though nearly bankrupt and without a boat, promptly entered. So did better-known yachtsmen like Bernard Moitessier, Robin Knox-Johnston and Nigel Tetley. Better organised, most of the other competitors left in June, with Crowhurst still fretting on land. Only late in May had he persuaded Stanley Best, an investor in his failing business, to fund a trimaran built to his specifications. And after many snags, on 3 September the forty-foot *Teignmouth Electron* was launched, with Crowhurst still basically a Sunday yachtsman. The last of the other competitors had already sailed when final trials in mid-October revealed serious basic faults in the new boat. But Crowhurst could not let himself back out. Just before 5 p.m. on the 31st, seven hours before the deadline, he set sail amid a cold drizzle.

The first week he made good speed, but hatches leaked, the self-steering equipment was unreliable, the electrics faulty, the pumping arrangements unreliable. After two weeks he had completed only 800 miles. During the third week he nearly docked at Madeira, but instead began to formulate an alternative plan, soon to involve keeping two logs – one true, the other false.

Thereafter the entries in his (later recovered) log grow sketchy, offering only broad hints as to his actual position. Tape-recording messages for the BBC, he affected a jaunty, swashbuckling image, and on 10 December jubilantly claimed to have sailed 243 miles in one day, a new record for a lone sailor. His broadcast of this claim led to maximum press coverage. Only a few critics, like Chichester, doubted the validity of his claim. As the real log later showed, his highest actual distance attained in one day was 177 miles.

Meanwhile he faked the false log so skilfully that an expert found nothing in it to seriously discredit either the navigational data or the narrative. This false log was begun on 12 December. Probably it was then he decided to risk faking the entire circumnavigation. On 17 December he transmitted more fake information: 'THROUGH DOL-DRUMS OVER EQUATOR SAILING FAST AGAIN.' By Christmas he was reporting himself some 550 miles ahead of his actual position off the north-east coast of Brazil, where he was trying to avoid shipping lanes. On Christmas Eve he radiotelephoned his wife Clare, but refused to give his position. Realising that a radio fix would reveal his hoax, he hinted at generator trouble and after 19 January kept radio silence for eleven weeks. Now he began writing notes suggesting his emotional distress. During the next month, aimlessly zigzagging off the Brazilian coast, he copied every message he could pick up on his set, knowing he would have to fake knowledge of weather conditions at every stage of his pretended journey. By now the *Teignmouth Electron* badly needed repairs. On 6 March Crowhurst landed illicitly on the estuary of the Rio Solado, within a hundred miles of Buenos Aires. The risk paid off: the repairs were made, the news never got out, but his mental state was poor. 'He laughed a lot, as though he were making fun of us,' said the wife of a French-speaking sergeant who helped him. On 8 March he set sail again, and continued south almost as far as the Falklands before turning north again. He had to kill time (while presumably sailing through the Indian Ocean) before he could plausibly resume radio contact from the Atlantic.

Meanwhile there were only three remaining competitors. Moitessier was in the lead, but dropped out for reasons of his own. Knox-Johnston had regained the Atlantic, and though now the probable winner of the Golden Globe he was going so slow it seemed more likely that Crowhurst or the third contender – Nigel Tetley, also in a trimaran – would get the money prize for the fastest voyage. Tetley, rounding the Horn on 20 March, was trailing Knox-Johnston home. In a dilemma, Crowhurst decided to let Tetley take the prize, fearing that if he was acclaimed victor scrutiny of his log would reveal the fraud. But on 21 May, Tetley's *Victress* sank in a storm near the Azores. Crowhurst, the only contender still in the race, was sure of the cash prize – if only he could get home.

From now on his log displays growing irrationality. With his radio now genuinely broken so that he could receive but not send messages, he was desperately anxious to speak to Clare. He began writing metaphysical ramblings preoccupied with God and his sense of sin. Back in Teignmouth, his press agent was preparing a hero's welcome. Receiving a cable that a hundred thousand people waited to greet him, Crowhurst retreated deeper into himself. By now, lounging naked in the tropical heat all day, he was almost out of food. Throughout June he drifted, letting his chronometer run down.

'During his lifetime,' he wrote, 'each man plays cosmic chess against the Devil.' Sensing that his end was near, on the night of 30 June he recorded his last confused notes. Having restarted his clock, at 11 17 00 he wrote his final words:

> It has been a good game that
> must be ended at the
> I will play this game when
> I choose I will resign the
> game 11 20 40 There is
> no reason for harmful

On 10 July the *Picardy*, a packet carrying mail from England to the Caribbean, came across the *Teignmouth Electron* drifting aimlessly some 1,800 miles from London. There was nobody on board. Donald Crowhurst had vanished. It was only when his log was read that the desperate hoax – and the tragedy – became apparent.

The Golden Globe celebration dinner for Knox-Johnston was called off; Knox-Johnston asking that the money prize be donated to a Crowhurst Appeal Fund. Later, journalists Nicholas Tomalin and Ron Hall gained the co-operation of all required to write the story of one of the strangest hoaxes of the century.[1]

1. *The Strange Last Voyage of Donald Crowhurst*, Nicholas Tomalin and Ron Hall, New York 1970.

D

'Get your facts first, and then you can distort them as much as you please.'

(Mark Twain)

DANCING DUCKS (*See* **REICHENBACH, Harry**)

DAVISON, Linda (contemporary) (*IMPOSTORS, LITERARY HOAXES*)

Archibald **Belaney** started something by pretending to be Grey Owl. Soon the fake cowboy Will **James** was also riding the literary range, and years later a rash of bestsellers by or about non-existent Indians appeared. First Carlos **Castaneda** invented the Yaqui *brujo* Don Juan, and the 1970s saw at least two more fake Native American sagas.

In *Crying Wind* (1977) devout Colorado mother of four Linda Davison feelingly told how her wise old grandma had raised her on a poverty-stricken Kickapoo reservation. The tale did so well that its publisher, Moody Press, soon issued the sequel, *My Searching Heart*. With a third book ready to be published and a fourth in progress, Davison launched an evangelistic ministry. Appearing in Indian garb at churches round the nation, she assured doubters that all errors were due to her poor memory. Yet complaints mounted and Moody Press investigated, to learn that 'Crying Wind' had grown up in Woodland Park, Colorado; graduating from high school in 1961. The family was not Indian and had never used Indian dress or names, insisted her uncle Paul Hamlet ('Uncle Cloud' in the books). In August 1979 Moody cancelled the series, saying that the books: 'extend literary privilege beyond [their] editorial standards'; yet in 1989 Harvest House reissued the first two as 'biographical novels', cataloguing them under 'Exciting True Stories'.

Linda Davison may have got her idea from *The Education of Little Tree* (1976), claimed as the autobiography of a Cherokee orphan born in Tennessee in 1930. Adopted by his 'Granma' Bonnie Bee (pure Cherokee) and 'Granpa Wales' (part Scots, like Grey Owl's father: odd, this hoaxers' passion for marrying Indians to Scotsmen), Little Tree had learned how to distil whisky, weave baskets, trap game, read 'Mr Shakespeare', and endure racism cheerfully. Unschooled, he had become a cowboy, then official Storyteller in Council to the Cherokee Nation. In 1976 he published his autobiography under his adult name, Forrest Carter. Praised in the *New York Times* and interviewed on TV by Barbara Walters, Carter died in 1979, but his 'true story' was reissued in 1986. In 1991, with a million copies in print, the American Booksellers Association gave it their ABBY reward for its humanitarian values. Only after it had been at the top of the paperback bestseller lists for weeks, with all royalties reportedly going to the Cherokees, did the ugly truth emerge.

'Forrest Carter' was Asa Carter from Alabama, a white racist and politician who'd worked all his life for the Ku Klux Klan. His supporters had attacked singer Nat King Cole on stage in Birmingham in 1956; in 1957 six of his associates had castrated a black man in a room decorated with his political posters; and in 1970, with Governor George Wallace said to have grown soft on race issues, Carter had run against him (and lost), stating: 'I am a racist.' He had shot a man, but witnesses had backed out and the case had been dropped.

And *Little Tree?* It was all a lie. There never was a post of Storyteller in Council to the Cherokee Nation, and the Cherokees never got any royalties. Asa Carter, said his brother Doug, had invented this lovable Cherokee guru (who stood for everything he opposed) to finance a political comeback! Indian chic was all the rage at the time, and Castaneda had proved there was a lucrative market for politically correct New Age Native American sages. So, calling himself *Forrest* Carter after a Klan founder, this master hypocrite had sat down to write what had become a bestseller – posthumous, fortunately.[1]

1. Lindskoog, *op. cit.*, pp.101–4.

DAWSON, Charles (*See* **PILTDOWN MAN**)

D-DAY LANDINGS (*See* **HOAXES IN WARFARE**)

DEAD SEA SCROLLS (*See* **CHRISTIANITY; SHAPIRA, Moses**)

DE HORY, Elmyr (1911–76) (*ART FORGERIES*)
The greatest art faker of the century? **Van Meegeren** or **Hebborn** may have been more skilled, but the most successful was Hungarian Elmyr de Hory. The only child of rich land-owning parents who divorced when he was sixteen, a Budapest art school led him to the Akademie Heimann in Munich, then to the Académie de la Grande Chaumière in Paris where,

taught by Fernand Léger, soon this charming homosexual knew all the great figures of the Parisian art world – Léger himself, Vlaminck, Derain, Matisse, Picasso. His own work sold well enough, and at the time there was no shortage of money from home. But now his fate took a turn for the worse.

Returning to Budapest in 1938 after Hitler's annexation of Austria, he was arrested as a political undesirable. Interned first in Transylvania, he was removed to a concentration camp in Germany, which he survived despite having a leg broken by the Gestapo. After the war he returned to Budapest, then Paris. He was forty now, and broke. One day he was visited in his room on the Rue Jacob by the widow of racing driver Sir Malcolm Campbell. 'Isn't that a Picasso?' she asked, seeing a line drawing he'd made of a young girl's head. Saying neither yes nor no, he sold it to her for the equivalent of $60 – then quickly produced another six.

Still unsure about this new line of business, he confessed his forgery to an old friend, Jacques Chamberlin, son of a well-known pre-war collector. Chamberlin persuaded him to produce more fakes, to be sold as the remains of his father's collection. De Hory began faking Picassos. All went well until he fell out with Chamberlin over money. Flying to Brazil, he tried to make it under his own name then, growing bored, went on to New York. His charm soon gained him entry to the smart set, but it was only on moving to Hollywood that he began making real money. Impeccably dressed with his gold-chained monacle and romantic Hungarian accent, now known as Baron de Hory, he turned from Picassos to drawings by Matisse and Renoir. Three days after reaching Los Angeles, he sold three Matisse pen-and-ink nudes to a Beverly Hills gallery. He prospered until in 1952 the dealer Frank Perls, studying his portfolio, became suspicious of a faked Modigliani and threw him out.

Again he tried to go straight, selling his own work. But one day when the rent was due he was broke. Quickly he drew a Modigliani self-portrait and within an hour sold it to the Dalzell Hatfield Gallery for $200. A month later he read that Chicago collector James Alsdorf had paid almost $4,000 for it.

In New York again, he sold three fake Matisse drawings for $500 each, then took an apartment in Miami. Calling himself L.E. Raynal, he wrote to galleries and museums all over America, saying he owned modern works, and over the next two years sold fake Braques, Derains, Vlamincks, Bonnards, and Renoirs. But after some seventy drawings had netted him $160,000, he got careless. Agnes Mongan, Assistant Director at Harvard's Fogg Art Museum, saw through 'L.E. Raynal' and alerted the FBI. It seems that *some* art 'experts' do know their business. What a relief.

He fled to Los Angeles, where Frank Perls was also after him. In Mexico City he was arrested as a suspect in the murder of a homosexual

Englishman. Back in New York, where he sold forged lithographs, he threw a party at which (with Marilyn Monroe among the guests), he met his nemesis – Ferdinand Legros, a young French-Greek conman, whom he instantly disliked. But by now his past had caught up with him. With his fakes hanging everywhere, nobody wanted his own work. Deeply depressed, he tried suicide.

Seizing his chance, Legros drove de Hory to Florida to recuperate, then became his fence. Between 1961 and 1967, taking forty per cent of all he could sell, Legros sold an estimated sixty million dollars' worth of de Hory oils, watercolours, and sketches. Thirty-two (Dufys, Modiglianis, Gauguins and Chagalls) went to Texan oil-man Algur H. Meadows. Trying to escape Legros, de Hory fled back to Europe, setting himself up in Rome as 'Joseph Boutin'. A year later Legros tracked him down in Paris. De Hory said he'd given up forgery. All his fakes were in a trunk in a New York hotel. Five days later he learned that Legros had flown to New York, claimed the trunk, and sold its contents.

Unable to sell his own work, back in Rome he turned again to faking and, with the proceeds settled on Ibiza in the Balearics. Again Legros caught up with him, and this time took over his life. Persuading him to stay on Ibiza, keeping him supplied with old canvas and materials, the dealer (his name means 'the fat man') even built de Hory a house – while always leaving him short of cash. Between 1964 and 1966 Legros made a fortune, mainly through Algur H. Meadows.

At last the astute millionaire got suspicious and invited genuine dealers, including Perls, to inspect his collection. Shocked, he learned it was all fake. Legros fled to Paris, then Ibiza. Insisting that Legros would never be tried, as the scandal would cause a crash in the art market, de Hory said he'd kill himself rather than go to jail. Yet in 1968 he was jailed on charges ranging from homosexuality to 'consorting with known criminals'. Freed after three months, he was deported from Ibiza for a year.

Extradited from Brazil in 1976, Legros was jailed in France for two years. In December that year, de Hory took a fatal overdose. All his efforts to go straight had failed, and it had been so easy to fool the 'experts'. Even now, nobody knows how many of his fakes hang as 'genuine' in galleries round the world.

DEMARA, Ferdinand Waldo (1921–82) (*IMPOSTORS*)
So good at being anyone but himself that in *The Great Impostor*, a 1960 biopic of his chameleon life, he was impersonated by actor Tony Curtis, this amazing man variously posed as a Canadian naval surgeon, cancer researcher, zoology graduate, village teacher, Trappist monk, doctor of psychology, assistant warden in a Texan prison, and dean of the School of Philosophy at Gannon College, Pennsylvania. Forging documents, degrees, certifications and letters of recommendation, in his various guises he used his remarkable memory and ability to pick up new skills

so well that few saw through him. Even when they did, they rarely blamed him. Though accused of military desertion, fraud, forgery, car theft, embezzlement, resisting arrest, vagrancy and public drunkenness, he never spent more than a few weeks in jail. Usually all charges were dropped, and more than once he was wanted back by those he'd deceived.

His most remarkable exploit (seemingly a desperate effort to avoid responsibility to the first woman he ever fell for) was to impersonate Surgeon-Lieutenant Joseph C. Cyr of the Royal Canadian Navy during the Korean War. Meeting Dr Cyr while posing as a physician turned theology student in New Brunswick, he offered to present the doctor's papers to the Maine medical board so that Cyr could practise in the USA, but used them to join the navy – as Dr Cyr. Assigned to HMCS *Cayuga*, he taught himself medicine and dentistry, and amid battle conditions performed many successful operations on badly wounded South Korean soldiers. Setting up a clinic ashore, his medical feats were written up in the Canadian and American press. In New Brunswick the real Dr Cyr read about the brilliant surgeon and identified him as Dr Cecil B. Hamann, the man he'd known and admired. Next, and worse still, in Kentucky the real Dr Hamann denounced him as a man expelled from St Louis University for cheating. Demara was in hot water – again.

He had begun his career by running away from New England when his family lost their home and status. Deserting from both the US Army and Navy, he'd been caught and court-martialled with threat of execution, but defended himself so movingly on the grounds of his religious principles that he'd got off virtually scot-free. Stealing the name of philosophy doctor Robert Linton French he'd joined a Trappist monastery in Kentucky, for two years enduring every discipline before breaking his vow of frugality by guzzling grapes in the vineyard. After that he'd left a trail of academics (like Hamann) saddened to learn that their brilliant subordinate was not what he seemed. And so at length – Dr Cyr.

Following a naval inquiry he was discharged and expelled from Canada, though the *Cayuga*'s crew sent him a Christmas card, on it quoting Berton Braley's poem 'Loyalty': 'He may be six kinds of liar . . . but I love him, Because – well, because he's my friend.'

Drifting south to Texas, in Houston he applied as and became a prison officer and, as Ben W. Jones, once again proved himself. Organising writing classes and sports days, he was asked by Director O.B. Ellis of the Texas Prison System to apply his progressive ideas at Huntsville Prison, the state's toughest. All went well until again his past caught up with him and he fled. 'He was one of the best prospects ever to serve in the prison service,' said Ellis, admitting he'd have the man back – if only he had proper credentials.

In Maine he set up a small college, again with false credentials, and when that fell through became the well-liked teacher of a small school on an island off the coast. After his arrest the islanders all wanted him back. He was the best teacher their kids ever had.

'Rascality, pure rascality,' he said when biographer Robert Crichton (*The Great Impostor*, 1959) asked him why he did it. But he also admitted that with every new role he felt he'd lost another part of himself. 'One of the last sad playboys of the Western world,' Crichton called him, wondering if Demara's brilliant impostures arose out of a desperate urge to regain the social standing his family had lost when he was young.

After Crichton's book and the movie were released, Demara again pretended to be a doctor – this time in a film, *The Hypnotic Eye*. But after that he tired of role-playing and turned instead to the profession which had once so nearly drawn him. Ordained as a minister in the church, at last Ferdinand Waldo Demara had an identity of his own.

D'EON DE BEAUMONT, Charles (1728–1810) (*IMPOSTORS*)

Charles Geneviève Louis André Timothée de Beaumont, a transexual spy whom almost everyone thought a woman, qualified as a lawyer before becoming a French agent. Though dark-bearded he put his effeminate looks to good use, turning up at the Russian court of Elizabeth the Great in 1755 as Mme Lia de Beaumont, chaperoned by Mackenzie Douglas, a Scot who claimed to be her uncle. Douglas was soon arrested and jailed as a French spy with Jacobite connections, but nobody, not even the Czarina, suspected the oddly chaste but lovely Lia. Pursued not only by court gallants but by painters wishing to portray 'her' as Aphrodite or to 'capture her pink and white complexion', he was ideally placed to pick up information, and on returning to France was honoured by Louis XV with an annual pension of 3,000 livres.

After serving in the French army he went to London, ostensibly as secretary to the French ambassador. In fact his job was to spy. Intercepting Foreign Office documents and obtaining War Office plans to work out routes for a potential French invasion of England, in 1763 his success was soured when he fell out with the new French ambassador, Count Guerchy, by refusing to hand over his secret files. Peremptorily ordered back to France and insultingly reminded how he'd served the king 'in women's garments', then believing himself poisoned by Guerchy, he approached the British, maybe offering his services as a double agent. But when Guerchy applied for his extradition, George III granted it, and the hapless Chevalier found himself without status. Court officers broke into his barricaded house to find only a cousin of d'Eon's and two women by the fire. The Chevalier was in drag again.

The war with Guerchy ended only when the ambassador was recalled to Paris, and with D'Eon and all his information still in London, argument raged not over his loyalties but over the far more interesting question of his sex. Gossips said he really *was* a woman; noting that he was not only not married but avoided affairs with women; that at birth he had been dedicated to the Virgin Mary; that his given names included the feminine Geneviève; and that he belonged to Sir Francis Dashwood's notorious Hell-Fire Club. Bets were offered in the clubs; but, given his reputation as a duellist and tales of him thrashing several London bookmakers, few dared ask him to his face. Though he swore an affidavit that he was male, in May 1771 a jury of aristocratic ladies gave him 'a most thorough examination' at Medmenham Abbey and declared his sex 'doubtful'. In 1777, amid a lawsuit over bets as to his sex, three respectable witnesses who included two doctors swore under oath that he was definitely a woman. Meanwhile the secretary of the king's adviser De Broglie (still trying to lure D'Eon and his secrets back to France) assured King Louis that: 'Sieur D'Eon is a woman and nothing but a woman, of whom he has all the attributes.'

Confusing, even by eighteenth-century standards. More important politically was that the debt-ridden Chevalier had given up his secret papers as security for a loan. Efforts to entice or kidnap him and his secrets back to France redoubled. De Broglie, it was said, had even hired an English chimney-sweep to hide in D'Eon's chimney and make groaning noises to make him think the place was haunted, but D'Eon thrust his sword up the chimney and made the sweep confess who had sent him.

Yet in time he returned to France – as a woman. Accounts vary. One says the deal was that he could return safely only if he agreed to spend the rest of his life as such. Another is that the decision was his (or hers) alone. The latter seems likely, for when early in the French Revolution he returned to England (after years as a humiliating public question which Voltaire called this 'nice problem'), it was as a woman – and he persisted as such the rest of his life. Only when he died in poverty in 1810 was the issue resolved (or was it?), a coroner's investigation declaring him to have been: 'without any shadow of doubt a male person'. At any rate, it is as a man that he was buried at St Pancras in 1810.[1]

1. McCormick, *op. cit.*, pp.46–52.

DISAPPEARANCES (See CONCORDANCE)

'DISGRUNTLED EMPLOYEE' SCAMS (*PRANKS*)

With trade unions broken or disempowered throughout Britain and the USA during the halcyon days of Reagan and Thatcher; with unemployment high and even the middle classes afraid of losing their jobs; and with millions working part-time or on short-term contracts for low pay and without job security, it may seem now that Big Business is getting everything its own way. Money matters more than people, and what can folk do but toe the line if they want to keep their jobs?

Yet pranking and sabotage by 'disgruntled employees' is a growth industry. Workers who realise they'll never get the promised raise steal without compunction from their companies. Programmers abused by supervisors plant 'logic bombs' in computer systems. Factory bosses threatening to fire workers complaining about unsafe conditions find their machinery breaking down, forcing them to buy new, safer equipment. Company property is deliberately destroyed, time is wasted, precision components are made to fail. Bored market research interviewers fake questionnaires; librarians invent non-existent books; reporters invent stories; clerks encourage shop-lifting or offer free services when the boss isn't looking. Everywhere employees are pulling scams, many of them described in *Sabotage in the American Workplace*, a book of interviews from which most of the following tales are taken. Understandably identified only by their first names, the motives of those interviewed range from sheer boredom to anger at low pay, management harassment, bad company ethics and working conditions, and rage at a system that denies all human values.

'There's a saying that we have at work,' explains Rita, a flight attendant with a major American airline: ' "The company knows the price of everything and the value of nothing." '[1]

'They could have my labor,' says a Chicago Transit Authority bus driver, describing how he and other drivers deliberately 'drag the street' (run the line slow), 'but they couldn't have my soul.'[2]

'They don't treat you like a human being, they treat you as a robot, and your function is to produce the profit,' says Eugene, explaining why he and his work-mates sabotaged the parts they made in a Detroit car factory. 'The [sabotage was] our way of equalising the situation. I caused a lot of damage. Not only did I teach and encourage others to do it, I caused many Americans strife and heartache and taught them the lesson not to buy from that particular company.'[3]

Often such sabotage takes the form of hoax or prank. One angry employee in a Georgia meat-packing plant sent a computerised message to day-shift workers that inside a week there would be huge lay-offs. So much time was wasted that day in anxious workplace discussion that thousands of dollars in company time were lost. Then there's the fired newspaperman caught inserting porn mags inside news-stand copies of the *Los Angeles Times* Sunday edition; or the undiscovered hoaxer who planted pamphlets depicting hard-core sex acts inside Cracker Jacks packets; or the employee with a company manufacturing fortune cookies who singlehandedly flooded Chinese restaurants with negative fortune cookie messages. From coast to coast people got messages like: 'You're a jerk and you know it!' and 'You deserve to die and *soon you will*!' The company had to recall all the cookies but never caught the hoaxer.[4] Likewise the young woman called Susan, who, working for Land of Plenty dates as a date-pitter, began filling the empty spaces in the dates she pitted with little messages like: 'Hi, I'm your pitter. Do you want to pitter-patter with me?'

A Michigan pickle-packer called Terry, working for the summer at Aunt Jane's Pickle factory, got so angry at the sweat-shop philosophy and at being told not to socialise with other workers as he worked that, finding out how to control the speed of the conveyor belts bringing pickles into the factory from the trucks unloading them, he slowed them down for the trucks and sped them up for the packers, so overloading the main belt with more pickles than could be packed. Realising that the bearings on the belts were worn, he threw pickles into them until the belts snapped, so stopping production. With the main belt fixed, he threw a case of glass jars into the tumbler – the machine that put pickles in the jars. The jars smashed; glass ended up in the pickle jars; work stopped for three days; the company lost thousands. 'Which one of you sons of bitches did this?' demanded the foreman, lining the workers up against a wall. Only Terry knew what had happened, and he denied it all (or he'd have been in a pretty pickle). He concludes: 'The beauty of it all was that I was a clean cut young man that looked forward when the foreman told me not to socialise. When he told me to be a robot, I was a robot. But I was a thinking robot.[5]

Immoral? Dangerous? Few such pranksters think so, or, even if they do, they don't apologise. Enraged at being blamed for not working fast enough when the problem was: 'one of the worst designed systems that I had ever seen', a Bank of America programmer called Lazlo went nuts when his pay was stopped. His revenge? He wrote a new program to delete the existing payroll program (a kind of electronic "Fuck you!" ', he calls it) so that, on pay day, nobody throughout northern California's PayNet system got paid. 'Granted,' he says, 'I fucked with the workers, but I really ruined Bank of America's credibility.'[6]

Less horrendous are the hoaxes played by bored librarians. One, called Art, tells how he and other librarians he knows put invented titles in the files for periodicals allegedly available through the system: titles like *Public Equanimity: Its Construction and Maintenance*, and *Roman Orgies: Then and Now*. He notes how the proliferation of computer systems makes it much easier for such 'titles' to assume a life of their own, so that people end up looking for publications that don't exist. And though such hoaxes don't hurt 'the system', but only waste other people's time, it's hard not to laugh at how, when the Iranians issued a death warrant against author Salman Rushdie for his book *The Satanic Verses*, Art infiltrated the records with: 'a special field which indicated that one of the library's copies was the special infidel edition, with an asbestos dust jacket.'[7]

Then there's Lee, a reporter with the *Burlington County Herald*, a newspaper in New Jersey. Making just $150 a week, he wasn't a 'happy camper', and became even less so when his editor: 'kept berating me for failing to write my lead paragraphs in two sentences with one-syllable words'. Assigned to the deadbeat police beat, Lee took the editor at his word, so that next day appeared two articles. One headline read: 'DEAD'. Under it, the copy ran: 'Dateline: Medford, New Jersey. That's what Harry Serbronski was after his car hit a telephone pole at eighty-six miles an hour.' The other headline (at a time when local police were busting pot growers) read: '300 POUNDS BURNT'. The copy ran: 'Dateline: Marlton, New Jersey. Flash fire went through a farm killing one obese woman weighing 304 pounds.' Sued for malice by the woman's family, the paper lost.

'I got fired the next day,' says Lee. 'I had no regrets. I didn't care.'[8]

Begin to get the picture? To preserve their individuality in a system that undermines it people will do almost anything. Thus at the Georgia-Pacific-owned Fort Bragg (in northern California) redwood sawmill in the 1970s, workers began calling in bomb threats on Friday lunchtimes. 'I put four charges of plastic in the powerhouse,' they'd claim. 'It goes off at 4.00. Nobody works today!' Then they'd hang up. So everyone got off early on Fridays, until after a while the tactic wore out through overuse. Nobody even looked for the bombs any more.[9]

Office workers also enjoy screwing up the system. Randall, an insurance file clerk, tells how, even with the boss watching him all the time, he still managed to let defaulted insurance policies go through by putting papers in the wrong file, or by writing down one wrong number, so that people unable to make their payments gained a little more time. 'A nice fire would have done that place some good,' he adds, 'but they had a good sprinkler system.'[10] Iris, a telephone surveyor, tells how often she and her co-workers don't do the interviews at all, but fill out the questionnaires with invented answers, then 'die laughing' when they see the published – and totally false – statistics.[11] Other office workers routinely draft fake sales reports, flush important documents down the toilet, or use company equipment to make money for themselves.

As for the financial world, what with the multi-million-dollar shenanigans of insider dealers like Ivan Boesky, it's easy to regard the entire industry as a hoax. Futures traders deal in commodities that don't even exist; hot-shot whizzkids in Wall Street, London and Tokyo decide the fate of nations by manipulating electronic data without relevance to anything in the real world; and total chaos is amazingly easy to cause. 'I've seen traders lose millions for the firm in minutes because they were hungover and mad at their bosses,' says an anonymous broker. 'You just pick up a phone on the trading floor and start hitting the keys. The touchtone phones are actually computer links to do block trades. One day I picked up some phones, pressed a bunch of buttons and then ran to a Telerate screen to watch the market plunge. I'll never know, but I may have caused a million shares of IBM to be sold that second. This became a big game and I enjoyed scrambling things in the trading department and then running to a screen to see the market fluctuate.'[12]

Other pranks are even scarier. Dennis, a model maker for the engineering contractor Bechtel, spent five years working on the complex and hugely expensive model for a coal-fired power plant in Coal Strip, Montana. Costing over five million dollars in time and materials by the time it was finished, the model ended up full of 'really ridiculous' fake equipment, inserted by Dennis and his friends simply to see how long it would be before an engineer or designer noticed. 'We were a bit of an uncontrollable crowd, which made it fun,' he says. Maybe so, but it makes the hair stand on end to read how, while working on the reactor core of the Hope Creek Nuclear Reactor, a friend of his modified the engineering drawings by inserting runs of piping that began and ended nowhere and had no function. 'There's a chance something like that could get onto the final model and even get out in the field and be partially built before somebody notices it,' says Dennis.[13]

Am I paranoid, or is *that* what happened at Chernobyl?

So it goes on. Most such pranks are harmless enough, undertaken more through boredom than for any deeper motive. Ron, floor manager (until he was fired) in a Florida toy store, cross-dressed Barbie dolls then repackaged them for sale. Finding a Barbie doll with half its leg chewed up, he attached a peg to her leg, and resold her as Peg-Legged Barbie. For the store's Christmas display, he dressed up the Ken doll in a clown outfit, tied Barbie to a balcony, and set Ken up so he was whipping her. 'I kept the other employees amused,' he said. 'I saw it as a necessity for surviving the type of job I had.'[14] And Tico, disc jockey and news director for an FM station in Ohio, had fun making up ever wilder news stories, like the one about a woman who attacked her cheating husband with an electric knife. Working it out with his engineer to play the sound of a Black and Decker saw and a man screaming on cue, he had every advertiser using that news segment for commercials ringing in to complain. Two pulled out. Tico kept his job – just.[15]

But few such scams help anyone. One that did (though in a way that sober, law-abiding citizens could never approve) was pulled by 'Zeke' who, having just got out of jail for dealing marijuana, got a job in the records department of the Arizona Division of Motor Vehicles – only to learn that he was supposed to be looking up vehicle registration numbers for cops investigating people. He didn't want to do it, but couldn't afford to quit. Soon after he started, a cop called up, gave him half a dozen numbers, and said: 'Yeah, we've got a pot party under observation and we're going to get these guys. Give me the information on them.' Thinking fast, Zeke made up fake names and addresses, and heard no more about it. The next week he did the same again when another narcotics agent called up. A friend began doing the same thing, and for ten weeks they fed the police fake information. It ended only when detectives appeared and talked to their supervisor, who called them in. 'Somebody is giving the police false information and we can't prove it's you,' she said, 'but if it happens again, we're going to fire everyone in the department.'

Rather than start giving correct information that would lead to pot-smokers being arrested, Zeke and his friend quit the job and were never brought to book.[16]

Another friendly scam (and one to end with) was pulled one slow Christmas Eve by a federal government officer, 'Bruce', who decided it would be a good idea if all federal employees got to go home early. So, masquerading as the fictitious 'Steve Watkins' of the Federal Executive Board – a body that sets policies for federal agencies in particular regions of the USA – he rang the regional manager of all northeast federal operations.

'Hello Ralph,' he introduced himself with more confidence than he felt. 'This is Steve Watkins with the Federal Executive Board. How are you?'

The Northeast Regional Manager apparently didn't realise he'd never heard of Steve Watkins, or, if he did, didn't want to let on that he hadn't. 'Oh, hi Steve, how are *you?*' he replied.

'Ralph,' 'Steve Watkins' went on, 'I thought I'd better call. We've decided that as of 3.00 p.m. you can let the chickens out of the coop.'

'Great!' said Ralph. He thanked the hoaxer for the call, they exchanged Christmas greetings, and it was done. Ralph called all his agency heads and passed on the good news. Soon even the smallest sub-offices over hundreds of miles in six different states had got the word. They could all go home early – official! As for Bruce, he still takes pride in: 'singlehandedly affording hundreds of federal employees a crack at some last-minute Christmas shopping.'[17]

He, at least, was one disgruntled employee who thought about all the other disgruntled employees – and did something about it. What you might call a bit of Christmas spirit . . .

1. *Sabotage in the American Workplace: Anecdotes of Dissatisfaction, Mischief and Revenge*, ed. Martin Sprouse, Pressure Drop Press, San Francisco 1992, p.11.All other references save 4 from same text, as follows: (2) p.10, (3) pp.113–14, (5) pp.21–2, (6) p.24, (7) pp.38–9, (8) p.51, (9) pp.55–6, (10) p.59, (11) p.62, (12), pp.136–7, (13) pp.85–6, (14) p.103, (15) p.118, (16) p.155, (17) p.154–5.
4. Vale and Juno (eds), *op. cit.*, p.60.

DOMELA, Harry (1904–?) (*IMPOSTORS*)
In the confusion of Germany's Weimar Republic during the 1920s this Latvian adventurer not only passed himself off as the grandson of ex-Kaiser Wilhelm, but delighted everyone by doing so. With his father already dead when Germany invaded Latvia in 1915 he lost contact with

his mother, to survive in a world gone mad. When the Germans withdrew in 1918 and the Red Army tried to take over he joined the Freikorps, raised by Graf von Brandis to restore the historic kingdom of Prussia. With German troops busy crushing workers' uprisings, he followed the Freikorps to Berlin. Their coup failing, he found himself broke, homeless, and without papers with prices and unemployment rising. Surviving on the streets by begging and sleeping rough, in Munich he met a horoscope-seller styling himself Baron Otto von Luderitz. Nobody, he noted, questioned the self-styled baron's credentials. Why should they? Thousands of ruined noblemen roamed the war-shattered land. Anyone could be a nobleman now, and when Luderitz told the blue-eyed, slightly-built Harry that: 'You look like a count, ergo you are one,' Harry listened.

Working for Luderitz and other swindlers by collecting money and drawing café portraits, he called himself Count Pahlen, but landed in jail. Released, he worked as a door-to-door cigar salesman, Count von der Recke. Again jailed for false pretences and again released, he made for Heidelberg. Times were hard, but the naive children of rich families still went there for their university education. Now presenting himself as Prince Lieven, after several weeks of being wined and dined by the snobbish undergraduates who thought he *must* be someone, he got out while the going was good. So he came to Erfurt, and signed in at one of the best hotels as Baron von Korff.

By now he was good at it. Offered a fourth floor room, he insisted angrily on a first floor suite with a private bath, then chanced a phone call to Prince Louis Ferdinand, one of the ex-Kaiser's sons, at the Cecilienhof palace near Potsdam. Luckily the prince was out, but the hotel staff noted the call. Eyeing a picture of the royal family in his office, the manager realised that 'Baron von Korff' was really the Kaiser's grandson, Prince Wilhelm von Hohenzollern. From now on Harry's every protest that he was only Baron von Korff stimulated the rumour that he was really Prince Wilhelm. Meeting his every wish, the hotel refused to let him pay the bill. Alarmed, Harry fled to Berlin and booked into the Habsburgerhof as 'the Baron', only to find that rumour trailed him. Soon everyone was calling him 'Your Highness'. Back to Erfurt he went, to dampen the speculation, but instead found himself signing the name 'Wilhelm, Prince of Prussia' in the town's Golden Book.

With his name now in the papers and the real Prince Wilhelm living just a hundred miles away, he was trapped in his role – but nobody questioned him. Politicians, bankers and industrialists fought to pay his bills and arrange banquets. Officers of the Reichswehr fawned on him, despite a ruling that the Hohenzollerns could keep their titles only if they avoided all connections with the military. He was everyone's favourite fantasy, but how long could he keep it up? The strain was telling. Then in Gotha one day he received a telegram. RESERVE QUIET ROOM FOR AFTERNOON. VON BERG. And Von Berg, he realised to his horror, was the chief administrator of the Hohenzollern estates!

Only later learning that Herr Von Berg was a Frankfurt businessman, he fled to the railway station, but there saw a man lurking by a shop. A detective! Taking a taxi back to Erfurt, at the Reichswehr barracks he persuaded the commandant to suppress embarrassing newspaper reports of his friendly relations with the army, a request he repeated to the commandant at Weimar. Yet by now he was exhausted. Deciding one night to become plain Harry Domela again, he bought a ticket to Berlin, meaning to vanish back on to the streets. But his imposture was already known. The police had learned that the real Prince Wilhelm was nowhere near the area. Leaving the train in Berlin, he saw headlines – FALSE HOHENZOLLERN PRINCE FOOLS DIE-HARD MONARCHISTS – and photographs, recognisably of himself, sur-rounded by aristocratic admirers.

Fleeing towards France, in the Rhineland he signed up with the French Foreign Legion, and was about to leave Germany with the other recruits when arrested by plain-clothes detectives. After seven months in jail, in July 1927 he was tried amid sensational publicity. Liberals used him to score points off Nationalists and Monarchists: witnesses from every town he'd visited said the presence of 'His Majesty' had stimulated optimism, a sense of prosperity, and greater trade. His jail sentence of seven months was immediately suspended, and on 23 July 1927 Harry Domela walked free. Offered 25,000 marks to write his memoirs, the success of the book let him buy a cinema, which in 1930 opened with a comedy, *The False Prince*. Later he starred in a play about himself and, though his subsequent history remains obscure – he may have emigrated to South America – before vanishing he introduced himself to the Hohenzollerns, via ex-Crown Princess Cecilie.

While awaiting trial in spring 1927 he had sent her a dozen yellow roses with the note: 'I was honoured to be taken for your Highness's son', and on his release later that year presented himself uninvited at the Cecilienhof. His exploits had brought undeserved ridicule on them, but the members of the ex-royal family invited him in to tea. Finding him 'a charming young man, with excellent manners', and while 'convulsed with laughter' at his exploits, his 'mother' confessed that one thing puzzled her.

'How on earth,' she asked, 'could people mistake him for our Wilhelm?'[1]

1.   Larsen, *op. cit.*, pp.107–19.

DONATION OF CONSTANTINE (*HISTORICAL HOAXES*)
Used for at least six centuries by the Popes of the Roman Church to support their claim to be the true rulers of Christendom, the authenticity

of the document known as the Donation of Constantine (*Constitutum Constantini*) was long unquestioned. Claiming to record the gift of half his empire to the Church in AD 315 by the Emperor Constantine, in gratitude for his conversion to Christ and Pope Sylvester's miraculous cure of his leprosy, it gave Rome spiritual authority over all other churches, and temporal authority over Rome, Italy, and the Western world. Those denying it would: 'be burned in the lower hell and shall perish with the devil and all the impious'.

First quoted by Leo X to support papal claims during a dispute that led the Eastern Orthodox Church and the Church of Rome to separate in 1054, the Donation was unknown before the ninth century, first appearing in a collection known, significantly enough, as the *False Decretals*. This did not stop nine Popes after Leo using it to assert Rome's authority, even after the ecclesiastical scholar Nicholas of Cusa (1401–64) proved it a fake, pointing out that Constantine's contemporary biographer, Bishop Eusebius of Caesaria, never even mentions this extravagant gift. Another tradition says it was first debunked by the scholar Lorenzo Valla, in about 1440. Even so, the argument raged until the end of the eighteenth century. It is now agreed to have been forged either in Rome or in the Frankish empire in about AD 760, and not even cleverly, in that it gives Rome authority over Constantinople before that city was even founded. The French philosopher Voltaire called it: 'the boldest and most magnificent forgery which deceived the world for centuries'. But whether the Popes who used it to their own ends were also deceived remains an open question.

DREYFUS, Alfred (1859–1935) (*See also* ANTI-SEMITIC HOAXES)

Victim of a particularly squalid hoax, Captain Alfred Dreyfus of the French War Office was hard-working and efficient, but also both rich and a Jew. His ordeal began in 1894, when the French General Staff intercepted a letter offering to sell military secrets to Colonel Max von Schwarzkoppen, German military attaché in Paris. Evidence suggested the traitor must be a junior gunnery officer who had been in several camps before joining the General Staff. Dreyfus fitted these requirements. His handwriting seemed to resemble that in the letter. In addition, he was a Jew in a time of mounting anti-Semitism, and many of his fellow officers resented his efficiency. He was arrested and court-martialled, but the evidence was poor. His record was exemplary, graphologists doubted the handwriting was his, and a police report that he was a gambler in fact referred to another Dreyfus. With his acquittal inevitable, something had to be done. Commander Hubert Joseph Henry, the intelligence officer in charge of the initial inquiry, now produced damning evidence – an 'intercepted' letter from the Italian military attaché, Panizzardi, to von Schwarzkoppen, referring to the traitor in the French War Office as 'that dirty dog, "D" '. Henry had forged it himself, but it was enough. Dreyfus was imprisoned for life on Devil's Island.

Two years later, with the Germans still obtaining French secrets, his file was reopened, a Colonel Picquart now investigating. When Picquart began to probe too deep, worried senior officers had him posted to Tunisia even as Henry – ignorant that Picquart had already had the document photographed – tried to cover his guilt by tampering with the Panizzardi letter. Arrested in 1898, Henry killed himself in prison a few days later, after first telling his wife he had copied the letter from an authentic original. As for Dreyfus, he languished on Devil's Island until 1906 when the real spy, a Franco-Hungarian officer named Esterhazy, fled to London. The conviction was annulled and Dreyfus was awarded the Legion of Honour. It must have been a great consolation to him.

DUPRE, George (1906–) (*LITERARY HOAXES*)
Soon after the Second World War ended the magazine *Reader's Digest*, as popular then as now, learned of the dramatic story of a young Canadian, George DuPre. Serving in the English-Canadian secret services during the war, he had parachuted into German-occupied Normandy and posed as a garage mechanic while working for the Resistance by smuggling allied airmen out of France. Captured by the Gestapo, he had been tortured for weeks but hadn't talked. Eventually he had escaped. Now back in Canada, he was a national hero, showered with honours and invited to speak to church groups and student organisations.

The *Reader's Digest* hired journalist and ex-war correspondent Quentin Reynolds to interview DuPre and write a piece for the magazine. DuPre showed him scars on his hand and throat. Nazi torture, he said. Reynolds believed him, wrote the piece, then approached Bennett Cerf, head of the publishers Random House, and suggested a book. Cerf agreed. In 1953 *The Man Who Wouldn't Talk* became what Cerf later called: 'a substantial success'. But then 'the man who wouldn't talk' did talk. One night Cerf got a call from the editor of the *Calgary Herald*. 'Your Mr DuPre has just collapsed and confessed that his entire story is a hoax,' said the newsman who (as told by Cerf in his 1977 autobiography, *At Random*), went on to say that DuPre was just a young country boy. He'd spent the entire war in Canada or England but had never been near France, inventing the entire saga using his imagination, aided by newspapers and spy magazines. Now his guilt was plaguing him. 'He is a nice little man and he didn't realise that his deception was going to be blown up to these dimensions,' said the editor, adding that the *Calgary Herald* would print the whole story next day. So Cerf promptly rang DeWitt Wallace, publisher of *Reader's Digest*, and suggested that the only answer was to laugh it off.

'I'm going to say, "Imagine this little man fooling all of us. Isn't it hilarious?" ' He said he would announce, in jest, that Random House would recategorise the book as fiction and change its name to *The Man Who Talked Too Much*. The plan succeeded. The press played it as a joke. Nobody was hurt, everyone enjoyed the tale, and the book sold five times better after the hoax was exposed.[1]

But did Reynolds himself believe in the tale? As an ex-war correspondent, surely he would have seen through a 'country boy'. DuPre, now admitting that his scars came from childhood accidents, had even claimed to have been given an enema of sulphuric acid. And was he just a 'country boy'? Another account calls him 'Pierre Dupont' (stating that this is a pseudonym), a French-Canadian lay preacher who began spicing up his sermons with his alleged real-life battles against adversity. These so impressed his congregations that soon, by repetition, his inventions became real to him and others.[2]

DuPre? Dupont? Even true tales about false tales vary so wildly that the original is easily lost under a weight of secondary accounts, like this. Remember what the Old Man of the Mountains (allegedly) said?

'Nothing is true. All is permitted.'

1. Goldberg, *op. cit.*, pp.214–16.
2. *The Pleasures of Deception*, Norman O. Moss, Chatto & Windus, London 1977, pp.115–16.

E

'There's one way to find out if a man is
honest – ask him. If he says yes, you know
he is a crook.'

(Groucho Marx)

EDWARD VII CORONATION HOAX (*PRANKS*)
When in 1901 King Edward VII succeeded at last to the English throne
several hundred leading citizens of Chicago received invitations to the
coronation, sent purportedly by the Earl Marshal of England, in fact by
liquor manufacturers Charles Dennehy and Co. Advising those invited
to pay 'particular attention to their attire', the 'Earl Marshal' also
required that: 'Titled nobility from America, such as merchant princes,
coal barons, trust magnates, lords of finance with their ladies, must
appear in costumes typifying the origins of their titles, and they may
carry tape measures, coal scuttles, oil cans, stock tickers, and may wear
stick pins, clothes pins, scarf pins, coupling pins, hair pins, rolling pins,
cuff buttons, shoe strings, picture hats, turbans, handcuffs, overcoats,
imitation lace scarfs, celluloid collars, hose or half hose as the case may
be, rhinestones, collar buttons of silver gilt, and golf capes edged with
two and one half rows of rabbit skin . . .'[1]
   Having waded through this, those spoofed learned they could drink
their toast to the new king in any way they liked so long as the base of the
drink was 'old underhoof rye, manufactured by Charles Dennehy and
Company of Chicago, USA'.

1. Quoted in Yapp, *op. cit.*, p.5.

EIFFEL TOWER, Sale of (*See* LUSTIG, 'Count' Victor)

ELLIS, Revd Wilfred (19th century) (*IMPOSTORS*)
Rector of Wetheringsett Manor in Suffolk from 1858 to 1883, Wilfred

Ellis epitomises the problem: when is an impostor no longer an impostor? A pork butcher by trade who had never taken holy orders, for twenty-five years he cared for his parishioners as well as or better than many another 'genuine' minister. Taking Sunday services and officiating at marriages, baptisms and funerals, when at last his fakery was revealed he showed no sense of shame. That in effect he had 'become' what he'd pretended to be was tacitly admitted when Parliament passed a bill legitimising the marriages he had blessed.

'THE EMPEROR'S NEW CLOTHES'

This famous fable by Danish folklorist Hans Christian Andersen (1805–75), in which nobody wants to be the first to acknowledge what should be obvious to all, that their emperor is naked, epitomises how many successful hoaxes rely not only on the skill of the hoaxer but on the self-deluding and herd-like tendencies of victims. As the condition called **'False Memory Syndrome'** also suggests, folk are capable of believing whatever they want to believe, whatever they think is expected of them, or whatever is suggested to them by authority figures. In the Andersen tale, the bubble of mass self-delusion is burst only when a naive child sees the obvious and declares it aloud, so that suddenly everyone sees what really they saw all along – that *'the emperor has no clothes!'*

END-OF-THE-WORLD SCAMS (*FAKE MESSIAHS*)

Through the ages charlatans have gained power by setting up pseudo-religious cults preaching the world's imminent end while offering salvation to obedient followers. With the apocalyptic round-numbered millennial year of AD 2000 now close at hand, such cults proliferate. Not all are deliberately exploitative, though self-deluding belief-systems seem central to most. Many fundamentalist Christians, especially in America, await the 'Rapture' when amid the Last Days they alone, they believe, will be raised up 'in the middle of the air' to be saved by Jesus. Sects like the Seventh Day Adventists or Jehovah's Witnesses command huge support even when, as with the Witnesses in 1975, the date foretold for the end comes and goes without event. The date is simply revised forward, or it is explained that 'the end' is metaphorical, as seen in the breakdown of social morality. The cult-belief offers such comfort that the believer will rationalise virtually any nonsense as true.

Many cults remain free of scandal. Yet recent tragic cases, like David **Berg**'s exploitation of the 'Children of God'; the suicide of 900 followers of Jim Jones in Guyana in 1978; the death by fire of over ninety Branch Davidians led by David Koresh at Waco, Texas in 1993; and the uproar over the **White Brotherhood of Kiev** (also 1993), plus mass suicides (or murders) in Canada and Switzerland during 1994, suggest the potentially terrible power of self-styled messiahs preaching The End.

But there is nothing new under the sun. Early **Christianity**, before

St Paul got hold of it, was a messianic Judaic cult expecting the End Times. For centuries thereafter (especially when times were hard) the expectation persisted. Fear of extinction was so great in Europe in AD 999 that rich men gave away their wealth in panic – but were quick to reclaim it when New Year AD 1000 dawned without calamity. Medieval Europe, especially during the Black Death of 1348–50 (in some areas half the population perished), was full of Joachites, Beghards, Beguins, Brethren of the Free Spirit, flagellants and others all certain that the end was nigh. Later arose radical Protestant cults like Anabaptists and Ranters who asserted that the imminent end allowed them (or their leaders) to do as they pleased.[1]

The eighteenth century (the 'Age of Reason') saw many new self-appointed messiahs exploiting their followers sexually, among the first of them Prussian gamekeeper Hans Rosenfeld. Calling Christianity a deception and its priests impostors, he declared he would depose Emperor Frederick the Great and rule the world with a Council of twenty-four Elders. Seven Messianic seals would then be opened by seven 'Angels of the Seals'. To prepare for this he asked his followers to provide seven beautiful girls (the 'angels') as his mistresses. He went too far only on demanding that one devoted follower offer up *three* of his daughters. The man did so but, increasingly impatient with the non-arrival of the promised Day of Judgement, provoked the Emperor to act against Rosenfeld, so hoping to make Rosenfeld use his supernatural powers against Frederick and begin the End Times. Arrested, Rosenfeld proved to own no such powers, and in 1782 was imprisoned for life.

Born in Devon in 1750, Joanna Southcott certainly believed herself destined to lead a genuine prophetic movement, but hypocritically professed horror at the promiscuity of others while less than chaste herself. Claiming in 1792 to hear voices speaking: 'words so dreadful that they made me tremble', she began prophesying. The success of some of her predictions, such as that the Bishop of Exeter, then in good health, would die before Christmas, won her a huge number of followers (14,000 on one mission alone). They believed her claim to be: 'the true and faithful Bride' of Christ who, by virgin birth, would bear a son, the Shiloh: an event which would presage the second coming of Christ. Those subscribing financially to the cause received 'seals' protecting them as 'heirs of God and joint-heirs of Jesus Christ'. In 1808, after vast success, the morals of her followers were denounced. One of her money collectors was Mary Bateman, seemingly a sober Quaker, actually a thief and abortionist. Arrested for murdering one Rebecca Perigo, Bateman was sentenced to death. Hanged despite her insistence on the gallows that an angel would rescue her, her body was viewed by over two thousand people who each paid threepence for the privilege.

Aged sixty-four Joanna announced herself pregnant and about to give miraculous birth to Shiloh. Doctors declared the pregnancy genuine.

Though insisting that the birth was virgin, as the 'pregnancy' advanced she decreed that Shiloh must have a foster-father. Choosing as husband John Smith, steward to the Earl of Darnley, she married him in her bedroom. All trace of pregnancy promptly vanished. She fell into a coma and died, despite which many of her followers long remained sure that she would be resurrected.

Declaring 1836 as the opening year of Christ's personal reign, the German founder of the Pietists, Archdeacon Ebel, created a church of woman. His chief disciple, the lovely Prussian countess Ida von der Gröben, agreed with two other women to watch over Ebel at all times and guard him from temptation. Permitting women to hear male confessions, grant absolution, and inflict penances; also to condemn masculine drinking, smoking, and snuff-taking, he formed a household with his three disciples. Describing Countess Ida as his: 'first wife, representing the spirit of Light'; Emilie von Scrotter as his: 'second wife, representing the spirit of Darkness'; and the third as his legal wife, 'representing the spirit of Union', his scam reminds one of David **Berg** a century and a half later.

In America, similar sexual conmen emerged. The Revd Jarvis Rider explained his succession of spirit-brides as: 'a necessary consequence of the Second Coming'. Sydney Rigdon, revivalist pastor of a church in Ohio, asserted that holy men had the right: 'to woo and win for themselves brides of the spirit as well as of the flesh'. John Humphrey Noyes, ex-Congregational minister and the founder of 'Pauline Communism', exercised his right to find 'his Paradise and his Eve' by flattering factory girls in a beerhouse by Lake Oneida into accepting the utopian delights he promised.

Also partial to women in his parish was the Revd Henry James Prince of Suffolk who, forced by outraged public opinion to quit two livings, in 1847 formed the 'Abode of Love' at Spaxton in Somerset. Proclaiming the imminent end of the world, he offered those supporting him financially an earthly paradise. His chief success was to persuade three out of five unmarried daughters whose retired merchant father had left them £6,000 each to join him. Enjoying a twenty-bedroom manor and the fruits of a profitable farm, Prince named his sect the Agapemonites, after a third-century sect which had scandalised even Romans with their 'love-feasts'. Known to his followers as the 'Beloved One', he took orphan Zoe Paterson as his 'Bride of the Lamb'; a purely mystic union from which, however, a child was soon born. The Agapemonites split, and their numbers dwindled, but after Prince died in 1899 he was succeeded by another fast talker, the Revd John Hugh Smyth-Pigott.

Deciding the Abode of Love needed a city address, at the Ark of the Covenant Church in Clapton in 1902 he proclaimed himself Messiah. Threatened by a hostile crowd, he retreated back to Spaxton. Here he lived lavishly, banning his wife Catherine from his private rooms where, as the new 'Beloved One', he entertained a succession of 'Brides of the Lamb' – mostly beautiful, young, well educated and well off.

Arraigned for immorality by the Church of England and in his absence unfrocked, Smyth-Pigott ignored public and ecclesiastical opinion. He went on enjoying a large number of 'Soul-Brides' not only at Spaxton but at other Abodes of Love in France and Norway until his death in 1927.[2]

Many recent cult leaders have followed the same exploitative pattern. David Berg, L. Ron **Hubbard** (founder of Scientology), **Rajneesh** and the leaders of the International Society for Krishna Consciousness have all taken advantage of their followers in one way or another. More tragically, in the late 1970s ex-San Francisco Housing Supervisor Jim Jones led his followers (mostly poor and black) to Guyana to escape investigation in the USA. When in November 1978 it became apparent that the authorities were closing in, he ordered his flock to drink kool-aid laced with cyanide. Those refusing were forced to drink. Only a few escaped with their lives. It is possible, though, that the long-accepted tale of mass suicide is, itself, a hoax. Other reports tell of mass murder, not suicide.

Quite as terrible was the fate of the Branch Davidians, breakaway Seventh Day Adventists led by guitar-playing bible-reading messiah David Koresh. Recruiting his followers (again, many black and poor) from England and Australia as well as the USA, he established a centre in a ramshackle compound at Waco, Texas. Preaching the imminent end of the world and sexually exploiting women in the sect, his and their fate was sealed in February 1993. Suspecting that the sect owned unlicensed guns, the ATF (the regulatory agency for alcohol, tobacco and firearms) raided the compound. Heavy fire led to the deaths of several agents and cultists, and to a fifty-one-day siege which ended only when the authorities attacked with tanks. The compound went up in flames. Over ninety Davidians died, only eleven survived. The official line was that the Davidians (awaiting the end of the world, remember?) had fired the compound themselves, yet rumours of official deception persist. Only the day before all fire trucks and ambulances standing by at the scene of the siege had mysteriously been sent back to their depots, while videos showed what looked like tank-fire shooting into the buildings.[3] Whatever the truth of the matter, for the Branch Davidians, that morning was indeed the end of the world.

1. *The Pursuit of the Millennium*, Norman Cohn, Paladin, London 1970.
2. McCormick, *op. cit.*, pp.90–111.
3. *San Francisco Weekly*, April 27, 1994, p.9.

EXPLORATION HOAXES (*See* **CONCORDANCE**)

F

'Each believes easily what he fears and what he desires.'

(Jean de la Fontaine)

FAKE MESSIAHS (*See* **CONCORDANCE**)

FAKE PROFESSORS (*See* **IMPOSTORS**)

'FALSE MEMORY SYNDROME' (*See also* **FREUD, PAST-LIFE MEMORIES, UFO ABDUCTIONS**)

The term 'False Memory Syndrome' (FMS) has come into use following many cases in which individuals accused of child abuse or ritual satanic abuse appear to be victims of fantasies judged objectively real, either by themselves or others. Such false memories are typically coaxed out of children or those accused of abusing children by zealous therapists or prosecutors claiming that traumatic memories, repressed for years in the unconscious, may later be recovered via hypnosis or intensive questioning. Yet many psychological experiments show how easily false memories can be implanted, often simply by insisting that some crucial event occurred and that the subject has forgotten it. In such cases the hoax is unconsciously imposed or self-imposed. Examples:

In the late 1980s in East Olympia, Washington, twenty-two-year-old Ericka Ingram broke down during an all-female prayer meeting at her fundamentalist church when another woman said she sensed, via the 'Holy Spirit', that one or more of them had been abused by a parent. After she'd accepted that her father, local deputy sheriff Paul Ingram, had abused her as a child, her eighteen-year-old sister Julie joined her in telling bizarre tales of satanic rituals involving their family and their father's friends. With prosecutors and therapists now at her, their mother Sandy initially resisted the tales, but under pressure produced her own catalogue of rapes and sodomies. Their brother Chad also denied any abuse, but when encouraged recalled a childhood dream in which a fat black-robed witch had sat on top of him so he couldn't move. Prodded further, he agreed that this and other fantastic dreams represented memory of abuse, but by then it didn't matter: his father had already confessed to every charge against him. A sceptical psychologist invented false charges to test Paul's memory: Ingram both agreed to and elaborated on these charges. The case collapsed, but not before Ingram had pleaded guilty to six counts of third-degree rape. Sentenced to twenty years in prison, he is eligible for parole in the year 2002.[1]

In 1993 Robert Kelly of Edenton, North Carolina, was found guilty of some of the 183 charges of satanic paedophilia he was accused of committing at his Little Rascals day-care centre. He received twelve consecutive life sentences despite the fact that three jurors refused to believe tales of children being microwaved or thrown into tanks full of ravenous sharks. The children's allegations, coaxed out over several months by parents and therapists, also led to another worker receiving a life sentence. Five others (including Kelly's wife Betsy) still awaited trial. Nobody visiting the centre had ever noticed anything unusual. Noting that most of the accusations came from stay-at-home mothers, Betsy Kelly felt that the accusations may have originated in their hatred of working women.

In April 1993 in New Zealand thirty-five-year-old Peter Ellis was accused of abusing over fifty toddlers between 1986 and 1991 at the Christchurch Civic Childcare Centre. His ordeal began in November 1991 when a child told his father he didn't like his teacher's 'black penis'. Ellis is Caucasian. Questioned, the child said this was 'just a story', but his parents turned to a 'community consultant', later revealed as co-founder of a private abuse therapy organisation called START. A month later Ellis (obviously unpopular with and even feared as a bully by some of the children he'd supervised) was suspended. Formally interviewed three times, the child made no direct allegations of abuse but, with concern spreading, in March 1992 Ellis was arrested. Soon forty-five indecency charges stood against him, many levelled over five long interviews by one six-year-old already in therapy before the case began. He told of being made to eat excrement; of being thrust by Ellis through a trapdoor into a maze where he met Spikehead and Boulderhead, two of Ellis's friends; and of children made to sit naked in a circle drawn on the floor of Ellis's house. Outside the circle stood slit-eyed guitar-playing adults in white cowboy suits who carried magic knives and who later put the children into ovens, pretending they'd be eaten. Asked why he hadn't mentioned these details earlier, the boy said: 'Oh, I just remembered today.' At the trial the judge, finding 'obviously correct' the Crown's assertion that no toddler could invent such tales, found Ellis guilty on sixteen 'proven' charges of sexual violation and indecent assault, and gave him ten years.

'I don't blame the children at all,' said Debbie Gillespie, one of four women also charged but acquitted. 'They don't think they are actually lying. They are emotionally manipulating their parents. Every time they disclosed they would get these cuddles . . .'[2]

In many such cases, as with reports of **'past-life memories'** or accounts by folk claiming abduction by alien beings into **UFOs**, the evidence is solely circumstantial, based either on unreliable witnesses or on procedures like hypnotic regression, too often conducted by therapists who ask leading questions to get answers that fit their theories. Some commentators, recalling the witch hunts of the sixteenth and seventeenth centuries, suspect a resurgence of mass hysteria like that leading to the Salem trials of 1692 or the remarkable self-induced confessions of the 'witch' Isobel Gowdie of Auldearn in Scotland in 1662. Gowdie, claiming to have had intercourse with the Devil, was obsessed with the black penis of the Evil One, 'as cold within me as spring-well water'. Hmm.

Here is an area of psychology so ambiguous that unconscious hoaxing or deception is omnipresent. Sigmund **Freud** himself, the father of modern psychoanalysis, has lately met renewed attack on the grounds that he projected his theories on to his female patients, encouraged them to tell him what he wanted to hear, then accepted whatever they said as objective proof of his theories. If so then, self-hoaxed, he hoaxed the willingly hoaxed.

Caveat emptor!

1. 'Memories of Hell', Jim Schnabel, *Fortean Times* No. 71, London 1993.
2. 'Bedevilled', Mike Dash, *Fortean Times* No. 72, London 1993.

FEY, Dietrich (20th century) (*ART FORGERIES*)

It can be hard to persuade hoax victims that they've been conned. On 2 September 1951 art restorer Dietrich Fey proudly showed West German Chancellor Konrad Adenauer the newly restored frescoes of the Marien-kirche in Lübeck. The originals had come to light amid the Second World War when incendiary bombs gutted the church, burned white-wash from the walls, and revealed scraps of thirteenth-century paintings. Despite a warning from a provincial curate that Fey could not be trusted, he and his team had been given the restoration contract. Now, it seemed, he had succeeded brilliantly in restoring the frescoes, claiming to have: 'added nothing but merely [to have] preserved what had survived'.[1]

With Christians and art lovers celebrating the event, and a special 5-pfennig stamp issued to commemorate it, the public flocked to see the 'restored' paintings of biblical scenes, mythical beasts, and images of the saints. Yet when Fey was awarded the federal Cross of Merit his colleague Lothar Malskat, enraged at his own lack of recognition, came forward in May 1952 to declare that the frescoes were entirely his own invention.

Nobody believed him. Critics said that neither he nor Fey had the ability to fake such beauty. The West German Association for the Preservation of Ancient Monuments was unwilling to accept that it had wasted $30,000 on a forgery. Even more enraged by this disbelief, Malskat (who before the war had faked Chagalls and other modern masters, with Fey selling them) now went to the insane length of instructing his lawyer to file charges against Fey and himself. His pride was upset, and at the trial he produced a film proving that the walls had been almost entirely bare when the work had begun. He showed that among the much-admired choir figures were portraits of Marlene Dietrich, Rasputin, Genghis Khan, and his own sister; and that in Schleswig Cathedral, parts of which he and Fey had restored before the war, he had painted a turkey – a bird unknown in Europe until after the discovery of America. When still the diehards insisted that the nave paintings must be genuine, Malskat bitterly explained that the old work had crumbled at the touch of a brush, leaving nothing to restore. Though widely viewed with sympathy, this angry artist got eighteen months in jail. Fey got twenty. What Fey had to say to Malskat about this betrayal is not recorded. After his release, Malskat made an honest living, painting in the style of the past wherever so required. He remained in great demand.

1. Hans Jürgen Hauser, quoted in Yapp, *op. cit.*, p.200.

FLYNN, Errol (*See* **HOLLYWOOD HOAXES**)

FOSSIL FORGERIES (*SCIENTIFIC SCAMS*)
The pressure of the competition to be first or on top is as powerful in science as in athletics, politics, exploration, or any other area of human activity. Such pressure often leads to hoaxes, and anthropological hoaxes are as common as in any other area of science. Typically, given the urgency of the academic need to learn more of human origins or to find out the stages by which ape became man, such hoaxes focus on the burial and subsequent 'discovery' of fake fossils or bones that seemingly prove claims to have found the 'Missing Link', or to have established some new chronology of human origination.

Perhaps the first hoaxers to use fraudulent fossils were Ignatz Roderick (Professor of Algebra and Geometry) and Georg von Elkhart (Head Librarian) of the University of Würzburg. In 1725, for reasons unknown, they decided to hoax Dr Johann Beringer (1667–1738), Dean of Faculty of Medicine and a fanatical fossil hunter. In a quarry where Beringer often sought remains of the past, they planted 'fossilised' birds, beetles and lizards then, as Beringer grew enthusiastic about his 'finds', they 'fossilised' stars, comets, and moons; also tablets of stone with the name 'God' inscribed in Latin, Arabic and Hebrew. It has to be remembered that the origin and nature of fossils were not then understood.

In 1952 Californian mystic George Adamski claimed the first human contact with extra-terrestrials. Later his new friends took him on a trip to the dark side of the moon – or maybe not. (*Fortean Picture Library*)

Said to have been a slave on the isle of Samos, the ancient Greek author of *Aesop's Fables* was himself fabulous, the *Fables* being a collection of tales by many different authors. (*Peter Newark's Historical Pictures*)

Enduring for centuries, irrational hatred of Jews reached its most vicious pitch in Nazi Germany. This 1933 poster suggests that 'A vote for the Nazis is a vote against the Jews'. (*Mary Evans Picture Library*)

Here seen addressing a First World War army recruitment rally (he charged £50 per rally), Londoner Horatio Bottomley's business frauds made him a wealthy MP. The epitome of jingoistic patriotism, after the war further frauds landed him in jail. There's some justice after all. (*Topham*)

James Barry's secret was revealed only on 'his' deathbed in 1865. Rising to the rank of Inspector General of Hospitals in Canada, this British Army doctor successfully masqueraded as a man all her life. (*Topham*)

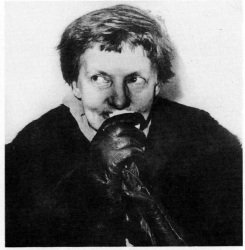

For half a century Anna Anderson claimed to be Anastasia, daughter of Russian Czar Nicholas II. Though probably murdered by Bolsheviks in July 1918 with the rest of her family, rumour said Anastasia had escaped. Surviving Romanovs denied Anderson's claim. (*Topham*)

How to raise money after Glastonbury Abbey almost burned down in 1184? Easy! Discover the grave of King Arthur and Queen Guinevere in the grounds. Pilgrim-tourists flocked in, and the abbey became medieval England's wealthiest. (*Janet & Colin Bord/Fortean Picture Library*)

Better known as 'Jack Bilbo', Hugo Baruch got rich by writing of his mobster life in *Carrying a Gun for Al Capone* (1930). In fact he'd never been near Chicago. When in 1934 he admitted the hoax, nobody wanted to know. Later he became an artist and owned a London art gallery. (*Topham*)

The author of the Sherlock Holmes stories may have been fooled by the Cottingley Fairies (*below*) but some suspect him of being behind the famous Piltdown Man 'missing link' hoax in 1912. (*Mansell Collection*)

There really *were* fairies at the bottom of their Yorkshire garden, claimed young Elsie Wright and Frances Griffiths in 1917 – and they had photos to prove it! Sir Arthur Conan Doyle made himself a laughing stock by believing them. (*Mary Evans Picture Library*)

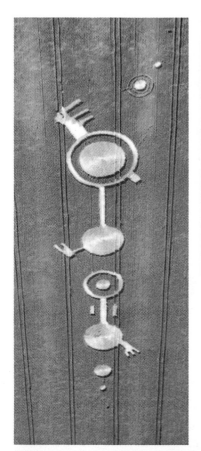

Above: Many people say Israeli psychic Uri Geller's spoon-bending stunts must be fake – but Geller has become rich dowsing minerals for multinational corporations like Rio Tinto Zinc. Would *businessmen* shell out millions if they didn't expect even more in return? (*Topham*)

Left: Was this elaborate 1990 crop circle at Alton Barnes in Wiltshire created by inventive human pranksters, or are *alien* hoaxers responsible? (*Frederick C. Taylor/Fortean Picture Library*)

Skilled at being anyone but himself, Ferdinand Waldo Demara's astonishing escapades led in 1961 to a Hollywood biopic, *The Great Impostor*, in which Tony Curtis impersonated him. Perhaps he should have been a movie star himself. (*Kobal Collection*)

Hans Christian Andersen's famous fable, 'The Emperor's New Clothes', suggests how successful hoaxers rely not only on skill but on the self-deluding and herd-like tendencies of their victims. (*Mansell Collection*)

In 1983 literary hoaxer Konrad Kujau admitted defrauding the German magazine *Stern* by selling them 'Hitler's diaries'. He'd written every word himself. *Stern* lost over nineteen million marks. (*Camera Press*)

In 1923 the world's greatest ever escapologist, Harry Houdini, was caught rigging an experiment so that he could prove the psychic Mrs Mina Crandon a faker. (*Topham*)

Attributing his discoveries to the work of God, Beringer devised the *lusus naturae* theory, by which some stones mysteriously imitate the forms of others. In the *Lithographiae Wirceburgensis* he wrote learnedly on his finds. Feeling their hoax had gone far enough, Roderick and Elkhart confessed. Refusing to believe them, Beringer accused them of scientific jealousy. They had to plant fossils with his name on them before he believed them. He spent the rest of his life trying to buy up and destroy copies of his book but succeeded only in making it a collector's item, republished in 1767 to an even greater sale. The hoaxers' motives are unknown: maybe it was a grudge that got out of hand.[1]

A century later a spate of new discoveries upped the stakes in terms of the kudos to be won via new knowledge of old fossils uncovered. In 1856 the leg bone and skull of what became known as Neanderthal Man emerged from a cave near Düsseldorf in Germany. In 1868 (after Lartet's 1864 discovery of a carved mammoth tusk began the process) the skulls and skeleton of Cro-Magnon Man were found in the Dordogne in France. In 1869 a hunting dog fell into a crack in the ground at the foot of the Cantabrian Hills of northern Spain. Finding the dog in a cave, the hunters told their master, Don Marcelino de Sautuola. He explored the cave, found nothing of interest, and forgot it – until at the Paris Exhibition in 1878 he was fascinated by a collection of Ice Age tools and engravings dating back 12,000 years. He began excavating the cave and after a year found a hand axe and some stone arrowheads. One day his five-year-old daughter Maria found a recess he'd ignored. On its walls were prehistoric paintings of bison in various postures – charging, living, dying. The cave (later known as Altamira) became famous. Even the King of Spain visited it. But academics like the prehistorian Cartilhac, unwilling to regard mere cavemen as artistically skilled, derided his find. Later, stunned by what he saw in newly opened caves in the Vézère Valley, Cartilhac went to Altamira to apologise to Marcelino, but too late. Marcelino was dead.

Less honest was Yorkshireman Edward Simpson (1815–?75), also known as 'Flint Jack', 'Shirtless' and 'Snake Billy'. Introduced to the study of fossils and prehistoric flint weapons and tools by local geologist Dr George Young, by 1840 he was collecting such items and selling them to dealers. Concluding it was easier to fake than find them, he soon found how easy it was to fool 'experts' with the fake arrowheads which got him the name 'Flint Jack'. Setting up a pottery near Bridlington he turned out numerous fake Roman and prehistoric urns, and even sold a piece of stone on which he'd scratched IMP CONSTANT EBVR ('Emperor Constantine, York'). Like George Hull, faker of the **Cardiff Giant**, he must have marvelled at his buyers' gullibility while selling fakes to the British Museum, working as a fossil collector for York Museum, and carving amber necklaces in the Lake District. Confronted in London in 1862 by a geologist, Professor Tennant, he admitted his forgeries but claimed he'd never tried to pass off his work as genuine. A heavy drinker, in March 1867 he was caught stealing, spent a year in Bedford prison, and a few years later died in obscure poverty, probably in a workhouse.[2]

In 1924, barely a decade after the discovery in England of Piltdown Man, a cow fell into a hole in the ground near Glozel in southern France. In it the landowners, farmers named Fradin, found pots, inscribed tablets and melted glass. It was: 'a kind of tomb', and locally explained as a cremation grave. An amateur archaeologist, Dr Morlet, who had lately found a skeleton in his own garden, offered to buy their finds and advised them to fence off the site, soon known as 'the Field of the Dead'. Excavation revealed inscribed tablets, images of reindeer carved in stone, marks like writing, the figure of a human being standing on an animal. But their association with Morlet led to accusations of fraud. Why sell to him, why fence off their land? For fifty years accusations persisted that the Glozel finds did not date from the prehistoric Magdalenian culture *c*.13,000 BC, but were frauds.

In 1974 Emil Fradin, seventeen at the time of the first discovery, announced that the antiquity of Glozel pottery was proved by a technique called thermoluminescence. This, involving measurement of trapped electrons from radioactivity, suggested to experts in Scotland and Denmark that the Glozel pottery was fired *c*.800 BC. Not Magdalenian, but not a fake either. Yet other tests gave different dates. Another new technique known as archaeomagnetism, which measures the relative geomagnetic field of fired objects cooled in different parts of the world, implied the Glozel pottery could not have been fired within the period 1500 BC to AD 1500. The case remains open.[3]

Piltdown Man remains the best-known palaeontological fake. In 1912 Charles Dawson, a Hastings solicitor and amateur fossil-hunter with a history of finding dubious artefacts in his quest for admission to the Royal Society (he was already known as the 'Wizard of Sussex'), wrote to his friend Arthur Smith Woodward, Keeper of Geology at the South Kensington Museum, that: 'I have come across a very old Pleistocene bed overlying the Hastings beds between Uckfield and Crowborough which I think is going to be interesting.' A few days later, with Sir Arthur **Conan Doyle** looking on, he wrote again to Woodward to report finding part of an early human skull. Woodward joined him at the Piltdown site. Their work excited local press interest: 'nobody could make out what they were up to'. Soon they had dug out not only fossilised animal bones and stone tools, but half a jaw both ape-like yet human. So emerged *Eanthropus dawsoni*, the Missing Link between ape and man. Announced on 18 December 1912 as the earliest-known human fossil, it was promptly accepted as such by the British scientific establishment. For years, with the local pub changing its name from The Lamb Inn to The Piltdown Man, nobody doubted it. Everyone wanted to believe.

Only in 1953 did it emerge that the jaw of 'Piltdown Man' had belonged to a young orang-utan, its teeth crudely filed down to look human. In *The Piltdown Forgery* (1955) J.S. Weiner blamed Dawson for the hoax, but admitted that somebody else might have tricked him. Later, articles in *Antiquity* pointed to J.T. Hewitt, who allegedly admitted his involvement to a friend. In 1986 *The Piltdown Inquest* blamed Lewis Abbott, a local fossil collector who'd claimed that pompous palaeontologists should be punished by clever fakes. Other suspects include the anatomist Sir Arthur Keith, the scientist Martin Hinton (whose career had been hindered by Woodward), and of course **Conan Doyle**. But whoever the hoaxer really was, the gullibility of experts must have frustrated him. Though fresh fakes were planted and found in the area in 1914 and 1915, nobody paid any attention, and those involved were long dead by the time the forgery was finally exposed.[4]

This profitable business endures. Following the discredited (but maybe genuine) discoveries in Java between 1891 and 1893 of the first-ever fossils of *Homo Erectus* by the Dutch anatomist Eugene Dubois, fake skulls began to emerge. Today the Javanese, using the skulls of hippopotami, are skilled at such fakery – a lucrative trade for folk who need to survive like anyone else. If the West wants fakes, they're happy to provide them . . .[5]

1. Yapp, *op. cit.*, pp.116–17.
2. *ibid.*, pp.105–6.
3. Newnham, *op. cit.*, pp. 146–50.
4. Lindskoog, *op. cit.*, pp. 159–62.
5. 'Boneheads', Pat Shipman, *Fortean Times* No. 70, London 1993.

FOX SISTERS (*See* **MEDIUMS**)

FRAUD (*See* *CONCORDANCE*)

FRENCH SOCIAL SECURITY SWINDLE (*See* **MORENO, Antonio**)

FREUD, Sigmund (1856–1939) (*SCIENTIFIC SCAMS*)
Was the author of *The Interpretation of Dreams* (1900) and father of psychoanalytic theory a hoaxer? Some recent critics doubt not only Freud's methodology but his integrity. In a 1993 article in the *New York Review of Books*, University of California Professor of English Frederick Crews claims he was: 'quite lacking in the empirical or ethical scruples that we would hope to find in any responsible scientist, to say nothing of a major one'.[1]

With psychoanalysis in institutional decline, the new image is of a man driven by the desire for fame who, interpreting evidence retrospectively to suit his theories, used his patients as pawns. The main charge concerns his theory of infantile seduction; the basis of what later he termed the Oedipus Complex. While initially believing the tales his mainly female patients told him of being abused as infants by their fathers, later, unable to accept that virtually all middle-class Viennese citizens practised incest, he decided that these were only fantasies. Or so it appeared for a long time. The issue now is not whether they were fantasies or not; but whether such 'memories' originated with his patients at all.

Freud himself, desperate to find the cause of neurosis and so make his reputation, revealingly remarked that: 'The principal point is that I should guess the secret and tell it to the patient straight out.' Having done that: 'We must not be led astray by initial denial.' Commenting on this inference that Freud *invented* the stories of abuse allegedly revealed by his patients, Allan Esterton in *The Seductive Mirage* points out that: 'The patients did not themselves report sexual experiences from infancy – these were inferences made by Freud himself on the basis of a theoretical postulate.'

This accusation, that Freud (knowingly or not) fabricated his evidence, is currently used to support the theory of what is now known as **False Memory Syndrome**. Freud himself hardly helped by insisting that all opposition to his theories arose not from intellectual but emotional sources: i.e., only a trained psychoanalyst can evaluate psychoanalysis. Nor has concealment by the Sigmund Freud Archives of documents possibly damaging to his reputation aided his case. As for the techniques he pioneered, one of his best-known cases, the 'Wolfman' Sergei Pankeev, in and out of analysis throughout his life, in the 1970s told a journalist: 'I am in the same state as when I first came to Freud, and Freud is no more.'

Was Freud a hoaxer? Is psychoanalysis just a con game? There is no clear verdict. Like it or not, his system is now part of modern intellectual life. Psychoanalysis may be seen as a form of conversation between two people: but what kind of conversation? Therapists dealing with 'patients' or 'victims' are in a position of power. Such power, as appears in some recent cases of alleged child abuse, can be abused by the projection of preconceived ideas or theories. Perhaps the main issue is this: how can therapists, from Freud on, be sure they are not hoaxing themselves?

1. Quoted in 'What's Up Doc?', Suzanne Moore, *Guardian Weekend*, London, 12 February 1994.

FURGUSON, Arthur (d.1938) (*CONMEN*, *see also* **LUSTIG, 'Count' Victor**)
Within a few weeks in 1925 this canny Scot sold three of London's best-known landmarks to American tourists. Cheapest was Big Ben at

£1,000; Buckingham Palace was a snip at £2,000; while Nelson's Column fetched £6,000. An actor who had appeared in repertory company melodramas in Scotland and the north of England, Furguson (or Ferguson, according to which account you read) had once played the part of an American conned by a trickster, and perhaps this gave him the idea when one day in Trafalgar Square he saw a rich American from Iowa gazing reverently at Nelson's Column. Appointing himself as guide, he explained that the statue atop the column was of England's great naval hero, victor of the Battle of Trafalgar in 1805. So unfortunate, he remarked, that it and several other landmarks had to be sold and dismantled to help repay Britain's vast war loan to the United States. He explained that he was the ministry official appointed to arrange the sale, which had to be kept secret, and could only be made to a gentleman who appreciated this great monument to Britain's former glory. Of course, there was already a long queue of potential buyers, but perhaps, if the gentleman from Iowa was interested . . .?

The American *was* interested. Slipping away to telephone his superiors, Furguson was soon back with the good news that Britain could accept a cheque for £6,000, right away. Leaving his client a receipt and the name and address of a firm who would dismantle the column and ship it to the States, Furguson immediately cashed the cheque while the buyer got in touch with the firm. Of course the demolition company laughed in his face, but it was only when Scotland Yard assured him he'd been conned that the light dawned.

Soon the police also heard from another American who had bought Big Ben, while a third complained he was unable to complete his purchase of Buckingham Palace despite a down payment of £2,000. Meanwhile, so delighted with his American clients that he emigrated to their country, Furguson soon leased the White House for ninety-nine years to a Texan cattle rancher at the knockdown rent of $100,000 a year – the first year's rent payable in advance.

He'd made enough to retire, but his ambition demanded that he pull off one more truly grand hoax. So in New York he explained to an Australian from Sydney that New York harbour was to be widened so that the Statue of Liberty, in the way of the proposed scheme, had to be dismantled and sold. Perhaps it would look good in Sydney Harbour. The price? A mere $100,000! The Australian immediately began trying to raise the money, but his suspicious bankers told him to tip off the police. And this time Furguson had made a bad mistake, allowing himself to be photographed arm-in-arm with his buyer, the Statue of Liberty in the background. At last the police caught up with him, and Arthur Furguson was jailed for five years. Released in 1930, he moved to Los Angeles, where a further string of confidence tricks allowed him to live in luxury until his death in 1938. As for his victims, hopefully they were all supple enough to kick themselves – hard!

G

'Ed could not have faked the pictures.'

(Dr Bruce Maccabee, US naval physicist
and UFO buff, speaking of the Gulf Breeze
UFO photographs)

GELLER, Uri (1946–) (*PARANORMAL HOAXES*)
On 23 November 1973 a young Israeli psychic named Uri Geller
appeared on a British TV show, the *David Dimbleby Talk-In*. Before a
national audience he started up broken watches and bent forks apparently by psychokinetic mind-power alone. The studio switchboard was
soon jammed by reports of children ruining the family cutlery by similar
means while watching the show. Overnight Geller was a sensation. Sober
scientists like Professor John Taylor of London University were
impressed; journalists asked if Geller should be banned from planes lest
he upset delicate electronic equipment. And American stage-magician
James **Randi** was encouraged in his enduring crusade to debunk all
paranormal claims. Clearly, Geller had something. But what?

His rise to fame began in 1971 when American psychic researcher
Andrija Puharich caught his stage act at a Jaffa discotheque. Impressed
only by his final trick of breaking a ring without touching it, in his
apartment next day he saw Geller raise the temperature of a thermometer
by gazing at it, by concentration move a compass needle, and reveal
already written down a sequence of numbers which Puharich thought he
had only just thought up.[1] Then letting Puharich 'regress' him hypnotically, in Hebrew he told how, in a Tel Aviv garden aged three, he'd seen
a shining bowl-shaped light above, then a bright faceless figure before
him. In his book *Uri*, Puharich then claims that he and his two
colleagues heard an 'unearthly and metallic voice' above them, and that
Geller, emerging from hypnosis to hear what had happened, snatched
the tape (which vanished from his hand) and ran off. Later he was found
confused and amnesiac.

Puharich reconstructed what the 'metallic' voice had said as: 'It is us who found Uri in the garden when he was three. He is our helper sent to help man. We programmed him in the garden for many years to come, but he was also programmed not to remember. On this day his work begins. Andrija, you are to take care of him.'[2]

Subsequent events included teleportation of Puharich's briefcase from New York to Tel Aviv, disappearing tape-recorders, and other bizarre miracles due to the Nine: the other-dimensional entities not only behind Geller's powers but all **UFO** activity. Published in 1974, Puharich's account led many to doubt his sanity, honesty, or both. Even Geller was sceptical, calling the Nine: 'clowns playing practical jokes'. Soon they ordered Puharich to abandon further tests on Geller, who now perhaps no longer needed him.

A fraud? Yet there were bent forks, started-up watches, and the reactivation of a flat battery belonging to famed rocket scientist Werner von Braun who, rejecting fakery as impossible, concluded that Geller could produce electricity.[3] And the tests conducted at the Stanford Research Institute in California by psychic researchers Russell Targ and Harold Puthoff. Geller's ESP successes were claimed as notable. Twelve out of fourteen times he 'guessed' correctly under which of ten empty cans a small object was hidden, and he accurately duplicated drawings sealed inside double envelopes.

Now the counter-attack. Both Randi and Charles Reynolds (another professional stage-magician) claimed that Geller's 'powers' were explicable by sleight of hand. Randi scathingly rejected Targ and Puthoff's methodology. Dismissing tests where Geller had failed, they had weeded out other ambivalent results to increase the percentage of 'hits'. But even Randi was baffled by: 'just how Geller fooled the experimenters during the tests done at SRI', though suggesting he'd been aided in trickery by Shipi and Hannah Strang, two assistants he'd trained in Israel, and by Jean Mayo, his devotee. All three were at the tests, a fact not mentioned in Targ and Puthoff's report.[4]

Yet Randi too (like **Houdini**) has used dubious methods in his crusade to prove *all* paranormal claims fake and, though soon enough Geller slipped out of the public eye, later reportedly he became a millionaire hiring himself out to multinationals to dowse for rare minerals. In 1986 he told author Bob Couttie that his success rate was thirty per cent. The *Financial Times* reported that his terms as a dowser were a £1 million advance against royalties, non-returnable. Among his clients were the mining company, Rio Tinto Zinc. It seems odd that hard-headed businessmen would shell out a fortune if they didn't expect to get something in return.[5]

Moreover, Geller's on-going (and various) legal actions against Randi's assertions have not been wholly unsuccessful. In 1993, with other actions still pending, he won a case for defamation of character, based on

Randi's false assertion in a 1989 interview with the Japanese magazine *Days Japan* that metallurgist Dr Wilbur Franklin, a believer in Geller's powers, had shot himself in shame when Randi 'discredited' Geller's powers. The truth was that Franklin had died from natural causes. Geller was awarded costs.[6]

1. *Uri*, Andrija Puharich, Futura, London 1974, pp.66–7.
2. *Ibid.*, pp.94–6.
3. 'Under the Eyes of Scientists', Colin Wilson, *The Unexplained*, Orbis partwork, London 1983, pp.666–9.
4. Randi, *op. cit.*, pp.136–9.
5. *Forbidden Knowledge*, Bob Couttie, Lutterworth Press, Cambridge 1988, p.8.
6. 'Geller Gets Randi', *Fortean Times* No. 69, London June–July 1993.

GIANT PENGUIN HOAX (*ALIEN ANIMALS*)

In February 1948 a resident of Clearwater, Florida, encountered a track of odd three-toed footprints which, emerging from the sea, meandered along the beach for two miles before returning to the ocean blue. About 14 inches long and 11 across, these odd tracks (associated with the tale that a young couple had been disturbed one night on the beach by a huge monster emerging from the sea) reappeared on neighbouring stretches of beach three times in March and April, and again in October, when they were found to run for 200 yards at Suwannee Gables, 40 miles up the Suwannee River.

Enter Ivan T. Sanderson, English zoologist and founder of the Society for the Investigation of the Unexplained. Investigating the Suwannee site for New York's WNBC radio station, he presented witnesses who said they'd seen the mystery beast. Two pilots had seen an odd animal swimming in the sea off Hog Island on 25 July. About 15 feet long, it had a 'very hairy body, a heavy blunt head and back legs like an alligator'. On an offshore island that August a Wisconsin couple had seen a neckless furry beast with a 'head like a rhinoceros', arms like 'flippers' and 'short, thick legs and huge feet' come waddling out of bushes and go down into the sea.

Then, looking out from a plane halfway between Suwannee Gables and the sea, Sanderson saw 'an enormous dirty-yellow creature . . . wallowing on the surface' of the river. About 20 feet long and 8 wide, it sank out of sight, but he'd seen enough to conclude (despite the Sheriff's Department insisting it was all a 'masterful' prank) that the mystery beast was, in fact, a giant penguin, displaced from its natural habitat by some natural catastrophe. Never mind the differing descriptions of other witnesses: he was sure it was a giant penguin, and so he later reported it in print.

Forty years later, with Sanderson now dead (1973) and the 'giant three-toed penguin' by now an enduring part of Florida's folklore, reporter Jan Kirby told in the St Petersburg *Times* (11 June 1988) how retired auto dealer Tony Signorini had confessed that he and his partner Al Williams (a well-known local prankster who'd died in 1969) had been inspired by photos of fossilised dinosaur tracks to create the hoax.

Using heavy iron three-toed feet (cast at a local foundry, and produced in evidence by Signorini – each weighed 30 pounds), they'd made the tracks, starting either from a boat offshore, or (for the inland up-river prints) from a car, using a palm frond to brush away their footprints.[1]

Yet, as *Fortean Times* editor Bob Rickard points out in his description of this good-humoured hoax, a mystery remains. The tracks were faked, but what of the various reported sightings of the unidentified swimming beast? Was every witness (including Sanderson himself) a liar? Possibly. Or do we see here the signature of the **Cosmic Joker**? What if a *real* alien animal manifested amid (or because of) the publicity? What if (as with the **Loch Ness Monster**) publicity itself triggers events, encounters or visions so impressive to the senses that 'witnesses' perceive as 'real' what otherwise exists only in dream or imagination? And can perception in and of itself create the reality of what is perceived?

Of course, such questions are best asked with tongue firmly in cheek . . .

1. 'Florida's Penguin Panic', Bob Rickard, *Fortean Times* No. 66, London 1992, pp.41–3.

GLOZEL MYSTERY (*See* **FOSSIL FORGERIES**)

GRAHAM, Dr James (*See* **CELESTIAL BED, The**)

GRAY, Muriel (contemporary) (*MEDIA HOAXES*)
In summer 1991 the energetic Scottish media personality Muriel Gray presented on Channel 4 TV a set of programmes called *ART IS DEAD – Long Live TV*. Inspired by the belief that too much bad art is taken too seriously, the initial name for the programme was ENC (**Emperor's New Clothes**), but this was thought too much of a giveaway. Filmed in Edinburgh (a city rich in art snobbery), the series consisted of five programmes, the first four highlighting particular 'artists'. Sculptor Kenneth Hutchinson's basic material was rotting carcases; novelist Laura Mason built her books from transcripts of telephone chat-lines; art-film maker Richard Bradley-Hudd offered a fridge-eye view of New York; and architect Hannah Patrizzio's bio-degradable houses were filmed apparently in Bavaria but in fact in Scotland. In the fifth and last programme an angry discussion between Gray and the four artists ended prematurely when one of the 'artists' threw a glass of wine in Gray's face. With the series so far accepted at face value by press, public, and the art

critics (some feigning prior knowledge of the four artists), Gray now revealed it as a hoax. Everyone but folk in the art world, yet again caught with their pretentious pants down, was highly amused. Maybe there's hope for the media yet.[1]

1. Yapp, *op. cit.*, pp.126–8.

GREENE, Graham (1904–91) (*LITERARY HOAXES*)

Another joke that got serious. In the early 1960s *The Times* published a letter about the Anglo–Texan Friendship Society, created to promote: 'cultural and social links between this country and the state of Texas', and claiming a special (though undefined) relationship between Britain and the Lone Star State. It was signed by John Sutro and novelist Graham Greene, acclaimed author of books like *Our Man in Havana* and *A Burnt-Out Case*. Not widely known as a joker, Greene had been working hard, and needed light relief. Thus this hoax, which the *New York Times* quickly spotted: 'We feel scepticism, like a calcium deposit, residing in our bones.' Yet (surprised?) others took the letter at face value: of sixty genuine replies received by Sutro and Greene one was from banker Sir Samuel Guinness, another from Attorney-General Sir Hartley Shawcross. So a genuine Anglo–Texan Society was formed, its elected officials including Guinness, and a programme of cultural events organised. The American ambassador gave Sutro the Texan flag at a barbecue given by the United States Air Force; the Duke of Edinburgh attended a London cocktail party; and a plaque was unveiled on the site of the old Republic of Texas Embassy in London's Pickering Street. Bemused by what they'd started, Sutro and Greene soon resigned, but the Society continued to flourish.[1]

1. Yapp, *op. cit.*, pp.40–1.

GREENLAND (*EXPLORATION HOAXES*)

More renowned for rape, pillage, and navigational skills than imagination, the sea-going Vikings were good liars. In the ninth century, reaching the world's largest island, they found a frozen, mountainous land mass within the Arctic Circle, eighty-five per cent of it permanently under ice. Only coastal areas were even marginally verdant, and then just in summer. And though a thousand years ago, before the Little Ice Age, the climate was a bit more pleasant than now, it was still a forbidding place. How could they attract settlers?

Simple! Call it *Greenland!*

Meanwhile another Viking party had found another island in the north Atlantic. Though at latitude 66 degrees north, this had green forests, fertilising volcanoes, and more hot springs than anywhere else on earth. It was a harsh land, but healthy and invigorating – the women there have the world's longest life expectancy (79.5 years). They decided to keep it for themselves. So, to dissuade other potential immigrants by making it out to be as cold as **Hell** (originating in Norse myth as the land of ice, snow, mist and gloom that lies north of the Abyss), they called it – what else? – *Iceland*.[1]

1. Goldberg, *op. cit.*, p.27.

GREGORY, Maundy (1877–1941) (*CONMEN*)

As humbly born and ambitious as Horatio **Bottomley**, Arthur John Peter Michael Maundy Gregory made a fortune selling titles to those desperate for honours. Eldest son of a Hampshire clergyman, he was a teacher then actor before in 1907 opening a theatrical agency. This failed, leaving him broke, but through it he made useful contacts. Collecting information on 'foreigners and undesirables', when the First World War broke out he gained an introduction to the security services in Whitehall where, oozing charm and confidence, 'his remarkable genius and delightful manner won him a high place in the opinions of men of experience and probity'.[1] Building up his image as a man of probity and influence by launching a stoutly anti-Communist magazine, *The Whitehall Gazette and St James Review*, and by starting his own club, The Ambassador, he opened a palatial office at 10 Parliament Street, close to Downing Street. Elegantly dressed with bejewelled fingers, an orchid in his buttonhole, and a gold watch-chain attached to a large jewelled watch, after the war and with various revolutions rending Europe he began specialising in the care of dethroned royals. Soon he was so well off he had a flat in Hyde Park Terrace, another in Brighton, and owned a hotel and two river launches.

Where did the cash come from? From his victims, to whom he sold honours. His going rate was £10,000 for a knighthood, £35,000 for a baronetcy, and £50,000 for a top-drawer peerage. He operated by discovering through his many contacts who was in line for an honour and whether the individual wanted it enough to pay for it. Then he sent the victim a letter suggesting a meeting to discuss a matter of confidence. Many paid up without ever knowing they'd have got the title anyway. Or he looked for rich businessmen anxious to be ennobled, then wangled their names onto the Honours List.

But, while governments could legally sell honours (Lloyd George's Coalition government had sold six million's worth to boost funds and pack the House of Lords with supporters), individuals could not, especially not after 1925 when Stanley Baldwin's new Conservative government made such trading illegal. But Gregory carried on anyway, even though the Conservatives infiltrated an official into his organisation to get the list of people to whom he'd promised titles. Soon it all began to go wrong. Paying £30,000 for a baronetcy, a client died before receiving it, and the dead man's executors demanded the money back. Then (threatened with blackmail for his homosexuality: a criminal offence at the time) in December 1932 he offered Lieutenant-Commander Edward Leake of the Royal Navy a knighthood for £12,000. Leake went to the police. Gregory was arrested. Tried at Bow Street under the 1925 Act, he pleaded guilty on advice of counsel. Fined £50 and serving two months in prison, on release he went to live in Paris as Sir Arthur Gregory, only to end up in a German hospital, where he died in 1941. Another unedifying tale.

1. *Daily Sketch*, 22 February 1933, quoted in Yapp, *op. cit.*, p.46.

GREY OWL (*See* **BELANEY, Archibald**)

GRIMM, The Brothers (*LITERARY HOAXES*)
Jacob (1785–1863) and Wilhelm (1786–1859) Grimm are famous for a collection of folk-tales, *Kinder und Hausmärchen*, in English *Grimm's Fairy Tales* (1812–22). Born at Hanau, they remain widely respected for laying the foundations of the study of folklore as a science. Hessian ambassador in Paris (1814–15), Jacob joined his brother to work in the Elector's library in Kassel, where they produced their ground-breaking collection of some 200 tales – drawn, they said, from the good old German oral tradition. They had listened to the peasants and simply written down what they'd heard. Following the success of the *Fairy Tales*, in later years they published many other collections of legend and ancient German, Norse, Irish and other texts, then philological works, dictionaries and grammars, all well received. They died with their reputations secure, well remembered for tales like *Hansel and Gretel*, *Rumpelstiltskin*, *The Frog-Prince* and *The Golden Goose*.

Yet these were gathered not from 'simple peasants', but from well-off friends and relatives, and every story had been radically rewritten for publication. Lying about their sources, they deliberately destroyed original material, then fibbed about their own revisions to their own published texts. The full story, which many remain understandably reluctant to accept (if we can't trust tellers of nursery tales then who *can* we trust?) is told by John M. Ellis, Professor of German Literature at the University of California, Santa Cruz, in his *One Fairy Tale Too Many* (1983). A *grimm* tale indeed.

GUERRE, Martin (d.1560) (*IMPOSTORS*)
This extraordinary imposture, filmed in France as *The Return of Martin Guerre* (1982) starring Gérard Depardieu, began *c.*1538 in the village of Artigat in the Ariège region of the French Pyrenees, when Bertrande de Rols married Martin Guerre. Both were young, not even fourteen. She

was a local girl of good family, but his family came from the Basque. And though after eight years at last he was a father, still he felt out of place. He had neither schooling nor country skills, and when he quarrelled with his father after thieving some of the old man's grain, he'd had enough. In 1548 he left.

Though looked after by both families, Bertrande was now in limbo. She couldn't remarry, and was too proud to fake news of Martin's death to do so. Then in 1556, after eight empty years, one day his four sisters heard that Martin was back, and fetched her. So they met again. But was this Martin? He'd changed so much. He was shorter, less agile – and what had happened to the scar over his eyebrow? Yet who could remember exactly what he *had* looked like? His sisters accepted him as Martin, his father was dead, and Bertrande was happier than she'd been in years. The village shrugged. He was Martin.

In fact his name was Pancette du Thil. From further north, he'd met Martin Guerre while both soldiered in Picardy for King Henri II, and already by 1553 or 1554 had been mistaken for the other man. Sensing opportunity, he'd begun to study Martin, who had no wish to return home, and so in 1556 reached Artigat, hoping for an inheritance larger than anything he'd get as poor (though golden-tongued) Pancette. Moving into the old parental home with 'their' son Sanxi, the couple soon had two daughters. Bertrande knew it was a fake marriage, but they were happy. Martin was good at helping run the Guerre family land, but when he decided that some ancestral property in the Basque could profitably be sold, he fell out with Uncle Pierre. Asked for the accounts he'd been keeping since his brother's death, the old man refused. Taking him to court, 'Martin's' right to see the accounts were upheld. Pierre accused him of being an impostor, and the local shoemaker agreed: the real Martin had bigger feet.

The dispute split the village. Alarmed, Bertrande and Pancette rehearsed their life together back to 1538, she coaching him in 'the most secret acts of marriage'. In late 1559 a landowner had Pancette jailed for suspected arson even as Pierre's inquiries produced two men who'd formerly known Pancette du Thil. Released from the arson charge, Pancette was seized by Pierre and his sons-in-law and carted off to another jail at Rieux. The abductors said Bertrande had agreed. Harassed by mother and stepfather, Bertrande could only accept the violent *fait accompli* and hope their agreed story would stand up at the hearing.

Among the 150 witnesses the don't knows prevailed, but there were more disbelievers than otherwise. But Pancette's *élan* was impressive. He was unworried by talk of his bigger feet and missing scar. 'Pierre Guerre told you to say that!' he retorted when Bertrande was made to call him impostor, though under oath she wouldn't deny him.

Yet he was found guilty. Pierre wanted only an apology and fine, but the King's attorney required a beheading. Pancette appealed to the Toulouse *parlement*, where his case re-opened in February 1560. His performance impressed the splendidly robed, experienced judges of ancient Languedoc's capital. He appeared 'truthful in everything', while Pierre looked shifty and overawed. After all, what was the main problem? The judges wished to sustain this obviously happy marriage and its three children. Clearly 'Martin' loved his wife; his manner showed he knew she'd been forced to speak against him. As for Pierre, he'd refused the accounts and attempted violence. They ordered him chained and secluded from 'Martin' and Bertrande, while pondering a decision, leaning increasingly towards Pancette.

Then appeared the real Martin Guerre.

As soon as this one-legged man back from the Flanders wars hobbled into court his eldest sister fell on his neck and wept. Pancette remembered his past better than he did, but the jig was up. Bertrande threw herself on the court's mercy. Pancette had tricked her and everyone! She had believed Martin's sisters, but the moment she'd realised the imposture she'd taken him to court! With 'a hard, wild face' Pancette heard her admit that the fault was hers alone. Sentenced to be hanged by the church at Artigat, he died bravely, eloquently confessing his sins and regrets. Martin and Bertrande were reconciled, and had another son – but the suspicion lingers that many in the village had always preferred the congenial Pancette to the dour Martin, and that even Pierre Guerre would have supported what he knew was imposture – if only the two of them hadn't argued.[1]

1. Newnham, *op. cit.*, pp.171–80.

GULF BREEZE UFO MYSTERY (*UFO HOAXES*)

An odd UFO event with even odder consequences began in the small Florida town of Gulf Breeze on 11 November 1987. Late that night, claimed builder-developer Ed ('Mr Ed') Walters, a top-shaped UFO appeared over his suburban home. His Polaroid was to hand, but the UFO shot out a blue beam that paralysed and lifted him from the ground. 'We will not hurt you,' a computer-like voice said in his head. He was dropped. The UFO vanished. In later meetings he met four-foot-tall humanoids. His UFO photos were pronounced: 'absolutely genuine,' by Dr Bruce Maccabee of the Washington-based Fund for UFO Research. 'Ed could not have faked the pictures.'

Mr Ed's headline tale led to a publishing contract with a six-figure advance; the TV mini-series was planned . . . then the cry of HOAX! went up. Young Tommy Smith told how Mr Ed had once asked him to help him fake UFO photos. A model flying saucer was found in the attic of Mr Ed's former home. Maybe both Tommy and model were plants, but the damage was done. Dr Maccabee admitted receiving ten per cent of the advance for writing the last chapter of the book. Confronted on the *Oprah Winfrey Show* by Philip Klass, a professional UFO debunker, Walters had to admit he'd spent nearly three years in jail for forgery. Exit book and mini-series. Many UFOlogists gave up.

But the real mystery was yet to dawn. On 9 July 1990, three weeks before Iraq invaded Kuwait, six US Army intelligence experts – communications analysts scanning foreign broadcasts, working with complex codes – left their posts in Augsburg, Germany and disappeared. Five days later in Gulf Breeze, stopping a van with a broken tail-light, a local policeman checked the offender's name. He was one of the missing soldiers. Reporting upward, the local station was ordered to hold but not question the man. Four of the other five unlikely deserters were located at the home of Anna Foster, a local psychic. The sixth, Annette F. Eccleston, was found camping alone on the beach. Questioned by Army Intelligence at Fort Benning, Georgia, the six said Armageddon was imminent and that they'd come to Gulf Breeze to meet alien spaceships presaging Christ's second coming, also to find and kill Antichrist – Mr Ed? Kenneth Beason, apparently group spokesman, had already told journalist Stan Johnson, from the same Kentucky town as himself, that war was about to break out in the Middle East. How did he know? Telepathic messages had been received by Vance Davis, another of the six. Sent to Fort Knox, the six were suddenly discharged and cut loose – perhaps because of the press coverage, or because the army realised they'd spent too long at the terminal: their software was gone.

Yet the mystery remained. Knowing in advance about Saddam's invasion plans didn't require alien telepathic input, especially not for military communications analysts, but how had they got through Immigration? How had they even got out of Germany? Who had colluded, and why? Would they have deserted solely on the basis of alleged telepathic messages?

Prominent UFO researcher Jacques Vallee suggests that they *did* hear messages, via the same coded channels they used in their military work – channels which, by definition, could not easily be tampered with or infiltrated. Had these military channels been compromised by cults or interests wishing to exploit UFOlogist naiveté, either to discredit UFOlogy or to promote a popular scare for reasons unknown? Yet who had the motivation, specialised knowledge, and political clout to access an encrypted network and send six apparently computer-shocked soldiers on a fantasy mission, then ensure that lower levels of authority played ball? And why were they cut loose? After all, they were deserters – or were they?

Later interviewed on TV in Gulf Breeze, the six said they'd merely decided to visit a friend. That was why they'd all simultaneously deserted and fled from Augsburg to Florida.

Forget the stuff about the Antichrist. The Pentagon's playing some strange games these days. Either that, or it's the **Cosmic Joker** again. Or maybe both.[1,2]

1. *Revelations*, Jacques Vallee, Ballantine, New York 1992, pp.210–17.
2. *Angels and Aliens*, Keith Thompson, Ballantine, New York 1993, pp.185–9.

H

'If I write Rembrandt's signature on a piece of
lavatory paper, there are Bond Street dealers
who will claim that Rembrandt used it.'

(Eric Hebborn, art forger)

HAMILTON'S AIRSHIP HOAX (*UFO HOAXES*)

Another long-running hoax dates from 19 April 1897 when, it was
alleged, an airship manned by 'six of the strangest beings I ever saw'
hovered over the Kansas farm of respected local man Alexander
Hamilton, and kidnapped one of his heifers. Later, a neighbour found
the beast's hide, legs and head, but there were no tracks in the soft
ground, and no clues as to its fate.

Hamilton's detailed account neatly fitted other 'mystery airship'
reports of the time, and was so widely believed that in time it became
a UFO core-myth. After all, ten local men as upstanding as Hamilton
himself had attested to its truth. So, with nobody finding any cracks
in it, eighty years rolled by. But in February 1977 *Fate* magazine's
associate editor Jerome Clark revealed how he'd traced Hamilton's
granddaughter, Mrs Elizabeth Hamilton Linde, to be told by her that
Hamilton, who had a 'darn good imagination', had made it all up with
the help of the editor of a local newspaper, the Yates Center's *Farmer's
Advocate*.

Next, *Fortean Times* editor Robert J.M. Rickard *fortuitously* received a
clipping from the *Buffalo Enterprise* for 28 January 1943 – of a letter by
Ben S. Hudson, son of Ed Hudson, the editor unnamed by Mrs Linde.
Following a re-run of the calf-napping tale, Ben had written to say that
Hamilton and his father, having concocted the story, had been delighted
to find it taken up by newspapers from New York to Berlin. Alerted by
Rickard, Clark sought new information – and from a Mrs Donna Steeby of
Wichita, Kansas, received a statement made by her ninety-three-year-old
mother, Ethel L. Shaw, who as a girl had been out at the Hamilton house

'that beautiful afternoon'. Returning from town, Hamilton had said: 'Ma, I fixed up quite a story and told the boys in town and it will come out in the *Advocate* this weekend.'

It emerged that Hamilton had belonged to a club of yarn-spinners called 'Ananias' (the Liar's Club). Not only had Hamilton's tall tale topped them all, but he'd got ten of his (all respectable) friends to sign an affidavit attesting to his veracity. No wonder he'd been so delighted – and (he died in 1912) doubtless he'd have been even more pleased to know that his hoax survived three-quarters of the twentieth century before being exposed . . .[1]

1. 'Fortean Corrigenda', *Fortean Times* No. 20, London 1977, pp.5–7.

HAMPSTEAD SEAL, The (*ALIEN ANIMALS*)

The first modern sighting of Scotland's **Loch Ness Monster** in 1933 was by two local hoteliers – and so too in London in August 1926 the tale of two seals caught in a pond near the fairground on Hampstead Heath's Vale of Health originated with a local hotelier, Fred Gray.

For some time before 25 August, a strange creature had been reported in the pond – a 'huge, black creature, with the head of a gorilla, and a bark like that of a dog with a sore throat'; or perhaps a 'phantom'. That night a local angler, one Mr Trevor, allegedly landed it. Lodged in an iron tank in Gray's hotel, it turned out to be a young seal. Though wild, it so enjoyed the free fish that it became known as 'Happy of Hampstead'. The papers speculated that this and other seals which Gray claimed had been heard barking in the pond had got there via the River Fleet, which connects with the Thames. It was unclear how the angler had singlehandedly unhooked the struggling, angry seal and carried it uphill to the hotel.

On 2 November 1926, the *Daily Chronicle* told of a second seal which, before an 'excited crowd', had been landed by an 'astonished angler', even as it 'fought like a lion and barked like a dog'. Rapidly expiring, its carcase was removed by the angler – so said Fred Gray who, again claiming that it must have swum up the River Fleet, said it had 'a lot of scales'.

Good silly-season stuff. Seals don't bark; they have fur, not scales; and even after heavy rain the Fleet never flows over a foot deep. Yet only in 1986 (long after Gray's death in 1941) did local sculptor Hubert Adamson learn the truth from Gray's grandson, Charlie Abbot, once part of a touring fair and still living with his family on Hampstead Heath's fairground site.

One of the fair's venues had been King's Lynn, on England's east coast. There, Abbot had been told by a friend called Bone (of a King's Lynn fisher family) how his family had caught a seal and, as a joke, transported it to Hampstead, where it ended up in Gray's tank. Probably it had never been in the pond at all. As for the second seal, Gray had invented it.

'I think it was all for fun,' commented Hubert Adamson, 'but it can't have done [Gray's] hotel trade any harm.'[1]

1. 'The Hampstead Seal', Paul Sieveking, *Fortean Times* No. 65, London 1992, pp.47–9.

HAMPTON, David (1964–) (*IMPOSTORS*)
Kicked out of his Buffalo home by his father, an attorney fed up with his rebellious precocity, David Hampton decided to take Manhattan by storm. It was 1981, he was just seventeen, and he knew he was a genius with a great theatrical career ahead of him. So naturally he was enraged when the doorman of the famous Studio 54 club refused him and a friend entry. He decided on revenge. Masquerading as the son of black movie star Sidney Poitier (who had only daughters, but who was to know?), he rented a stretch limousine and pulled up at the club. Out jumped his friend, telling people to make way for Poitier's son. Not recognising the teenagers they'd just rebuffed, the guards deferentially ushered them in. There was no ID check, drinks were on the house, and Hampton realised he was on to a good thing.

Showing up at the door of an actor-director who was house-sitting actress Melanie Griffith's apartment, 'David Poitier' said Melanie always let him stay when he was in town. He got away with this too.

Next, freeloading on the Connecticut College campus, he stole a rich student's address book and so gained access to the most exclusive Manhattan homes. Introducing himself as a friend of their daughter Josie to Lea and John Jay Iselin (then president of New York's public TV station, WNET), he said he'd been mugged on his way in from the airport. They took him in and lent him money. A day later Osborn Elliott, dean of Columbia University's Graduate School of Journalism, was conned the same way.

So it went on, Hampton flamboyantly presenting himself as a celebrity guest in numerous households, until at last it emerged: Sidney Poitier had no sons! His furious victims pressed felony charges. Plea-bargaining led to a suspended sentence: the deal was that he left New York and never returned. But, unable to see Manhattan surviving without him, still as David Poitier he returned, checking into a New York hotel. This led to a two-year stretch in less elevated conditions. Did he learn? No way. Released, claiming he'd spent three years as a gigolo in London, Paris and Rome, he went back to the Big Apple and immediately drew attention by refusing to pay a cab fare. Arrested, he failed to turn up in court, claiming he'd been hospitalised by a traffic accident. When finally he did conde-scend to appear, he offered written proof of his ambulance trip. Fined

$500 for not paying the fare and given another suspended sentence, he was about to walk free when it was spotted that his written proof was forged. He was immediately arrested again.

None of this would have interested the world except that, fascinated by Hampton, playwright John Guare wrote *Six Degrees of Separation*, a play based on his impostures. Nominated for a Tony award, this comedy-drama played to packed houses. Hampton, not unreasonably claiming that without him there wouldn't be a play, sought a court injunction to halt the production until he got his share of the profits. The case was thrown out, but he went on hogging the headlines, enjoying celebrity appearances on TV and radio – but to date the great theatrical career he once so confidently expected has eluded him.[1]

1. Madison, *op. cit.*, pp.97–103.

HANAU, Marthe (*c.*1890–1935) (*FRAUD*)

Quite as remarkable as Thérèse **Humbert**, what this daughter of a Lille industrialist lacked in looks she made up for in ambition and will. Marrying businessman Lazare Bloch before the First World War, she invented a beauty cream which he successfully marketed. By 1914 their factory employed a hundred workers. The war took the workers to the trenches, and her lesbian tastes ended her marriage; but Bloch remained her closest friend and associate when, with the war over, she bought an ailing financial weekly, the *Gazette du Franc et des Nations*, and attracted good journalists by paying well. Taking a radical political line, soon the *Gazette* was a paper that nobody interested in money could ignore.

But her real plan was that the information the *Gazette* offered would influence readers to buy shares in companies run by her associates. The scheme worked brilliantly. Stock-market gamblers after quick profits rarely look into the products or services of share-issuing companies, and Madame Hanau's firms, all vaguely named, made and did nothing useful. But nobody minded so long as the share prices rose, encouraged by the demand created among *Gazette* readers. As for the journalists who wrote the articles creating the demand, Madame paid up to ten times more than other editors. Few of them were rich. Many had expensive lifestyles. They were happy to advise whatever she wanted.

Now creating a network of publications manipulating investments and share prices, she founded a press agency to handle financial information: the Agence Interpresse. With this she challenged the mighty Agence Havas, which supplied most big French newspapers with their financial columns. Offering better terms, she captured some of these papers and by 1928 felt strong enough to float, under her own name, an issue of short-term bonds at eight per cent, offering investors a profit-sharing scheme promised to yield up to forty per cent. But this time she went too far. Even as she enjoyed her wealth, the banks realised the danger and with Havas prepared for war. Rumours about Madame and her hollow companies began circulating, and though for a time she scotched these by bribes from her 'reptile fund' (the 'reptiles' being corrupt politicians on her secret payroll), soon so many charges stood against her that the public prosecutor could no longer ignore them.

Despite fears that the sudden collapse of her empire would create a national financial crisis, Madame Hanau, Lazare Bloch and several associates were arrested in December 1928, and charged with conspiring to obtain money by fraud for investment in companies connected with the *Gazette*. Fascinated, France watched her fight her corner with spirit. Asserting that the judge was financially ignorant, that the charges were merely vindictive, and that if left in peace she'd pay back all her clients' money, nonetheless after fifteen months in custody at the St Lazare prison she was committed for trial. She promptly went on hunger strike. Transferred to the Cochin Hospital at Neuilly, she persisted despite the efforts of twelve male nurses to force-feed her. On the twenty-second day she took coffee and milk – and, that night, tying bed sheets to the radiator, left by the window. 'Disgusted with the violence to which I have been subjected, I am leaving,' read her note.

Now at large, what did she do? She took a taxi back to the St Lazare prison and asked for 'hospitality'. Allowed in, she collapsed, having eaten nothing for three weeks. The papers called her escapade a 'refreshing practical joke', but Chiappe, the President of Police feared that if she died it would rebound on him. In April 1930 he recommended her provisional release on bail. She regained her strength in a nursing home as the trial preparations still dragged on. Facing enraged creditors, she assured them that, if acquitted and allowed to resume her business, they would all be paid. Half of them cheered her, half shouted her down.

When the trial began on 20 February 1931, it proved impossible to exclude the names of every 'reptile' involved. The scandal was huge. She was sentenced to two years in jail (mostly already served), and fined a mere 3,000 francs. Bloch got eighteen months, the others were acquitted. Freed, she bought a journal called *Forces*, and in April 1932 was again arrested. Publishing a piece on disreputable aspects of the money market, she'd quoted a secret police report about herself. Cross-examined, she refused to say how she'd got it, and declared that French justice was the most corrupt on earth. When it emerged that the file from which she'd quoted had been in the drawer of Minister of Finance Flandin, she said only that: 'Someone had a key'. Sentenced to three months for receiving a stolen document, she appealed. With the appeal denied she fled, but was caught and jailed.

On 19 July 1935 Marthe Hanau was found dead. Sleeping pills had been smuggled to her. The day before she died she'd said: 'I shall always be mistress of my fate.'[1]

1. Larsen, *op. cit.*, pp.152–61.

HARTZELL, Oscar Merril (d.1943) (*CONMEN*)
Perpetrator of one of the twentieth century's most lucrative hoaxes, in 1913 this ambitious farmer's son left Madison County, Iowa, and moved to Des Moines, where he met Sudie B. Whiteaker, a resourceful widow who'd made $65,000 selling shares in a dormant estate she said she could claim – the estate of Sir Francis Drake, the seadog and circumnavigator of Elizabethan England. Borrowed from the annals of conmanship, this scam fooled hundreds of Iowa's citizens before it fell through and she was jailed.

Hartzell, impressed, kept it in mind throughout the First World War, and in 1921 embarked on the same venture. But where Mrs Whiteaker had been amateurish, he was much better organised and thinking on the grand scale. Moving to England and sending all correspondence by American Express (it being a federal offence to use the US Mail for fraudulent purposes), he targeted only people who might possibly believe themselves the descendants of the great hero. Selecting names from Mid-Western trade directories, he sent letters to potential victims called Drake or related to someone of that name. He said he'd made an amazing discovery; that Sir Francis Drake had had an illegitimate son who, jailed to avoid scandal, had been robbed of his rightful inheritance. Released only after solemnly swearing never to reveal his father's name, he had married and fathered a son, a descendant of whom was still alive! Claiming to have traced this true heir to the estate, now worth $22,000,000, Hartzell said this man, who wished to fight in court for his heritage, had appointed himself, Oscar Merril Hartzell, as his representative. The man's name, of course, could not be revealed, lest the 'secret courts of England' try to stop him claiming the estate. Lacking money to fight the case, the heir had authorised Hartzell to raise it by selling shares in the estate. Contributions, he wrote, would be repaid at the rate of $500 for every dollar invested. However, the heir stipulated that contributions could be accepted only from people named Drake or with Drake blood in them. The 'donators', as Hartzell called them, would have to sign a paper swearing to send money only by American Express and pledging themselves to 'silence, secrecy, and non-disturbance'. Anyone breaking that pledge would forfeit their contribution and be struck from the list of beneficiaries.

It worked like a dream. Adna Shepherd *née* Drake, among the first to be hooked, mortgaged her home to invest $5,000, and other Iowan Drakes (none, it seems, had heard of Sudie B. Whiteaker) contributed $166,775. Appointing the Shepherds as the first of fifteen agents operating in nine states, he demanded that they raise $2,500 a week to cover his investigations and the forthcoming legal battle. Sending 'progress reports' at intervals to keep his victims happy and expectant, for eleven years Hartzell maintained his scam. Nobody, it seems, asked the obvious question: how, after over three centuries, could there only be a single heir among all the Drake descendants? Not only that, but why had none of them ever met Hartzell in person?

His inventiveness never flagged. Suggesting that every ripple in the shaky British economy was linked to the on-going legal battle, he increased the value of the fictitious estate to $400,000,000,000, implied that Elizabeth herself had mothered Sir Francis's illegitimate child, and hinted at the involvement of the British Royal Family. Yet, doubtless recalling Abe Lincoln's aphorism about the impossibility of fooling all the people all the time (by now there were over 70,000 'donators'), and soothing his own fears by paying thrice-weekly visits to Miss St John Montague, a well-known crystal ball reader, Hartzell knew that soon he would have to pull out and vanish. So in summer 1932 he prepared his flock by cabling his agents that the final settlement of the estate claim had been definitely fixed for 1 July 1933. But then it all collapsed. Several agents, carelessly using the US Mail, were arrested. Those still free held secret meetings of the hopeful, some attended by up to 4,000 people. Hartzell sent cables urging them to write to their congressmen, to the Attorney-General, even to President Roosevelt. It was too late. By now the State Department was after him. Extradited from Britain in February 1933, in New York he was arrested by the FBI then charged with fraud in Iowa. Told that his ordeal proved the legitimacy of his claim and that Washington and London were in cahoots, the faithful went on coughing up. Hartzell received another $130,000, enough to pay his bail bond, hire lawyers, and live comfortably until 1 July 1933, when the great day came and went with no settlement of the Drake estate.

Brought to trial, Hartzell was accused of defrauding 270,000 people. Witnesses prepared to swear they'd given him money were readily available, but all wished to attest on his behalf. Their faith in him survived their irretrievable losses. Sentenced to ten years in jail, on the grounds that he had: 'caused to have sent mail to defraud', he began his time in January 1935, but by now the hoax had a life of its own. Money for Hartzell and for investment in the Drake fund went on pouring in. When his former US headquarters were raided it emerged that $350,000 had been contributed since his conviction: another $25,000 arrived in the three days after the police raid. It seemed unstoppable. The story spread that a leading radio station had reported the forthcoming settlement of the claim. It was rumoured that a ship in the Galveston docks had brought the first consignment of gold from England. Even when local 'donators' were shown that the ship in question held only oil pipes, they concluded that this was just another government trick, that soon the truth would be revealed, Hartzell freed, and the money paid out. Some died still believing it.

The hoax, which netted over two million dollars, was never completely exploded.

Serving his sentence in Fort Leavenworth, he suffered increasingly from delusions of grandeur and, removed to a mental institution, died there in 1943.[1]

1. Larsen, *op. cit.*, pp.209–18.

HEARST, William Randolph (1863–1951) (*MEDIA HOAXES*, *see also* **HOAXES IN WARFARE**)
This American newspaper baron (the model for *Citizen Kane* – see **Welles**) was happy to provoke war between the USA and Spain over Cuba to increase circulation of his papers and promote his political future. To this end in 1896 he sent painter Frederick Remington to Cuba to depict Spanish atrocities. Finding none, Remington wired Hearst: 'Everything is quiet. There is no trouble here. There will be no war. I wish to return.' Hearst wired back: 'Please remain. You furnish pictures. I'll furnish the war.' Remington did as he was told, and Hearst succeeded. The pictures published in his papers so incited anti-Spanish feeling that when the US warship *Maine* was blown up in Havana harbour, the US government readily declared war.

In 1913 Hearst papers carried a photo of Mexican children standing in water up to their knees with their hands raised. The caption claimed they'd been herded into the ocean to be shot by Mexican *federales*. In fact it was a tourist photo of children bathing in British Honduras. And in 1936, when the Spanish Civil War broke out, Hearst ran photos showing atrocities supposedly committed by the Loyalists against Franco's followers. Atrocities *were* being committed – but by Franco's troops against the loyalists.[1]

Such devotion to the truth led to Hearst's style of reportage being branded 'Yellow Journalism'. It's widely thought this arose from his sponsorship of the Spanish–American War. In fact it originated with his theft from the rival *New York World* in 1896 of a comic-strip character, 'The Yellow Kid'.[2] Like many a successful entrepreneur, he paid attention to the small things too.

1. Goldberg, *op. cit.*, p.51.
2. *The Penguin Book of Comics*, George Perry and Alan Aldridge, Penguin, London 1989 (1971).

HEBBORN, Eric (1934–) (*ART FORGERIES*)
Born to a large, poor, unhappy family, this English faker of Old Masters always liked to draw, at school using a struck match dipped in ink.

When the headmaster caned him, suspecting potential arson, he decided to commit the crime for which he'd been punished. Setting fire to the school cloakroom, he was sent to Borstal. Happily his talent flourished, and in 1957 he was accepted by the Royal Academy of Art, where he won all the drawing prizes. Leaving Britain in 1964 he settled in Italy, first in Rome, then twenty-five miles away in Anticoli Corrado. Here he established the Pannani Galleries, and settled down to a sun-drenched life of professional 'copying'.

Feeding art dealers drawings which he lets 'experts' attribute to Old Masters, he has mastered many old styles – French, Flemish, German, Swiss, English, Italian – and claims to have fed at least a thousand drawings into the market. Many, sold by auctioneers like Sotheby's and Christie's now grace leading collections and museums, wrongly attributed as Renaissance or to Old Masters. He is bemused by the greed of dealers and the gullibility of 'experts', but not above enjoying being a hoaxer. 'I don't think you'll find an honest man who is also a dealer,' he told a BBC interviewer in 1991, and: 'Only the experts are worth fooling, and the greater the expert, the greater the satisfaction.'[1]

Once he bought a 'real' Breughel for £40, realised it was a fake, made his own improved copy, destroyed the original, then sold his version to a dealer. In time it reached the Metropolitan Museum of Art in New York. Hebborn has admitted it as his own work, yet the Museum, testing the paper and ink (Hebborn makes his own; the paper comes from the flyleaves of old books), still insists that it is a genuine Breughel. The National Gallery of Denmark still claims as genuine a Hebborn 'Piranesi', having paid £14,000 for it in 1969. Another of his 'copies', a 1970 'Van Dyck', ended up in the British Museum.

Hebborn has not done as well from his fakery as the dealers. Producing thirty drawings for an Italian dealer who gave them false attributions, for one of them he received just £750. Later it sold for £9,000. Not surprisingly, and like fellow English faker Tom **Keating**, he sees himself as more honest than most of the people he meets in his work – and, though there may be self-deceit in his claim that he just makes honest copies and lets other rascals make the false attributions, it's not hard to agree with him.

1. 'Portrait of a Master Faker', *Omnibus*, BBC TV, November 1991.

HELL (*See also* **CHRISTIANITY**)
Religions other than Christianity posit afterlife realms in which folk suffer eternal agony or enjoy eternal felicity according to their acts while alive, but Christian dogmatists have made particularly good use of the concept to control social behaviour by stimulating hope or fear in folk. Be good and you'll go to heaven, be bad and you'll go to hell!

Heaven is harder to imagine than hell. The abode of God or the gods, to which the risen Christ is said to have ascended bodily, it implies a perfected state for those who've lived impeccable lives. The popular image is of white-bearded St Peter with his keys at the pearly gates, beyond them a paradise full of harp-strumming angels. In *The Divine Comedy*, the Italian poet Dante (1265–1321) describes ten heavens of paradise – nine the heavens of space, in which spirit is manifested; the tenth the heaven of light and love, beyond human conception.

But nothing ever seems to happen in heaven. Dante's *Inferno* is much more interesting than his *Paradisio*, just as seventeenth-century English poet John Milton's *Paradise Lost* is much more vivid than his *Paradise Regained*. Why? William Blake (1757–1827) remarks in *The Marriage of Heaven and Hell* that: 'The reason Milton wrote in fetters when he wrote of Angels & God, & at liberty when of Devils & Hell, is because he was a true poet and of the Devil's party without knowing it.'[1] So too the Russian novelist Nikolai Gogol (1809–52). In *Dead Souls* he succeeded in portraying hell on earth, but his follow-up attempt to portray heaven caused him such despair he burned the manuscript uncompleted, and died of melancholy only days later.

As for hell, the Church was always in favour of it, opposing the dualist assertion that there is no realm of perpetual torment for sinners after death, but that *this* world is the real hell, ruled by a false god. During the Middle Ages the pious were ever ready to save the souls of those holding such ideas by burning them alive, thus maintaining a deception by which folk were terrorised into obedience. And though Islamic and Hindu traditions also speak of a realm of eternal suffering, few if any of the older pagan religions had promoted such a belief. The Underworld or Afterworld was merely the Land of the Dead. No punishment was involved.

The name 'hell' derives from the Scandinavian *Hel*, a place of ice, snow, mist and gloom, said to be a land of the dead north of the abyss from which the world was born. Later, 'Hel' became the goddess who ruled this realm, but it was left to Christians to appropriate her name, changing mist and snow to hellfire and demons with pitchforks. As if this were not enough, the Roman Church also invented another realm of dubious attraction: purgatory, an afterlife state between heaven and hell, in which those who have lived 'without praise and without blame' (Dante, *Purgatorio*) must endure fires of purification before (via penance, privation, and prayers of aid sent by the still living) earning their heavenly rest. Belief in this nasty half-world became official dogma in 1245, and led to the sale of indulgences – payments made by folk so their dead relatives might more speedily go to heaven. It was this particular scam that Martin Luther denounced in 1517, so stimulating the Reformation.

The taxes we have to pay in this life are bad enough without having to pay up to be saved from a dubious afterlife torment from which nobody can return to prove it exists. But there you are. The best hoaxes are always those which nobody can prove as such.

1. *Poems and Prophecies*, William Blake, Dent Everyman, London 1972.

HELL (UNDER SIBERIA) *(See also* **HELL**)
So nobody really believes in hell any more? The August 1989 edition of a Finnish monthly, *Ammenusastia*, told of a geological team led by Dr Dimitri Azzakov drilling in Siberia (purpose undisclosed) when they found their drill spinning in emptiness at a depth of 14.4km (8.95 miles). Calculating temperatures of about 2,000°F (about 1,100°), Azzakov reportedly said: 'This is ten times higher than anticipated.' More amazing still, when the team lowered microphones into this unexpected hollow vault under the earth, they picked up what sounded like thousands (or millions) of human voices screaming in pain.

'Hopefully,' said Azzakov, 'what we found will stay there.'

Elaborated by fundamentalist newspapers and broadcasting networks across the USA to claim the scientific discovery of hell as a real subterranean location, this bizarre tale was further developed in a letter (later repudiated as a hoax) dated 7 January 1990. In it Age Rendalen Jr ('Special counsellor to the Minister of Justice in Norway') said he heard of hell's discovery in a Trinity Broadcasting Network programme while in California. Returning to Norway he found: 'the newspapers full of reports about this incident'. The letter quoted an interview with Bjarne Nummedal, chief seismologist on the project. In the 4 January 1990 edition of *Asker og Baerums Budstikke* ('Norway's largest and most reputable newspaper'), sixty-five-year-old Nummedal was said to have seen: ' a fountainhead of luminous gas shooting up from the drill site', from which, he claimed, erupted: 'a brilliant being with bat wings'. Nummedal also said he'd seen ambulance teams in the area, and that one ambulance driver had told him they were there to administer a drug erasing short-term memory. Finnish and Norwegian geologists on the team had been instantly dismissed and bribed (by the Ministry of Religious Affairs) to keep quiet or risk their lives.

This was reported (and elaborated) in *The Midnight Cry* (April/July 1990), *Christianity Today* (July 1990), *Biblical Archaeology Survey* (November/December 1990), and other Christian newsletters across the USA. Additions included fangs, evil eyes, screeching, and sky writing. In one version the brilliant bat-winged being revealed itself with the Russian words: 'I have conquered' shining against the dark Siberian sky.

Summarising the tale in *Fortean Times* (No. 72: December 1993), Paul Sieveking comments that the basis of the hoax may be the Kola borehole. Begun in 1970 on the Kola Peninsula north of the White Sea in Soviet Lapland, by 1984 this had descended 12 km (7.46 miles), and was still meeting rock. The temperature at ten kilometres was only 180°C. Large amounts of hot, mineralised water were encountered, also small gas flows – but not, apparently, any damned souls in torment.

HELLMAN, Lillian (1905–84) (*LITERARY HOAXES*)

Posing as a liberal humanitarian, in 1973 this successful American playwright published *Pentimento*, her second volume of memoirs. In it she recalled Julia, a school-friend who, becoming an ardent socialist, persuaded Hellman to help her liberate prisoners of the Nazis before herself being killed by them. In 1977 this dramatic tale of heroism was filmed as *Julia*, with English actress Vanessa Redgrave portraying Julia. The movie was a hit, but what the public didn't know was that Hellman had made it all up.

Or not quite. The real 'Julia' was American-born Muriel Buttinger who, studying psychiatry in pre-war Vienna, worked against the Nazis before in 1939 returning to settle in New Jersey. Hellman had never met her but heard of her through a mutual acquaintance. Buttinger read *Pentimento* when it came out, and wrote to Hellman pointing out how much Julia resembled herself. Hellman never replied, and Buttinger dropped it.

In 1980 on *The Dick Cavett Show* author Mary McCarthy impugned Hellman's honesty. Hellman immediately sued her for $2,225,000. McCarthy's friends began to dig, and Buttinger herself concluded that Hellman had filched her story, published in 1983 by Yale University as *Code Name Mary*. By 1984 it was clear that 'Julia' was indeed a fiction, but Hellman – whose life had been full of fraud, deception, and cruel exploitation of others – conveniently avoided further embarrassment by dying.[1]

1. Lindskoog, *op. cit.*, pp.197–8.

HERSCHEL HOAX, The (*MEDIA HOAXES*)

In August 1835 the New York *Sun* ran a series of scientific articles (by journalist Richard Adams Locke) purportedly reprinted from the *Edinburgh Journal of Science*, which had ceased publication two years earlier. Allegedly by the famous English astronomer Sir John Herschel, the articles reported that Herschel had built a huge new telescope with a magnifying power of 42,000X, letting him study the Moon's surface as if from only a hundred yards away. The first article, setting up the hoax, was crammed with diagrams and technical language that lent an air of authenticity. In the second, 'Herschel' reported discovering on the Moon an inland sea with white beaches, hills and fields covered with poppies, thirty-eight species of forest trees, pyramids of amethysts and a temple made of sapphire. With the *Sun*'s circulation soaring, the third article described heavy-lidded bison, horned bears, tiny reindeer, moose, unicorns, and beavers that walked on their hind legs and lived in lodges with chimneys. On 28 August the fourth instalment, with the *Sun* that day selling 19,360 copies – more than any other paper in the world – Locke had Herschel discover *vespertilio homo* – bat-people, furry, friendly, and four feet high.

With the *Sun*'s competitors frantically reprinting the articles and Locke claiming that Herschel had forty pages of scientific calculations based on his Moon studies, two soberly suspicious scientists from Yale turned up at the *Sun* asking to see these calculations. Sent on a wild-goose chase, they gave up and went home. Three weeks later the *Sun* confessed its hoax, scolding its rivals for copying the articles without giving credit. Some claim that ninety per cent of the *Sun*'s readership believed the articles. This argues a degree of human gullibility that stretches the imagination. Maybe it was only eighty-nine per cent . . .[1,2]

1. Yapp, *op. cit.*, pp.104–5.
2. Lindskoog, *op. cit.*, pp.75–6.

HESS, Rudolf (1894–1987?) (*IMPOSTORS*, *see also* HOAXES IN WARFARE)

On 17 August 1987, in Berlin's Spandau Prison, Prisoner Number Seven hanged himself. His name, said the records, was Rudolf Walter Richard Hess. Once Hitler's deputy and private secretary, he was the last of seven high-placed Nazis held in Spandau. Or was he? Was it the real Rudolf Hess who flew to Scotland on a self-appointed peace mission in 1941? Or was the pilot a double who'd sustained the lie ever since?

Born in Egypt, schooled in Germany, wounded (in the lung, later causing bronchial trouble) then trained to fly during the First World War, in 1920 this most intellectual of Hitler's inner circle was among the future Führer's first recruits. Involved in the attempted Nazi coup (the 'Beerhall Putsch') against the Bavarian government in 1923, he was jailed for eighteen months in the Landsberg fortress with Hitler, helping him to write *Mein Kampf*. When Hitler seized power in 1933, Hess became his deputy. He was as close as anyone to the Führer. Advocating military expansion eastward, he was against war on two fronts. When France capitulated in 1940 and with the invasion of Russia planned, he thought the war with Britain dangerous and unnecessary. So, without Hitler's knowledge, on 10 May 1941 he vanished from Berlin and flew to Scotland on a self-appointed peace mission.

A likely story.

Parachuting into a field near Glasgow, 'Hauptmann Alfred Horn' gave himself up, saying he had an important message for the Duke of Hamilton. Next day the captured German officer told Hamilton they'd met in Germany during the 1936 Olympics and then at a party at his house. Hamilton was puzzled. Now revealing himself as Rudolf Hess, the prisoner said he was on a 'mission of humanity' to negotiate peace between Britain and Germany. A mutual friend, Dr Albrecht Haushofer, had suggested Hamilton as a contact. Haushofer's visiting card was among his confiscated belongings. Also there was the letter Haushofer had sent Hamilton, inviting him to a secret meeting in neutral Portugal.

Hamilton *had* received that letter (after MI5 intercepted it), and the prisoner did look like Hess – but it seemed too good to be true. The Deputy Führer give himself up? What if it was a trick, using an impostor to sound out British willingness to continue the war? Why had he no identification other than Haushofer's card and some photos of Hess as a child?

Flying to inform Churchill in person, Hamilton concluded that only the real Hess would know of Haushofer's letter. He and Haushofer were known colleagues. 'The worm is in the bud,' Churchill muttered. Back in Glasgow with Ivone Kirkpatrick, who as a Berlin embassy official from 1933 to 1938 had often met Hess, Hamilton heard from Foreign Secretary Sir Anthony Eden of a German public radio broadcast. It said Hess had taken off from Augsburg at 18.00 hours on 10 May and not returned. He had left a letter showing 'traces of mental disorder'. He must have 'crashed or met with an accident'. Eden said the British government was about to issue a statement headed: 'Rudolf Hess in England'. A trick it might be, but nobody could imagine what such a trick might achieve. It seemed logical to assume that 'Hess' was exactly who he said he was.

Though not at first recognising Kirkpatrick, as they talked the prisoner mentioned incidents they'd witnessed together in Germany. Hamilton and Kirkpatrick were convinced. This was Hess. Yet Churchill refused even to meet him. It would look bad. He was to be treated like any other prisoner of war. The British government had no interest in him.

After several suicide attempts in prison Hess spent the rest of the war in a mental hospital. His condition supported the Nazi assertion of 'mental disorder', but grounds to doubt his identity remained. His amnesia was perhaps a convenient ploy. He was slovenly; Hess had been neat. He ate anything; Hess had been a vegetarian. Receiving a letter from him sent via neutral Switzerland his wife, Ilsa Hess, said later the handwriting seemed to be Rudolf's, but that he'd seemed oddly anxious to convince her that he really *was* Hess.

Facing the War Crimes Tribunal in Nuremberg in October 1945 he suffered a total memory loss, failing to recognise Göring or Karl Haushofer. Then suddenly his memory returned. Refusing to see Ilsa or his son then or for another twenty-three years (when at last she did meet him she was surprised that his voice had deepened), he was found guilty of conspiracy and crimes against peace, but not of war crimes, and sentenced (with Funk, Donitz, Raeder, von Schirach, von Naurath and

Speer) to life imprisonment in Spandau.

Spandau, in British-occupied West Berlin, was administered jointly by France, Britain, the United States and the Soviet Union. Control alternated monthly between these four nations. By 1966 the other prisoners had all been released – but not Number Seven. The Russians demanded that he stay in Spandau until he died. He gave them a legitimate toehold in West Berlin. That toehold vanished on 17 August 1987. Number Seven's long ordeal was over at last. By then it was widely agreed that he *was* an impostor. In 1973, finally allowed to give him a complete medical check-up, Dr Hugh Thomas of the British Military Hospital in Berlin found no sign of the lung wound from the First World War, no bronchial trouble, nor any of the scars noted in Hess's medical records. 'What happened to your war wounds?' asked Thomas. 'Too late, too late,' muttered Hess.

Studying the documents about the flight to Scotland, Thomas concluded that a Messerschmitt 110D could never have made the 850-mile journey had Hess made as many detours as he'd claimed. A photograph of the plane as it took off, taken by Hess's adjutant Pintsch, showed no spare fuel tanks.

In his book *The Murder of Rudolf Hess*, Thomas suggests that Hess never left Germany, but was killed there and replaced by a double. If so, why, and by whom? Göring detested Hess, and Himmler, head of the SS and ambitious to replace Hitler, wanted Hitler's deputy out of the way. Hess truly wanted peace with the British – in July 1940 he had gone to Lisbon to discuss it with the Duke of Windsor – and it is known that Hitler too wanted peace with the British, in order to concentrate on Russia. It may be that Hess truly did mean to fly to Scotland but that his enemies, getting wind of his plan, had him eliminated, perhaps on the night of 9 May. Hitler, who would not have tolerated the murder, had to be kept in the dark, meaning that 'Hess' had to seem to arrive in Britain – and duly did, the double being hastily coached and despatched, probably from a Danish airfield. Landing in Britain, he didn't fool the intelligence services, who made no attempts to use him for propaganda purposes.

Then why did this double not end his deception after the war? Thomas mentions Himmler's habit of eliminating whole families of 'traitors' to the Reich – reason enough to keep quiet before the Nuremberg trials and Himmler's execution. Thereafter, confused and mentally exhausted following a series of breakdowns and suicide attempts, he may simply have lapsed into a state of blank indifference as to his fate. Who'd believe him anyway? Everyone wanted him to be Hess, especially the Russians. It was: 'too late, too late'.

Yet, if he really was an impostor, it seems odd that no evidence or even the hint of a clue as to his real identity has yet emerged.[1]

1. Wilson and Wilson, *op. cit.*, pp.124–36.

HEWITT, Marvin (1922–) (*IMPOSTORS*)
Though less versatile than Ferdinand Waldo **Demara**, this American
impostor found it just as hard to be himself. Son of a Philadelphia
policeman, a loner already versed in advanced mathematics aged ten, he
longed to go to college, but routine schoolwork bored him, and his
family was too poor to send him. Leaving school at seventeen, for six
years he worked in factories and goods yards then, seeing an advertisement for a senior preparatory school teacher at a military academy, he
applied, claiming to be a Temple University graduate. Getting the job,
he enjoyed the respect of pupils and colleagues alike. Next, borrowing a
name and qualifications from a universities *Who's Who*, he applied as an
aerodynamicist at an aircraft factory and got this job too. But the name
he'd chosen was too well known: he was found out.

It didn't dent his confidence. Stealing the name and qualifications
of Julius Ashkin of Columbia University, he began teaching physics at
Philadelphia College of Pharmacy and Science. His capacity to do
complex calculus in his head was admired; his classes did as well as
any others in the annual exams, but surely 'Ashkin' was worth over
$1,750 a year! Approaching other colleges, he enhanced his prospects
by introducing the Christie Engineering Company to his references –
simply by getting letterheads printed and hiring a secretarial service
to handle mail. Minnesota Bemidji State Teachers' College inquired,
and Christie sent a glowing testimonial. Now, with a job paying
$4,000 a year, he married, telling his wife that because he'd qualified
under an assumed name he had to keep using it. She accepted this,
but he hit a snag. The Bemidji president had been at Columbia, just
like Ashkin, and kept wanting to discuss the good old days. Time to
move on, this time to the physics department at St Louis University at
$4,500 per annum, teaching nuclear physics, statistical mechanics,
and tensor analysis to Ph.D level. Again, he was well liked, but one
day a colleague returned from Argonna National Laboratory in
Chicago, saying he'd run into an old friend who'd worked with
Ashkin at Columbia, and remembered him.

Hewitt survived this, but in 1948 read in the journal *Physical Review* a
paper by the real Julius Ashkin, an assistant professor at Rochester
University. This he explained by saying that he'd signed it from Rochester
as he'd done its background work there. Hewitt moved on to the University
of Utah, where his St Louis and Columbia references landed him a
$5,800-a-year job as a full professor. But the fates are not mocked. Just a
month later a letter came addressed to 'Dr Julius Ashkin(?)'

It was from the real Julius Ashkin. He demanded an end to the
imposture, while promising not to 'take any immediate steps to notify
the university officials'. But one of Ashkin's colleagues was less merciful.
Hauled before the Utah president, Hewitt had to admit the truth. And
though offered work as a research fellow to qualify for his former post

legitimately, or a transfer to another college, he was too shaken to accept either offer.

After eighteen months at his mother's home in Philadelphia, 'George Hewitt' was born. He had a D.Sc from John Hopkins and had been 'research director of the Radio Corporation of America'. Inventing an RCA vice-president as reference, he began teaching electrical engineering at Arkansas University – until an RCA chief came seeking recruits.

Back in Philadelphia, now with twin baby sons to support, next he was Clifford Berry, Ph.D, teaching at New York State Maritime College, then Kenneth Yates, Ph.D, teaching at the University of New Hampshire. Here a student grew suspicious of lapses in his knowledge, and from the *American Men of Science* catalogue learned that the real Yates worked near Chicago for an oil company. Again Hewitt owned up and resigned, but this time the media picked up the story. His career as a fake professor was over for good.

Why did he never take the trouble to gain real qualifications, of which he was clearly capable? That's one for the psychoanalysts. 'If only they'd let me be a professor, I'd never want anything else or lie,' he said wistfully. 'I lied only to get those jobs. I was a good teacher. I've never really hurt anyone.' Except, perhaps, himself and his family.[1]

1. Blundell, *op. cit.*, pp.166–9.

HISTORICAL HOAXES (*See* *CONCORDANCE*)

HITLER DIARIES, The (*LITERARY HOAXES*)
As if the publishing world hadn't already burned its fingers in 1971 with Clifford **Irving**'s fake biography of Howard Hughes, in 1981 the German magazine *Stern* spent a fortune on diaries purportedly by Adolf Hitler. For almost two years it made virtually no effort to authenticate them. Then in 1983 the truth emerged: they were a total fake.

The hoaxer was Konrad 'Konni' Kujau. Born in the Saxon town of Loebau (from 1946 to 1991 in East Germany), in 1957 he fled to the West to avoid arrest for petty theft. Settling near Stuttgart as 'Peter Fischer' and twice jailed for minor offences, with fellow refugee Edith Lieblang he opened the Pelican Dance Bar in 1962. This failed and he was again jailed, for forging luncheon vouchers. Edith started the Lieblang Cleaning Company, and he went straight until a 1968 police check revealed 'Peter Fischer' as Konrad Kujau, wanted for evading a jail sentence. Back behind bars he went, but when he got out, the cleaning company began making a profit. He and Edith were able to visit his family in Loebau – and there he had the Big Idea.

Advertising for old Nazi memorabilia, he smuggled into West Germany so many relics – uniforms, helmets, medals, flags – that by 1974 his apartment was full. Moving to a shop in Stuttgart's Aspergstrasse, he began forging documents of authentication so as to justify raising his prices. For a rusty old First World War helmet he faked a note by Rudolf **Hess** saying Hitler had worn it in 1917. He began faking not only paintings by Hitler, but the Führer's handwriting. He was good at it.

Enter Fritz Steifel, owner of an engineering works. Finding Kujau's shop in 1975, over the next six years he paid 250,000 marks (furtively transferred from his company account to the Lieblang company as 'cleaning costs') for 160 drawings and paintings, plus manuscript poems, letters and speech notes, all supposedly by Hitler. Thus encouraged, in 1978, in pencil and ink and using a 1935 Nazi Party yearbook, Kujau copied out a chronology of Hitler's daily life from January to June of that year. Steifel readily bought this as 'Hitler's Diary' – and then in 1980 was visited by Gerd Heidemann.

In 1955 this Nazi-obsessed photo-journalist had joined Hamburg's *Stern* magazine. An obsessive collector, in 1971 his second wife left him, tired of sharing their home with his war games and toy soldiers. Two years later, buying Göring's old motor yacht the *Carin II*, he'd met the Nazi chief's daughter Edda and begun an affair with her. Now amid a circle of former Nazis he found the yacht's upkeep costly. Leaving Edda for Gina, an ex-airline stewardess, in 1979 he honeymooned in South America, seeking Martin Bormann and Josef Mengele, Auschwitz's 'Doctor of Death'. Instead he found Klaus Barbie, the 'Butcher of Lyon'. Back home with his debts now astronomical, a friend put him in touch with Steifel – and he saw the 'Hitler Diary'. Instantly hooked, he wanted to know more.

Refusing to name Kujau, Steifel hinted at another twenty-six volumes, and inferred (as Kujau had told him) that the source had highly placed relatives in East Germany. Heidemann knew that one of the last flights out of beleaguered Berlin on 20 April 1945, carrying Hitler's personal papers to his 'Alpine Redoubt' near Berchtesgaden, had crashed near Börnersdorf on the Czech border. He concluded that the diaries must have been among these papers and in East Germany ever since. So on 15 November 1980, with Thomas Walde, editor of *Stern*'s historical department, he visited the East German graves of the plane crew. An intermediary said he thought the diary had come from a dealer called Fischer, and agreed to pass on an offer of two million marks for the other volumes.

On 15 January 1981 this intermediary rang with Fischer's phone number. Tense, Heidemann called. Yes, answered 'Fischer', he not only had the diaries but also other Hitler manuscripts, such as a third volume of *Mein Kampf* and an opera the Führer had composed in his youth, *Wieland der Schmied* ('Wayland Smith').

Bypassing *Stern*'s editor Peter Koch (who'd told him to drop his Nazi obsessions), Heidemann went with Walde to three senior executives of Grüner and Jahr, the owners of *Stern*. Excited by their dossier, managing director Manfred Fischer authorised payment of 85,000 marks for each diary volume, 200,000 for *Mein Kampf* part three, and 500,000 for the remaining archives. Heidemann flew to Stuttgart with 200,000 marks and Göring's dress uniform (a gift from Edda), and so met 'Fischer', alias Kujau. As excited by the uniform as the cash, Kujau promised to get the rest of the diaries, and promptly set to work.

Drawing on his huge reference library, in three weeks Kujau forged the first three. They consisted of lists of official engagements, personal notes, and trivia as dull as it was worthless. Fixing on the covers a red wax seal of a German eagle and a note by Hess declaring the diaries to be Hitler's property, he took them to Heidemann on the *Carin II*. Next day the five men in on the secret at Grüner and Jahr, though unable to read the old Germanic script of the diaries, all agreed they were undoubtedly genuine.

Over the next two years, whenever Kujau said a new consignment had arrived from East Germany, Heidemann would fly to Stuttgart, collect and photocopy the diaries, then put them in Grüner and Jahr's company safe. Only he knew he was paying Kujau just 50,000 marks per volume and pocketing the other 35,000 himself. With Manfred Fischer promoted, his successor Gerd Schulte-Hillen was let in on the secret, and in August authorised payments to Heidemann of 565,000 marks. When Heidemann said the price per volume had gone up to 200,000 marks because the East German general supplying them had to pay large bribes, Schulte-Hillen handed over another 600,000 marks.

Meanwhile Walde and his assistant Leo Pesch began turning the utterly banal material into a book, the source of sensational articles to be published in January 1983, the fiftieth anniversary of Hitler's rise to power. The date passed, and only in February, with syndication rights being marketed to magazines round the world, did *Stern* decide to focus on the story of *how* the diaries had been found. Three 'experts' had already asserted that the handwriting was Hitler's, but now more detailed authentication was required. On 28 March a police expert said six of nine specimens revealed a paper whitener not in use until after the war. Rung about this, Kujau seemed unbothered, while neither Heidemann or Walde told *Stern*. Meanwhile in London, rights to the story having been offered to Rupert Murdoch's Times Newspapers, on 1 April the assistant editor of *The Times* asked Lord Dacre (Hugh Trevor-Roper, author of *The Last Days of Hitler*) to authenticate the diaries.

Examining the fifty-eight volumes lodged in a Zurich bank, Trevor-Roper declared himself: 'satisfied that the documents are authentic'. Within the day, visiting the bank himself, Murdoch offered $3.25 million for the English language rights. Then *Newsweek* offered $3 million for the American rights. Planning to launch the story on 3 May, *Stern* demanded $4.25 million from both of them. It was a mistake. The rivals walked out, with *Newsweek* already owning the text of the articles and ready to publish. Advancing the story to its 25 April issue, *Stern* went back to Murdoch who, now offering only $1.2 million, planned to announce his scoop in the 24 April edition of the *Sunday Times*.

By now there were doubters, like David Irving, a far-right English historian who held that the Holocaust was a myth propagated by the Jews. On 22 April he declared on BBC TV that the diaries were fake. And when Trevor-Roper, by now also dubious, called *Sunday Times* editor Frank Giles, Murdoch's reply would have delighted **Hearst**. 'Fuck Dacre!' he said. 'Publish!' *Sunday Times* circulation immediately went up by 60,000 as Heidemann, another 300,000 marks in hand, collected the last four diaries from Kujau.

But the jig was up. Even as *Stern, Paris Match, Newsweek*, the *Sunday Times* and other periodicals published their first instalments, new forensic evidence proved the diaries fake. Cancelling publication, *Stern* questioned Heidemann for hours before he admitted Kujau's existence and phone number. Heidemann was sacked and a week later Kujau gave himself up. Their trial began a year later, Kujau charged with receiving over 1.5 million marks; Heidemann with having stolen between 1.7 and 4.6 million marks. Kujau was jailed for four and a half years, Heidemann for four years and eight months. *Stern*, said the judge, had been so reckless as in effect to be an accomplice to the hoax. Over five million marks of Grüner and Jahr's money was lost; *Stern* ultimately lost over nineteen million. Murdoch, who'd never cared if the diaries were genuine or not, alone was happy.

HOAXES IN WARFARE (*See also* **HESS, JONES, MUSSOLINI**)

'In wartime,' declared Winston Churchill, 'truth is so precious that she should always be attended by a bodyguard of lies.' This famous quote from the Second World War led to the label 'Bodyguard' for the deception operation mounted by the Allies to persuade the Germans that the real D-Day invasion of Europe would take place at the Pas de Calais a hundred miles from the actual beach-head selected for the landings. But in fact Churchill didn't invent the phrase. He told one of his private secretaries he'd got it from Stalin, who claimed it as an old Russian proverb, and who'd also told Roosevelt and Churchill himself that in fighting the Nazis the Russians had: 'made considerable use' of dummy tanks, aircraft, and airfields, and that: 'radio deception had also proved effective'.[1]

The use of hoax in warfare goes back a long way. The climax of Europe's earliest prose epic, the *Iliad* by Homer (*c.*850 BC) tells how, after a ten-year siege, the city of Troy was finally taken by the besieging Greeks only when, all direct assault exhausted, Ulysses persuaded the Greeks to build a giant Wooden Horse, leave it before the city gates, and withdraw. The Trojans, believing the Greeks had abandoned the war and left this odd gift to acknowledge their bravery, opened the gates and dragged in the artificial beast, at which the Greek warriors hidden inside it leapt out and seized the initiative. So Troy fell.

In the fourteenth century there was another siege. During the Hundred Years War between England and France, the French town of Angoulême was in English hands under the Earl of Norwich, but the besieging French under the Duke of Normandy had forced the English to the point of surrender. So Norwich requested an interview with his opponent, who assumed he wished to surrender. 'No,' said Norwich, 'but as tomorrow is the feast of the Virgin, to whom I know that you, sir, as well as myself, bear a great devotion, I desire a cessation of arms for that day.'

This being agreed, next day Norwich told his men to pack their bags and marched them out towards the French camp. The French, thinking they were betrayed and attacked, ran to arms, but Norwich sent a messenger ahead to remind the Duke: there was to be no fighting today. The English (known, incidentally, as: 'the bare-bottomed army' due to the dysentry so plaguing them that it wasn't worth keeping their britches on) only wished to leave without being killed. Normandy, whose men had been relishing the slaughter ahead while he'd anticipated the ransom to be won for noble English hostages like Norwich, was furious at the trick, but his honour allowed no option. 'I see the Governor has outwitted me,' he said through gritted teeth, 'but let us be content with gaining Angoulême.' So the English army passed safely, and lived.[2]

Such a trick wouldn't work today, nor (in the First World War) were many English commanders as smart as Norwich. The youth of Britain ('Lions led by donkeys', the Germans called them) obeyed the call that YOUR COUNTRY NEEDS YOU! and died in the trenches of Flanders, sent over the top by generals who rarely left their well-appointed coastal villas. Among them was Percy **Toplis**, the 'Monocled Mutineer'.

Despite the murderous deadlock on land, the British sea blockade of Germany secured the safety of Allied shipping. Convinced that the only way to beat the British (with the USA not yet in the war, and France and Russia reeling) was to cut their trade routes, the Germans resorted to ruse.

At dock in Hamburg in 1916, the three-masted windjammer *Maletta* seemed quite innocent. The timber on her decks carried the names of Norwegian lumber yards; the crew's worn clothing, with Norwegian labels, hid letters and snapshots from family homes in Norway; there were pictures of the Norwegian king and queen on the cabin walls – even the captain's underwear was embroidered: Captain Knudsen of the *Maletta*.

In fact the *Maletta* was the *Seeadler* ('Sea Eagle'), a German warship. Built in Glasgow in 1888 and captured by a U-boat in 1915, now with a Norwegian-speaking German crew under Count Felix von Luckner, the

Seeadler's mission was to run the naval blockade and sink British shipping with its hidden 4.2 inch guns. There were secret rooms everywhere. The wardroom deck, on a hydraulic lift, could vanish below at the touch of a button. The log was genuine, stolen in Copenhagen from the real *Maletta* by von Luckner himself. And should the British board, 'Captain Knudsen' even had a wife, Jeannette, to be acted by seaman Hugo Schmidt, complete with powder, wig, and falsies.

On 23 December 1916, *Seeadler* sailed. South of Iceland she was boarded and cleared by British inspectors. On 9 January she met a British coal-freighter, the *Gladys Royal*. Bringing down the Norwegian flag and running up the Imperial German Navy ensign at the very last moment to diminish risk of radio alarm, von Luckner took his prize, captured the crew, then sunk the freighter. Next day he took and sunk the sugar-carrying *Lundy Island*, and in the next two months took and sunk another ten ships. The only man to die was an American, killed when gunfire hit the freighter *Horngacth*. *Seeadler* became overcrowded. Transferring his captives to a French sailing ship, the *Cambronne*, von Luckner headed for the Pacific. The *Cambronne* alerted the British, who sent cruisers after the raider, but it was a freak wave, not enemy fire, that finished the *Seeadler*. While von Luckner and his crew were ashore on the Pacific isle of Mopeha, the wave smashed in and ruined the ship on the reefs. Later the Germans were captured in Fiji by a British steamer.

The Second World War saw the odd case of Major William Martin, RM – the dead man who won a battle. With the Allies taking North Africa in 1942, it was obvious to the Nazis that Sicily was next. It was the logical stepping stone to Italy. To make them think otherwise, British Intelligence suggested that the body of a courier seemingly killed in a plane crash at sea, fake top-secret papers on it, should drift ashore on the coast of neutral Spain for the inspection of local German agents. To simulate the victim of a drowning, the corpse of a pneumonia victim was obtained and 'reborn' as Major William Martin of the Royal Marines. He carried two letters, one from the Vice-Chief of the Imperial General Staff explaining to General Alexander in North Africa why he could not invade Sicily, the invasion target being elsewhere; the other from Lord Mountbatten to Sir Andrew Cunningham, Admiral of the Fleet, with the subtly indiscreet sentence: 'He might bring some sardines (Sardinia) with him.' So, on 30 April 1943 'Major Martin' was consigned to the sea from HM submarine *Seraph*. Found by a fisherman on a beach near Huelva, the Spanish told the British. Major Martin was buried with full military honours. Meanwhile German agents *had* picked up the letters. Even Hitler was convinced that Sardinia was the main allied target. With German forces scattered, and with another hoax suggesting an invasion of Greece, the allied invasion of Sicily was met by only two German divisions.

Then there's the tale of 'Black Radio'. German troops enjoyed the forces' radio station, Gustav Siegfried Eins (GS1). The music was good, the news well covered, and it spoke for the ordinary soldier. They listened when it condemned profiteering back home 'while our brave troops are freezing to death in Russia', or praised doctors whose work at camps for bombed-out civilians had cut the death rate from cholera and typhus to just sixty a week, or described methods used by deserters on the run to get into neutral countries.

The broadcasts came from English transmitters strong enough to drown out real forces' broadcasts. Blending truth with lie, they played on the fears of men far from home even as each night British aircraft dropped *News for the Troops*, a well-faked newssheet resembling a real German forces' paper. Meanwhile the Nazis had hired Swiss astrologer Karl Ernst Krafft to forge verses allegedly by the famed French prophet Nostradamus (1503–66) predicting their victory. The Allies hired novelist Louis de Wohl (*see* **Past-Life Memories**) to do the same, in reverse.

Many other such scams were invented by both sides, but most effective of all were the deceptions that kept the Nazis off track in the crucial months before the Allied invasion of Europe on 6 June 1944. Targeted for Normandy, the invasion risked the lives of almost 200,000 men. Five thousand ships and 9,000 planes were involved. Of fifty-nine German divisions in France, on D-Day only six were in Normandy. The Allies had persuaded the Germans that the real thrust would be at the Pas de Calais, where screens filled with the false images of approaching planes and ships. On that morning, the Allies 'attacked' near Cherbourg. The airborne assault: 'consisted of three British paratroopers, hundreds of exploding dummies, a chemical preparation exuding smoke, and a battery of Victrolas amplifying recordings of gunfire, soldier talk, and troop movements.[3] So a German infantry division was diverted from its position behind Omaha Beach, allowing the US Marines to take it. Meanwhile the BBC broadcast messages to the French Resistance that the Normandy thrust had been contained; that forces meant for the Pas de Calais had been diverted there, but were being replaced by fresh American troops poised to invade as soon as enough Nazi troops had been diverted to Normandy. A British agent code-named Garbo gave out news of the Normandy attack four hours before it began, but suggested it was only a diversion for the Pas de Calais assault. Learning of this, Hitler countermanded his own previous orders, so keeping the Fifteenth Army away from Normandy. The Pas de Calais beaches were pounded by bombers as the Normandy landings began. Allied losses were 2,500 dead, not the 20,000 or more Churchill had feared. Under a year later the Second World War ended.

Did Homer know what he'd started?

1. Goldberg, *op. cit.*, pp.58–9.

2. McCormick, *op. cit.*, pp.15–16.
3. *The Secret War Against Hitler*, William Casey, Regnery Gateway, New York 1988, as quoted in Goldberg, *op. cit.*, p.57.

HOFFMAN, Abbie (contemporary) (*PRANKS*)

Ironic prankster and radical political organiser since first springing to the horrified attention of Middle America by releasing pigs in the streets of Chicago during the riotous Democratic Party Convention of 1968, Abbie Hoffman declares that: 'Pranks are symbolic warfare.' The author of *Revolution for the Hell of It*, he is also responsible for the classic prankster's manual, *Steal This Book*, which was banned in England and Canada. Of this ban, he comments: 'They're democracies – what do you expect?'

A founder of the tongue-in-cheek Yippie movement and defendant in the notorious Chicago Seven trial after the 1968 Convention, seven years on the run from a jail sentence before resurfacing with new subversive campaigns to make people think, he adds: 'When I go for the emperor I try to pull his pants down.' Yet his more serious radical brethren have not always approved. In France he found his idea that 'revolution could be fun' denounced as: 'Only an American could be so goddamned silly.' His response to this is that the only way to get a point across in the USA is: 'to render unto Caesar's Palace that which is Caesar's Palace'.[1] Thus in an early prank *c.*1966 he and other Yippies (Youth International Party; an ironic take-off of 'hippies') got into the public gallery of the New York Stock Exchange and from it threw 200 single dollar bills to the floor below. Trading stopped for six minutes as stockbrokers and dealers fought for the bills that fluttered down. Subsequently a bullet-proof shield was built in front of the gallery.

Another prank attributed to Hoffman as a way to embarrass 'Caesar's Palace' is to rent a bank safety deposit box, insert a packet of frozen fish, and not come back. Soon the entire vault will stink of dead fish but, by law, the bank is forbidden to go through the boxes to find and quench the source of the stench.

One Valentine's Day prank: with friends he sent 3,000 joints of marijuana to 3,000 people randomly picked from the phone book, complete with instructions on how to smoke them, and ending with the advice: 'Oh, by the way, just holding this joint qualifies you for five years in prison in this state.' Someone held up one of the joints on TV: the police broke into the studio and arrested him. A special squad was set up to track down the recipients of the supposedly deadly weed.

Another time, seeking a negotiating platform over other issues, the Yippies threatened to seed New York City reservoirs with the hallucinogen LSD. All hell broke loose. Six thousand National Guards patrolled the reservoirs. Told by Hoffman that this was a waste of time; LSD simply doesn't dissolve so easily, the Deputy Mayor admitted: 'I *know* it can't happen, but we can't take any chances anyway'. The myth of awful LSD, Hoffman points out, had superseded reality.

With such pranks (irresponsible? dangerous?) his aim was to provoke absurdly over-the-top official reactions. Why? To reveal, as he sees it, the lunacy underlying the taken-for-granted 'normality' of the social system – and to make people laugh, then think.

Later he turned to environmental issues, fighting acid rain, nuclear waste transport, and toxic dumping. In upstate New York, with the Army Corps of Engineers threatening to destroy river-island communities for an Army project, he started a group, 'Save the River'. He promoted a letter-writing campaign, but the conservative local folk under threat were all out with their chainsaws, cutting winter wood supplies. Nobody wrote. Then the movie *The Texas Chainsaw Massacre* gave him an idea. A friend dressed up in a dayglo-bright Pink Panther suit, white patent-leather pumps, blonde beehive hairdo and so on, placed an ad in the local paper. 'FREE ARMY SURPLUS CHAIN-SAWS,' it ran. 'Pay postage only. Call or write Walter F—, Army Corps of Engineers, Buffalo, New York.' It also gave the phone number. The Army was swamped with calls from people claiming free chainsaws. 'BUFFALO CHAINSAW HOAX', ran the local headlines.

It was only then that the farmers, realising who'd done it, and both amused and now stirred up by the prank, began writing letters of protest objecting to the Army plans.[2]

Pranks work best, says Hoffman, 'when people don't know if you're serious or not . . .' He's joking, of course.

1. Vale and Juno (eds), *op. cit.*, p.66.
2. *Ibid.*, p.67.

HOFMAN, Mark (1954–) (*LITERARY HOAXES*)
In September 1823 the founder of Mormonism, Joseph Smith, had a vision in which the angel Moroni led him to buried golden plates, on them written the message and history of the religion later based in Utah. In 1972 Mark Hofman, of a devout Mormon family, joined the Melchizedek priesthood and completed a mission to England. But his belief was not deep. Dropping out of Utah State university he began to collect (and forge) Mormon memorabilia. With interest in Mormon history and 'faith-promoting' documents growing, he produced a transcript that Smith claimed to have hand-copied from the golden plates, then a letter from the Prophet's mother confirming the account. Selling these and other documents to Salt Lake City dealers and directly to the Church, by 1985 his expensive lifestyle had led him into debt. Announcing a fictitious chestful of materials removed by a disillusioned early Mormon, he pledged it to a dealer for $185,000 even as, unaware that Hofman was a faker, a devout local financier, Steve Christensen,

became involved with him. Yet by now, in bad need of cash, Hofman had decided to 'discover' a literary rarity – the 'Freeman's Oath'.

This, the earliest (1639) broadsheet in English published in America, had long been thought lost. In March 1985 Hofman planted a forged ballad sheet, 'The Oath of a Freeman', in a browsing bin in a New York bookstore, then bought it with other items, taking care to get an itemised receipt headed with the shop's name. Informing his New York dealer of his good luck he set about the detailed forgery. Taking a modern facsimile edition of the 1640 *Bay Psalm Book*, printed by the same Massachusetts press which a year earlier had produced the 'Freeman's Oath', he photographed several pages then cut up the enlargements one letter or group of letters at a time. So building a text of the 'Oath' and reducing it to the right size, he had a line block made, drilled and ground down certain letters to produce irregularities, then made ink to his own formula to evade detection by dating tests. Printed on paper of the period, by April his 'Oath' was being scrutinised at Washington's Library of Congress. The experts were satisfied but the price tag of $1.5 million was too steep. The Library declined to buy it.

Hofman's earlier pledge, of that chestful of materials, was now long overdue. He was already selling items supposedly from it and soon, via Steve Christensen, the Church would learn the truth. On 15 October, with Hofman's cheques bouncing, a bomb killed Christensen at his office. A second bomb, meant for Christensen's boss, killed the man's wife instead. Their company was in trouble: was the killer a crazed creditor? When next day a car bomb wounded Hofman, the police were not fooled. His tale of a package falling to the car's floor matched neither the state of the car nor his injuries. His trial began in April 1986; in January 1987 he was jailed for between five years and life for murder and fraud.

As for the 'Oath', its authenticity fell apart not through scientific analysis but via the witness of a man who knew about old printshop practice. Of various giveaways, the most damning was that the ornamental border round the 'Oath' was far too close to the type area of the text. Packed with so many metal letters and spaces, the type frame (forme) would have demanded tightening wedges (furniture) between border and text. Hofman had been clever, but not clever enough.[1]

1. Newnham, *op. cit.*, pp.158–61.

HOLLYWOOD HOAXES (*MEDIA HOAXES*, see also REICHENBACH, Harry)

World centre of an industry devoted to the creation and sale of celluloid fantasy, drama and dream, Hollywood and hoax (of one sort or another) are synonymous. What to make of a multibillion-dollar-a-year business based on optical illusion and sited in a region that a century ago was desert? Everything that comes out of Hollywood is a sort of mirage. nothing is as it seems. 'Motion pictures' are produced from 'stills'. Fake towns are built on sets with nothing behind the façades. 'Family values' are promoted by producers who wouldn't know a family value if they saw one. Publicists promote the glamour of movie 'stars' whose carefully presented public lives are the opposite of those they live in private.

Take all those macho, handsome leading men whose screen virility made women swoon the world over for half a century. How about Errol Flynn? Not only a Nazi spy but the lover of handsome Tyrone Power. Cary Grant, alias Archibald Leach? He shacked up for years with Randolph Scott. As for Rock Hudson, alias Ray Scherer, for years his screen courtship of Doris Day fooled millions of fans, before his miserable death from AIDS. James Dean, like Rudolf Valentino, was privately shy and insecure, not so dashing at all. And how would folk feel about John Wayne, Kirk Douglas, Omar Sharif, and Karl Malden were their real names more widely known: Marion Morrison, Isidore Demsky, Michel Shalhouz, and Mladen Sekulovich? Would it matter?

Deception is so much part of Tinseltown that even those writing about it aren't what they seem. For years Hollywood's biggest columnists, making or breaking careers, were Louella Parsons and Hedda Hopper, born Louella Oettinger and Elda Furry.

Sometimes it's understandable. Stefanie Powers gave up not-so-easy-to-pronounce Stefania Federkiewicz; suave, oh-so-English Laurence Harvey would have had problems getting across as Larushka Mischa Skikne. Or would he? Gina Lollobrigida resisted every studio demand that she should change her name, and she did all right for herself.

Is it a surprise to learn that Clara Bow, Tyrone Power, Clark Gable, Ava Gardner, and Alan Ladd all used their real names? But they all worked in the world of deception too. Alan Ladd was so short that in love scenes with tall actresses he had to stand on a platform or she had to stand in a trench. Johnny Weissmuller (Tarzan) may be congratulated for not changing his name to Johnny Savage; also for the five gold medals he won swimming for the USA in the Olympics of 1924 and 1928. The problem is, when he won those medals he was not an American citizen. All his life he said he was born in Windber, Pennsylvania, but in fact he was born (2 June 1904) in Freidorf, then in Hungary, now in Romania. Not even his five wives got to hear of it, far less his only son, Johnny Jr – but then, Tarzan always was the strong, silent type.[1]

Hollywood is always careful to project a collective image of glamour and success, but sometimes the façade cracks. Marilyn Monroe (no, that wasn't her real name either, and she was a brunette, not a blonde) projected sexy assurance, but her life was sad as her death was suspicious. Was she murdered? Had she been threatening to blackmail Jack and Bobby Kennedy? Both were deep into Hollywood secrets, into layers of deception. Their father Joe had owned a studio, actor Peter Lawford was an in-law.

Lawford, of course, ran with the Sinatra 'Rat Pack'. So how did Ol' Blue Eyes get famous? Because in 1942 publicist George Evans hired twelve young bobby-soxers at $5 each, trained them to scream, moan, and faint when Frank sang, packed a theatre by giving away hundreds of tickets, then alerted the press. It worked better than he could ever have imagined. When the trained twelve faked the screaming faint, another eighteen girls in the audience fainted for real. Mass hysteria. Soon, with publicity everywhere, every time Sinatra appeared he was besieged by thousands of screaming, fainting girls.[2]

Ambition and cruelty go hand in hand. Publicist Al Horwitz loved sending struggling actors a wire reading DISREGARD MY PREVIOUS TELEGRAM. ZANUCK. His victims, assuming the wire came from movie mogul Darryl F. Zanuck, were thereafter plunged into a morass of false hope followed by anguish and disappointment. They had, in short, been 'spiegeled' – a Hollywoodism for being lied to, derived from the name of the movie mogul responsible for many great movies from *The African Queen* to *Lawrence of Arabia* – Sam Spiegel. Claiming to be Austrian (in fact Polish), for years after his illegal arrival in Hollywood in 1939 he avoided the Immigration Service by using the name S.P. Eagle. Casting his movies he secured top stars by falsely assuring them that other top stars had already signed up. Yet that's small beer compared with the shoddy case of David **Begelman**. Swindling his actors by forging and cashing $10,000 cheques in their names, this Columbia president should have been jailed for years. Instead, after a year's probation he got an even better job, as head of MGM. That's showbiz.

Charlie Chaplin too was once cruelly hoaxed. Introduced in Germany to the new star Pola Negri, he whispered to a not-so-friendly friend: 'How do you say in German, "You are the most beautiful woman I have ever seen"?' '*Du bist ekelhaft*', came the reply. So, bowing, Chaplin tried this line – and got his face slapped. Bemused, only later he learned that what he'd really said was: 'You are disgusting.'

But one of the biggest Hollywood hoaxers of all was swashbuckling actor Errol Flynn – not because he changed his name (he didn't) or was bisexual (he was), but because before and during the Second World War he was a Nazi spy. Calling Flynn 'the number-one-son-of-a-bitch' of all the people he ever met, veteran journalist George Seldes claims that some 200 US government documents now available under the Freedom of Information act reveal that Flynn routinely took photos of US naval installations and sent them to Japan.

Meeting Seldes in the main Paris police station as they waited for permits to enter Spain during the Spanish Civil War, Flynn said he was going to Madrid with over a million Hollywood dollars to supply a Republican hospital. Also he had medicine and food for the International brigade. At the front line, Seldes noted that Flynn preferred the comforts of a 'good, clean whorehouse' when the bullets started flying, maybe sensible enough, but next day Flynn sent to Paris what seemed an innocent telegram. It carried a code triggering a hoax prearranged in Hollywood. 'ERROL FLYNN KILLED ON SPANISH FRONT,' reported the New York *Daily News* next day; a statement soon modified by Warner Brothers in Paris. Flynn wasn't dead, only injured. Appearing in Barcelona with an ostentatiously bandaged left arm, bold Captain Blood milked the publicity then left rapidly.

As for Flynn's stated objectives, Seldes notes that: 'There were no ambulances, no hospital, no medical supplies, no food for the Spanish Republic, and not one cent of money. The war correspondents said bitterly it was the cruellest hoax of the time. Flynn was one of the most despicable human beings that ever lived, and had used a terrible war just to advertise one of his cheap movies.'[3]

When years later this tale emerged, Flynn only dropped a $2 million libel suit when Seldes and others threatened to testify against him. When aged fifty he died in 1959, *Life* magazine remarked that: 'the truth was not in him when a lie made a better story'.[4]

That's showbiz. That's Hollywood.

1. Goldberg, *op. cit.*, pp.179-201, quoting the following:
2. *His Way: The Unauthorised Biography of Frank Sinatra*, Kitty Kelley, Bantam, New York 1986.
3. *Witness to a Century*, George Seldes, Ballantine, New York 1987.
4. *Errol Flynn: The Untold Story*, Charles Higham, Doubleday, New York 1980.

HOME, Daniel Dunglass (*See* **MEDIUMS**)

HOOK, Theodore Edward (19th century) (*PRANKS*)
This poetic prankster of Regency London at the turn of the nineteenth century was not averse to involving celebrities and even royalty in his japes. He was not popular with theatre-goers. Once at Drury Lane Theatre he hid under the stage as a tragedy was performed and, when the leading actor began the crucial soliloquy, accompanied him on the penny-whistle. Another night he walked onstage amid the play and gave the leading man a letter to say he'd won a fortune. Jubilantly declaring his good luck, the actor exited: end of play.

In November 1810 he pulled off one of history's better hoaxes. He bet a friend that he could make an ordinary house in an ordinary street – like the one they were in, 54 Berners Street – 'the most famous address in the whole of London'. His wealthy friend didn't believe him. The stake of £1,000 seemed a sure thing.

Writing letters to hundreds of people, high and low, Hook rented a room in a house opposite, and on the morning of 10 November he and his friend began to watch from the window. On the stroke of nine, the coalman arrived with sacks of unordered coal – then the fishmonger, butcher, florist, and many other merchants. Soon the street was jammed with men of every profession, vehicles of every sort. Hour by hour, more and more of the people to whom he'd written poured into Berners Street, each at the hour appointed. First the merchants, then the professionals, then – his greatest triumphs – the leading citizens of the land. The Governor of the Bank of England came to keep his appointment with a criminal with inside information on a major fraud. The Archbishop of Canterbury arrived to collect a large donation, and next the Lord Mayor of London, on a similar mission, followed by the Lord Chief Justice, then the Lord Chancellor. Each came, then departed, mystified. By now the crowd was huge, and the best was yet to come. Into Berners Street rattled a detachment of guards, escorting not only the chief of police but the Duke of York, son of King George III and Commander-in-Chief of the British Army. They too milled about amid the confusion as, with the area brought to a complete standstill, Hook's friend had to admit he'd lost the bet. On that particular day, 54 Berners Street was certainly London's most famous address – and only two people knew why. But, with one of them poorer by £1,000, Hook thought it best to take an extended foreign holiday. He could, after all, afford it.[1]

1. Blundell, *op. cit.*, pp.181–3.

HOSKINS, Cyril Henry (*See* **RAMPA, Lobsang**)

HOUDINI, Harry (1874–1926) (*PARANORMAL HOAXES*)
Remembered for feats nobody else has ever duplicated, that this great escapologist faked evidence to discredit **mediums** remains less well known.

Son of a Hungarian rabbi, Wisconsin-born Erich Weiss read the memoirs of famed stage-magician Robert-Houdin and took the name *Houdini* on beginning his remarkable career. Without fail he escaped whatever restrictions police, lock-makers, or other experts imposed on him. On 2 December 1906 he leapt handcuffed from the Old Belle Isle Bridge at Detroit into icy water, yet freed himself. On 26 August 1907 he was thrown into San Francisco Bay, hands tied behind his back and seventy-five pounds of ball and chain attached to his body, but emerged safely. 'Handcuffs might have been made of jelly,' records Sir Arthur **Conan Doyle**, 'so easily did his limbs pass through them.'[1]

How did he do it? How, in 1926, did he survive underwater in a sealed container for over an hour? Saying all he did was breathe deeply before the box was closed and then relax, he did admit to an 'inner voice' telling what he could or couldn't do, claiming that: 'so long as he obeyed the voice he was assured of safety'. 'The greatest physical medium of modern times', claimed Conan Doyle, so implying a psychic power.

Such power, in himself or others, Houdini denied so vehemently that he was willing to resort to trickery. Courageous and generous, yet vain and intolerant, his motives remain a mystery. He wrote *The Unmasking of Robert-Houdin* to demolish the reputation of his boyhood hero, distorting fact to do so. After his mother died in 1913 he obsessively consulted spiritualist mediums, but when she did not 'come through' began attacking all mediums as fakes. At his suggestion in 1923 the *Scientific American* offered $2,500 for: 'the first physical manifestations of a psychic nature produced under scientific control'. Mrs Mina Crandon (as 'Margery' then America's best-known medium), agreed to the challenge. With psychic researcher Hereward Carrington and three others, he tested her in Boston, having already declared he was going to expose her. Yet if he was so sure she was a fake, why did he try to rig the tests?

Shut in a box locked by eight padlocks, her arms alone protruding through holes on either side, she was required to ring an electric bell – possible only by pressing down a wooden flap out of her reach. A pencil rubber was found stuck in the flap so it couldn't descend to ring the bell. Who had put it there? Before the test was resumed Houdini was seen to pass his hand along her arm into the box. With even her arms now inside and only her head protruding, again she was to try to ring the bell. Before the attempt was made, a two-foot folding rule was found lying in the box. It hadn't been there before. Had the bell been rung Houdini would have demanded a search of the cabinet: the rule would have been found. This, if held between the teeth, would have let a faker reach out and press the flap of the bell-box. Unable to claim her guilt (she had asked for the cabinet to be examined after entering it), Houdini could only pretend it had got there by accident.[2]

Still he claimed to have 'exposed' Mrs Crandon, though never specifying how. It did his reputation no good. Was he a genuine fakir who thought all fakirs fake? Or did he fear that to admit his own psychism would harm his career?

More recently Canadian-born American stage-magician James 'The Amazing' **Randi** has similarly resorted to dubious methods to prove his assertion that all psychics are fakes.

1. *The Edge of the Unknown*, Sir Arthur Conan Doyle, Putnam's, New York 1930, p.25.
2. *Ibid.*, pp.15–18.

HUBBARD, L. Ron (1911–86) (*FAKE MESSIAHS*)

The life of Lafayette Ron Hubbard, inventor of the pseudo-religion Scientology, was one long catalogue of deception. Claiming descent from the Norman nobleman 'Count de Loupe' and that his father was a US naval commander, he said he'd grown up in the wilds of Montana (in fact Iowa), had been adopted by an Indian tribe, had wandered the East and been taught by a personal disciple of **Freud** – all as much a lie as his claim to have been sunk four times and wounded as often fighting the Japanese in the Dutch East Indies during the Second World War. In fact, though a naval lieutenant, he never saw action.

What *is* true is that during the 1940s he wrote 'space operas' for pulp science fiction magazines, but that despite his speed in turning them out he never made much money. 'I always knew he was exceedingly anxious to hit big money,' editor Sam Merwin later recalled, 'he used to say he thought the best way to do it would be to start a cult.'[1]

So he did. In the April 1950 edition of *Astounding Science Fiction* he unveiled *Dianetics*, boosted by editor John F. Campbell as a psycho-therapy capable of revealing the superman latent in us all. 'It is,' Campbell wrote with wild inaccuracy, 'a coldly precise engineering description of how the human mind works.' Claiming his system could release 'engrams' (coded unconscious memories) from the 'reactive' mind, Hubbard's book *Dianetics, the Modern Science of Mental Health*, offered the solution to all ills. Though verbose and confusing, the book became a craze. You could 'audit' (psychoanalyse) your friend and uncover deep memories, then get your friend to do it for you – supposedly.

Soon the charismatic Hubbard was making big bucks. Undaunted by bankruptcy and FBI investigation, he unveiled the Church of Scientol-ogy, so gaining tax exemption and initial freedom from official harass-ment. Claiming 'scientifically-validated evidence of the existence of the human soul', he created an entire cosmology, declaring that our true self is an immortal 'thetan'. Over millennia the universe-creating thetans occupy many thousands of bodies but, enmeshed in matter, forget their omniscient origins. Scientology aims to restore ('clear') its gullible devotees to the level of 'operating thetan' ('OT') by using the 'E-meter', a galvanometer providing technical glamour (and later implicated in reports that devotees were being brainwashed). 'For compressed non-sense and fantasy it must surpass anything hitherto written', commented a 1965 Australian government report on Hubbard's cosmology. Yet the cult's followers (by 1980 reportedly six million worldwide) bought it all. Literally. Many still do. Fifty hours of auditing can cost well over $2,000. Some members have paid over $30,000 in seeking to be audited through to 'Clear' status.

Forced to flee the USA, in 1959 Hubbard relocated the cult at East Grinstead in Sussex, England. Media exposés of its dubious practices, kidnapping of its members, and claims to be 'the world's largest mental health organisation' led to a 1965 Australian ban on Scientology and to demands in Britain for an official enquiry. In 1967 Hubbard took to the seas with a private navy. Served by nymphets in hot-pants who dressed and undressed him and relayed orders in his tone of voice, his paranoia grew. The tale of this 'Sea Org', the cult's later settlement in Florida (under the name of the 'United Churches'), its infiltration of US government agencies, and Hubbard's own disappearance in 1980 is absurd, but not funny. Those breaking cult rules were humiliated, those trying to leave it were pursued, those on the 'enemies list' were described as fair game to be eradicated by any means.

Still in hiding, Hubbard died on 24 January 1986. Even this fact was disputed by the cult's new leaders. Truth is hard to come by where Scientology is concerned, save that Hubbard exploited the gullible to make a fortune.

1. *Bare-Faced Messiah*, Russell Miller, Sphere, London 1988.

HUGHES, Howard (*See* **IRVING, Clifford**)

HUMBERT, Thérèse (1860–1917) (*FRAUD*)
Gilbert Aurignac of Beauzelle near Toulouse in southwest France was not really a poor peasant farmer, he told everyone, but d'Aurignac, of noble birth, as proved by the family deeds in his brass-studded oak chest. This could only be opened when he died. In 1874 his sons Emile and Romain, and daughters Thérèse and Marie, duly opened the chest. But in it was only an old brick. Thérèse was impressed.

Plain and dumpy yet with an iron will, she worked as a washerwoman, then got a job in the house of Gustave Humbert, an ambitious lawyer and already Mayor of Toulouse. There she attracted Humbert's son Frédéric by telling him that when she was younger an old woman, Mlle de Marcotte, had taken a fancy to her, making her the chief beneficiary in her will. When Mlle de Marcotte died, Thérèse would be rich. Believing her, Frédéric married her against his father's objections. Moving to Paris, he practised as an advocate while she spent his money. Their debts grew. When their creditors learned there was no Mlle Marcotte and no inheritance, Gustave Humbert, now Minister of Justice in the government, had to pay his son's debts to avoid scandal. He was furious, but Thérèse had a talk with him, persuading him of her sincerity. She must have been very convincing.

Of course, she said, there was no Mlle de Marcotte. That was a fiction to hide the true story. Two years earlier in 1879 she'd been on a train when an elderly American in the next compartment had a heart attack. She'd saved his life and the American, Robert Henry Crawford, had taken her name and address. Now, she went on, the executors of his will had been in touch with her. He had been a Chicago millionaire. His fortune was to be divided between his two nephews and her sister Marie, still a schoolgirl. Out of their inheritance these three heirs were to pay

Thérèse an annual income of nearly $100,000. The securities and bonds representing Marie's share were assigned to the Humberts, to be kept in a sealed safe until Marie came of age.

On the strength of this improbable story of the 'Crawford inheritance', Thérèse and Frédéric began borrowing on a huge scale. Moving into a mansion on the Avenue de la Grande Armée and spending a fortune on clothes and jewellery, Thérèse repaid her loans by raising larger loans at higher interest. Soon cracks began to appear in the façade. A Lyon banker, Delatte, who had already advanced her large sums, paid a visit. Where did the late Mr Crawford's nephews live? In Somerville, a Boston suburb, she lied quickly.

Visiting America, Delatte found nobody who knew the nephews in Somerville, nor any trace of the dead millionaire. Writing to a friend in Paris, he was about to start proceedings but was murdered in New York. The friend, also one of Thérèse's creditors, showed her the letter. She bribed or talked him out of going public, and when in 1883 a newspaper article cast doubt on the existence of the Crawford fortune, she announced that she had quarrelled with the late Mr Crawford's nephews, who had started a lawsuit to force her to lodge the fortune in the safe with the Crédit Lyonnais Bank. With her husband assembling a team of lawyers, and actors playing the role of the 'nephews', she won the case. Then the 'nephews' began new litigation, keeping both case and safe locked up.

Now, with Marie's twenty-first birthday fast approaching, Thérèse invented a new scheme – the *Rente Viagère*, an insurance company specialising in life annuities. Launched by brothers Emile and Romain from a fine building in the Boulevard des Capucines, a staff of slick salesmen ensured that money poured in – to the Humbert coffers. Not a franc was invested in securities, all annuities being paid out (as with Jabez **Balfour**) from the cash inflow. Unbelievably, for nearly twenty years the company prospered, Madame Humbert too. In that time, spending sixty-four million francs of other people's money, 'La Grande Thérèse' had everything she could possibly want. Her parties were the most successful in Paris. Marie's twenty-first birthday was long past, none of her creditors had got their money back; but there was always the American litigation to stop Thérèse opening the safe.

At last Jules Bizat, a senior official at the Bank of France, concerned by growing rumours, asked Madame where the insurance company invested. In gilt-edged securities, she said. He checked, and found that no such securities had been cashed to collect interest due. They didn't exist. He approached the Prime Minister, Pierre Waldeck-Rousseau, who, to avoid a financial crash, decided against attacking Madame Humbert directly. Instead he 'inspired' a series of articles in the newspaper *Le Matin*, some by Emile Zola.

Threatening to sue the 'slanderers' for libel, Madame's lawyer, Maître du Buit, declared that he would scotch all rumours by opening the safe in her bedroom before the principal creditors. This was the last thing she wanted. On 8 May 1902 a mysterious fire broke out in the Humbert mansion. Next night she collected her entire family and vanished to Spain. The following morning du Buit and Madame's main creditors assembled in the mansion's burned out bedroom, where the fireproof safe was opened.

It was empty – but for a brick.

Seven months later the family was found living under assumed names in a Madrid lodging house. Extradited, on 9 March 1903 Thérèse, Frédéric, Emile and Romain stood in court in Paris, charged on 257 counts of forgery and financial misdealing. When the trial opened on 8 August all Europe was rapt. How had a peasant woman fooled so many for so long? The question remained unanswered. There was no sign of the magnetic *grande dame*. Plump and sallow, lisping in her provincial accent, Madame had no answers. A journalist described her as 'the typical French cook'. All four were found guilty. Thérèse and Frédéric each got five years, Romain three, and Emile two.

With the safe displayed for a year in a shop window in the Rue Blanche, the last the world saw of La Grande Thérèse was a stout old woman in black, waiting to board a train after her release from jail. Still proclaiming her innocence, she died forgotten in 1917.[1]

1. Larsen, *op. cit.*, pp.143–51.

HURKOS, Peter (1911–88) (*PARANORMAL HOAXES*)

In 1943 house painter Pieter van der Hurk fell from a ladder and fractured his skull. Emerging from coma in a Hague hospital, when he shook hands with a fellow patient about to be discharged he 'knew' the man was a British agent about to be assassinated by the Gestapo. So he claims in his autobiography, *Psychic*, though the State Institute for War Archives in Amsterdam has no record of any British agent being shot at the place and time given.

So flooded with images of other people's lives that he could no longer concentrate or hold a job, as 'Peter Hurkos' he emigrated to America in the 1950s to begin a successful career as psychic counsellor to **Hollywood** stars. Specialising in psychometry and the blindfold description of pictures, for at least two decades he maintained a high profile despite continual deceptions and failures as a 'crime sleuth'. When in December 1950 the Stone of Scone was removed from Westminster Abbey by Scottish Nationalists, he 'clairvoyantly' tracked it to Glasgow. Later it was found in a ruined cathedral at Arbroath, eighty miles away. Nor did his famed 1951 detection of a firebug in Njimegen, Holland, occur as claimed. He identified seventeen-year-old Piet Vierbroom only after the arsonist's arrest, not before.[1] Likewise, the only times he ever correctly identified murderers by 'psychic' means was when they were already in custody. His claim to have identified the Boston Strangler was as false as his claim to have been tested for ESP at Duke University with one hundred per cent success – he was never tested at Duke. He told supporter Henry Belk, the department store heir, that two of his stores would do well and that Belk's missing daughter was alive and well. The stores failed; Belk's daughter was found drowned. As for his prophecy that he would die on 17 November 1961, that too failed to check out. Few parapsychologists were ever convinced by him, save Andrija Puharich, discoverer of Uri **Geller** and Arigo (*see* **Psychic Surgery**), who called him: 'one of the greatest telepathic talents of modern times'.[2] Perhaps embarrassed by such praise, in later years Hurkos had the decency to assume a very much lower profile.

1. 'Less sensitive by half?', Piet Hein Hobens, in *The Unexplained*, Orbis partwork, London 1983, pp.2754–7.
2. Randi, *op. cit.*, pp.270–3.

I

'They believe. They've got to believe or
they'd never get a night's sleep.'

(Clifford Irving, literary hoaxer, speaking of
the publishers he duped)

ICELAND (*See* **GREENLAND**)

ICE WORM FESTIVAL, The (*MEDIA HOAXES*)
Working as a journalist in Dawson, Alaska in 1898, E.J. Stroller White
was asked by the editor of the *Klondike Nugget* to invent absurd tall tales
for times when news was slow – a common occurrence in Dawson. After
a particularly violent snowstorm – also a common occurrence in Dawson
– White produced a piece about ice worms, attracted by the sudden fall
in temperature, coming down to town from nearby glaciers. 'The little
critters came to the surface,' he wrote, 'to bask in the unusual frigidity in
such numbers that their chirping is seriously interfering with the
slumber of Dawson's inhabitants.'
   The ice worms are still fondly remembered in February each year at
the Ice Worm Festival in Cordova, Alaska, when Main Street is visited
by a multi-legged ice worm, one hundred and fifty feet long.[1]

1. Yapp, *op. cit.*, p. 29.

IMPOSTORS (*See* **CONCORDANCE**)

INVISIBLE COLLEGE, The (*See* **ROSICRUCIANS**)

IRELAND, William Henry (1777–1835) (*LITERARY HOAXES*)
In the 1790s this young man went further than John Payne **Collier** in the
annals of **Shakespearean** forgery by trying to pass off his play, *Vortigern
and Rowena*, as a formerly undiscovered play by the Bard himself. The

son of London antiquarian engraver and bookseller Samuel Ireland (d.1800), his motives remain obscure. Maybe he wanted to impress his father, who said he had no talent; or maybe he wanted revenge on the old man for refusing to explain the mystery of his unknown mother until his twenty-first birthday. He never did learn about his mother. By the time his twenty-first birthday arrived, he and Samuel had fallen out amid the scandal over the hoax, and they never spoke again.

Impressed by **Chatterton**'s tragic fate, following a visit with his father to Stratford in 1794, he decided to try to emulate Chatterton's forgeries. Back in London that autumn, in the office where he worked this seventeen-year-old began by writing on the fly-leaf of an Elizabethan tract a letter of dedication to Queen Elizabeth. To his delight, his father thought it genuine. Next, using old rent-roll parchment and a wax seal, and a deed from the reign of James I (1603–25) as his handwriting model, he faked a mortgage document involving Shakespeare and an actor called John Heminge, whose name he signed with his left hand. Samuel also accepted this as genuine, as did Sir Frederick Eden and the Heralds Office. Increasingly confident, by the end of January 1795 he had produced more 'finds'. These included letters between Shakespeare and the Earl of Southampton, a letter from Shakespeare to his wife Anne Hathaway, a letter to the Bard from Queen Elizabeth and, more daring, revisions to *Hamlet* and *King Lear*. He told his father that a Mr 'M.H.' had given him access to these documents on condition that his identity remained a secret. Samuel swallowed this fib too.

He was not alone. On publicly displaying his son's findings, literary giants like the Poet Laureate Pye and Johnson's biographer Boswell also thought them genuine. Boswell was so impressed by Shakespeare's alleged *Profession of Faith* that he went down on his knees and kissed: 'the valuable relics of our bard to thank God I have lived to see them'.

Much cheered, William now wrote a blank verse play, *Vortigern and Rowena*, and followed it up with a tragedy, *Henry II*, both supposedly by Shakespeare, and in his hand. There were close shaves, however. His friend Montague Talbot caught him in the act of forgery but agreed to keep the secret. An office visitor dropped and broke the mortgage seal: until it was repaired it was obvious how it had been split open and refilled. Then, soon after in December 1795 Samuel published the finds, a genuine signature of John Heminge emerged. It was wholly unlike William's fake. Doubts grew, while critics like Edmond Malone had denounced the finds as forgeries from the start. Yet already in September the playwright Richard Sheridan had agreed to produce *Vortigern and Rowena* (based on the legend of a fifth-century Celtic king who invited the Saxons into Britain) at Drury Lane. Convinced it was a fake, the theatre's actor-manager Richard Kemble wanted to hold over the first night until **April Fool's Day**. When rehearsals began, the astute actresses Mrs Siddons and Mrs Palmer declined their parts on grounds of ill-health. The production went ahead due only to the support of the Duke of Clarence and other gullible aristocrats with money to waste on lost causes.

On opening night (2 April 1796), Drury Lane was packed out. It was a disaster. The bald language and banal plot provoked increasing mirth. When in the final act Kemble had to speak the line: 'And when this solemn mockery is o'er', the derisive uproar ended only when the curtain fell. There was no second performance. The Irelands were overwhelmed by public ridicule. William confessed the fraud to his sisters, who in turn told his father, but still Samuel refused to believe that his dull son was capable of such a hoax. Leaving home, William wrote a pamphlet admitting his forgeries and exonerating his father – but still the old man denied that he'd been conned. Ridicule and contempt pursued him to the grave, but he never accepted (at least in public) that the plays were fraudulent.

William survived as a minor poet, but in France not England, where he was never forgiven for taking the name of the Bard in vain – especially not by those he'd fooled.[1]

1.   Stephen and Lee (eds), *op. cit.*

IRVING, Clifford (1930–) (*LITERARY HOAXES*)

In December 1970 this expatriate American author (already known for *Fake!*, his exposé of art forger Elmyr **de Hory** who also lived on the Mediterranean isle of Ibiza), met his friend Dick Suskind at Palma on the nearby isle of Mallorca. He mentioned a wild idea triggered by an article he'd just read in *Newsweek*, 'The Case of the Invisible Billionaire'. It was about Howard Hughes, supposedly the world's richest man.

Born in 1905, his fortune from oil and engineering, in earlier years Hughes had built a giant wooden-framed seaplane, the *Spruce Goose*, which had never flown; and as a Hollywood producer had promoted sex bomb Jane Russell. Since 1955 he had lived as a recluse on the top floor of the Desert Inn in Las Vegas amid an entourage of Mormons. Running his empire solely by telephone or memo, nobody knew what he looked like or even if he was still alive. He hadn't been interviewed for fifteen years. Lately, with his airline TWA in trouble, its major investors had sued him for mismanagement. Paying $145 million in costs and damages out of court, he'd fled from Las Vegas to a hideaway in the Bahamas. This was the substance of the article.

Meeting Suskind, Irving suggested proposing to his New York publishers, McGraw-Hill, that Hughes had commissioned him to write an authorised biography, but would refuse all personal communication with the publishers. Irving would be the sole contact. In the first place, this was a joke. Soon it got out of hand. Suskind's enthusiasm led Irving to write to his McGraw-Hill editor to say he'd sent Hughes a copy of

Fake!, and had received a note of thanks. 'Do you know if there is any biography of Hughes,' he asked, 'or anything in the works for the near future?'

Studying a *Life* magazine photo of the billionaire's handwriting, and with a pad of legal paper as used by Hughes, Irving wrote himself three letters suggesting Hughes's interest. 'It would not suit me to die without having certain misconceptions about my life cleared up and without having stated the truth about my life,' stated the third. 'I would be grateful if you would let me know when and how you would wish to undertake the writing of my biography you proposed . . .'

McGraw-Hill jumped at it. Excited by the letters and by Irving's account of phone calls from Hughes, Vice-President Albert Leventhal offered $100,000 on signature, $100,000 on delivery of a transcript of interviews, and $300,000 for the manuscript of the biography. At a New York meeting Irving told McGraw-Hill he was flying to the Bahamas to meet Hughes. In fact his assignation was with Nina von Pallandt, of the Danish folk-singing duo Nina and Frederick. His on-off lover over the years, she'd just met him in New York. With no Nassau flights available, instead they flew to Oaxaca in Mexico. In Mexico City, where they changed planes, he had his photo taken. Back in New York, he showed McGraw-Hill a notebook recording two meetings with Hughes ('Señor Octavio'); the draft of a contract for the book; and the photo of himself emerging from a plane – taken, he said, by a Hughes aide. McGraw-Hill were hooked. But their lawyer said that Hughes' signature must be bank-documented or notarised.

Back in Ibiza, Irving phoned Suskind. 'The ball game's over,' he said. Then his editor called him to say McGraw-Hill could accept the signature made, in his presence, by 'Octavio'. Irving flew to Puerto Rico, to meet 'Hughes', then in New York presented two copies of a contract signed 'Howard R. Hughes'. It contained clauses demanding that the project be kept secret, and a provision that: 'The money will be deposited as designated verbally or in writing by H.R. Hughes for deposit in any bank account of H.R. Hughes.'

Meanwhile Irving had photographed his Swiss wife Edith in a black wig. She also had a spare passport. This he doctored in the name of 'H.R. Hughes', even as McGraw-Hill asked *Life* magazine to pay $250,000 for pre-publication magazine rights. Edith opened an account with the Crédit Suisse Bank in Zurich as 'Helga Hughes', then flew to Düsseldorf, where the younger of her two daughters by her previous marriage lived with her ex-husband and his new wife, Hanne. Stealing Hanne's German identity card, back in Zurich she opened another account in the name of 'Hanne Rosencrantz'.

Later Irving claimed almost a hundred secret meetings with Hughes in motels and parked cars throughout Latin America. In New York late in May, left alone with the *Life* magazine files on Hughes, secretly he photocopied over three hundred unpublished reports on the billionaire's life. Back in Ibiza, he and Suskind spent the rest of the summer taking turns to play Hughes in rambling tape-recorded interviews, freely inventing the transcript on which the book would be based. They worked hard to capture Hughes's arrogance, to reveal his business secrets, and to provide anecdotes from each period of his life. In short, they did as any other 'unauthorised biographer' does, except in claiming to have Hughes' personal authorisation.

The work went well. But disaster loomed when in August McGraw-Hill rang to say another publisher had been offered a Hughes biography, as told to Robert Easton, ex-husband of Hollywood actress Lana Turner, once one of Hughes's lovers. Taking the bull by the horns, Irving and Suskind flew to Palm Beach (near Nassau, where Hughes was still genuinely holed up). From there they telegraphed McGraw-Hill to say that Hughes, having learned of the serial rights deal with *Life*, now wanted his advance upped to $1 million. In a second telegram 'Hughes' denounced the legitimacy of the Easton biography.

On 12 September Irving and Suskind delivered their transcript. It took McGraw-Hill executives a week to read the 999 manuscript pages. They were hooked, and when Irving (just) survived a lie-detector test, Leventhal raised the advance to $750,000, 'but not a penny more'. Taking the cheque for 'Hughes' to Zurich, Edith paid it into the H.R. Hughes account, and two weeks later transferred it into the Rosencrantz account.

In November McGraw-Hill rang in alarm. The *Ladies' Home Journal* was to publish extracts from the Easton book in January. The company wanted Hughes to let them announce that they were the sole publishers of an authorised biography. Irving sent them a letter from 'Hughes' ranting about their incompetence. The same handwriting expert who a year earlier had studied the genuine Hughes letter published in *Life* assured them that: 'The chances that another person could copy this handwriting even in a similar way are less than one in a million.' Once again, so much for 'experts'.

When on 7 December McGraw-Hill announced forthcoming publication, lawyers acting for Hughes immediately denounced the book as a fake. McGraw-Hill had expected this, Irving having assured them that Hughes had kept the project secret from all but a few confidantes. Then it was learned that Chester Davis, an attorney representing Hughes, had telephoned Time Inc. (publishers of *Life*) to say Hughes would talk to Frank McCulloch, a reporter who had interviewed him in the 1950s. Now worried, McGraw-Hill submitted the original 'Hughes' letters to New York's leading handwriting analysts – Osborn, Osborn, and Osborn, who declared the documents genuine. Yet again, so much for the 'experts'.

Soon after Christmas Hughes gave his first press conference in over fifteen years. By telephone to journalists in a Los Angeles studio he denied ever meeting Irving. Fighting to save his neck, Irving insisted on CBS TV that the voice on the phone did not belong to the billionaire. But now the fraud rapidly unravelled. Attorney Chester Davis, noting that Harold McGraw held a cheque cancelled by Crédit Suisse counter-signed 'H.R. Hughes', put Intertel (Hughes's own detective agency) on the trail. The bank divulged private information. Learning that 'H.R. Hughes' was a woman, Intertel went to the Swiss police. Edith was questioned on Ibiza, and the Irvings fled to New York.

The final nail in their coffin came when Jim Phelan, author of an unpublished Hughes memoir, saw Irving's manuscript and realised that some of its best stories came from his own unpublished work. Irving had got it the previous summer from a literary agent called Mayer. In New York, Phelan confronted Harold McGraw, who had to admit that the fit was too close for coincidence. McGraw-Hill had been duped.

Clifford Irving, his wife Edith, and Dick Suskind, appeared before two grand jury hearings on 7 February and 3 March, and made a full confession. Between them they owed over one and a half million dollars to McGraw-Hill, the taxman, and their lawyers. On 16 June 1973 Clifford Irving got thirty months in jail, Suskind six months, and Edith two years. All but two months of her American sentence was suspended, but she received (and served) a two-year sentence in Zurich. The Swiss don't like con artists.

The Autobiography of Howard Hughes was never published. Yet in 1977, with Irving released and back on Ibiza, he and Suskind wrote and published *Project Octavio*, their account of this extremely bold hoax. Edith by then was seeking a new life elsewhere.

As for Howard Hughes, whose own life had been just as bold, even before the hoaxers had pleaded guilty he had fled from Nassau to Nicaragua. Still in seclusion, he is said to have died on 5 April 1976, on a private Lear jet flying from Acapulco to Houston. The circumstances of his death, as of his life as a whole, remain unknown.[1]

As for Irving, he's made a comeback. Look around UK bookstalls, and you'll find the name 'Clifford Irving' heading a new bestselling thriller (Christmas 1994). The biographical data says he now lives in Mexico. There's no mention of his past. Good luck to him. He took it all the way.

1. '*Project Octavio*', Clifford Irving with Richard Suskind, Allison and Busby, London 1977.

J

'If you think fishermen are the biggest liars
in the world, ask a jogger how far he runs
every morning.'

(Larry Johnson, TV personality, quoted in
Reader's Digest)

JAMES, Will (1892–1942) (*IMPOSTORS*)
What Archibald **Belaney** ('Grey Owl') did for the Indian, Will James
did for the cowboy. Noted first for *Smoky the Cowhorse*, a 1927
children's book which he wrote and illustrated, in 1930 appeared *Lone
Cowboy: The Autobiography of Will James*. This bestseller told how,
orphaned aged four in Montana in about 1896, he was reared by
Bopy, a French-Canadian trapper. Trapping in winter and prospect-
ing in summer, lodging in cabins from Canada to Mexico, young Will
learned all the skills of a backwoodsman before Bopy disappeared,
thought drowned in a creek. By then our hero was old enough to be
hired as a cowboy, becoming a bronco buster before writing his life
story.

Lone Cowboy was a success. James's later life was not. Buying the
Rocking R Ranch in Montana, to the despair of his friends he went on
benders and ended up broke, dying of alcoholism aged fifty in Hollywood's Presbyterian Hospital.

Yet his books remained well loved, and few people realised he was a
fraud until 1987 when, in *Ride for the High Points: The Real Story of Will
James*, author Jim Bramlett revealed that 'Will James' had really been
Joseph Ernest Nepthali Default, son of a middle-class French-speaking
Quebec family. Reading about the West in pulp fiction, aged fifteen he'd
left home to become a cowboy, trying various aliases before settling on
Will James. When his artwork didn't sell, his wife Alice suggested
writing down one of the yarns he loved telling and sending it to *Scribner*'s
magazine. Scribners paid $300 for it and, having sworn his family in

Quebec to secrecy, Joseph Default had been Will James thereafter.[1]

1. Lindskoog, *op. cit.*, p. 100.

JAVA SKULLS (*See* FOSSIL FORGERIES)

JONES, Jim (*See* END-OF-THE-WORLD SCAMS)

JONES, Reginald (20th century) (*PRANKS*, *see also* HOAXES IN WARFARE)

Later professor of natural philosophy at Aberdeen University and scientific adviser to successive British governments, this academic hoaxer's career began in the 1930s when, as a research physicist at Oxford's Clarendon Laboratory, he was assigned to disrupt an important Oxford seminar. Posing as a boiler-room mechanic he phoned the seminar chairman to warn that due to a pressure block in the steam pipes the radiators were likely to blow up. Taken in by this scientific nonsense, the scientists quickly closed their meeting and evacuated the building.

Another time he showed his colleague Gerald Touch how easy it is to make an intelligent scholar do absurd things just by talking to him over the phone (*see* **Telephone Hoaxes**). One evening, with Touch visiting a well-known Oxford professor, his host's phone rang several times. Each time nobody answered when the professor picked it up. Calling again, now posing as a telephone engineer notified of a fault on the line, Jones said that due to a staff shortage nothing could be done for at least a week. When the victim begged for a faster repair, the 'engineer' said if the problem was a leak to earth, it could be repaired immediately, but this would involve testing by the owner. Touch now watched amazed as Jones had the professor tap the phone with a pen, take off his shoes and tap it, stand on one leg and tap it with a rubber, and so on. Finally, with the man about to lower his phone into a bucket of water, Touch could no longer control his laughter. Upset, his host informed Jones he had a: 'young friend here who's trying to stop me. I think he's a bit drunk. He says it'll damage the telephone if I put it in the water.' Learning that the 'young friend' was a physicist, Jones was scornful. 'Physicists!' he declared. 'They're the bane of our life here in Oxford. They always think they know about telephones, and they're always wrong.' So he talked the scholar into lowering his phone into the bucket of water.

Working for Air Ministry Intelligence during the war, he learned that the Germans were using directional beams from the Continent to guide their bombers to British targets. Duplicating one signal, he sent it out from London. The bombers went off course and dropped their bombs on to empty fields. Another wartime hoax concerned a navigational device that helped Allied bombers to seek out U-boats. The Germans knew the RAF had something new. 'Inventing' an infra-red beam to locate submarines, Jones ensured that the enemy learned of it. So the entire U-boat fleet was specially painted to counteract the non-existent rays (*see* **Hoaxes in Warfare**).

Jones once delivered a lecture at London's Institute of Physics entitled: 'The Theory of Practical Joking: Its Relevance to Physics'. 'The object,' he said, 'is to build up in the victim's mind a false world-picture which is temporarily consistent by any tests that he can apply to it, so that he ultimately takes action on it with confidence.'[1]

1. *The Pleasures of Deception*, Norman O. Moss, Chatto & Windus, London 1977.

JURADO, Señorita Concepción (1864–1931) (*IMPOSTORS*)
Sharing the same Mexico City grave, Don Carlos Balmori and Señorita Concepción Jurado both died the same day at the same time – 27 November 1931. A memorial service is still broadcast over leading Mexican networks on the anniversary of their deaths.

Reportedly the world's richest man, with money from holdings in sugar, tin, opium and other commodities, Don Carlos was also famed as the world's greatest lover. 'Nothing is as it appears to be,' he was fond of saying. 'Nothing is real. Not even I.'

As for Concepción 'Conchita' Jurado, daughter of Don Carlos's gardener Ignacio, when she died aged sixty-seven she was unmarried. She had never even been Don Carlos's mistress. So what was the secret? Until Don Carlos died, it was known only to members of an exclusive club, initiation into which could prove highly embarrassing. Take the case of Señor Carlos Arturo Rodriguez, a newspaper magnate hoping to persuade Don Carlos to invest in a new publication.

Brought one night by his friend Don Adolpho to a luxurious soirée held in two small rooms in the house of Don Carlos's gardener, as soon as he arrived he found himself being quizzed by Don Carlos in front of all the other elegant, wealthy guests. Before he knew what had happened, the astonished publisher heard the billionaire agree to invest two million pesos – four times as much as he was asking. Within minutes the cheque for the full amount was offered. He reached for it, but Don Carlos snatched it back, asking: 'Are you a member of the Masons?' Puzzled, Señor Rodriguez said no, but he was a member of the Lodge of the Moose, at which Don Carlos demanded that he show everyone the size of his antlers. 'But I am a Moose in name only,' he protested. 'It is a brotherhood.'

'You call yourself a moose but you have no antlers?' Don Carlos was outraged. 'How can I go into business with someone who has no antlers! Show me your antlers or I'll keep my cheque!' The bemused publisher waved his arms over his head. 'A two-legged moose?' Don Carlos asked.

Soon he had Señor Rodriguez crawling on his knees while imitating antlers with his arms. Drawing him up with the cheque again extended, and eyeing the dupe's magnificent moustache, Don Carlos said he could never do business with a man whose moustache was larger than his own. The distressed publisher agreed to lose his pride and joy for the sake of the cheque, and soon his upper lip was bare.

Don Carlos wasn't done yet. 'I've been robbed!' he cried. 'My diamond tie-pin is missing! No one move!' The chief of police, who was one of the guests, stepped forward, dipped his hand into the publisher's pocket – and out came the missing pin. Amid cries for his arrest from the delighted guests, the terrified Señor Rodriguez protested his innocence. 'I am no thief!' And he begged his tormentor, now standing on a chair in the middle of the room, for mercy. Don Carlos smiled down. 'This is true, my dear sir. You are no thief, just as Don Carlos Balmori, the renowned Spanish millionaire, is neither Spanish nor a millionaire – in fact, not even a man!' And off came the hat, then the fake moustache, to reveal a slender older woman with long, greying hair.

'In truth, I am Conchita Jurado – daughter of the gardener Ignacio, in whose home you are now, and "sister" of your host,' declared 'Don Carlos'. 'Thank you, Señor Rodriguez, for allowing us an evening of pleasure.'

So, humbled and astonished, the arrogant Señor Rodriguez now learned what was known to everyone else in the room. One day many years before the then young Conchita had dressed up to impersonate the real Don Carlos Balmori, fooling her parents so well that she had continued with the deception at family gatherings. When the real Don Carlos died, she persisted with the impersonation, keeping his memory alive. With the help of friends, in time Balmori's history became so well developed that the ever more extravagant tales of 'his' exploits grew famous. By 1925, 'his' club in the gardener's rooms attracted the great and good of Mexico City, all of whom kept the secret. It was an ideal way to shame the pompous, arrogant, and greedy: just bring them to the Jurado household, where Balmori would deliver a *balmoreada*.[1]

1. Madison, *op. cit.*, pp.58–65.

K

'It used to be said that Camille Corot
painted 800 pictures in his lifetime, of which
4,000 ended up in American collections.'

(*Time* magazine)

KAMMERER, Paul (1880–1926) (*SCIENTIFIC SCAMS*)
The suicide of Austrian biologist Paul Kammerer on 23 September 1926
seemingly ended the controversy caused by his work with the midwife
toad (*Alytes obstetricians*). Supporting the thesis advanced in the late
eighteenth century by Jean Baptiste Lamarck that acquired characteristics are heritable, his experiments had infuriated neo-Darwinians, who
held (and still hold) that evolution proceeds by chance mutation alone.
As Kammerer had apparently been caught out in experimental fraud, his
death seemed to clinch it. Orthodoxy had prevailed, and Lamarckism
has been derided ever since.

Yet it's not so simple. Did Kammerer fake the evidence, or was he
betrayed? Did he kill himself because of the scandal alone? And what of
the politics and personalities involved? Highly strung and emotional,
Kammerer's musical background and socialist principles had no more
endeared him to orthodox biologists than his success in keeping experimental animals alive and in breeding them through several generations.
No biologist since has been able to reproduce his work. Whatever the
truth, the case as a whole sheds unflattering light on the alleged
'objectivity' of science and scientists.

Born in Vienna to a wealthy family, in 1902 this gifted amateur
composer joined the Biologische Versuchsansalt ('Institute for Experimental Biology'), known in Vienna as the 'Sorcerers' Institute'. Organising the laboratory aquaria and terraria as models for the care of
experimental animals, his early work with salamanders led him to claim
to have induced modifications in their mating habits, colour, or physique
by breeding them in artificial environments radically different from their

natural habitats. This caused a sensation, with neo-Darwinians finding the theory that organisms might alter their own chromosomal structure as absurd as his thesis (*Law of Seriality*) that 'coincidences' can be meaningful.

But the real uproar was caused by his work with the midwife toad which, unlike other toads, usually mates on land. To get a grip on the female, the males of water-mating species grow rough, blackish, horny pads on their hands. By making several generations of midwife toads mate in water, Kammerer claimed, the hands of their offspring had also developed these pads. This outraged neo-Darwinians like English biologist William Bateson, who after 1910 attacked Kammerer viciously in the pages of *Nature*, casting doubt on his procedures and hinting (as yet without proof) at fraud.

Was Bateson jealous? Failing to breed midwife toads himself, aged twenty-six in 1886 he'd gone to Asia, seeking evidence of acquired characteristics. Failing, instead he'd pioneered Mendelian genetics in England, arguing that the units of heredity – 'genes' – do not blend, but are like hard, static marbles that combine in mosaic patterns. Yet his dispute with the anti-Mendelians (ironically, it later emerged that Gregor Mendel had doctored statistics to 'prove' his theories) was nothing to the war waged on Kammerer – a war with political overtones. For while his enemies were mainly American or English, Kammerer's reputation remained high in Austria, Germany, and (after 1917) in the fledgling USSR. Indeed in 1925, a year after he published *The Inheritance of Acquired Characteristics*, he was invited to set up and direct a research institute in Moscow, mainly on the recommendation of psychologist Ivan Pavlov.

Before he could go east the blow fell. In August 1926 Dr Kingsley Noble of the American Museum of Natural History, running tests on the remaining specimen of *Alytes*, found the crucial discoloration of its nuptial pads to be caused by an injection of indian ink – clear evidence of fraud. And when a month later Kammerer shot himself on a hill outside Vienna, that seemed to clinch it. He'd killed himself in shame at being exposed.

Yet evidence offered by Arthur Koestler in *The Case of the Midwife Toad* (1973) suggests that person or persons unknown made the injection to discredit him. Kammerer himself denied any deception. 'Who besides myself had any interest in perpetrating such alterations can only be very dimly suspected,' he wrote to his would-be Russian hosts the day before he died. And, as Koestler notes, this unstable and passionate man had already tried to kill himself in 1923, depressed by a love affair. Just before he died, Grete Weisenthal, solo dancer with the Vienna Opera, had refused to go to Moscow with him. Additionally, his finances were parlous, the Austrian economy having collapsed. Disappointment in love, money worries, then ruinous accusation of fraud – all may have played a part in his death.

Now, though many are unhappy with neo-Darwinism, the situation remains as described a century ago by Samuel Butler: 'Lamarck has been so systematically laughed at that it amounts to little less than philosophical suicide for anyone to stand up on his behalf.'

In the case of Kammerer, the suicide was actual.[1]

1. *The Case of the Midwife Toad*, Arthur Koestler, Picador, London 1973.

KAROLY, Hadju (1920–81) (*IMPOSTORS*)
Arriving in England after the Second World War, this Hungarian-born son of a tailor took the name Baron Carl Hadju. Did he realise the pun? Soon married, in 1956 he raised money to send 'freedom fighters' from Britain to support the Hungarian revolt against the USSR, but none of the money ever got there. Accused of embezzlement and in 1957 declared bankrupt, he reinvented himself as man-about-town Michel Karoly, author and hypnotherapist, complete with Mayfair office. Dining with the rich and sleeping with a marchioness, all went well until in 1965 both his wife and mistress died. Bound over for a year for being found dressed as a woman in Hertford, in 1966 he was jailed for two months for obtaining credit while an undischarged bankrupt. But again the phoenix arose. In 1968 appeared Dr Charlotte Bach, formerly a lecturer in philosophy and psychology at Budapest University. This personality lasted thirteen years, though occasionally he doubled as the redoubtable Daphne Lyell-Manson, whose spanking service supplied many satisfied customers. As Bach he compiled a dictionary of psychology which, hailed by Colin Wilson as: 'one of the greatest intellectual advances of the twentieth century',[1] centred on the idea that sexual imbalance is evolutionary, and that sexual frustration is literally the mother of invention. To deal with such chaotic inner conflict, claimed 'Bach', people shunt it aside and block it (deviation); cage it in low equilibrium (normality); or, as in 'asexual' shamans and great artists, harness and resolve it at a higher level as unified creative force.

Well, if anyone should have known, it was him. Or her.[2]

1. *Mysteries*, Colin Wilson, Grafton, London 1989, pp.514–23.
2. Yapp, *op. cit.*, p.88.

KAWA, The cruise of the (*LITERARY HOAXES*)
Perhaps distressed by the plethora of banal travel-books promoting the wonders of the sun-kissed lagoons, sparkling coral atolls, and happy natives of the South Sea Islands, in 1921 George S. Chappell and publisher George Palmer Putnam pulled a neat little hoax with a book called *The Cruise of the Kawa* by 'Walter E. Traprock'. Claimed by Putnam in his Introduction as: 'a supreme, superlative epic of the South

Seas' which stood: 'pre-eminent in the literature of modern exploration', the authors introduced the *Kawa* and its crew of five – world-wanderer Reginald K. Whinney, Bohemian artist Herman Swank, the redoubtable Captain Ezra Triplett, First Mate William Henry Thomas, and Traprock himself, a native of Derby Connecticut who had also written *Jumping Jean*, the book of a musical version of *Les Misérables*.

Travelling o'er the ocean blue, this intrepid crew came to the formerly undiscovered Filbert Isles, so named for its abundance of filbert nut trees. Here the natives, who could stay under water for hours, spoke Filbertese, or nut-talk, a lively tongue with words like *oo-pa* (a vegetable cream puff); *hoopa* (a delicious milk, twenty-seven per cent proof); and *alova* (a flower with scent so strong that one inhalation produced the kick of three old-fashioned mint juleps). Meeting Baahaabaa (Durable Drinker), and Zambao-Zambino (Young-Man-Proud-of-his-Waistline), they also encountered the coconut-milk-drinking ooza snake; the fatuliva bird which laid cubic eggs with the pattern of dice on them; crabs big enough to pull boats; pearls the size of onions; and the tiny dew-fish which, rising to the surface of the sea at sunrise, turn: 'the entire ocean to a pulsating mirror of silver'.

Yet eventually the mariners had to return to civilisation. Sadly they sailed away, leaving behind them the child-like, illiterate islanders. It goes without saying that more than a few literate but gullible Westerners took the tale seriously. Traprock was even asked to lecture by the editorial board of the *National Geographic* in Washington DC . . .[1]

1. *The Cruise of the Kawa*, Walter E. Traprock, George Putnam & Sons, London 1921.

KEATING, Tom (1917–84) (*ART FORGERIES*)
Son of a poor London house-painter, this celebrated faker took up his father's work before serving in the Far East as a ship's stoker during the Second World War. Invalided out with nervous strain in 1944, after the war he studied art at Goldsmiths' College in London, but failed his diploma exams for lack of 'original composition'. Unable to afford frames when the Wildenstein gallery offered to exhibit his paintings, he became an art restorer, and as such was welcomed into several Scottish houses and castles. Like Eric **Hebborn** enraged by how shoddily dealers and the art establishment treat painters, early in the 1950s he began using his skills as a restorer to fake a wide range of artists – Rembrandt, Goya, Constable, Turner, Gainsborough, Renoir, Degas, and especially Samuel Palmer. Later insisting that his purpose was not to make money (he said he gave away more work than he ever sold) but to mock the so-called experts, he regarded himself as belonging to an immortal painterly brotherhood, his mission being to avenge artists bilked by dealers and dying in poverty. He had the mystical sense that these artists

of the past would 'come down' to him to inspire new work. One morning he awoke to find on his easel what looked like a Degas self-portrait, replacing the canvas he'd been working on the day before – apparently he'd done it in his sleep.

Over a quarter century feeding two and a half thousand fakes on to the market, on many of his 'Sexton Blakes' ('fakes' in Cockney rhyming slang) he would write, in white lead paint that would show up under X-ray, the word 'fake', or sign his own name. In others he included tiny portraits of the artist he was forging. Thus he admitted his forgeries to anyone smart enough to spot them.

Nobody did until 1976, when all at once he released thirteen previously unknown Samuel Palmers on to the market. The paper was modern: he no longer cared, and when exposed by Geraldine Norman, salesroom correspondent of *The Times*, he was quick to acknowledge what he'd been up to, and gladly collaborated with her in writing *The Fake's Progress*, a tongue-in-cheek account of his career. Yet at the same time he refused to issue a list of his fakes: why make things easier for the despised experts?

Tried for criminal deception in London in 1977, after five weeks the case was abandoned due to concern over his physical health. Yet while it lasted the press had a field day exposing crooked dealers and ignorant experts: all England rocked with laughter at the discomfiture of the art establishment, which could only foam in impotent rage as Keating became a popular celebrity. White-bearded and with an endearing sense of humour (which hid his deep sense of insecurity and sudden mood swings), soon he even had his own TV series, explaining the tricks of his trade and demystifying art to a fascinated public. Yet two days before the first programme was aired he died of a heart attack.

Just two months previously, in December 1983, he'd had the satisfaction of seeing Christie's auction a hundred and fifty of his paintings for almost £100,000. Months later, in September 1984, a second Christie's auction of 204 Keatings netted over a quarter of a million pounds. A 'Monet' and a 'Van Gogh' both fetched £16,000; a 'Keating' self-portrait £7,500. Nor was that the end of it. Soon forged Tom Keatings began to appear on the market.[1]

1. Newnham, *op. cit.*, pp.167–70; Yapp, *op. cit.*, pp.133–5.

KORESH, David (*See* **END-OF-THE-WORLD SCAMS**).

KRUGER, Bernhard (*See* **COUNTERFEITERS**)

KUJAU, Konrad (*See* **HITLER DIARIES**)

L

'If there were no falsehood in the world, there would be no doubt; if there were no doubt, there would be no inquiry; if no inquiry, no wisdom, no knowledge, no genius.'

(Walter Savage Landor, philosopher)

LANG, David (*DISAPPEARANCES*)

Two compilations of weird events published in the 1950s assert as true the sudden disappearance on 23 September 1880 of Tennessee farmer David Lang. Leaving his house and crossing a field in full view of his wife and children, abruptly he vanished. Driving a buggy up an adjacent lane, Judge August Peck and a friend saw him wave just before he disappeared. Despite a thorough search, he was never seen again, though one evening in April 1881, about seven months later, his children noticed a circle of stunted yellow grass (about fifteen feet in diameter) where he'd vanished. Eleven-year-old Sarah called out, and they were amazed to hear him, calling faintly for help, over and over, until his voice faded and was never heard again . . .

This unreferenced version appears in *Stranger than Science*, by Frank Edwards (1959), a year after another account, given in *Strange Mysteries of Time and Space*, by Harold T. Wilkins who, not naming the judge, identifies Peck's friend as Lang's brother-in-law. Dating the sequel as August 1881, not April, Wilkins describes the grass of the circle as 'high and rank', not 'stunted and yellow', and says neither animal nor insect would come near. Hearing their father's voice, the children told their 'startled mother'. Her calls were answered by her invisible husband for several days until at last his voice faded away. Though claiming to have summarised his account from several contemporary newspapers, Wilkins names none of them.

Investigating this story in 1976, Fortean researcher Robert Forrest checked Tennessee public records and contacted Herschel Payne of the Public Library of Nashville and Davidson County. Payne, it turned out, had also looked into it, to learn it had probably been fabricated in the 1880s by a travelling salesman, Joe Mulhatten – a champion liar in contests where men vied for the title of 'biggest liar'; the tale of David Lang had been his best lie. There was no proof that Lang, his family, or Judge Peck had lived; no surviving pictures of the farm; no journalistic documentation at all. It seems both Wilkins and Edwards had presented as true a tale which, some seventy years earlier, had won a lying contest – so highlighting the assertion that: 'History is the lie commonly agreed upon', and the weird way by which fables may be elevated to a level of spurious authenticity.[1]

1. 'Fortean Corrigenda', *Fortean Times* No. 18, London 1976, pp.6–7.

LESSING, Doris (1919–) (*LITERARY HOAXES*)

Often the name on the cover counts more than what's inside. Just as often authors may use more than one pseudonym to publish different books, either to evade contractual requirements, or to publish material at odds with their public image. The prolific American horror novelist Stephen King published several non-horror novels as Richard Bachman. Bachman's books did all right, but did much better when 'Bachman' was revealed as King.

Take Doris Lessing, one of the best-known, most inventive British novelists of recent years. Reportedly considered for a Nobel Prize in Literature, books like *The Golden Notebook* and the *Children of Violence* series, plus her exploratory *Briefing for a Descent into Hell* and the *Shikasta* science fiction series, have kept her name before the literary public for thirty years. In 1983 she perpetrated a hoax to show how hard life is for serious writers without a name. She gave her agent a new manuscript, *The Diary of a Good Neighbour*. This Michael Joseph (her usual publisher) at first turned down flat. Why? Because it was by 'Jane Somer'. It was only accepted when Lessing's authorship was revealed. Both Michael Joseph in Britain and Alfred Knopf in America colluded in the hoax. There were few reviews, none good: the book sold just 1,500 copies in Britain and 3,000 in the States. A year later 'Jane Somer' brought out a sequel. Copies were sent to reviewers claiming to be experts in Lessing's work. None guessed. Both reviews and sales were poor. Later she revealed the hoax and reissued the books under her own name. Point made and taken.

LEVITATION (*See* MIRABELLI, Carlos)

LEWIS-SMITH, Victor (contemporary) (*MEDIA HOAXES*)

Assuming the protean persona of Sir Clint Lucioni Rees-Bunce, this English hoaxer specialises in pranking the media. Rees-Bunce has appeared on TV as a gynaecologist dressed as Batman; as an Arab sheikh who runs an Islamic rock band; and in radio phone-ins as the driver of a Ford Capri with its windscreen totally obscured by cactus plants; or a man who's run up £200,000 in credit-card debt, his house invaded by loan sharks as he broadcasts. Like Reginald **Jones** he specialises in the **telephone hoax**. Phoning experts and always presenting Rees-Bunce as an idiot, he has masqueraded as the owner of a Picasso found in his loft from which he sawed off a piece, it being too large for his uses; as an aspiring DJ on Vatican Radio, and as a paraplegic playing 'The Sailor's Hornpipe' on the bass trombone in three seconds flat. Cultivating situations where his victims are given the chance to be kind, superior and tolerant to the ignoramus the other end of the line, Lewis-Smith told author Nick Yapp that: 'It's a version of the woman whose car has broken down on the motorway, standing on the hard shoulder and using her sexuality to get help.'[1] Once he and his partner Paul Sparks began writing letters of complaint to food companies, and in return got free food – but they were less lucky when complaining to a soup company of finding a condom in a can. Alarmed by recent sabotage in the food industry, the company stopped production and investigated the complaint. Soon the police arrived on Lewis-Smith's doorstep.

'But it was all right,' he told Yapp. 'They were pissing themselves when they left.'

'And you,' said Sparks, 'were shitting yourself when they arrived.'[2]

Finding it increasingly hard to think up hoaxes so bizarre or in such bad taste that the media would reject them, in November 1990 Lewis-Smith killed off Rees-Bunce after one last call to the Associate Producer of the TV show *Beadle's About*, to suggest that the show's front man, Jeremy Beadle, go to Maryland State Penitentiary's Death Row to film a prisoner playing the fairground game of moving a loop along a wiggly copper wire without touching it. 'If he manages it,' suggested Rees-Bunce, 'he goes free, but if he doesn't, it's not a bell that rings. The whole circuit's connected to his electric chair and he gets 20,000 volts through his frontal lobes.'

There was silence, followed by a horrified 'Oh dear, no. No, we couldn't *possibly* do that.'

'Why not?' Rees-Bunce asked.

'Our budget. It doesn't extend to foreign trips.'[3]

1. Yapp, *op. cit.*, p.66, author's interview with Victor Lewis-Smith.
2. *ibid.*, p.67, author's interview with Victor Lewis-Smith and Paul Sparks.
3. *ibid.*, p.67, quoting the *Sunday Correspondent*, 25 November 1990.

LLOYD, Sophie (contemporary) (*MEDIA HOAXES*)
Furious that women were denied entry to England's Magic Circle

association of magicians, no matter how good their act, in 1989 English stage-magician and agent Jenny Winstanley decided to do something about it. Too well known to members of the Circle to disguise herself, she persuaded Sophie Lloyd, who played a twelve-year-old boy in their double act, to invent Raymond, a not-too-bright sixteen-year-old obsessed with magic. A school, family, and social history was invented for him while she studied the characteristics of young men and practised being Raymond in everyday life. At last Raymond was ready to perform, with a club date booked for his debut. Wearing glasses, gloves, a wig and a body harness to suggest a youth, 'Raymond' succeeded, and for a year toured London with his act. At last Winstanley and Lloyd applied for his admission to the Magic Circle. Tested before 200 people in South London, Raymond passed the exam, even successfully mixing with the other magicians afterwards. Admitted to the Magic Circle, he received his badges and certificates.

When soon afterwards the Magic Circle declared women eligible for membership after all, Winstanley and Lloyd revealed the hoax. Were the members of the Magic Circle amused? Not a bit of it. Withdrawing Raymond's membership, they threatened Lloyd with legal action. There was even a threatening late-night call telling the two women: 'You will never work again in this business.' It wasn't an idle threat. They've found bookings hard to come by ever since. It seems some jokers just can't take a joke.[1]

1. Yapp, *op. cit.*, pp. 67–9.

LOCH NESS MONSTER (*ALIEN ANIMALS*)

Nessie a hoax? As a Scot, how can I say it? Could the saintly Adamnan have been deluded when, in his seventh-century *Life of St Columba*, he describes how in AD 565 Columba dismissed a monster that rose from the loch with: 'a great roar and open mouth'? Or the chronicler a millennium later who, telling of the death of Scotland's last dragon after a 'sair tussle', added that: 'No one has yet managed to slay the monster of Loch Ness, lately seen.' Nor, surely, can it be suggestive that in April 1933 the first modern sighting of this mainstay of Scottish tourism was by two hoteliers. Their report of: 'an enormous animal plunging and rolling' in the loch by Abriachan appeared in the *Inverness Courier* on 2 May. By October, with over twenty further sightings, Nessie was world news. Most sightings reported an unknown animal with long neck, tiny head, and a huge black body, but few believed it – until the publication round the world in 1934 of the famous photographs taken that April by respectable London surgeon R.K. Wilson.[1]

One of these, the 'Surgeon's Photograph', was so clear it seemed to clinch the matter. There *was* a monster, even if Wilson claimed only to have photographed an object 'moving in the water'. Why was he so reticent?

We'll get to that. For now, with monster-hunters flocking northward, even tight-lipped locals, who had long whispered fearful tales of the kelpie (water-horse) were admitting that: 'There's many a queer thing in that loch.'[2]

The sightings continued. Zoologists were baffled. Had a colony of prehistoric animals (plesiosaurs?) been cut off from the sea and stranded? Was it some kind of giant eel or slug? But what did it feed on? Despite salmon and trout aplenty, Loch Ness is sparse in aquatic vegetation and plankton. And why had no body, floating or beached, ever been found? The mystery was compounded by the nature of Loch Ness itself. Britain's largest freshwater loch is deep, dark and cold. Twenty-two miles long, up to one and a half miles wide, at one point almost a thousand feet deep, its waters are so peaty that the strongest light penetrates hardly at all. Unknown creatures could easily exist undetected in it. So the argument raged. Most scientists denied that such a beast could exist, but believers pointed out reports from some 300 other lakes round the world of similar creatures – the Bunyip in Australia's Lake Modewarre, and Champ in Lake Champlain in Canada. And while ignoring the weirder theories, distinguished naturalists like Gerald Durrell (calling the evidence 'incontrovertible'), David Attenborough, and Sir Peter Scott were sure there was *something* in Loch Ness. So was Robert H. Rines of the Academy of Applied Science, Boston. Setting up underwater sonar linked to a camera with a flashlight designed to take pictures once every fifty-five seconds so long as any large moving object remained in photographic range led, on 8 August 1972, to underwater colour photographs apparently showing a diamond-shaped paddle or flipper, four to six feet long. Its rhomboid shape led Scott to suggest the name *Nessiteras rhombopteryx* for the monster. Did he realise that this is a perfect anagram of 'monster hoax by Sir Peter S'?[3]

Whether he did or not, all such evidence was dismissed by zoologists of London's Natural History Museum as being of 'small gas bubbles' produced by 'the larvae of phantom midges'. Gerald Durrell concluded that, faced with evidence that: 'something large and unknown exists in the loch', the scientific fraternity: 'nervously takes refuge behind a barricade of ripples, leaping salmon, shadows, dead stags, logs of wood and what must surely be the most agile and acrobatic strings of otters ever seen . . .'[4]

Over the years there had been many hoaxes, each claimed by opponents as 'proof' of the Monster's non-existence. Yet in 1994 a killer punch was landed when the *Sunday Telegraph* offered proof that the best-known evidence, the 'Surgeon's Photograph' of April 1934, was part of an elaborate joke which had got out of hand. The perpetrator was not Wilson at all, but the flamboyant Marmaduke Arundel 'Duke' Wetherell, self-styled big-game hunter and film producer. Hired in December 1933 by the *Daily Mail* to produce evidence of the Monster, within forty-eight hours of his arrival at Loch Ness he'd found two footprints of an amphibious animal in soft mud near Fort Augustus at the south end of the loch. These were proclaimed as Monster-prints – until on 4 January the Natural History Museum, having tested plaster casts of the prints, announced them to be those of a young hippopotamus – probably part of an umbrella stand.

Hoaxed, Wetherell became a hoaxer himself. 'All right,' he told his twenty-one-year-old son Ian, 'we'll give them their monster.' So they did. It consisted of a toy submarine, with head, neck, and body of the monster formed by moulding plastic wood over the conning tower. In February or March 1934 Ian and Duke Wetherell returned to Loch Ness, floated the 'monster' in shallow water, and took the famous photographs. But for the hoax to work, a fellow conspirator was needed, someone respectable who'd enter into the spirit of the joke and act as front man. A friend suggested Robert Wilson, who agreed to take part. Giving the four plates to an Inverness chemist to be developed, he launched the myth. But those involved were unprepared for and overwhelmed by the publicity. Wilson, warned by the British Medical Association that the story could damage his professional standing, warded off all enquiries by hinting that his companion that April morning had been a married woman. Nobody ever approached the Wetherells. As for the 'monster', after taking the photographs, Duke sank it. No doubt it lies rusting in the depths of Loch Ness to this day.[5]

None of which proves, of course, that there isn't a *real* monster.

1. *The Loch Ness Story*, Nicholas Witchell, Corgi, London 1989, p.29.
2. *ibid.*, p.70.
3. *Alien Animals*, Janet and Colin Bord, Granada, London 1980, p.30.
4. *op. cit.*, Foreword by Gerald Durrell.
5. 'Nessie and a big-game hunter's ego', James Langton, London, *Sunday Telegraph*, 13 March 1994.

LUSTIG, 'Count' Victor (1890–1947) (*CONMEN*)

One of the greats. Victor Lustig not only swindled Al Capone and lived, but sold the Eiffel Tower for scrap. Son of the Mayor of Hostinne in Bohemia, a natural linguist educated at a Dresden boarding school, when sent to Paris to 'complete his studies' he turned to gambling to maintain his expensive lifestyle. Masquerading as 'Count' Victor Lustig, he met Nicky Arnstein, an expert at 'working the boats' – preying on rich Americans making the trip to Europe by transatlantic liner. Skilled at bridge, poker, and billiards, he mastered his trade, and after the First World War moved with Arnstein to America, where their last joint operation left him with $25,000 in government bonds.

Now on his own, in Kansas he found a way to use these bonds. One day a small-town banker named Green, who'd just foreclosed on a farm, was visited by a well-dressed, monocled foreigner, Count von Lustig.

Driven from his Austrian properties and seeking a property, he said he'd sold his family heirlooms for $50,000 of government bonds. Viewing the farm and delighted by it, back in Green's office he produced two packets. He opened one. It contained $25,000-worth of genuine bonds. 'I shall need some working capital, of course,' he said. 'Can you cash the other $25,000?'

That evening he wined and dined Green and another bank director at his hotel. The deeds were signed, $25,000 in cash was counted out, and the bankers left. By the time they learned that only the bonds at the top and bottom of the two packets were genuine, Lustig had left too. But he failed to cover his tracks. In New York a lawyer and a private detective forced him to return with them to Kansas. En route he persuaded the lawyer that people would lose all confidence in the easily duped bankers if the tale got out. Furious, the bankers agreed by phone to forget it if he repaid the $25,000. He did, but demanded $1,000 to compensate for the 'distress and inconvenience' he'd been caused. He got it.

A racecourse swindle in Montreal brought him to Paris with his 'private secretary', 'Dapper' Dan Collins. Reading a paper one morning in a Champs Elysées café, he had the same idea that, over in London, would soon occur to the Scot Harry **Furguson**. 'I think, he said, gazing at the Eiffel Tower, 'it's time we went into the scrap iron trade.'

He'd read that the French government was thinking of scrapping the Eiffel Tower due to the huge cost of much needed repairs. Posing as Deputy Director of the Ministère des Postes et des Télégraphes, he sent forged letters to five leading scrap dealers. Meeting him a week later at the Hotel Crillon and invited to submit tenders, they all did so. Chosen as the sucker due to his obvious desire for social acceptance was a M André Poisson. Yet when Collins told him his tender was accepted, he seemed suspicious. So Lustig had Collins phone him, asking him to meet the 'minister' at the hotel. It was a matter so private, said Collins, that they couldn't meet at the ministry. On arrival, Poisson heard the minister complain of his 'inadequate salary'. He understood immediately. Handing over a large cash bribe, a few days later he sent his cheque. Cashing it, the Count and Dapper Dan were quickly out of France.

Next, in Miami, he told a young actress he was a successful Broadway producer. Taking her to Havana, at parties and in casinos he let it be known he was preparing a new musical. A star-struck Rhode Island millionaire, dreaming of being the toast of Broadway, offered $34,000 in backing. Pocketing this in cash in a Rhode Island hotel, Lustig took his victim to a speakeasy, where a message came that an urgent phone call from New York awaited him in his hotel. Saying he'd be back, Lustig absconded.

By the time the victim went to the police, he was in Palm Beach, California, in a Rolls Royce with a hired Japanese chauffeur. Soon he met Hermann Loller, a millionaire with business difficulties. Again the Austrian count who'd lost his lands, he hinted that he knew how (literally) to make money. Unaware that Lustig knew of his problems, Loller pressed him. Reluctantly the Count admitted he had a machine able to reproduce bank notes, and in his hotel room showed Loller a well-made box, a narrow slot at either end. Setting dials and turning knobs, into one slot he fed a real $100 bill and a blank piece of bank note paper. Explaining that the photochemical reproduction process would take six hours, later he pulled a lever, and out came two identical bank notes. Suggesting that Loller change them to confirm that the banks couldn't detect the forgery, Lustig warned him not to change them at the same bank, as both had identical serial numbers (he'd changed two threes on one note into two eights). Begged to sell the box, the Count grudgingly accepted $25,000 in cash. Back on his yacht Loller found the box empty but for two rubber rollers and sheets of blank paper. Lustig was gone – and Loller could hardly go to the police.

So to the attempt to con the mobster Al Capone. It was a challenge which, despite the danger, the Count would never have forgiven himself for ducking. Months later, gazing at the shuttered windows of the Hawthorne Inn, Capone's Chicago headquarters, Lustig was spotted, 'invited in', frisked, and escorted into Capone's presence. Impressing the gangster with his elegant self-possession, he improvised a yarn about a Wall Street scam he planned. It was guaranteed, he said, to double anyone's money in fifty days.

'What's the minimum stake?' asked Capone.

'Fifty grand,' said Lustig.

Counting out $50,000 in cash, Capone pressed a button on his desk. A wall panel slid aside. Behind it stood a hoodlum armed with a machine pistol.

'Sixty days,' said the most dangerous man in America. 'Understand?'

In fact Lustig had no plan at all. It was the challenge that had made him do it. Back in New York with Capone's money, he knew he couldn't touch it. Lose any, and he was dead. When the sixty days were up, he took a gamble. Returning to Chicago, he let it be known where he was. Summoned before a furious Capone, he hung his head in shame.

'I'm so sorry, Mr Capone. I had some trouble. The scheme didn't work.'

'You've lost my money?' Red in the face, Capone reached for the button.

Lustig stayed calm. Producing the $50,000, he laid it down on the desk, and with a mournful shrug apologised, saying how embarrassed he felt and how much he'd have liked to have made money on the scheme. 'As for myself,' he added, turning away from the amazed mobster, 'You can imagine how much I need it.'

'Hold it!' Capone himself was fooled. 'You're in a fix?'

The Count smiled ruefully. 'I must admit that I am.'

'Here's five,' said Capone. 'Will that help?'

'You are a gentleman, Mr Capone,' said the elegant Victor Lustig, bowing deeply as he pocketed the five one thousand dollar bills – and then he was gone.

That was his greatest hour. After that, it was all downhill. Despite a fat FBI file, so far he'd avoided conviction because his shamefaced victims refused to testify against him. But in 1934 the US Treasury put together a team to track down **counterfeiters** flooding the market with fake $100 bills. The trail led to a high-class brothel off New York's Park Avenue. The house was watched, the phone tapped. When a 'Mr Frank', speaking in a cultured European voice, rang to announce his visit, the agents closed in. Spotting them as he arrived in his chauffeured car, Lustig fled. Captured, he was charged with conspiracy and locked up in the Manhattan House of Detention. Soon he escaped it via a rope made of bedsheets. Sliding down from an upper window, he bowed politely to the astonished passers-by, then hurried off.

Three months later 'Robert Miller' was arrested in Pittsburgh. It was Lustig's forty-eighth arrest, and his last. In December 1935 he was tried in New York with the forger, William Watts, who told the court that Lustig: 'was the best distributor of counterfeit money that ever lived'. Dejected by this unwanted praise, he changed his plea to guilty, and got twenty years. Eleven of these he spent in Alcatraz, where Al Capone was also held, for tax evasion. In 1947, aged fifty-seven, Lustig fell ill. Transferred to the Medical Center for Federal Prisoners in Springfield, Missouri, this most elegant and stylish of swindlers died of pneumonia. (See page xvii for his 'Ten Commandments for Conmen'.)[1]

1.   Larsen, *op. cit.*, pp.190–203.

LYSENKO, Trofim (1898–1976) (*SCIENTIFIC SCAMS*)

About **Kammerer**, doubt remains. About Trofim Denisovish Lysenko, there is none whatever. Rising to prominence as a Soviet agronomist at a time when millions of Russians were starving under Stalin's new regime of collective farming, with Mendelian geneticists and neo-Darwinian biologists declared 'class enemies', Lysenko attempted to make nature obey Marxist ideology. Just as human nature was said to be malleable, so too, he argued, it should be possible to show that the nature of plants can be moulded by their environment, whatever their genetic make-up.

Assigned to a remote agricultural station in the north Caucasus, from 1923 on he set about trying to find a good winter crop by promoting 'vernalisation', a process involving pre-soaking and pre-chilling winter wheat to allow spring planting, thus gaining a bigger yield. The method was known already: what he did was to extend it from wheat to every kind of crop. In fact, as the farmers he lectured soon discovered, his theories didn't work. But that didn't matter. They were *ideologically* correct. Transferred in 1929 to the Odessa Institute, then to the Moscow Institute of Genetics, he was so enraged by academic criticisms that he'd made no 'discovery' at all that from now on he refused to submit his articles and data for scientific scrutiny, instead asserting his ideas to the reporters of mass-circulation newspapers. Made President of the Academy of Agricultural Sciences in February 1938 and director of the Genetics Institute in 1940, his power (he had Stalin's complete support) grew to the point that those daring to criticise his theories not only lost their jobs, accused of the 'wreckage of Soviet agriculture', but in some cases were tried and executed. Whole institutes were closed down; the science of genetics in Soviet Russia was virtually destroyed. Meanwhile the real wrecker maintained his authority. Surviving the death of Stalin in 1953 and even the fall of Khrushchev in 1964 (though then losing his post as Director of the Institute of Genetics), he remained unchallenged until 1965.

In September that year, following investigation of a Lysenko research station which had reported butterfat yields from the offspring of Jersey bulls crossed with large domestic cows, an official inquiry concluded that the Jersey station was a fraud and Lysenko's herd of cattle a showpiece, consisting of specially selected cattle given a highly intensive diet. It also reported that data had been deliberately falsified. Despite Lysenko's fury, the investigations, now begun, could not be stopped. At the end of 1965 the Academy of Science and the Soviet Ministry of Agriculture nominated a state review board. Discovering dishonesty in the experimental design of his tests, it denounced his methods as 'economically unsound' and his recommendations as 'erroneous'. Lysenko and his supporters had gained recognition for their ideas by: 'distortion of facts, demagoguery, repression, obscurantism, slander, fabricated accusation, insulting name calling and physical elimination of opponents'.[1]

At last, though twenty-five years too late for Soviet agriculture as a whole, he was disgraced, and his criminal hoax revealed.[2]

1. *The Rise and Fall of Lysenko*, Zhory Medvedev, Columbia University Press, New York 1969.
2. Kohn, *op. cit.*, pp.63–74.

M

'No normal human being wants to hear the
truth. It is the passion of a small and
aberrant minority of men, most of them
pathological. They are hated for telling it
while they live, and when they die they are
swiftly forgotten. What remains to the
world, in the field of wisdom, is a series of
long tested and solidly agreeable lies.'

(H.L. Mencken)

MACGREGOR, Gregor (1786–1845) (*FRAUD*)
A vast fraud based on one of the biggest cock-and-bull stories of all time
began in 1811 when Venezuelan patriot Simón Bolívar came to London
seeking British aid in his war of liberation against Spain. Among those
joining up was the scion of an old Highland family, Gregor MacGregor.
Arriving in Caracas to serve under General Miranda – a sixty-year-old
Spanish rebel who years earlier had fought with the American colonists
against the British – the young man heard of Miranda's dream of creating
a new Inca empire. Maybe this was what set MacGregor thinking. But
the fraud lay years ahead. For now the war grew desperate. With the
Spanish fighting back in 1812 an earthquake devastated Caracas, and
many interpreted it as God's revenge on the revolutionaries. Whole
garrisons of Bolívar's troops went over to the Spanish. So did Miranda,
to end his days in a Cadiz prison. As for MacGregor, he not only
remained loyal but, promoted to general for his bravery and military
skill, played a decisive part in Bolívar's rout of the Spanish at Araure.

The immediate danger over, with money raised in the USA he hired
mercenaries to seize Florida from Spain. This venture failing, he
returned to Venezuela where he was again needed, the Spanish having
been reinforced. At the head of British recruits he won decisive battles
and, with Venezuela free at last, the hero married Bolívar's daughter.

What happened next seems inexplicable. Did he conceive his fantastic scheme after nearly dying in an attack on Spanish Panama in 1820, or had Miranda suggested it years earlier with his talk of a new Inca empire? Or was it suggested by his experience raising money in the USA? It is as impossible to be sure as it is to guess why this brave, resourceful soldier now embarked on one of the biggest scams in history. For later in 1820 he led a small, non-military force to Nicaragua's Atlantic coast. This swampy, desolate land, known as the Mosquito Shore after a local tribe and nominally a British protectorate since 1655, had been abandoned by European settlers for years. Apparently it suited his purpose exactly. Persuading the chief of the Poyais Indians of the interior to grant him a coastal concession for colonisation, when a while later he appeared in London he was no longer plain General Gregor MacGregor but Gregor the First, sovereign Prince of Poyais.

Exploiting general ignorance of Central America and a common eagerness to invest overseas, he spun the yarn that Poyais (the Mosquito Shore) was a paradise. Ringed by great gold-veined mountains, rich with mahogany and cedar, the fertile land fed vast herds of cattle and grew cotton, sugar, maize, tropical fruits – whatever you planted in it. There was a fine capital city at the mouth of the Black River with palace and parliament, opera house and cathedral, boulevards, bridges, banks and port installations. The government was democratic, with three elected chambers, and the Chief of State was – who else but Gregor the First, sovereign Prince of Poyais and Cazique of the Poyer nation!

And he was believed. Nobody asked why nobody in Whitehall or in shipping circles had ever heard of Poyais – nor did MacGregor give anyone time to think. He moved fast. Promoting investment and colonisation, as 'Gregor the First' he sent his henchman William John Richardson ('The Commander of the Most Illustrious Order of the Green Cross') with letters of credence to his 'brother sovereign' George IV. Richardson was received. Diplomatic recognition of Poyais was organised via discreet bribes; engravings of the capital of Poyais were sold on London and Edinburgh streets; pamphlets describing the land and emphasising the money to be made went to businessmen and bankers; a handbook for would-be settlers was produced by another conspirator, Thomas Strangeways. MacGregor even hired ballad-singers to sing the praises of Poyais on street corners. Immigration offices were set up in London and Edinburgh, land was sold to would-be colonists at four shillings an acre; and in September 1822 the first fifty sailed from Leith in the *Honduras Packet*. Among them were farmers who'd sold up to pay for the crossing, and craftsmen whose trade had slumped with the arrival of mass-production techniques.

So off they all went to paradise even as early in 1823 MacGregor persuaded the London bankers Sir John Perring and Co. to float a loan of £200,000 'for the purpose of consolidating the state of Poyais'. The share issue was a success, soon fully subscribed. Perring never questioned the securities, described as 'the general resources of the State of Poyais'. After all, why should he doubt a man who'd been received by the king and lately knighted in consideration of his services to Great Britain's relationship with Poyais?

Meanwhile the *Honduras Packet* settlers reached the Mosquito Shore to find empty beaches and arid, sun-blasted hills. Where was Poyais? Where was the golden city? They sent a scouting party west as another ship arrived from Scotland, with 150 colonists. As soon as they landed a hurricane swept both ships out to sea, stranding them. Many died before news of their plight got to British Honduras, 300 miles further north. The rescue ship from Belize arrived just in time to prevent their total annihilation. Other ships went out to intercept another seven colonising vessels, diverting them to existing ports or turning them back. From autumn 1824 on hundreds of disillusioned settlers were back to tell their angry tale and seek out the culprit. But by now he was in France, pulling the same scam. The first group of French colonists sailed from Le Havre late in 1825. How the scandal took so long to erupt defies belief, as does the fact that in London a further loan was floated, this time for £300,000, with the non-existent 'gold mines of Paulaza' as security. Again, investors rushed to buy into it.

But at last the tale did get out, and when MacGregor rashly returned to London in 1827 he was arrested and jailed at Tothill Fields. Yet the Great and Good who'd involved themselves with him and received their rake-off were desperate to avoid publicity. All charges were dropped, he was released and advised to return to Paris, where exactly the same thing happened. For several years he lay low, enjoying his ill-gotten gains, but in 1836, incredibly, attempted a comeback. It failed. Nobody was interested in Poyais any longer. Broke, in 1839 he applied to the Venezuelan government for citizenship, restoration of his former military rank, and a life pension. These were granted. He settled in Caracas, an honoured, respected veteran of the War of Liberation, and spent the rest of his life at ease. Sir Gregor MacGregor, Prince of Poyais, had got away with it, scot-free.[1]

1. Larsen, *op. cit.*, pp.71–81.

MACPHERSON, James (1736–96) (*LITERARY HOAXES*)

The longest-lived literary hoax (though in a sense no hoax at all) of the mid-eighteenth century relied on nostalgia. With the Industrial Revolution's 'dark satanic mills' on the march, romantics dreamed of an ancient world full of brooding bards and noble savages as popularised by Jean-Jacques Rousseau. The Celtic lands, especially Highland Scotland which in 1715 and again in 1745 had erupted in support of Jacobite claims, were an ideal locale for such a world – and in Edinburgh in 1760 appeared a dramatic publication: *Fragments of Ancient Poetry, Collected in the Highlands of Scotland, and Translated from the Gaelic or Erse Languages.* Sparking immediate controversy throughout Europe, in December 1761 it was followed by the London publication of *Fingal, an Ancient Epic in Six Books, Composed by Ossian, Son of Fingal*; and in 1763 by a third volume, *Temora.*

Purportedly translations from the original Gaelic of heroic poems by the legendary third-century bard Ossian, they were soon denounced as fake by London's literary critics. It was, after all, just sixteen years since Bonnie Prince Charlie's Highlanders had invaded England as far as Derby. English critics could hardly accept such a militant Scots epic as genuine. This prejudice blighted and slanted the controversy thereafter.

The 'translator' was James Macpherson, a Gaelic-speaking farmer's son from the Central Highlands. Failing to graduate either from Aberdeen or Edinburgh universities, disliking his work as village teacher and private tutor, in autumn 1759 this fluent versifier met the author John Home. Quoting Gaelic verses from memory, he showed Home other verses in manuscript, collected in the Highlands. Encouraged by Home, he produced sixteen translated pieces, published in Edinburgh in July 1760 as the *Fragments.* These were well received and accepted as genuine, though one critic did doubt: 'whether they were the invention of antiquity or of a modern Scotchman'. In the introduction Hugh Blair, Professor of Literature at Edinburgh University, hinted at another work, a 'heroic poem' in epic form relating the wars of Fion or Fingal. This might, he said, be recovered and translated: 'if encouragement were given'.

Macpherson didn't want to take it further. To make the Fingal poem historically credible involved reversing history to suggest that the protagonists (Cuchullin, Cairbar, Fingal and Ossian) were in origin Scots, and only later adopted by the Irish as Cuchullain, Cairbre, Fionn and Oisin. Though part of Scottish lore since the Irish invasion of Argyll ('Coast of the Gael') *c.*AD 500, he would have to portray them as the heroes of an earlier Caledonian invasion of Ulster *c.*AD 200. The first poem would therefore have to describe the Scots king Fingal aiding the Irish against Norse pirates. But this in turn meant putting back the earliest-known Norse invasions by some five centuries. All very tricky.

But with £60 raised by subscription, he was persuaded (mostly by Home) to start the search. Travelling to the remotest reaches of the Highlands and Hebridean isles, he wrote down poems as he heard them, and translated others from old manuscripts. Back in Edinburgh, on 16 January 1761 he said he'd found 'a pretty complete poem, truly epic, concerning Fingal, and of an antiquity easily ascertainable'.[1]

Describing the invasion of Ireland by Swarin, King of Lochlin (Denmark) in the purplest of purple prose ('His armour rattled in thunder; and the lightning of his eyes was terrible'), *Fingal* was an instant hit in Ireland and on the Continent, but was denounced as spurious and bombastic in England. Publication in 1763 of a sequel, *Temora*, fuelled the controversy. Writing to Blair from London, the philosopher David Hume said the poems were taken to be: 'a palpable and impudent forgery', and later described Macpherson as 'most perverse and unamiable'.

Scorning his doubters, Macpherson refused Blair's suggestion that he solicit the sworn testimony of those who'd given him his materials. Challenged to produce the Gaelic originals, he left manuscripts with his publishers, advertised the fact, and promised to print them if subscribers came forward. None did. Taking back the manuscripts, he withdrew from the fray, and ignored the charges of fakery. Thereafter, only Samuel Johnson could get under his skin. The good doctor still smarted at how another Scot, James Lauder, had duped him in 1748 with 'proof' that Milton had plagiarised *Paradise Lost* from older Latin manuscripts. Now, calling Gaelic: 'the rude speech of a barbarous people who had few thoughts to express', in his *Journey to the Western Isles of Scotland* (1775) he denied the existence of original Gaelic texts, said there were not 500 lines in all Gaelic over a hundred years old, and derided Macpherson's audacity as: 'the last refuge of guilt'.

Infuriated, Macpherson (a big man) challenged him. Johnson bought a stout oak stick. 'I received your foolish and impudent letter,' he replied, declaring that he would repel violence and 'never be deterred . . . by the menaces of a ruffian.'[2] But the dispute (of which Walpole wrote that Macpherson had been as much a bully as Johnson a brute) went no further. Turning to politics, Macpherson defended Lord North's American policy and in time retired wealthy to his native Badenoch. The final irony came when he died. Buried in Westminster Abbey (an odd last resting place for a militant Gael), he ended up right next to Johnson! No doubt their ghosts argue still.

Set up in 1797 by the Highland Society of Scotland to examine the issue, in 1805 a committee reported that the legend of Fingal and Ossian was ancient in Scotland; that Ossianic poetry remained abundant in the Highlands; and that Macpherson had embroidered genuine original material – as he'd admitted in his preface to *Fingal*. Much later, the 1862 publication of *The Book of the Dean of Lismore* showed that Macpherson had used this early sixteenth-century collection of some 11,000 verses of earlier Gaelic poetry. Though basing only four of his Ossianic passages on *Lismore* (apparently he thought its allusions too modern), it seems this was the text he'd lodged with his London publishers when challenged to produce sources. In effect, there was no hoax. Though never finding the epic he claimed, and while freely arranging the fragments he collected, the original material was genuine, though not from the third century. Few read *Fingal* now, but the controversy has endured. As late as 1983 Macpherson's work was attacked by English historian Sir Hugh Trevor-Roper. Is it coincidence that (as with Johnson over Lauder before him) in April that year Trevor-Roper had been mortified to learn that the **Hitler Diaries**, which earlier he'd accepted as genuine, had been proved to be . . . a fake?

1. Stephen and Lee (eds), *op. cit.*
2. *Norton Anthology of English Literature*, ed. M.H. Abrams, Norton, New York 1968, p.1898, quoting Boswell's *Life of Johnson*.

MAESTRI, Cesare (1929–) (*EXPLORATION HOAXES*)

During the 1950s, even as massively organised expeditions scaled most of the great Himalayan peaks, another kind of climbing developed at the southern tip of the Andes in Chilean Patagonia, where dramatic granite spears soar between eastern pampas and western icecap. Though none are higher than 11,073 feet, they are terrifyingly steep and lashed by some of the world's worst weather. In 1952 climbing the highest, Fitzroy, from its summit Lionel Terray and Guido Magnone saw nearby a needle-like pinnacle. Called Cerro Torre, at 9,908 feet it had never even been attempted. Terray later said he thought it might never be climbed, and more than one expert reckoned it the hardest mountain in the world.

In 1958 two rival Italian teams accepted the challenge. One consisted of Walter Bonatti and Carlo Mauri, two of the world's finest climbers. They were at the peak of their form. But Cerro Torre beat them. Reaching a high pass on the southwest flank which they called the 'Col of Hope' they crawled on up before admitting defeat with several thousand feet still to go. The other team, led by Cesare Maestri, attacked from the opposite, eastern side. Bonatti's equal technically, Maestri was the superior solo climber. Cerro Torre beat him too, but unlike Bonatti he decided to return. He was not one to be seen to be beaten.

Born in Trento, his mother had died when he was seven. His father, who ran a travelling theatre, fled with his son to Bologna when the Nazis seized Trento. Cesare was always a loner. Beginning to climb after the war, later he bragged that having followed a leader on his first six routes, he never again, save for one climb, went second on the rope. He began soloing not only up his routes, but back down again. His climbs on the Dolomites, northern Italy's steep limestone crags, were so daring that soon he was known as the 'Spider of the Dolomites'.

The 1958 attempt on Cerro Torre was his first major climb abroad. For the 1959 attempt he invited as his partner the brilliant Austrian Toni Egger. Renowned for his fast, daring ice routes and for his 1957 alpine-style ascent of Jirishhanca in the Peruvian Andes, when he had eschewed fixed ropes, Egger had never climbed with Maestri. They'd met only once, in a hut on the Dolomites, and though he'd be the only

Austrian in an Italian expedition, he was eager to try Cerro Torre. But by the time they got there, he'd developed a foot infection. So, with Argentinian Cesarino Fava, in January 1959 Maestri reached the base of the gigantic eastern precipice (three camps were needed to get even that far), then climbed higher to fix ropes. Despite his infection Egger joined Maestri to push on up a 1,200-foot diagonal groove. For two weeks the weather got so bad they had to leave the mountain, returning on 26 January to find a cache of pitons lost under new snow. Maestri was in a dark mood when on 28 January they pushed up the diagonal groove towards the north col, christening it 'the Col of Conquest'.

Only he knows what happened next. Seeing the icy upper wall rising 2,500 feet at a dizzy angle, Fava gave up and descended to await the other two in the ice cave at Camp 3. He had to wait six days. For three the weather held, then a warm wind blew up, melting summit ice and sending avalanches crashing down. On the sixth day, sure they were in trouble or dead, he left the cave to descend to the base camp for help – and found Maestri, buried in snow at the edge of a crevasse, almost delirious. Recovering, Maestri said he and Egger had reached the summit, and amid terrible conditions had descended almost to the highest fixed rope when an avalanche had swept Egger away, with both rucksacks.

Word of the ascent spread rapidly. Terray called it: 'the greatest climbing feat of all time'. Maestri told how on the ascent he had, for the first time in years, let someone else lead, Egger being lighter and the ice crust thin. At the top of each pitch Egger had dug through the ice to the rock beneath, laboriously hand-driving a drill hole for an expansion bolt to serve as anchor. Each bolt, said Maestri, had taken 500 hammer blows to drive. They'd reached the summit late on the third day. Warm winds had begun to blow so hard their ropes were blown out horizontally. With avalanches roaring on all sides they'd struggled down as far as the diagonal groove when, said Maestri, Egger had been swept away, along with all their gear – including the camera recording their climb.

Doubts began to surface when in an Italian climbing magazine Maestri's 1958 rival Carlo Mauri implied that Cerro Torre remained unclimbed. Scepticism grew. Increasingly it seemed unlikely that anyone could have climbed that last 2,500 feet. And Maestri, so vague about the details, seemed to have lost his nerve. He climbed slowly now, using too many bolts. The controversy intensified in 1968 when a strong British team, using new gear and techniques which had revolutionised mountaineering so that once desperate routes were now almost routine, failed on Cerro Torre's southeast ridge, well below the summit. They'd found it fiendishly hard. Then Japanese and Argentine expeditions failed well below the British high point. In 1970 Carlo Mauri returned. Surmounting a tower of rock and ice like a shoulder on the main peak, he found the way blocked by 'cauliflowers' of ice 600 feet below the summit. Declaring he'd never return, scornfully he implied that no human being had yet stood on the summit. To silence his detractors, Maestri returned. Armed with a gasoline-powered compressed-air drill for placing bolts, his team stormed the southeast ridge. For fifty-four days they persisted, winching up behind them almost 300 pounds of gear. Forced to retreat just above the high point of the 1968 British expedition, five months later Maestri returned, to reach a ledge 150 feet below the summit. Here his way was blocked by a huge mushroom of ice. Dismissing it as: 'just a lump of ice, not really part of the mountain – it'll blow away one of these days', he claimed the ascent. The climbing world was appalled. 'Cerro Torre: a Mountain Desecrated' claimed the British journal *Mountain*. More than ever now his 1959 ascent was doubted. Interviewed at his home by *Mountain* editor Ken Wilson and three others, Maestri refused to mark his 1959 route on a photograph.

In 1974 an Italian team reached the summit ice-mushroom which Maestri had denigrated. Conquering it after a long battle, at last they stood on the summit. They did not find the tin can in which Maestri and Egger had supposedly left their names in 1959. That same year American Jim Donini and Englishman Mick Coffey found the remains of Toni Egger in a glacier, a mile and a half from Cerro Torre. The next year Donini returned with two others. Following the 1959 route, they found gear left by Maestri and Egger everywhere. At last just below an ice field on the east face, at the top of a pitch they found a pack containing pitons, wedges, and rope. And then, nothing. There was no further evidence of progress by Maestri and Egger in the final 5,000 feet of the climb.

When did Egger die, and how? What happened? Maestri alone knows. The only thing that seems sure is that he never reached the summit of Cerro Torre in 1959.[1]

1. Roberts, *op. cit.*, pp.136–51.

MAJESTIC 12 (*See* **ROSWELL INCIDENT, The**)

MALETTA, The (*See* **HOAXES IN WARFARE**)

MALSKAT, Lothar (*See* **FEY, Dietrich**)

MANDEVILLE, Sir John (d.1372) (*LITERARY HOAXES*)
The Voyage and Travels of Sir John Mandeville, Knight, the original volume of armchair discovery, was the most popular book of its time. With those able to read eagerly devouring tales of journeys to remote, exotic lands, as by Marco Polo and Friar Odoric of Portenone, Mandeville became known as the greatest traveller of all. But by the sixteenth century he had gained a new reputation – as the greatest liar of all.

In the earliest-known manuscript (French, 1371), he tells how between 1322 and 1356 he left England to visit the Holy Land by way of Paris, Constantinople and Egypt. Looting earlier works for detail, he went on into romantic, unknown Asia, unapologetically borrowing from the *Travels* of Friar Odoric, current bestiaries, and classical authors like Pliny. He visited an isle of dog-headed men, a land of headless people with eyes and mouths in their backs, and the exotic realm of Prester John. From the Land of Darkness he passed through the country of the Vegetable Lamb to find the Ten Lost Tribes of Israel, long ago imprisoned by Alexander the Great in the Caspian Mountains. He saw the giant reeds of the Isle of Panten, served the Great Khan, and drank from the Fountain of Eternal Youth – which seems at odds with the explanation in his introduction that, being now crippled by gout, he writes his memoirs as a solace for his 'wretched ease'.

A rattling good yarn. Everyone loved it. It was a bestseller.

Yet who *was* 'Sir John Mandeville'? He claimed to be from St Albans in England, but, though the name 'Mandeville' was then common round St Albans, there is no trace of him in local records, and the legend of his burial there is a later invention. More probably he lived and wrote in France, was called Jean de Burgoyne, and was buried at the Church of the Guillemins in Liège, demolished in 1798. Before then many authors recorded seeing in it the tomb of 'Jean de Mandeville', and on it the date of his death: 17 November 1372.

In his 'General Chronicle', Jean d'Outremeuse (1338–99) says Mandeville lived in Liège after 1343 as 'Jean de Bourgogne dit à la barbe'. A copy of a treatise on the plague by 'Jean de Bourgogne dit à la barbe' was part of the 1371 Paris manuscript of the *Travels*, written at Liège in 1365. The name appears in the Latin Vulgate version of the *Travels*, while d'Outremeuse also tells how, in his will and on his death-bed, Jean de Bourgogne revealed himself as: 'Messire Jean de Mandeville, chevalier, comte de Montfort en Angleterre'. He said that, having killed an unnamed English count or earl, he had traversed 'three parts' of the world before settling in Liège.

No Mandeville was ever an English Count of Montfort, yet there *was* a John de Burgoyne – the chamberlain of John, Baron of Mowbray, who in 1321 rebelled against King Edward II's favourites, the Despencers. Mowbray was executed: de Burgoyne, who had joined his master in the rebellion, would have had good reason to flee England in 1322, the date 'Mandeville' says he left England.

So the *Travels* were a fake, and likewise the name of the author. But this never stopped anyone enjoying the original rattling good yarn.[1]

1. Stephen and Lee (eds), *op. cit.*

MARTIAN HEAD, The (*UFO HOAXES*)
Do astronomers and the American space agency NASA downplay the

significance of a giant human head which, sculpted in the Martian Plain of Cydonia, stares out into space? Some conspiracy theorists insist that this is so. This extraordinary feature, photographed on 25 July 1976 by a NASA Viking probe, certainly exists – but is it artificial or natural? It looks very impressive with its large, domed forehead like that of a porcelain buddha, its darkly brooding eyes, its nose with identifiable nostrils, and its weak chin. Apparently earless, its cheekbones are also missing – doubtless due to erosion over the millennia since an alien species carved it and left it there for humanity to discover.

Why would the authorities wish to cover up or downplay such a find? Obviously, because NASA is afraid to admit a potential encounter with a technologically superior race of beings like those in the movie *2001*. It would cause panic (remember the 1938 radio broadcast of *War of the Worlds* by Orson **Welles**?). It would undermine authority. It would require a rethinking of our ideas about the universe. It must be kept secret.

Is this why, on 21 August 1993, three days before it was about to start orbiting the planet, the $1.5 billion Mars Observer spacecraft just vanished? Launched eleven months earlier, it would have conducted a detailed photographic survey of the Martian surface lasting one Martian year (687 days). Its transmitter switched off for the orbital manoeuvre and failed to switch on again. Equally mysterious were the failures in 1989 of the two Russian Phobos spacecraft.

But did Mars Observer *really* fail? The lobby group 'Mars Mission' formed by Richard Hoagland suggests that information is filtering back to Earth to be processed by those in the know, and being kept from the rest of us. Hoagland, whose group accuses NASA of a 'billion dollar cover-up', asked Jodrell Bank to break the NASA monopoly on Mars data and confirm that Mars Observer is still transmitting. Sir Bernard Lovell, founder of the British radio observatory, did not mention this when telling reporters that Jodrell Bank's attempts to pick up signals from the lost probe had failed. Just as unsuccessful was the attempt by those attending the National New Age, Alien Agenda and Cosmic Conspiracies Conference in Phoenix, Arizona, to revive the probe by beaming 'loving energy' to it.

Hoagland has also suggested that a secret 'isolationist' group within NASA sabotaged the probe to prevent confirmation of the existence of the Martian metropolis which doubtless lies under or round about the Face.[1]

Percival Lowell, the astronomer who popularised the theory that ridges and hollows detected on the Martian surface by telescopes a century ago were the water-bearing canals of an advanced civilisation, would follow the controversy with interest were he still alive.

And one other thing. In *The Mayan Factor*, New Age mystic José Argüelles points out that in 1947, long before the Face was first seen in

1976, Japanese-American sculptor Isamu Noguchi proposed a monumental sculpture a mile wide of a face looking skyward, to be called *The Sculpture to be Seen from Mars*. This project was never executed – or was it? Perhaps Noguchi was hired by the Martians.[2]

1. 'Martians Zap Orbiter', *Fortean Times* No. 73, London 1994, p.16.
2. *The Mayan Factor*, José Argüelles, Bear & Co, Santa Fe 1987.

'MARTIN, Major William' (*See* **HOAXES IN WARFARE**)

MCGRADY, Mike (20th century) (*LITERARY HOAXES*)
In 1966 this Long Island *Newsday* reporter decided with twenty-four colleagues to write a blockbuster satirising the steamy productions of Harold Robbins and Jacqueline Susann. Setting out to tell the tale of Gillian Blake, a radio talk-show hostess who takes revenge on her sleep-around spouse by seducing married men, McGrady insisted that: 'there will be unremitting emphasis on sex. Also, true excellence in writing will be blue-pencilled into oblivion.' Written in a fortnight ostensibly by Long Island housewife Penelope Ashe (in reality McGrady's sister-in-law), *Naked Came the Stranger* was soon bought by Lyle Stuart (publisher of two of the three Howard Hughes biographies to escape the billionaire's lawyers). He saw through the hoax immediately but loved it, spending $50,000 on promoting the book. After it rapidly sold 20,000 copies McGrady blew the whistle and admitted the hoax. The result? That same day another 9,000 copies were sold. With over 100,000 sold in hardback, Dell bought the paperback rights for a six-figure sum: McGrady was offered half a million dollars to write the sequel. Horrified by the implications of his success, he refused, instead producing *Stranger than Naked, Or How to Write Dirty Books for Fun*.
'America', he lamented in it, 'sometimes I worry about you.'[1]

1. *The Pleasures of Deception*, Norman O. Moss, Chatto & Windus, London 1977, pp.115–16.

MEANS, Gaston Bullock (1880–1938) (*CONMEN*)
A suave, baby-faced southerner from North Carolina, this ex-cotton broker and part-time lawyer was 'the greatest natural detective ever known'. So his boss at the Burns Detective Agency called him. But after he set up his own agency in 1915 he became one of the greatest natural heels ever known, using his reputation to swindle and worse.
In 1917, eager to meet heiress Maude R. King (who'd married a millionaire fifty years older and was now a wealthy widow), he hired a thug to mug her, then attacked and saw off the mugger, so endearing himself to her. Becoming her manager and protector, he dipped into her purse so often (to the tune of $150,000) that even she became suspicious.

So he took her on a hunting trip in the woods back home – then staggered out of the woods alone, sobbing to former friends and neighbours that she'd shot herself while fiddling with his Colt automatic. He'd put it in the crook of a tree to kneel at the creek's edge for a sip of water, then looked round to see her twirling it playfully. His warning shout had so startled her she'd dropped the gun and it had gone off, shooting her neatly behind the left ear. Nice one, Gaston, but few believed it. Yet he knew what he was doing. Indicted for murder before jurors he knew were mostly Ku Klux Klan members, with the artistry of a true conman he gave them a lot of racist flim-flam, so winning their sympathy that they not only found him not guilty but declared Maude King's death a suicide.

Seizing the opportunity offered by America's entry into the First World War to offer himself to the British as a master spy, he was hired, then went to the Germans, told them he was a British spy, and offered them his services too. As being a mere double-agent was not enough, he also signed on with the US Army Intelligence Service. Regrettably from his point of view the war ended, but after it he was contacted by his former boss, William J. Burns. Likely soon to be named head of the US Bureau of Investigation (forerunner of the FBI), Burns wanted Means to work with him. So Means went to work in Washington, blackmailing enough congressmen to ensure that Burns (and thus he) got the job. Enjoying his work, he learned that President Harding wasn't sleeping with his wife alone, and threatened to go public if not paid $50,000. The President died before he could pay, but Mrs Harding coughed up over $35,000 to keep Means quiet.

Did it work? No. Helping the ex-President's paramour to write a book about her love child with Harding, he himself wrote a bestseller insinuating that Mrs Harding had poisoned her husband. The success of *The Strange Death of President Harding* enabled him to move his wife, son and himself into a luxurious three-storey home in one of Washington's better neighbourhoods, whereupon this thoroughly nasty individual now hit on a new scam – sending anonymous death threats to millionaires then offering his services as master detective. But at last he went too far when Evalyn Walsh McLean, wife of the *Washington Post*'s publisher, hired him to find the kidnapped Lindbergh baby. Though assuring her he'd return the baby to his parents, he both failed and absconded with over $104,000 of her money. Scandalised, she had him prosecuted. Put away for fifteen years in Fort Leavenworth, he died still refusing to say where he'd stashed her cash.[1]

1. Madison, *op. cit.*, pp.155–9.

MEDIA HOAXES (*See* **CONCORDANCE**)

MEDIUMS (*PARANORMAL HOAXES*)

In spiritualist terminology, mediums are human intermediaries between the living and the dead. Allegedly they channel messages from the dead, are possessed by the dead, or even manifest phantasms of the dead. The practice is ancient and widespread, though in modern form it began in 1848 in a house in Hydesville, New York, when, with John and Margaret Fox and their seven children upset by phantom footsteps and knockings on the walls, it was noticed that the knockings pursued daughters Margaretta (fourteen) and Kate (twelve). Kate began to talk to 'Mr Splitfoot', the unquiet spirit, who began to respond. Asked to count to ten, ten raps would follow. Using a code of raps, the invisible guest said he was a pedlar who'd been murdered in the house and was buried in the cellar.

The news spread. Clairvoyance and occultism were already of such public interest that, though diggings in the cellar flooded and proved inconclusive, the Fox Sisters became celebrities. The family moved out, but the rappings followed them. Spirit messages said they were chosen: 'to convince the sceptical of the great truth of immortality'. Though denounced and even assaulted, in June 1850 (directed by older sister Leah and championed by editor Horace Greeley) they took New York by storm. During their many sittings no fraud was proved even as new mediums emerged everywhere. The craze spread so fast that in 1854 a Parisian journalist reported that hardly a table between the Champs Elysées and Montmartre remained unturned. By 1855 the term 'Spiritualism' was in use, and though much later in 1888 Kate and Margaretta publicly admitted their mediumship had been fraudulent (retracting this admission a year later), it hardly mattered. By then or soon afterwards eminent men like Sir William Crookes, Sir Oliver Lodge, William James, and Sir Arthur **Conan Doyle** had publicly endorsed their personal experience of the reality of spirit-survival and communication. The Society for Physical Research (SPR) had been founded to investigate claims. The battle between belief and disbelief was on.

For, though at first sceptical of events like apports, **levitation**, table-rapping, physical materialisations, spirit-possession, direct voice-communications and messages from the dead, these men became certain of the reality of survival, though fraud was and is common. Mediums holding seances in dim-lit rooms used many trucks, like sheeted masks to ape materialised spirits; cheesecloth hidden in the mouth to produce 'ectoplasm' (a term describing the transitory matter produced by mediums in physical materialisation); hidden strings or wire which when tugged would produce fake psychokinetic effects. Such tricks persuaded sceptics that the phenomena were *always* the result of fraud, for fame or gain. The case was not improved by mediumistic appeals to 'spirit guides' purporting to be discarnate Tibetans, deceased Red Indian chiefs (*see* **Roy**), or jocular Scotsmen.

Nor did the cheating of mediums like Florence Cook or Eusapia Palladino help. Physicist Sir William Crookes (1832–1919) almost ruined his reputation by endorsing as genuine in 1874 the materialisations by pretty Florrie Cook of Katie King, long-dead daughter of a pirate. Persuading Cook's parents to let her move into his house 'for further study', it seems plain enough that it was not her materialisations he was studying – Cook later admitted that the seances were a fraudulent cover for an affair between them.

As for Palladino (1854–1918), the phenomena associated with her were so violent and exhausting that she cheated whenever she could, so that during her seances she was usually tied to a chair. In his book *Death and its Mystery* the French astronomer Camille Flammarion tells how, when she got angry, sofas, tables, and lesser objects rushed about the room; a man was thrown from his chair which 'came up on the table with a great clatter'; limb-like extrusions appeared from her body.[1] Everard Fielding of the SPR, who with several colleagues conducted eleven seances with her in Naples in 1908, later wrote: 'I have seen this extraordinary woman held hand and foot by my colleagues, immobile, except for the occasional straining of a limb, while some entity has over and over again pressed my hand in a position clearly beyond her reach.'

Palladino's open eroticism also stood against her. Sexual prejudice (many mediums being women) has always made clear evaluation difficult. To many, science seems honestly masculine, as clear as sunshine; mediumship seems shady, lunar, and inherently disreputable. Some mediums suffered fraudulent attempts to prove them frauds. Mina Crandon took up **Houdini**'s challenge to produce genuine physical manifestations, but Houdini was caught out rigging the tests against her. Yet others, like Daniel Dunglass Home (1833–86), Eileen Garrett (1893–1970), and Leonore Piper (active *c*.1900) were not only never caught out despite stringent examination, but produced so many phenomena and so much information unavailable by normal means that serious investigators (i.e., those unswayed either by prior credulity or incredulity) usually concluded that genuine mediums had access to knowledge inexplicable save by telepathy, or by the survival of death of those with whom contact was sought.

Scepticism comes easily, but disbelief in every case is possible only if one asserts that *all* observers in such cases were naive dupes. D.D. Home demonstrated levitation of himself and of furniture, held burning coals without harm, produced percussive noises from thin air, induced musical instruments to play and pens to write by themselves, and so on. Unbelievable? Yet he was admired by Lytton, Ruskin, Thackeray and Longfellow. Ralph Waldo Emerson called him a 'prodigious genius'. He was never, not even once, and in an era when mediums were routinely exposed, accused of fraud.

Nor was Boston-born Leonore Piper ever accused of charlatanry. In

1885 the psychologist William James (1842–1910) concluded that either she could read his mind or was transmitting information from dead relatives. In 1901 the philosopher James Hyslop (1854–1920), also considering telepathy, concluded his study of her powers by stating: 'I prefer to believe that I have been talking to my dead relatives in person: it is simpler.'[2]

Today the process known as channelling combines mediumship with so-called New Age thought to put clients in touch with their personal 'guide', said to be a spirit between incarnations with whom the client has had close karmic contact in a former life. In a recent survey, author Joe Fisher concludes (following disenchanting personal experience) that any fakery involved in such work is caused not by the mediums but by the spirits. He concludes that such spirits are unhappy souls denying their deaths, clinging to earth-life by tormenting and pranking the living – reminiscent of the activities of the so-called Men in Black, and of John Keel's theory that some **UFO** activity is generated by those same mischievous sprites who in ages past were said to lure humans into the fairy-hills.[3]

So there you have it. Plenty of fakery goes on in mediumship – but is it always the medium who's doing the faking? Yet again, the spectre of the **Cosmic Joker** . . .

1. *Death and its Mystery*, Camille Flammarion, Unwin, London 1923.
2. *The Infinite Boundary*, D. Scott Rogo, Aquarian, Wellingborough 1988, pp.32–5.
3. *Hungry Ghosts*, Joe Fisher, Grafton, London 1990.

MEIER, Eduard 'Billy' (1937–) (*UFO HOAXES*)

This prominent New Age guru claims that as a young Swiss farmer he often met extraterrestrial entities, in particular a four-hundred-year-old lady named Semjase from the planet ERRA, located in the star cluster called the Pleiades, or Seven Sisters. This cluster, in the constellation Taurus, consists of very young stars radiating in the ultra-violet and violet range of the spectrum. The energy they emit is so intense that it would make life very problematic for any life forms in the neighbourhood. Perhaps this is why the citizens of ERRA are not hedonists, but live under a moral system as stern as Calvinism. Adultery, for example, is punished by exile. The men go to an all-male planet, and the women to an all-female planet. It's hard to see the attraction in this, yet Meier, who 'proves' his tale with many colour photographs of Pleiadian spaceships hovering over lush Swiss pastures, is sought out by thousands of believers who admire his simple rural wisdom, as described in books like *Light Years*, by Gary Kinder, or in the lavish productions published by a retired USAF officer, Colonel Wendelle Stevens.

Simple rural wisdom? Meier, as sceptical UFOlogist Jacques Vallee points out, is not as simple as he'd like true believers to think. In trouble with the law at an early age, he was jailed, and in France joined the Foreign Legion. Deserting in Africa, he became a soldier of fortune, a sailor, and a racing driver. Losing an arm in a bus accident in the Middle East, on a Greek isle he fell in love. With his bride he returned to Switzerland to find the Pleiadians manoeuvring over his rooftop. Whipping out his camera he took the sharp, high-quality photographs which, insists Wendelle Stevens, 'could not be faked for a million dollars'.[1] That, at least in the experienced Vallee's opinion, the Meier photos are 'consistent with the behaviour of small models suspended from strings', doesn't impress the guru's followers any more than the unlikelihood of virgin birth impresses fundamentalist **Christians**. Though apparently no longer in regular contact with the Pleiadians, Meier is now a media celebrity, surrounded by disciples who (much like the original Calvinists of nearby Geneva) brook neither doubt nor questions.

Well, whatever keeps folk happy . . .

1. *Revelations*, Jacques Vallee, Ballantine, New York 1992, p.211.

MENCKEN, H.L. (*See* **BATHTUB HOAX, The**)

MENDEL, Gregor (*See* **KAMMERER, Paul**)

MESMER, Anton (1734–1815) (*SCIENTIFIC SCAMS*)
His theory of 'animal magnetism' made the eighteenth-century Austrian physician Anton Mesmer a fortune. Positing a psychic ether that pervades space, he said the heavenly bodies cause tides in this 'fluid', which as magnetism flows through the world and all organic bodies. The free movement of these bodily tides results in health; their blockage causes sickness. Trying the effects of magnetism on his patients, he concluded that their bodies were magnets, and that he could cure them by moving the stagnant 'fluid' round their bodies by using magnets (and his hands). Since apparently he believed this as much as his patients did, cures *did* occur. His fame spread rapidly, and with the demand for his attentions growing, he devised an apparatus: a vat of dilute sulphuric acid from which protruded magnetised iron bars to which his patients clung. Apparently it worked (like a primitive form of electric shock treatment?), but the process was violent, involving convulsion, hysteria, and (claimed prudish sceptics) overmuch fleshly contact between the patients – explained by Mesmer as being necessary to spread the 'animal magnetism.'

In 1784 a committee of Parisian doctors concluded that, though Mesmer possessed strong powers of suggestion (thus *mesmerism*), there was no evidence of a magnetic fluid. Mesmer was denounced as a fraud; his self-confidence, and through it his capacity to heal, declined long before his death. Yet it seems harsh to call him a faker. Though sensing that much illness arises from a blockage of natural forces, and that cure involves setting those forces in motion again, Mesmer didn't understand what force he'd tapped, any more than the mechanics of hypnotism are understood today. His talk of animal magnetism may have been deluded, but there's no evidence that he meant to defraud his patients.

MICHAEL, Jerry Dean (contemporary) (*IMPOSTORS*)
Setting up office in an expensive part of Los Angeles in 1974, Elizabeth Carmichael caused uproar in the American motor industry by announcing that she was about to produce a revolutionary new design of car, the Revette. 'My car is going to make me the Henry Ford of the 1980s,' declared this widowed, attractive mother of five from Indiana. 'Anything a man can do, I can do better.' Displaying a scale model of the Revette on TV, she'd hold up twelve one-hundred dollar bills and announce: 'That's all the car is going to cost you.' Naming her company the Twentieth Century Corporation, she began selling agencies. Options for the first few thousand Revettes off the production line were snapped up. The cash flowed in. Then disaster struck. The promotion manager was found dead in his office, shot through the head. Inquiry revealed his criminal record, and with another member of staff charged with the killing, Mrs Carmichael said she'd known nothing about their background. To escape the scandal she moved to Dallas, opening up a new office and factory. But now she was closely watched. The 'factory' turned out to be a warehouse full of junk, while the 'Revette' was a fake. Charges were brought, but by the time the police reached her apartment, she was gone. Yet a search revealed not only the expected feminine clothing and cosmetics, but wigs, padded bras, and an electric razor.

Finding no record of an 'Elizabeth Carmichael' on their wanted lists, and deciding that 'she' might be a he, the police reworked a photograph of Carmichael by painting out the hair and cosmetic details, rephotographed it, and compared the result with mug shots in their files of wanted men. It resembled a certain Jerry Dean Michael, wanted for forgery and absconding on bail. Tracking him down to a Miami apartment, they found him still in women's clothing. 'I look on myself as a woman,' he told them. 'You can call me Liz.'

It turned out he was a transvestite who'd run away from Indiana years earlier with a girlfriend, Vivienne Barrett, who'd since borne him five children. For years they'd lived together amicably while he began to change his sex with hormone treatment, at which point he'd dreamed up the Revette promotion stunt. With Jerry Dean now in jail awaiting trial, his wife Vivienne insisted she'd stand by him. 'He has been a good husband and father,' she said, 'and he has always looked after us and shown us every consideration. We all love Liz just as much as we love

Jerry, and the kids call him Mother Liz, while I'm just plain Mom. I
suppose you could say we are like sisters rather than man and wife.'[1]

1. McCormick, *op. cit.*, pp.207–10.

MILLER, Glenn (1904–44) (*DISAPPEARANCES*)

On 24 December 1944 an official press release reported that: 'Major
Alton Glenn Miller, Director of the famous United States Army Air
Force Band, which has been playing in Paris, is reported missing while
on a flight from London to Paris. The plane in which he was a passenger
left England on December 15 and no trace of it has been found since its
take-off.' So the world learned of the death of the renowned dance-band
leader, and for years thereafter nobody seriously questioned the tale of
his mysterious death at sea.

Born in Clarinda, Iowa, in March 1904, Miller had learned the
trombone at the age of thirteen and turned pro at twenty, over the next
decade becoming known in New York as an arranger. A dance orchestra
he set up for Ray Noble in 1934 became popular, but none of his own
orchestras succeeded until in March 1939 suddenly it all clicked. Playing
at the Glen Island Casino in a New York suburb his band caught the
middle-class audience with its syrupy brass textures. Radio broadcasts
spread his fame via numbers like *Moonlight Serenade*, while a younger
generation enjoyed 'hot' numbers like *In the Mood*.

Rich at last, he went to Hollywood, where he befriended actor David
Niven, and in 1942 joined the air force. Assigned to entertain the troops
abroad, he was sent to London, where Niven was appointed to organise
his tours. In charge of hotel and travel bookings, however, was
Lieutenant Don Haynes, his former booking agent.

One such tour was due to open in Paris on Saturday, 16 December
1944. But, Haynes later said, on 12 December Miller told him he wanted
to be in Paris a day earlier for a social engagement. Next day, the story
goes, he met Lieutenant-Colonel Norman Baessel who, serving at RAF
Milton Ernest near Bedford, said he'd be flying to Paris on Thursday –
the 14th. Offered a lift via Haynes, Miller accepted, and despite foul
weather they took off early on Thursday afternoon. Experiencing engine
trouble, the plane ditched in the sea some six miles west of Le Touquet.
A small prop-driven plane called a Norseman, it was located on the sea
bed in 1973 and examined by a diver seven years later. He reported its
propeller missing. Due probably to a hydraulic leak, it had 'oversped'
and fallen off.

On Monday the band arrived late (due to the bad weather) at Orly
airport in Paris. Haynes was puzzled. Where was Miller? Nobody knew.
Failing to find him, Haynes contacted General Ray Barker, in charge of
US military personnel in Paris. Two days later the band opened without
him. Three days later his death was announced.

After the war his wife Helen, still puzzled by his disappearance, made enquiries. She learned he'd been cleared to fly from Abbots Ripton Field near Huntingdon, not to Paris, but Bordeaux. Why Bordeaux? She could learn nothing else. Nor could anyone else. Over the years the rumour of a cover-up began to spread. One researcher, John Edwards, late of the RAF, found it oddly hard to get hold of the official file about Miller's death. Another, Squadron Leader Jack Taylor, obtained the MACR (Missing Air Crew Report), but the typing was blurred and the signature illegible. Other documents showed that there had been no search for the missing band leader. In 1986 Taylor approached novelist Wilbur Wright, also late of the RAF. Wright wrote to the United States Air Force Inspection and Safety Center in Norton, California, for the accident report. The reply to this and a second letter said they had no record of a Norseman missing that day, nor of any accidents involving a Norseman in December 1944. But another document listed no fewer than eight Norseman planes lost that month. Further inquiry made it clear to him that there had been a cover-up, and that it was still in place. But why?

Wright now recalled that the actor David Niven, Miller's friend, had arranged that final tour. Yet Niven, in his autobiography *The Moon's a Balloon*, didn't even mention Miller. Odder and odder. This and other details either omitted or altered by Niven, who'd been in Paris when Miller vanished, led Wright to conclude that Niven knew Miller hadn't drowned at sea. Studying many scenarios (described in *Millergate*: 1990), Wright concluded that Miller *had* reached Paris. But what had happened once he'd got there?

One story was told by a man called Dennis Cottam. Drinking one night in 1954 in Fred's Bar, near the Hotel Olympiades in Montmartre where the Miller band had stayed, he heard from the bartender that: 'You English think Glenn Miller died in the Channel on December 15th, 1944, yet he was drinking in here that same evening.' Sent to a blue door the other side of the street, Cottam found himself in a brothel. The Madame there told him that in 1944 her boyfriend, a Provost Marshal Captain, had seen and identified the murdered body of Glenn Miller in another brothel, killed: 'Because he knew too much about the Black Market.' But that made no sense at all. If Miller had only been in Paris for twenty-four hours, what could he have known about the Black Market?

Other leads convinced Wright that Miller had flown to Paris that Thursday, but in a Dakota, not a Norseman (Miller hated small planes), and had been met by Niven. A further angle emerged when, writing to the New Jersey State Registrar for details of the death of a Major Alton Glenn Miller, he received a letter confirming that Alton Glenn Miller had died in December 1944 – but in Ohio. Pursuing this, he ran into further obstruction. A typist had made a mistake. He'd been sent not

Miller's place of death, but his place of birth.

Then emerged another oddity. In 1949 Helen Miller had purchased a six-grave burial plot in Altadena, California – for her parents, herself, and the son and daughter she and Glenn had adopted. That made five. So who was the extra grave for? Asked to deny that Glenn Miller was buried there, the cemetery officials took fifteen months to do so; while the response by Miller's adopted son Steve to Wright's inquiry was to write an angry letter to Miller's brother, Herb, saying: 'Get this guy off our backs.'

The story that kept emerging was that Miller had been in a brawl in a Paris brothel, and had died (though not in Paris) of a fractured skull. Being 'a bit of the lad with the ladies', he'd gone to Paris two days early to enjoy female companionship. When Haynes, later involved in the cover-up, reached Paris, he'd been genuinely perplexed: where was Miller? After a frantic search the badly injured band leader was located. If he died, there would be a scandal. Why ruin his reputation? Besides, given the war, the news might be demoralising. So he was flown to a military hospital in Columbus, Ohio, as the cover-up began. The loss of the Norseman explained his non-appearance at the Paris concerts. By the time its disappearance was announced, he'd already died in Ohio. Helen, refusing to believe the official story, pursued the trail after the war and eventually learned the true story from the authorities, later purchasing the six-grave plot. Miller was reburied there, and she joined him in 1966. As for Niven and Haynes, why should they collude in the posthumous public disgrace of their friend? Much better to agree that Miller had died in an airplane accident at sea rather than in a squalid brawl in a Paris brothel.[1]

1. Wilson and Wilson, *op. cit.*, pp.254–66.

MIRABELLI, Carlos (1889–1951) (*PARANORMAL HOAXES*)
Can folk lift themselves or be lifted off the ground by mind-power alone or while in ecstatic trance? History is full of such reports. **Christ**'s bodily ascension to heaven is the most remarkable example. He just kept going up and didn't come down again. Examples from later centuries include St Joseph of Copertino (the 'flying monk') and the nineteenth-century **medium**, Daniel Dunglass Home – said never once to have been caught out in trickery.

Yet while recalling the Fortean Principle that folk who need to *dis*believe are just as credulous as those who need to believe, perhaps it's a relief to be able to prove at least *one* levitator a faker – the Brazilian medium Carlos (Carmine) Mirabelli.

Said to produce automatic writing in twenty-eight languages and trance speeches in twenty-six, also complete materialisations of identifiable people known to be dead, playing billiards without touching the cue and apparently able to travel at near light-speed, Mirabelli was also an accomplished levitator. Or so he claimed. In 1934 the sceptical Society for Psychical Research (SPR) sent its research officer Theodore Besterman to investigate. So in his opinion he did. 'Mirabelli left me in no doubt that he was purely and simply fraudulent,' Besterman wrote to author Guy Lyon Playfair in 1973. Yet while failing even to investigate printed evidence about Mirabelli's earlier history, he did bring back one useful photograph, lost in the SPR archives until disinterred in June 1990 by American researcher Dr Gordon Stein. It shows Mirabelli apparently poised in mid-air, arms stretched out and eyes lifted, head almost touching the ceiling of a room at least fourteen feet high (as verified by Playfair). Inscribed 'To Mr T. Besterman from Carlos Mirabelli', and dated 22 August 1934, it shows clear signs of retouching either to the negative or to an earlier, rephotographed print. The outline of clothing and shoes is sharpened, and just below the shoes is the evidence. There, the wallpaper pattern behind Mirabelli, elsewhere in sharp focus, is blurred. Why? Because that's where the top step of the step-ladder he'd been standing on had been erased or painted out. On a photocopy or under a magnifying glass, Playfair notes, all doubt vanishes. Mirabelli faked that one at least.[1]

Yet that doesn't prove the same of St Joseph, St Teresa, or Daniel Dunglass Home. So, believe or not, as you please.

1. 'The Great Mirabelli', Guy Lyon Playfair, *Fortean Times* No. 71, London 1993, pp.43–5.

MISSISSIPPI PLAN, The (*See* **SOUTH SEA BUBBLE**)

MONA LISA (*ART FORGERIES*)
'You can sell anything to Americans and Englishmen,' said the grandson of French painter Jean François Millet when convicted of art forgery in 1935. 'They know nothing about art; even their experts know nothing. All you have to do is ask a fabulous price.'

Exaggeration? Hardly. In 1911 no fewer than *six* Americans each paid $300,000 for what each thought was Leonardo da Vinci's masterpiece, the *Mona Lisa*. What made each of them think they'd bought the real thing is that on 21 August that year the world's best-known painting had vanished from the Louvre in Paris. Dressed as workmen, the thieves – Italian Vincenzo Perrugia and two accomplices – had emerged from their overnight hiding place in the museum's basement and made off with it, just like that.

The burglars had been hired by art forger Yves Chaudron and his partner, Eduardo de Valfierno, a self-styled marquis. They'd begun working together in South America. A former picture restorer, Chaudron specialised in faking paintings by the Spanish artist,

Bartolomé Esteban Murillo, which Valfierno would then offer for sale to rich Argentinian widows to be placed in churches as memorial bequests. Having saturated Argentina with fake Murillos, they'd moved on to Mexico City, where they'd perfected their technique. Pretending to be art experts, they'd ask a gallery owner to let them examine a picture. While it was in their hands, Valfierno would line the back of the genuine canvas with Chaudron's forgery of the original. Returning with a prospective buyer, they'd urge the crooked victim to mark the back of the canvas, so he'd be sure the painting delivered to him was the one he'd marked. Of course the dealer had marked the back of the fake. If later he asked why the original still hung in the gallery, Valfierno would say the gallery had put up a copy, and would also send him a fake press cutting reporting the theft. It was foolproof. Even if he realised he'd been duped, the victim could never go to the police and admit being party to such a shady deal.

Reaching Paris, Valfierno and Chaudron had begun selling pictures 'stolen' from the Louvre, Valfierno by now supplying clients with forged documents on Louvre paper, including a confidential report that a masterpiece had been stolen and a copy substituted. Soon, inspired to try this brilliant scam on the *Mona Lisa* itself, they enlisted Perrugia's aid. He'd worked in the Louvre, knew his way about it, and as a glazier had put the glass in the box protecting da Vinci's masterpiece. And the theft went like a dream.

Chaudron and Valfierno made $1,800,000 selling Chaudron's six faked copies, but they never got the chance to sell the real *Mona Lisa*. Perrugia fled with it to Italy, where on 13 November he tried to sell it to a Florentine dealer, who contacted the police. The gang was jailed, and the *Mona Lisa* went back to the Louvre. Replaced under heavy guard and behind a thick glass panel, it remains there today, surrounded by electronic alarms.

Yet there is another *Mona Lisa*, smiling mysteriously down from the wall of a flat in Kensington, London. Its custodian, art connoisseur and inventor Dr Henry Pulitzer, says it is not a reproduction, but another version by da Vinci, who habitually did several versions of his portraits. First he'd painted Mona Lisa del Giocondo, wife of a Florentine noble. Mourning a dead child, she wore a transparent veil during the sitting. Some years later he portrayed Constanza d'Avalos, mistress of Guiliano de Medici. While resembling Mona Lisa only slightly, she too was called 'La Gioconda' – 'The Smiler'. Completing it, Leonardo then adapted the earlier portrait, turning Mona Lisa's face into that of Constanza. Abandoning Constanza to make a profitable marriage, Guiliano refused to buy the picture, which Leonardo took with him to Paris. This second version may be the one in the Louvre. The original portrait eventually reached London, in time to be bought by a Swiss syndicate to which Dr

Pulitzer belongs. Microscopic photography techniques show that finger-prints on the canvas match up with those on other authenticated paintings by Leonardo.

Catalogues list over sixty other alleged *Mona Lisas*, most attributed to the school of Leonardo. The six fakes with which Chaudron fooled the millionaires are not among them.

MONK, Maria (1817–49) (*IMPOSTORS, LITERARY HOAXES*)
In January 1836 a nineteen-year-old Canadian woman with a babe in arms caused a sensation in New York City's Protestant community. Allegedly a nun daringly rescued from a Montreal convent by a man named Hoyt, her terrible tale was written down by Hoyt as *The Awful Disclosures of Maria Monk*. This titillating exposé told how the convent cellars were connected by tunnels to a neighbouring monastery, and how nuns resisting the demands of lustful monks had been killed and buried there. Impressed, the pastor of New York's Collegiate Dutch Reformed Church and his wife not only took poor Maria into their home, but put up the cash needed to get the book published by Harpers. After it became a bestseller, Maria ran off with a clergyman named Slocum who, realising that royalties from the book were going to the Dutch Reformed pastor's ministry, sued Harpers for part of the loot. But at the trial the truth emerged: the *Awful Disclosures* was a pack of lies. Maria's mother testified that her daughter had been a pathological liar ever since suffering a head injury aged seven. She'd lost all her jobs because of her lying, and after time spent in reformatories had turned to prostitution. The baby's father was probably a Montreal policeman. As for Hoyt, he had expanded Maria's own tall tales with scurrilous European myths connecting convents and torture. With the hoax exposed, Slocum lost his case, and the pastor washed his hands of Maria.

Unabashed, next she found herself enslaved in a Philadelphia convent, as described in the *Further Disclosures of Maria Monk*. Tricking her, Hoyt went to London and made a mint selling the foreign rights to both books. Meanwhile Maria became a drunken down-and-out prostitute in the Bowery, went to jail for picking pockets, and died there aged thirty-two.

As for the *Awful Disclosures*, to date they have sold some 300,000 copies, and are still considered to be true by some gullible, Catholic-hating Protestants.[1]

1. Lindskoog, *op. cit.*, pp.105–6.

MORAN, Jim (20th century) (*IMPOSTORS*)
When in 1947 the Crown Prince of Arabia visited Hollywood, prankster Jim Moran decided that the royal imposture already successfully pulled in England by Horace de Vere **Cole** and in the States by Stanley

Weyman was due for another outing. Recruiting three actors, on the evening of the real prince's departure he reserved a table at Ciro's and arrived in a limousine and in full regalia. With every eye upon him he spilled a pouch of jewels on the table and sent a genuine amethyst (worth $30) to the band leader. Having wined and dined and enjoyed his royal self, on his way out over the dance floor he dropped the pouch. What looked like a fortune in gems scattered in all directions. Impatiently signalling to his companions not to bother retrieving these mere baubles, the scandalously rich Prince departed, leaving Ciro's clientele scrambling all over the floor to grab the gems – which turned out to be nothing but coloured dime-store glass.

MORENO, Antonio Jiminez (20th century) (*FRAUD*)
Western governments operating welfare systems for the unemployed or disabled are always inveighing against those claiming benefits to which they're not entitled. Tales of cheats making a mint at the expense of the honest tax-payer are a dime a dozen – but rarely does such fraud display any real artistry or imagination. In the USA Dorothy Mae **Woods** (the 'US Welfare Queen') has demonstrated a flamboyance above the merely ordinary, but for sheer audacity Spanish gypsy Antonio Jiminez Moreno (known as 'El Chorro', 'The Fountain') must surely be crowned the King of Welfare Cheats. By forging birth certificates and school registration forms, between 1960 and 1968 he invented 197 non-existent families and over 3,000 children for whom he claimed benefits worth over $3,500,000 from the French Social Security system.

Roaming over France from Spain and stopping wherever there was temporary work to be found, El Chorro's gypsy tribe had many children. With the French birth rate being so low, the French Social Security system makes child-bearing a profitable business. Large families are encouraged. In the 1960s a father could draw about $10 a month for each of the first two children, more for the third, and more again for the fourth. The sum paid per child didn't rise thereafter, but remained constant at the upper limit, no matter what the number of children. Residence but not French nationality was required to make such claims. Being of no fixed address gypsies could register their children anywhere.

The situation Moreno exploited developed when, with France having lost its North African empire, many illiterate gypsies unaware of their rights entered the country. Acquiring the identity card of one Vicente Cortez, Moreno applied for the benefits due to Cortez' six children. When, in a town where his tribe was staying overnight, a social worker came to check on the family, Moreno produced six children of the right ages from his and other families – children for whom benefit was already being legally collected. Expanding the scam, he acquired a pack of blank cards stolen from a Social Security office and created 3,000 imaginary children. Other gypsies soon copied his methods to register at least another 500. In addition, the 'mothers' of the invented children collected pregnancy and maternity compensation, doing so by having one pregnant woman register in a dozen different towns, each time under a different name. To avoid mistakes, Moreno meticulously recorded marriages, births and deaths in a single ledger.

For several years the scam worked like a dream. It collapsed only when police, investigating a killing in a knife fight between two gypsy men, were alerted by finding so much wealth in the gypsy camp, and began a search ending in the discovery of the ledger. By then El Chorro had not only vanished but had salted away much of his ill-gotten gains in Spain, where soon he reappeared. Jailing twelve other gypsies, the French demanded that Spain arrest and extradite the mastermind. Moreno spent three months in prison for owning a revolver but, with extradition demands denied on the grounds that a country does not extradite its own nationals, was free to purchase and thereafter enjoy the pleasures of a magnificent villa near Barcelona. As for the French Social Security system, gypsy families today find their every application for benefit minutely and suspiciously scrutinised.[1]

1. McCormick, *op. cit.*, pp.191–4.

MORGANWG, Iolo (1746–1826) (*LITERARY HOAXES*)
Like James **Macpherson** a gifted Celt insulted by Dr Samuel Johnson, the Welsh scholar Edward Williams took the bardic name Iolo Morganwg (Iolo of Glamorgan). An eccentric dreamer, laudanum user, and republican, as a youth this asthmatic stonemason's son rapidly mastered the Welsh language and literary tradition and soon published his own poetry. Following his father's trade in England for some years after his mother's death, in 1781 he returned to Wales to marry Margaret Roberts, a remarkable woman who often scolded him in sarcastic doggerel for building castles in the air. Ignoring her advice, he undertook business ventures that all collapsed, and for over a year (1786/7) was jailed as a debtor. In Cardiff Prison he began studying and imitating the fourteenth-century poetry of Dafydd ap Gwilym, and in 1789 published a modern edition of Dafydd's works. That he'd forged many of his 'discoveries' went undetected for over a century.

Thereafter, while promoting the need for radical political reform, he continued enthusiastically producing 'ancient' poetry of high quality, while his recreation or invention of supposed old bardic traditions led to the birth of the Eisteddfod – the Welsh language cultural festival, still annually celebrated. Known by 1788 as the best-read man in Wales and by now calling himself Iolo Morganwg, increasingly he built new castles in the air, elaborating his bardic and druidic fantasies in which, it seems, he believed totally.

Now pretending to be descended from older Welsh poets, in 1791 he abandoned his family to poverty and moved to London where, though denounced for writing pacifist poetry and viewed as a potential traitor during the war against revolutionary France, still he invited the Prince of Wales to druidical meetings on Primrose Hill. When in 1791 a Dr John Williams revived the tale of how a twelfth-century Welsh prince, Madoc (*see* **Columbus**) had visited America and sired the Mandans, a Welsh-speaking Indian tribe, Iolo promptly forged papers supporting the claim. These papers were so convincing that Williams had to rewrite his book, and a young Welshman called John Evans set out to find the Welsh-speaking Indians. Making his way up the Missouri, in 1799 Evans died in New Orleans without finding any Mandans, but Iolo lost no sleep over this tragedy.

Back in Wales with his family in 1795, he set himself up as a bookseller. When this business collapsed, he took work as a surveyor. Stumping about the countryside loaded with satchels, he collected folklore and preached druidism, establishing a *Gorsedd* of bards wherever he could. Still occasionally working as a mason, in time the now aged and venerable Iolo persuaded the Cambrian Society of Dyfed at Carmarthen to associate the *Gorsedd* with the Eisteddfod; and in 1820 this most persistent of forgers demanded the establishment throughout Wales of local societies to collect all known traditions: 'with fidelity, the collector not to adulterate them by blending them with own conjectures'.[1]

Was he serious? Apparently. Like Macpherson in Scotland, Iolo didn't see himself as a hoaxer, but as the interpreter of traditions otherwise sure to be lost. Part of the reason he was never exposed as a hoaxer during his lifetime lies in the fact that he was far and away the best Welsh scholar of the time, who at his death left behind him a vast number of manuscripts. His work has to be treated with caution, but (at least in Wales) he remains well respected. The bardic system he promoted was a fabrication, but his potent self-delusion still underpins many of the 'ancestral' beliefs of modern Welsh traditionalists.

Perhaps the most effective way to fool others, after all, is first to fool yourself.[2]

1. *Glamorgan Historian*, Vol. III, Stewart Williams, Cowbridge 1966, p.29.
2. *Iolo Morganwg*, Prys Morgan, University of Wales Press 1975.

MORRISON, J. Bam (20th century) (*CONMEN*)
Arriving one hot July day in 1950 in the sleepy burgh of Wetumka, Oklahoma, this charismatic conman knew right away that he'd found the perfect place to pull the classic 'circus advanceman' scam. Striding into the local newspaper office, he claimed to be the advance publicity man for Bohn's United Circus, which would hit town in under three weeks,

on 24 July. With the excited town council immediately setting up a special emergency meeting of the local chamber of commerce, Morrison warned everyone to stock up on supplies. Soon Wetumka would be flooded by crowds from miles about, all come to enjoy the travelling circus – which, he claimed, would willingly buy all its necessities from Wetumka merchants! Anyone buying advertising space on the circus billboards or on the sides of the Big Top would be eligible to sell the circus his products or services! There were vast profits to be made by everyone in the community!

With his every promise believed, this gregarious, smooth-talking rogue settled in as the town's guest. The owner of the tiny Meadows Hotel invested in new mattresses; the butcher stocked up with hot dogs and the baker got in extra flour for hamburger buns; the feed shop owner ordered a mountain of hay for the circus animals; while, as a reward for buying a vast amount of advertising space, restaurateur Louis Charlton got the contract to feed all the circus personnel. After two weeks, his wallet crammed with the townsfolk's money, Morrison knew it was time to get out. Announcing that he had to get back to the circus to make final publicity preparations, he left town even as the newspaper proprietor, printing full-page ads announcing the imminent arrival of Bohn's United Circus, hired Boy Scouts to distribute thousands of handbills throughout the region.

On the great day Wetumka was crammed and doing a roaring trade. By noon the main street was thick with people eagerly awaiting the big parade. No circus materialised. With the crowd growing impatient, the mayor received a postage-due package containing a handful of hay and a card that read: 'Regards, J. Bam Morrison.'

Realising the only way to stop a riot was to admit they'd all been conned, the town council did so and, announcing the advent of Wetumka's first annual Sucker Day, told the concessionaires to give away everything free – the hot dogs, soda pop, balloons, banners and other goods bought in expectation of the bonanza. In return, the now well-pleased crowd spent in Wetumka all the money they'd brought to spend at the circus – and suddenly there was more cash in Wetumka than anyone had ever seen! What should have been a disaster had turned into a huge success, so that on 24 July ever since Wetumka has celebrated Sucker Day. As for Morrison, soon afterwards the law caught up with him over another scam. The sheriff of a Missouri town phoned Wetumka asking if they wanted him extradited after he'd served his sentence in Missouri, but the Oklahomans replied that not only were they bringing no charges but that they'd be happy to have him as their Guest of Honour at the next annual Sucker Day – so long as, this time, he paid his own way![1]

1. Madison, *op. cit.*, pp.119–25.

MUNCHAUSEN, Baron von (*See* **RASPE, Rudolf Eric**)

MURPHY, Bridey (*See* **PAST-LIFE MEMORIES**)

MUSSOLINI, Benito (1883–1945) (*See also* **HOAXES IN WARFARE**)

Fascist leader of Italy for twenty-three years, Benito Mussolini felt that propaganda (meaning hoaxes and lies) was the essence of his grip on power. Packing his audiences with 'applause squads' to provoke the necessary mass enthusiasm, his main problem was that he let fantasy replace reality. Preparing for Italy's entry into the Second World War, on 21 April 1940 he had his spokesman, Virgion Gayda, declare that: 'the whole of the Mediterranean was under the control of Italian naval and air forces . . .' It wasn't. He told Hitler that over eight million soldiers and seventy divisions were available, and that Italy could produce twice this number if Germany could help equip them. It couldn't. The real numbers were one million men and under twenty divisions. He spoke of having eight million bayonets; in fact Italy lacked sufficient bayonets to equip the 1.3 million rifles then available. Implying that he had three armoured divisions including twenty-five-ton tanks of advanced design, so he did – in his imagination. The largest Italian mobile armour consisted of a 3.5 ton armoured car copied from the British, armed only with machine guns, and with a skin so thin that small-arms fire could penetrate it. As for Italy's 8,530 warplanes, this too was a slight miscount: Italy had 454 bombers and 129 fighters. The Italian navy *did* have eight battleships and the world's largest submarine fleet in 1939, but the battleships had been built for speed at the expense of armour protection and range, while the submarines proved useless, being too slow to submerge. Only two of the battleships were ever involved in conflict, off the Calabrian coast on 9 July 1940. The battle lasted only a few minutes, but Mussolini told the Germans that half the British navy in the Mediterranean had been destroyed. Later the chiefs of the rival Italian air force claimed that: 'not a single shot fired from these vastly expensive battleships ever hit an enemy vessel during the entire war'. And, in a meeting with German Foreign Minister Joachim von Ribbentrop in Rome on 10 March 1940, Mussolini claimed that: 'almost the entire civilian life of the Italian people had been sacrificed to the production of armaments' – when in fact nothing at all was being done to increase the strength of the army.

Knowing what a windbag Mussolini really was, to fill his sails and blow him into the war as their ally, the Germans hoaxed him in return. Early in 1940 Hitler informed Il Duce that Germany was ready to attack in the west with over 200 fully equipped divisions and that they meant to win the war that summer. Mussolini, who loved looking on the bright side, believed him, joined the war, and so five years later found himself hanging from a lamppost with a rope round his neck, strung up by infuriated Italian partisans who, with the war lost, were tired of his lies.[1]

1. *Mussolini's Roman Empire*, Denis Mack Smith, Longman, London 1976.

MYTHICAL HOAXES AND HOAXERS

The world's myths are so full of hoaxers, tricksters and situations in which nothing is as it seems that volumes couldn't exhaust the huge variety of tales. In culture after culture tales of trickster gods, people, and humanised animals epitomise the long-held and universal perception that appearances cannot be trusted and that there's one born every minute – starting with Adam. As the Book of Genesis has it, the Lord God put Adam in the Garden of Eden, telling him he could eat of any tree but that of the knowledge of good and evil, 'for in the day that you eat of it you shall die'. But his wife Eve, manufactured from his rib, soon meets the Serpent, who asks if the fruit of any tree in the garden is forbidden. Eve explains, and the Serpent tells her: 'You will not die. For God knows that when you eat of it your eyes will be opened, and you will be like God, knowing good and evil.' So Adam and Eve eat of the tree, and do not die, at which the Lord God, no doubt as furious at the discovery of his hoax as at their disobedience, curses all three. Given the fact that clearly it is the Lord God and not the Serpent who is proved to be the liar, it seems odd that the Serpent has always since taken the rap as 'That Old Liar, Satan'.

In Greek myth there's so much hoaxing it's amazing that anyone ever believed anything. Prometheus, arbitrating a dispute between men and the gods as to which part of a sacrificial ox the gods should be offered, tricks Zeus into choosing the bones by hiding the tasty flesh under the unwanted stomach, and the bones under tempting fat. Zeus is so angry that he forbids mankind the use of fire, which Prometheus then steals from the sun. Zeus, meanwhile, never tires of seducing mortal women, invariably via trickery. Danaë falls for Zeus in the form of a shadow of gold; to Europa he appears as a bull; to Leda as a swan. As for the ugly smith-god Hephaestus, when his lovely wife Aphrodite has an affair with the war-god Ares, he takes his revenge by tricking them into bed and netting them as they sleep together, then displays the humiliated pair to the delighted Olympians. Nor is Greek myth alone in loving tricksy villains. In Norse myth the trickster Loki fools blind Hodur into hurling the mistletoe dart that slays Baldur the Beautiful; then wittily disguises Thor as a blushing bride so that the thunder-god may recover his stolen hammer from the Frost-Giants. In Irish lore the great warrior

Cuchulainn, forbidden either to eat dog flesh or ever to refuse a feast, is brought down at last when three old hags invite him to a feast – of dog flesh. And so on. Tricksters stride everywhere, through every tradition, often as humanised animals. The cunning of Reynard the Fox, or Coyote or Raven in Native American lore, or African spider-gods like Tule or Anansi, is proverbial. Never lost for an answer or unable to get out of a tight spot (though often victims of their own deceit), they are usually amoral, greedy, lustful and selfish.

In Eskimo lore, Raven persuades a whale-cow to shut her eyes and open her mouth. In his raven-clothes and with his fire-sticks he darts inside her to find himself in a lamp-lit room. Here sits a beautiful girl, the whale's soul. Forbidding him to touch a tube running along the ceiling, when she goes out he licks a drop of sweet oil from it, then breaks off a piece and eats it, so killing the whale, this being its heart-artery. With the corpse washed ashore, men cut it open. Raven leaves unseen, but realises he left his fire-sticks behind. Taking human form to help the men butcher the whale, when one finds the fire-sticks Raven cries that to find fire-sticks in a whale is bad luck. Running away, he scares the men into doing the same – then returns to enjoy the feast on his own.

The doyen of animal tricksters is the Native American figure of Coyote. Typical motifs in Coyote tales include: contests won by deception; scaring folk from food to eat it himself (like Raven); tricking his victim over a cliff; pretending magic powers to win a bride; and many tales in which, too clever for his own good, his own tricksiness betrays him. He is a buffoon, his fate a warning to all. Yet, though often killed, he always returns to life to continue working mischief – the chief pleasure and purpose of tricksters.

The Yoruba of West Africa tell how one day the god Edshu walks between two fields, a farmer working in each. He wears a hat, red one side, white the other, green before, black behind (symbolizing the four world directions). Later one farmer asks the other: 'Did you see that old man in the white hat?' The other insists: 'It wasn't white, it was red!' They end up disagreeing so furiously that they try to kill each other, and it's only when they're taken before the headman to be judged that Edshu reveals himself. Showing the hat, he laughs, 'They couldn't help but quarrel. I love causing trouble.'

The moral is simple: don't trust the evidence of your senses.[1]

Such tales are told as much to amuse as to edify. Popular in Islamic lands are the stories of the Mullah Nasruddin – originally Sufi teaching devices designed to jolt the mind into lateral thought. So it is told how, day by day for a year or more, Nasruddin crossed a certain frontier, his donkey laden with straw-packed bags. With every trip he grew richer and richer, but the puzzled customs official, though sure Nasruddin was a smuggler, never found anything in the bags but straw. At length Nasruddin retired to live in luxury. Years later the official, also now retired, met him and asked him what he had been smuggling.

'Donkeys,' said Nasruddin.[2]

1. *The Hero with a Thousand Faces*, Joseph Campbell, Abacus, London 1975, pp.41–2.
2. *The Exploits of the Incomparable Mullah Nasruddin*, Idries Shah, Picador, London 1970.

N

'I'm not a crook.'

(ex-US President Richard M. Nixon)

NAUNDORFF, Karl (1785–1845) (*IMPOSTORS*)
By late January 1794 only one prisoner remained in the fortified Parisian
tower called the Temple. The eight-year-old boy had been there since
the autumn of 1791. At first, though they were prisoners of the
Revolution, it hadn't been so bad. His mother and father and sister
Marie Thérèse had been there with him. There had been a garden. He'd
been quite cheerful and healthy. But in autumn 1792 his father had been
removed for trial, and they'd seen him only once again, on 20 January
1793, the eve of his execution. In July that year he'd been separated from
his mother and sister, and lodged alone, guarded by a shoemaker family
called Simon. Then he, his sister, and their aunt Elizabeth had been
made to sign a document accusing his mother of terrible crimes; in
October his mother and aunt had been guillotined; and his sister had
been sent to Austria, leaving only the Simon family. Now they were gone
too, and not replaced. He was on his own. Nobody visited, except
government commissioners. One, De La Meuse, reported that he was
withdrawn, unresponsive. His limbs had swollen badly and he had
rickets. In March 1795 doctors were called. The first, doubting the boy's
identity, died a few days later. The boy was moved to a better room, but
too late: on 8 June 1795 he died. With the cause of death established as
scrofula (two of the doctors signing the certificate hadn't even seen him),
he was buried in an unmarked grave at St Marguerite's. The site was
lost, and the original certificate, citing the date of death as 10 June, also
vanished.

The name on the certificate? Louis Charles, son of Louis XVI and
Marie Antoinette, heir to the French throne and known as the Dauphin.

Such mystery over his end soon bred tales that he hadn't died, but had
escaped, or been rescued. In time, over forty impostors came forward,

including the American John James Audubon, later the expert on birds. But the only at all convincing claimant was Karl Wilhelm Naundorff, a tenacious individual of genuine mystery in that no background could ever be found – no birth certificates, no relatives other than his own six children, no proof that he wasn't the Dauphin. His tale was that sympathisers had put him in a secret room in the Temple attics, leaving a mannequin in his bed. Discovering this, the authorities had replaced it with a deaf-mute – the sick child reported by De La Meuse. With the substitution suspected, an attempt was made to poison the child. Growing suspicious, the first doctor was also poisoned. With the substitute's corpse stowed in the attic, the real Dauphin had been smuggled out in the coffin, to be hidden by royalists first in the Vendée and later in Italy. The death certificate was signed by doctors who did as they were told, while the empty coffin went into an unmarked grave. The Dauphin was officially dead. There was no longer a direct male Bourbon heir to the throne – very convenient for the revolutionaries.

Emerging with his claim when the revolutionary turmoil ended, Naundorff's vague recollection of the lost years did not help his cause, but he persisted, parading himself as the 'Found Dauphin' first in Italy, then in England. In 1812 he settled in Berlin as a watchmaker, a skill seemingly inherited from Louis his 'father'. Married, soon with a large family, by 1824 his claim attracted attention, but letters to his 'sister' Marie Thérèse and 'cousin', the Bourbon heir de Berry, went unanswered. Arrested and jailed for false pretences in Brandenburg, on his release he wrote another unanswered letter, this time to King Charles X. So in 1833 he went to Paris, convincing several prominent people with his tale. These included Mme de Rambaud, the Dauphin's governess, while Mme Simon the shoemaker's wife recognised him at once. They noted the features he shared with Louis Charles: a mole on the thigh, a scar on the upper lip, protruding teeth, triangular vaccination marks. He described the Temple precisely, and knew many unpublished details about the Bourbons. Pressure mounted on Marie Thérèse to see him. Sent to inspect him, the Vicomte de Rochefoucauld remarked on the clear resemblance, but Marie Thérèse refused to meet him, saying that it would serve no purpose, her brother being dead.

Failing to reach her, in 1836 Naundorff issued a civil court summons to Marie Thérèse, her husband, and the former king Charles. Two days later he was deported to England, where he spent most of the rest of his life. Devising a new explosive, when the English did not want it he went to the Dutch, and spent his last months in Holland before being buried in Delft. 'Here lies Louis XVII', begins the inscription on his gravestone – yet the battle wasn't over. Granted the name Bourbon, his Dutch-naturalised descendants continued to contest the claim, over a century later in 1950 opening the grave to seek clues from his anatomy when the French Court of Appeal upheld the 1795 death certificate.

Maybe he was Louis Charles, and maybe he wasn't. It has never been proved that the Dauphin escaped the Temple, nor that Naundorff wasn't who he claimed to be.[1]

1. Newnham, *op. cit.*, pp.186–9.

NEWBOROUGH, Stella (*See* **CHIAPPINI, Stella**)

NEWBURGER, Morris (20th century) (*PRANKS*)
Annoyed by press coverage given to backwoods American football teams, in 1941 wealthy New York stockbroker and football fan Morris Newburger decided to invent a team of his own, the Plainfield Teachers. Phoning the *New York Herald Tribune* with a report of how the Teachers had just beaten Beacon Institute 20–0, he found his call so well received that he then contacted the *New York Times*, United Press and Associated Press, giving each of them similar reports. Thus encouraged, he drew up a list of imaginary fixtures and 'From the Desk of Jerry Croyden' began filing reports on the progress of the Teachers. Coached by Ralph 'Hurry Up' Hoblitzel and using his unique W formation, the team (including one Morris Newburger as tackle) went from strength to strength. The star was a 'full-blooded' Chinese-American, Johnny Cheung, 'The Celestial Comet'. Telling how Cheung consumed bowlfuls of rice at half-time of each game, 'Croyden' predicted the player's All-American future so persuasively that genuine sportswriters picked up on the story. It got to the point where Herb Allen of the *New York Post* wrote a feature article on Cheung, a man he'd never met and who didn't exist (cynics may claim that in any case this is standard tabloid practice).

   But with the Teachers heading for the Blackboard Bowl Championship, the hoax fell apart. One tale is it was betrayed to Caswell Adams of the *New York Herald Tribune* by a friend who, working for the phone company, heard Newburger admit it while making a private call. Adams broke the story on 14 November 1941; and *Time* magazine told Newburger they were about to expose him. Apparently he begged *Time* to hold off till the end of the football season, but *Time* refused to play. So, in a final report 'From the Desk of Jerry Croyden', sporting fans learned that six Teachers, including Johnny Cheung, had been declared ineligible for the team on failing their mid-term exams, forcing Coach 'Hurry Up' Hoblitzel to cancel the season's remaining games.[1]

1. Yapp, *op. cit.*, pp.30–2.

NEWTON, Isaac (1642–1717) (*SCIENTIFIC SCAMS*)
The founder of modern physics a faker? Sadly for those who view the 'discoverer' of the Law of Gravity as the epitome of scientific probity and reason, the answer is yes. Examination of his monumental *Principia*

(published in three editions: 1687, 1713, and 1726) shows beyond doubt that corrections in his calculations were made *a posteriori*; that is: knowing what the result should be, he adjusted the data to fit his predictions. So, in his calculation of the velocity of sound he corrected the air:water density from 1:850 in the first edition to 1:870 in the second. As for his calculations on Earth's precession of equinoxes, known to be about fifty seconds, historian Richard S. Westfall points out: 'Without even pretending that he had new data, Newton brazenly manipulated the old figures on precession so that he not only covered the apparent discrepancy but carried the demonstration to a higher plane of accuracy.' Westfall goes on: 'Not the least part of the *Principia*'s persuasiveness was its deliberate pretence to a degree of precision quite beyond its legitimate claim.'[1]

Worse, he used deception to silence opponents like British chemist Robert Boyle and German philosopher Gottfried Wilhelm Liebnitz (1646–1716). To advance his claim that he and not Liebnitz had invented calculus, in 1712 he had the Royal Society issue a report, said to be by a committee of impartial scientists. Supporting Newton and accusing Liebnitz of plagiarism, the report's preface stressed its impartiality. In fact Newton (who just happened to be the president of the Royal Society) had written both preface and report.

On 16 April 1676 he wrote to warn the Royal Society that an observation by Boyle published in the Society's *Philosophical Transaction* that February could do great social harm. Boyle had noted that heat was produced when mercury was mixed with gold dust. Newton's objection? As he was then conducting alchemical experiments, he feared Boyle or another might beat him to the discovery of the 'Philosopher's Stone' (a mythic substance said to promote the transmutation of metals), and so abused his authority to prevent dissemination of Boyle's findings.[2]

Liebnitz and Boyle were not his only victims. Sir Isaac ruined more than one career with his vicious machinations. Unable to control his emotions and suffering two nervous breakdowns, it may be that when that apple fell on his head it not only triggered discovery of the Law of Gravity but contributed to a state of serious mental instability.

1. 'Newton and the fudge factor', Richard S. Westfall, *Science* 179:751 (1973).
2. Kohn, *op. cit.*, p.39.

NIXON, Richard M. (1913–94) (*FRAUD*, *see also* **RICHARD III**)
A nauseating spectacle of establishment and media obsequiousness took place in late April 1994 with the death of US ex-president Richard Milhous Nixon. Though in 1973 impeached and driven from the office he disgraced for his part in the Watergate cover-up, twenty years later the Great and the Good decided not only to forget and forgive, but to

eulogise the man once described by former President Harry Truman as: 'a shifty-eyed, goddamn liar', and by former Republican senator Barry Goldwater as: 'the most dishonest individual I have ever met in my life'. It seemed President Clinton and the four former presidents with him (Bush, Reagan, Carter and Ford), all at hand to praise and bury Nixon with full honours, had forgotten how, as Goldwater goes on: 'Nixon lied to his wife, his family, his friends, long-time colleagues in the US Congress, lifetime members of his own political party, the American people, and the world.'[1]

There's something very odd here. Despite his deviousness and paranoia, Nixon was remarkable. Not just the only American president to be impeached, he remains the one American elected twice to the vice-presidency and twice to the presidency. What that says about US politics one doesn't wish even to contemplate. Beginning his career during the McCarthy era by attacking Alger Hiss as a Communist, he used every dirty trick in the book to climb the greasy pole. Known even during his period as vice-president under Eisenhower as 'Tricky Dick', it is one of history's ironies that his close defeat in the 1960 presidential race against John F. Kennedy was probably due to vote-rigging at the Chicago polls, arranged by JFK's father's old Mafia contacts. What also stood against him in that race was his shifty appearance on TV, compared with JFK's clean good looks. With heavy jowls and permanent five-o'clock shadow, he didn't look like a man you could trust. But you can't keep a bad man down, and in 1968 he was back, repackaged so successfully by the Republican PR men that at last he became president.

'Let us begin by committing ourselves to the truth', he lied when accepting the Republican Presidential nomination in Chicago in 1968 as riot raged on the streets, 'to see it like it is and tell it like it is – to find the truth, to speak the truth, and to live the truth.'

Five years later, on 17 November 1973, with the Watergate scandal breaking round him, this Prince of Liars told a convention of newspaper editors that: 'People have got to know whether or not their President is a crook. Well, I'm not a crook.' But by then everyone knew if Nixon said something *was* so, almost certainly the opposite was the case.

His downfall began when in June 1972 five men were arrested for breaking into the Democratic Party national headquarters in the Watergate office complex in Washington D.C. Found to be working for the Republican Committee to Reelect the President (CREEP), the finger of suspicion pointed at Nixon himself. There is no hard evidence that he ordered the break-in, but he authorised the cover-up that followed, and the programme of lies and dirty tricks it required. Ironically, the most damning evidence against him and his aides came from Nixon himself. Wanting his place in history, and jealous of Secretary of State Henry Kissinger's international reputation, he'd taped every conversation that took place around him – both to provide material for his memoirs and as a source of proof to counter any attempt by Kissinger to steal his glory.

Why he never destroyed the tapes as the scandal mounted is a mystery. Perhaps he couldn't bring himself to do it. They were his record. They were his 'truth'. They were also his downfall, and that of others. Of twenty-nine people indicted in connection with Watergate offences, twenty were found guilty, including his closest aides. Nixon, though the only US President ever to be impeached, was pardoned by his successor, Gerald Ford – maybe because of his obvious devotion to the truth. For one of the tapes, so full of deviousness and lies, records Nixon giving excellent reasons for telling the truth. Instructing John Dean, the young White House counsel, on how to conduct himself during the forthcoming investigations, on 16 April 1973 Nixon recalled the Hiss case which had set him on his career. (In 1948, accused by Whittaker Chambers of working with him in a Communist spy ring of the 1930s, Alger Hiss had sued for libel; but Chambers proved his case, and Hiss, hounded by Nixon, was jailed for perjury.)

'Tell the truth!' Nixon told Dean. 'That is the thing I have told everybody around here – tell the truth! That Hiss would be free today if he hadn't lied. If he had said, "Yes I knew Chambers and as a young man I was involved in some Communist activities but I broke it off a number of years ago." And Chambers would have dropped it. If you are going to lie, you go to jail for the lie rather than the crime. So believe me, don't ever lie.'[2]

This too turned out to be a lie, though inadvertently so. Nixon never went to jail for his lies. Others went instead. And so, when he died twenty years later, the US media and establishment indulged in a revolting orgy of posthumous rehabilitation, as if all possessed by the ghost of Tricky Dick himself. Nixon lied all his life to the American people and, when he died, the American people lied about Nixon to themselves. At least, some of them did.

1. *Goldwater*, Barry Goldwater, Doubleday, New York 1988.
2. Goldberg, *op. cit.*, pp.86–91.

NORWICH, Lord (*See* HOAXES IN WARFARE)

O

'As long as there are people about with
empty brains and full pockets, my kind will
always succeed.'

(Solun Osmun, Turkish conman)

ORTON, Arthur (*See* **TICHBORNE CLAIMANT, The**)

OSMUN, Solun (20th century) (*CONMEN*)
Completing the triumvirate of outrageous conmen who specialise in
selling off famous landmarks like Nelson's Column (Arthur **Furguson**)
or the Eiffel Tower (Victor **Lustig**), meet Solun Osmun, once Istanbul's
most persuasive salesman. Though in the 1960s he went straight at last
after spending twenty-five years of his professional life in prison, in his
heyday he specialised in selling to visitors the city's best-known landmarks, monuments, and mosques. Among the items he sold to the
gullible were the famous Galata Bridge that crosses the Golden Horn and
links the two sides of Istanbul, two Byzantine fire-towers, the clocks in
the city squares, the university building, plus such other minor items as
the underground railway, various tram cars, and the entire Simplon-
Orient Express.

Some of these items stretch the imagination, but his description of
how he sold the clocks in the squares will give some idea of his methods.
Waiting under one of the clocks until a passer-by stopped to correct his
watch, he'd step forward and ask for 2.50 lira. Asked by the victim why
he should, Solun would tell him: because he owned the clock. Amid the
argument an accomplice would come up, set his watch by the clock, and
pay him 2.50 lira, whereupon the stranger would also pay him. In one
case the victim was an Anatolian trader who, engaged in further
conversation over coffee, asked Solun how much the business was worth.
A fortune, said Solun, who in this case ended up by selling the man two
clocks in Beyazit Square for the equivalent of a hundred pounds.

Attributing his success (if you call twenty-five years in Turkish jails 'success') to his ability to judge rapidly how naive a person is, he maintained that: 'As long as there are people about with empty brains and full pockets, my kind will always succeed.' Released from jail in a general amnesty in the early 1960s and deciding to go straight, he was helped in this ambition both by the police who'd spent years trying to catch him, and by the city's newspapers whose columns (and thus sales) had been enlivened by his exploits. Clubbing together, they collected enough money to buy him a shop. So at last he settled down, no doubt repaying the compliment by occasionally advising the people on how to prevent just those activities in which formerly he'd been so expert.[1]

1. McCormick, *op. cit.*, pp.167–8.

OTREFIEF (d.1606) (*IMPOSTORS*)

Anna **Anderson** and other impostors claiming to be surviving members of the Russian royal family murdered by the Bolsheviks in 1918 are far from being the first royal impersonators in Russian history. Indeed, over the centuries there have been so many that it is no wonder that in the early days of the 1917 Revolution the Bolsheviks feared the appearance of pretenders claiming to be Czar Nicholas II or his son Alexis.

Of them all, the most successful was a monk named Otrefief, the virtual double of Dmitri, younger son of Ivan the Terrible. At Ivan's death, his weakling eldest son Feodor had succeeded, but soon died. Boris Godunov, once one of Ivan's closest lieutenants and married to Ivan's sister, cleared the way to the throne by murdering Dmitri. At first his rule was popular and successful. Winning the support of the *boyars* (nobles) in 1597, he went about the conquest and colonisation of Siberia, and founded a university in Moscow. But when famine and plague came to roost on Russia later in his reign, his popularity waned.

At this point Otrefief began his imposture. Because of his extraordinary likeness to the murdered prince, he had little trouble persuading people, especially Boris's increasing number of enemies, that he really was Dmitri, and had escaped the assassination attempt by the substitution of another youth in his place. Nor was he lacking in personal qualities. A contemporary chronicler said of him that: 'his figure was fine, his manners prepossessing, and his eloquence forcible'. Seeking allies in Poland, he received promises of aid from all sides, got the support of the Polish king, and was promised the hand in marriage of the daughter of a wealthy noble, Sendomir, whenever he became Czar.

Leading a small army of Cossacks and Poles, in 1604 the fake prince advanced into Russia against Godunov's much larger force. Showing great courage and leadership, and an unexpected tactical skill, his fame spread so rapidly that soon many of Godunov's men began deserting to him. Despairing, Godunov killed himself by taking poison, and Otrefief entered Moscow in triumph, duly to be crowned Czar Dmitri – one of history's few royal impostors to make it all the way to the top.

It didn't last. It was hard enough for legitimate czars to survive, let alone fakes. Otrefief started well, and appeared to have genuine ability, but made the mistake of paying too much heed to his lowliest subjects and listening to their grievances. With the *boyars* already muttering, his second mistake was to start lavishing honours on the Poles who had aided his cause. Detesting this Polish influence at their court, the Russian nobility under Count Schisky launched a counter-revolution. The palace was stormed and Otrefief died.

Still, he'd had a good run for his money.

P

'I do not suppose that we can swear that we
are exactly at the Pole.'

(Robert E. Peary, 7 April 1909)

PALLADINO, Eusapia (*See* **MEDIUMS**)

PARANORMAL HOAXES (*See CONCORDANCE*)

PAST-LIFE MEMORIES (*PARANORMAL HOAXES*)
So what's so great about being born over and over again? Buddhist
believers view the prospect with anxiety, for 'all life is suffering', and
who wants to suffer? Texts like *The Tibetan Book of the Dead* exist
expressly to teach folk how to avoid rebirth. Yet the doctrine of
reincarnation is not just Eastern, but is found worldwide, and even
today, in the secular West, there are those who claim not only the reality
of rebirth, but memory of their past lives – memory typically evoked by
means of hypnotic regression techniques.

Yet the value of such hypnotically induced 'evidence' (as in **UFO
abduction** cases) must be doubted. The phenomenon of **False Memory
Syndrome** indicates the suggestibility of the human mind and its power
to invent 'evidence', especially if prompted by the leading questions of
an unwary researcher or one with preconceived ideas. That unconscious
'self-hoaxing' can occur is highlighted by the work of Cardiff hypnotherapist Arnall Bloxham, who in the 1970s claimed to have 'regressed'
several patients to their former lives. 'The Bloxham Tapes', a 1976 BBC
TV documentary, examined dramatic tape-recorded accounts made
during regression. Swimming instructor Graham Huxtable 'became' an
eighteenth-century sailor caught up in battle with a French ship. He
screamed in agony as he was 'wounded'. But the most instructive case
was of a young woman, 'Jane Evans', who recalled seven past lives:
especially those of Livonia, a Roman matron in fourth-century Britain;

Rebecca, a York Jewess murdered in a church crypt during a 1190 massacre; and Alison, servant to a fifteenth-century French merchant prince, Jacques Coeur. Her detailed knowledge convinced Bloxham, herself, author Jeffrey Iverson and others. It was claimed that as Rebecca she had died in a crypt of York's St Mary Castlegate, not found until after her public account of it.[1] A vaulted space *was* found, but errors in her tale and fresh evidence suggested cryptomnesia – a state in which the subject taps previously absorbed information which, consciously forgotten, is falsely attributed to personal experience. For later it emerged that her 'memories' came from historical novels she'd read and forgotten. 'Livonia', for example, came from *The Living Wood*, a 1947 novel by Louis de Wohl (hired by the Allies to forge anti-Nazi Nostradamus quatrains: *see* **Hoaxes in Warfare**). She'd so deeply absorbed and (unconsciously) edited de Wohl's characters that, under hypnosis, she recalled them as her own 'far memory'. No historical proof of the existence of any of her 'former selves' later emerged. She had hoaxed herself – and others.

The most famous case involving apparent regression to a former life is that of Bridey Murphy. Hypnotised in the 1950s by Colorado businessman Morey Bernstein and suddenly speaking in an Irish brogue, Mrs Virginia Tighe identified herself as Bridey Murphy who, born in County Cork in 1798 and later wife of a Belfast barrister, had died in 1864. In six tape-recorded sessions Mrs Tighe provided colourful detail about Victorian Ireland; named Belfast shops later found to have existed; used now-redundant terms then in use; and described songs, farming methods, books, coins and furniture of the time.

Serialised in the *Chicago Daily News*, in 1956 Bernstein's book *The Search for Bridey Murphy* became a bestseller. Yet efforts to trace Bridey were hampered by the fact that records of Irish births and deaths began only two years after her supposed death. Meanwhile a rival newspaper, the *Chicago American*, uncovered Virginia Tighe's identity and claimed she'd grown up in Chicago with an aunt: 'as Irish as the lakes of Killarney' who'd told her Irish tales. They'd lived opposite an Irishwoman, Bridey Corkell, whose maiden name was Murphy, and with whose son, John, Virginia had been infatuated.

The case collapsed. Virginia was assumed to be a fraud or unconscious romancer. Then a *Denver Post* journalist, investigating the exposé, found that most of it was a pack of lies. Virginia's aunt, Mrs Mary Burns, had grown up in New York and never even met Virginia until the girl was eighteen; both she and Virginia denied the 'Irish tales'. Mrs Corkell (whom Virginia said she'd never met) refused to be interviewed; and her son John turned out to be the Sunday editor of the *Chicago American*. None of which proved that Virginia really had been Bridey. What it *did* not prove was how easy it is to destroy such a case, given either a predisposition to disbelief or unrevealed commercial interest. Hoax had been used to ridicule what the hoaxers had assumed was a hoax. So, whatever the truth or otherwise of reincarnation, once again we have to invoke Fort's Principle: a predisposition to *dis*believe shows as much credulity as a predisposition to believe.[2]

1. *More Lives Than One?*, Jeffrey Iverson, Souvenir Press, London 1976.
2. *The Search for Bridey Murphy*, Morey Bernstein, Hutchinson, London 1956.

ST PAUL (*See* **CHRISTIANITY**)

PEARY, Robert E. (1856–1920) (*EXPLORATION HOAXES*)

Something about the North Pole – maybe the fact that it's only a compass reference point amid the frozen Arctic wilderness, with nothing dramatic to distinguish it from any other point for hundreds of miles around – seems to encourage fraud. **Cook**, already derided for claiming Mount McKinley, was even more derided when in 1909 he said he'd reached the Pole; while **Byrd**, though his 1926 claim to have overflown it was widely accepted (at least in the USA), was equally deceitful. Which leaves us with Peary, still the acclaimed conqueror. It remains widely assumed that on 7 April 1909 this obsessed explorer at last achieved his dream, leading his dogsledging team of Eskimos and Matthew Henson, the only non-Eskimo he chose to accompany him on his final dash.

Yet Henson was Peary's former servant. He was also a rarity in the Arctic: a black man. Peary sought the Pole only with those he saw as subservient. This is plain from his ghostwritten account, *The North Pole*. He says Henson had not, 'as a racial inheritance, the daring and initiative of Bartlett . . . or MacMillan, or Borup' – experienced men he'd rejected for the last push. As for the Eskimos, 'Of course they could not lead, but they could follow and drive dogs better than any white man.' And at the 'Pole', with Henson ordered to lead 'three rousing cheers', they were: 'childishly delighted with our success'. What he doesn't say is that none of those with him knew how to take bearings – a skill in which his fellow explorer, Bob Bartlett, was expert. But Bartlett wasn't there.

Peary's early history is eerily similar to Cook's. Cook lost his father aged five, Peary aged two. Both had a lisp. Both felt socially inferior to others. Peary's mother was domineering and smothering. Never remarrying, after her husband's death she returned to her native Maine, bringing 'Bertie' up almost as a girl, pulling him out of one boarding school after another. When he went to college, she announced: 'I am going to college.'

No wonder he fled to the Arctic. But she was hard to escape. Taking work with the Coast and Geodetic Survey in Washington aged twenty-three, when offered a post the next year on an upcoming survey of the proposed Panama Canal, he asked her permission to go. She refused, and he obeyed. Only in 1881, aged twenty-eight, did he get himself 'ordered' on an expedition to Nicaragua, still against her wishes. Five years later came the first of his Arctic trips, to Greenland. She opposed this too but, oddly, lent him money to undertake it. Meanwhile in 1882 he'd met Josephine Diebitsch, daughter of a Smithsonian scholar. When in 1888 they married, Mother came on the honeymoon.

Josephine joined him on two of his expeditions, and in Greenland in 1893 gave birth to their 'Snow Baby' – so nicknamed by the Eskimos. At least there they were out of reach of Mother, but Peary still sought her approval. Yet despite his devotion to Josephine he took a fourteen-year-old Eskimo girl, Allakasingwah, as a mistress. She bore him at least one child, and Greenland gossip suggests that he shared other beds too.

Meanwhile his passion to reach the Pole so intensified that while still young he'd lost all but two of his toes to frostbite. His drive was such that, by one estimate, in all he sledged a total of over 13,000 miles. And though on such frequent extended leave from the navy that his career with it was a joke, he had the knack of drumming up support for his expeditions. By 1908 he could rely on the 'Peary Arctic Club' to finance his expeditions and generate publicity for the forthcoming push to the Pole. His well-chosen team included George Borup, Donald MacMillan, Matthew Henson, and Captain Bob Bartlett. He was ready to go when he heard of Cook's planned expedition. All his colleagues felt Cook was travelling too light to succeed, but Peary was furious. By now he'd been in the wastes so long he felt the route was his, as were 'his' Eskimos and 'his' dogs. Also he knew that this time it was now or never. He wasn't getting younger. And maybe he was worried about his increasing reliance on the Newfoundlander Bartlett. The plan, for this polar attack, was that Bartlett would leave land first and break trail all the way to the last point of possible retreat. It remained unclear if he'd go on to the Pole himself.

On 6 July 1908 the party left New York on the *Roosevelt*, the President himself first coming on board. Enduring the winter at Cape Sheridan on Ellesmere Island, on 28 February Bartlett led the first group north across the ice. Others followed. There were 24 men, 19 sledges, and 133 dogs on the expedition, with varying tasks. By mid-March only two parties still pushed north: Bartlett's and Peary's. The strain showed. The best day's march was 17 miles. By 1 April Bartlett was only 133 miles from the Pole. That was when Peary said he had to go back. There was no room for the extra weight; he'd use up supplies. Bitterly disappointed, he begged to go on, but Peary refused. Magnanimous in his autobiography, he said: 'Don't forget that Henson was a better dog-driver than I. So I think Peary's reasoning was sound; and I have never held it against him.'

Peary's decision has always puzzled Arctic students. Nobody deserved the Pole more than Bartlett who, that **April Fool's Day**, unwillingly turned south. 'Goodbye, Captain,' Peary told him. 'If we get there it will be the South Pole next and you as leader.' So Peary went on, and when he regained the *Roosevelt* on 26 April, just two days behind Bartlett, he did so, apparently, as leader of the first party to reach the North Pole.

Later he claimed that on that final dash north his party made twenty-five miles a day. Odd, given that before Bartlett's departure the highest distance in a day had been seventeen. In the diary he later showed the world he'd written: 'The Pole at last. The prize of three centuries. My dream and goal for twenty years. Mine at last.' Planting five flags and leaving records in a glass bottle that commemorated: 'the last of the great adventure stories – a story the world has been waiting to hear for nearly four hundred years', his triumphant party had started back south at 4.00 p.m. on 7 April 1909. Remarkably, they returned to the *Roosevelt* at a speed almost twice that of the northbound trip – or so Peary later claimed. Most remarkable of all had been their initial march, back to the point where Bartlett had left them – 133 miles in two and a half days: over 50 miles a day.

With ice breaking up, the *Roosevelt* started home. At the Greenland settlement of Etah, Peary was furious to learn that Cook had already claimed the Pole. Questioning the two Eskimos who'd been with Cook, Borup learned that he'd never left sight of land. Peary, who had, felt well vindicated. Reaching Labrador on 6 September, he cabled the news of his success – but Cook, stopping over in the Shetlands en route to Copenhagen had, five days earlier, already claimed the Pole. Congratulating Peary for getting there after him even as Peary attacked his claim, at first Cook seemed the winner. A poll of readers by a Pittsburgh newspaper produced 73,238 supporters of Cook, and only 2,814 for Peary.

But Cook's claim crumbled. Though both men refused to produce records proving their respective claims, and despite the anger of their quarrel, soon it was clear that Cook (already the demonstrated hoaxer of Mount McKinley) couldn't have reached the Pole. Which meant, according to a simplistic either-or process of public thought, that if one man was a liar, the other had to be honest. The possibility that *both* were liars was too awful to contemplate. With Cook out of the running, Peary's records were scanned by a National Geographic Society sub-committee unwilling to scan them too closely. Two years later his supporters lobbied the House of Representatives to pass a bill officially crediting him with the Pole and retiring him from the navy as a rear admiral. Despite questions that had him squirming, the bill was passed, 154 to 34. On an annual pension of $6,500 for life, Rear-Admiral Robert E. Peary retired with his wife and two children to Eagle Island, Maine. He spent his last years troubled only by doubters like North Dakota Congressman Henry Helgeson, who died before his bill to strip Peary of his honours could be introduced.

With Peary now as much a national monument as Byrd became a

decade later, the doubts of men like Helgeson and (more pertinently) Amundsen were not allowed to disturb his fame – though, according to his own report, to have gained the Pole and then returned from it his party must have travelled 429 miles between 2 April and 9 April – an average of over 53 miles a day, in polar conditions, by men close to exhaustion.

His achievement, like Cook's, was remarkable. Probably he got within a hundred miles of the Pole. But this fanatically determined man was as unreliable as Cook. Why, with nobody about him to check his calculations and with no landmark to say if he had or had not gained his goal, should he not lie to say that he had, especially to people who had not endured his hardships? It had been hard to get away from Mother. He deserved it!

As for Henson, in an article for the *Boston-American*, he told how he and two Eskimos had 'witnessed the disappointment' of their leader after Peary made observations from the last camp (later claimed as only six miles from the Pole). 'His face was long and serious,' wrote Henson who, perplexed by Peary's refusal to speak, asked: 'Well, Mr Peary, we are now at the Pole, are we not?' Peary said: 'I do not suppose that we can swear that we are exactly at the Pole,' then abruptly confessed surprise at being so close. But when Henson shook his leader's hand: 'a gust of wind blew something into his eye . . . and with both hands covering his eyes, he gave us orders not to let him sleep for more than four hours.' Thereafter: 'From the time we knew we were at the Pole Commander Peary scarcely spoke to me.'

If Peary faked the last hundred miles, he knew it, even if nobody else did.[1]

1. Roberts, *op. cit.*, pp.107–25.

PERCY, Bishop Thomas (1729–1811) (*LITERARY HOAXES*)
It seems sometimes that just about everyone in eighteenth-century Britain able to write was forging antique poetry. **Chatterton, Ireland, Macpherson, Morganwg** – the list stretches on. And at the same time that Macpherson was enraging Johnson, in 1765 there appeared the *Reliques of Ancient English Poetry*, an anthology of material (including the famous 'Ballad of Chevy Chase') purportedly four or five centuries old, and collected from the oral tradition. But in all probability only a quarter of the poems were genuinely old, the rest being written by Thomas Percy, a bishop in the Church of England.

Born the son of a Bridgnorth grocer named Piercy, he had assumed the rather more elevated name of *Percy*, and happily let people think him a scion of that illustrious family. As chaplain to the Earl of Northumberland and then to George III, he had risen through the ecclesiastical ranks to become Dean of Carlisle and finally Bishop of Dromore. A genuine

Tried in 1977 for criminal deception, English art forger Tom Keating had Britain rocking with laughter at the way he embarrassed the art world and humiliated its so-called 'experts'. (*Syndication International*)

This supreme artist (author of 'The Ten Commandments for Conmen') not only twice sold the Eiffel Tower for scrap, but got away with conning gangster Al Capone. Yet like Capone 'Count' Victor Lustig ended up behind bars, where he died in 1947. (*Topham*)

Long thought to have perished in an English Channel plane crash in December 1944, big-band leader Glenn Miller probably died following a Paris brothel brawl. The truth was covered up to avoid posthumous scandal. (*Peter Newark's American Pictures*)

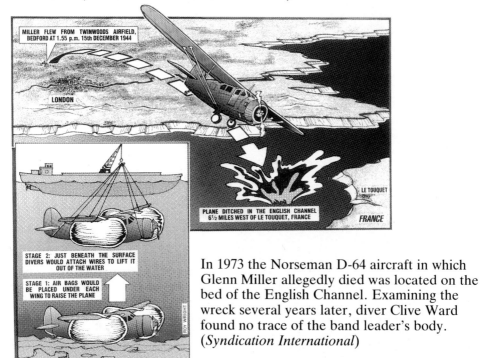

MILLER FLEW FROM TWINWOODS AIRFIELD, BEDFORD AT 1.55 p.m. 15th DECEMBER 1944

LONDON

PLANE DITCHED IN THE ENGLISH CHANNEL 6½ MILES WEST OF LE TOUQUET, FRANCE

LE TOUQUET

FRANCE

STAGE 2: JUST BENEATH THE SURFACE DIVERS WOULD ATTACH WIRES TO LIFT IT OUT OF THE WATER

STAGE 1: AIR BAGS WOULD BE PLACED UNDER EACH WING TO RAISE THE PLANE

In 1973 the Norseman D-64 aircraft in which Glenn Miller allegedly died was located on the bed of the English Channel. Examining the wreck several years later, diver Clive Ward found no trace of the band leader's body. (*Syndication International*)

Here Swiss UFO cult leader Eduard 'Billy' Meier is shown with a framed photo of his lady friend Semjase. Four hundred years old, she hails from the planet ERRA in the Pleiades star cluster. (*Fortean Picture Library*)

Despite his claim in 1959 to have scaled the 'unclimbable' Patagonian peak Cerro Torre, it now seems certain that Italian mountaineer Cesare Maestri never got near the top. What drives men like Maestri, Peary and Cook to make false claims? (*Topham*)

Shown here visiting Hitler in 1937, Italian Fascist leader Benito Mussolini claimed many more soldiers, aircraft, tanks and guns than he really had. This tendency to look on the bright side so ruined Italy that, with the war lost, Italian partisans strung him up – from a lamppost. (*Mary Evans Picture Library*)

AMERICUS VESPUTIUS

In 1503 Amerigo Vespucci said he'd reached mainland America in 1497. He hadn't, but as Columbus still believed he'd got to the Indies, in 1507 Amerigo had *two* continents named after him when, needing a name for South America, a map-maker named it 'America', 'because Amerigo discovered it'. (*Mary Evans Picture Library*)

When philandering US televangelist Jim Bakker was jailed for fraud, rival preacher Jimmy Swaggart was quick to cast the first stone – until prostitute Debra Murphree recognised him on TV as one of her regulars and he too was caught with his pants down. (*Popperfoto*)

Face of Christ, or fourteenth-century fake? Radio carbon dating suggests that the Shroud of Turin was almost certainly manufactured between 1260 and 1390, but believers remain unconvinced by the scientific evidence. (*Mansell Collection*)

Claiming that on 7 April 1909 he had reached the North Pole, American Robert E. Peary convinced most people that he was first to have done so – but almost certainly he never got within a hundred miles of it. (*Topham*)

Did the apple *really* fall on his head? If so, it may have caused brain damage. Sadly Sir Isaac Newton, famed discoverer of the Laws of Gravity, was not above deceit, cooking calculations to fit his theories and using foul play to discredit opponents. Is *nothing* sacred? (*Antman Archives/Topham*)

'I'm not a crook', said US President Richard Nixon in 1973 at the height of the Watergate scandal that ruined him. By then everyone knew that if he said something *was* so, almost certainly the opposite was true. (*Hulton Deutsch*)

If Indian guru Bhagwan Sri Rajneesh really was a 'godman', as he claimed, why did he need a hundred Rolls-Royces? Whatever the reason, they did him no good. Indicted for fraud and deported from the USA, his death in 1990 was perhaps due to poison, or AIDS. (*Popperfoto*)

Slain at the Battle of Bosworth Field, 1485, and succeeded by the first Tudor, Henry VII, was King Richard III the cruel, scheming hunchback of legend, murderer of the Princes in the Tower – or is this Tudor propaganda? (*Topham*)

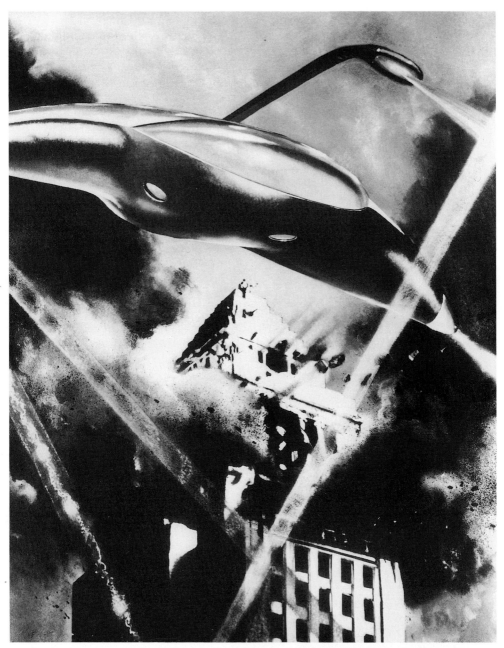

On 30 October 1938 millions of Americans panicked when, tuning into Orson Welles' radio dramatisation of *The War of the Worlds* by H.G. Wells, they thought that Martians (this still is from the 1953 movie version) really *were* invading. (*Kobal Collection*)

scholar who'd already published volumes of Chinese, Norse, and Hebrew poetry, at one time he'd been tempted to expose George **Psalmanazar**, but 'laid aside my Intention on account of the Age and Poverty of the Author'. Maybe also he stayed quiet on account of the fact that his own volume of fake medieval poetry was about to be published. He had no need to worry. Though some saw through the pretence, the Johnsonian literary clique in London eagerly embraced the *Reliques* as a new weapon in their war against Macpherson and other upstart Scots. It was one thing, that dreadful farmer's son from the Highlands trying to foist *Fingal* on them, but Percy was a *bishop*, and these were *English* poems – and as such were warmly received. Forgery? Of course not! Just poetic licence![1]

1. Yapp, *op. cit.*, pp.146–7.

PICKARD, Rawson (d.1963) (*PRANKS*)

Few in the US scientific world were surprised when the famed J. Fortescue of San Diego declined to attend a banquet honouring him or to accept in person the $10,000 Fleischmann prize for his outstanding research into yeast. A known recluse who preferred to pursue his research into polio, the sexual habits of American males, and other arcane topics without interruption, Fortescue (President of the International Board of Hygiene and a keen mycologist) received a glowing biographical write-up in the 1936 *Who's Who in San Diego*, and was also written up in the *San Diego Medical Society* magazine by one of the few colleagues who knew him well, Clifford Graves M.D. Among his exploits, during Prohibition and strictly for scientific purposes, he had crossed the Mexican border into Tijuana to conduct research into local beers, and on his discovery that one of the *cervezas* was calorie-free, San Diego advertisers promoted it as a slimming drink.

What they didn't promote was what they didn't know; J. Fortescue existed only in the mind of Rawson Pickard M.D., a pathologist of La Jolla, California. He and his thirsty friends, including Clifford Graves, had dreamed up their reclusive scientist in a Tijuana bar the night they'd declared one local beer calorie-free. They'd based him on the British jurist Sir John Fortescue (1385–1479), the man who first asserted the principle that it is better the guilty escape than the innocent be punished. Thereafter he served as cover for their pranks, including invention of the fake International Board of Hygiene, for nearly thirty years until Pickard's death in 1963.[1]

1. Madison, *op. cit.*, pp.56–8.

PILTDOWN MAN (*See* FOSSIL FORGERIES)

POITIER, Sidney (*See* **HAMPTON, David**)

PONZI, Carlo (1883–1949) (*FRAUD*)

Around 1900 Brooklyn swindler William Franklin Miller invented the pyramid scheme scam. At first known as Peter-to-Paul, in 1919 along came a conman who ran it so well that it has been named after him ever since: the Ponzi.

Already a compulsive gambler and dandy when aged eighteen he left Italy and made for New York, Carlo Ponzi never believed in making an honest living. As a waiter he saved enough money by cheating on customers' bills to get him to Canada where, working in a bank, he wrote too many cheques on its clients' accounts and ended up in jail. Released in 1919, despite his record he became a clerk with a Boston import-export company. Dealing with international reply coupons (whereby foreign customers can reply to requests without cost by redeeming the coupon for stamps at their post office), one day the light dawned when, sent a coupon from Madrid, he discovered that there it currently cost one US cent, but that in New York it bought ten cents worth of stamps.

Setting himself up as an investment counsellor, he promised potential investors that he could double their money in three months by making bulk purchases of postal coupons in foreign countries, then bringing them into America and selling them at profit. It worked. Within ninety days the initial investors got double their money – straight from the pockets of new investors who, hearing of this great new scheme, flocked to give Ponzi their cash. Within five months over a million dollars a week was flooding into Ponzi's grand new offices. Bought abroad by hundreds of agents, quite how the coupons were redeemed for cash on reaching the States remained his secret. Exchanging postage stamps for cash was illegal – officially. But no doubt he had no trouble persuading somebody, somewhere, that rules are made to be bent when the scent of cash is in the air.

Before the first year was out he rode a cream-coloured limo and was so eagerly sought by would-be investors that, by one account, whenever he was stopped at the lights, he was deluged by bank notes thrust through the windows. No doubt he kept them rolled down even in bad weather! Hailed by many as 'The greatest Italian of them all', he bought heavily in land and property, and soon had a country mansion with swimming pool and wine cellar. But no pyramid can last forever.

In August 1921, after a *Boston Globe* reporter exposed the scam, the crash came. Paying off $15 million of the $20 million he'd taken in the first year, he was arrested, charged with fraud in a Federal court, and sent down for five years. On release, he was rearrested by the State of Massachusetts and jailed for a further seven years. From prison he wrote personally to his 40,000 creditors, but when in 1934 he came out it was to meet a mob screaming for his blood. The police could barely hold it back; the safest course was to deport him. So back to Italy he went, there to die alone and close to poverty, leaving behind him nothing but his name as that of a scam – the Ponzi.

POPE JOAN (*HISTORICAL HOAXES*)

It was widely believed in the Middle Ages (some folk still believe it today) that in the ninth century a woman called Joan so successfully disguised her sex that she became Pope John VIII. Reigning for twenty-five months between AD 855 and 858, it is said she followed Leo IV and preceded Benedict III, and that her downfall came about only because she got pregnant. Concealing this misfortune up to the last moment, she gave birth during a procession to the Lateran, to be dragged out of Rome by the enraged mob and stoned to death. Another version is that this distinguished predecessor of James **Barry** died on the spot in childbirth, was buried where she died, and that later papal processions avoided the street where this shocking and iniquitous event had occurred.

In fact, as so often, the truth is otherwise. Only weeks elapsed between the death of Leo IV (847–855) and the accession of Benedict III (855– 858). The tale seems to have been invented by a thirteenth-century French Dominican friar, Stephen of Bourbon, who dated her election at *c.*1100. It may be he had heard tales about the influence wielded by a tenth-century Roman senator, Marozia, and her equally powerful mother, Theodora. With the story developed by itinerant friars, by the early fourteenth century it was generally agreed that Joan had been an Englishwoman who, born in Mainz in Germany, had fallen in love with an English Benedictine monk and dressed as a man to follow him to Athens. There she'd become so learned that, moving on to Rome while maintaining her masculine disguise, she'd become first a cardinal and then Pope.

The legend was widely believed as late as the seventeenth century. Protestants used it to attack Rome during the Reformation, and only in 1647 was it openly questioned, by a sceptical Calvinist, David Blondel. It cannot be put down to deliberate hoaxing, more to collective wishful thinking. People *wanted* to believe in it, and therefore asserted it as true.

PRESIDENTIAL NUCLEAR LAUNCH AUTHORITY *HOAXES IN WARFARE*, (*see also* COMPUTER FRAUD)

'It is necessary that the prince should know how . . . to be a great hypocrite and dissembler,' wrote Italian statesman Niccolò Machiavelli in 1513. 'For men are so simple, and yield so much in immediate necessity, that the deceiver will never lack dupes.'[1]

Never was this more apparent than in this Cold War government-engineered hoax, aimed at covering up the alarming fact that the United States Strategic Air Command at all times retained the autonomous capacity to launch a major nuclear strike against the Soviet Union, and presumed the authority to do so should military computers signal that a Soviet missile attack was under way. Since the decision to launch would necessarily be taken before the first impact of the suspected missiles, this imposed a timeline of about ten minutes after the first warning of a submarine-based Soviet attack.

False warnings plagued the system, triggering alerts in which missile crews were ordered to insert their keys in their launch locks, and in which nuclear command planes took off. On one infamous occasion in 1979 a massive attack warning was caused by the input of a war-games simulation tape. It may be that this was an attempted ultimate **computer** con, one that could have ended the world we know. The official finding was that the input was a tape operator's inadvertent mistake, but his name was never made public, nor was action taken against anyone on account of the near Armageddon.

A mistaken warning six months later was triggered by a single 46-cent computer chip getting stuck on the digit '2'. First it reported 2 attacking missiles, then 22, and then 222, and the Strategic Air Command again readied its launch crews for imminent launch orders.

The Pentagon's hoax was that these launch procedures required Presidential authorisation, a legend which mainstream media preferred not to question. In the official scenario, only the President held the requisite launch codes on a plastic card, which he would insert into an encoded transmitter carried by a military aide, always at his side, in a black bag called the 'football'. According to the legend, such a state of readiness was sustained that, at a moment's notice from the Strategic Air Command, the President could and would take a meaningful and constitutional launch decision, and have a whole minute to decide on and select a retaliatory option (including 'all-out') from a 75-page black book kept with the football – even in the event of a submarine-based missile attack first targeting Washington, D.C., which implied less than five minutes' flight time.

Good authority (*Washington Post*, 13 December 1981) related that President Reagan was himself fooled by this hoax, expressing surprised anger after he was shot in 1981 by John Hinckley when he learned that the military had no interest in his plastic card. It was a dummy. The military (perhaps not foolishly) didn't trust the President.

This situation led to the occasional congressional question regarding the President's human frailties, and so, on top of this transparent hoax, the Pentagon overlaid a second, intellectually more credible hoax. The second hoax was the official Department of Defense policy, most subtly expounded in the late 1970s by Undersecretary of Defense for Policy Fred Ikle, an ex-RAND Corporation nuclear strategy whizz-kid.

This policy began with an express concession that it was impossible for anyone – President or general – to validate a missile attack warning with one hundred per cent certainty in the brief time before the forecast first impact. It continued with the firm assertion that procedures were in place guaranteeing that no accidental launch could occur, thus inviting the conclusion that the firm policy was *not* launch on warning of attack. To support this conclusion, the Strategic Air Command vehemently affirmed that it did not have a launch on warning policy. But on much rarer occasions it was quietly mentioned that United States policy was also *not* to 'not launch on warning'. To justify this while perpetuating the hoax, the policy was completed by the clever affirmation that keeping the enemy guessing was sufficient gain to justify keeping secret the implied policy not to launch on warning.

In other words, secrecy was represented as a beneficial hoax, even if the policy was not to launch on warning. The Air Force, at first stand-offish towards the civilian-devised policy, soon realised the advantages of this position, which let them claim perfect conduct and yet do whatever they chose under a cloak of utter secrecy.

By this point, Machiavelli was doubtless sitting up in his grave and applauding enthusiastically. The hypocrisy and reversed layers of deceit involved were, in their own way, little short of brilliant. Yet that this policy was a hoax not on the enemy but on the American people became quite clear in the mid-1980s, when evidence emerged establishing that the Strategic Air Command indeed had the capacity to launch on warning, and had ever-ready launch-on-warning drills that *forced* the taking of a retaliatory decision in an incredibly brief timeline. The policy guidelines meant that the decision-makers had to assume that any 'confirmed' attack warning was valid. They had no jurisdiction to question the validity of a confirmed warning, it being the duty of others to issue a 'confirmed' attack warning if ever two sensor systems simultaneously reported an attack under way. This policy was obscured by its official name: 'dual phenomenology'.

In plain words, this required the issuance of a confirmed attack warning, and thus the taking of a retaliatory launch decision, if only two false alerts (as mentioned above) had ever occurred at the same time. Moreover, Personnel Reliability Programs policies assured that nuclear launch orders would be carried out immediately upon receipt.

For example, a Major Herring (a would-be missileer who'd distinguished himself in air raids over Vietnam), was ignominiously discharged just for asking how he could be sure that a launch order really came from the President. He was told that his question was impertinent, and that an answer was 'beyond his need to know'.

This hoax of pretended Presidential authority was almost adjudicated in a lawsuit suing the Pentagon for unsafely delegating the nuclear launch decision to military drills governed by error-prone computers, thus usurping the exclusive constitutional powers of Congress to declare war, and of the President as Commander in Chief to order a nuclear strike in time of war. The Pentagon first responded by arguing that it had an implied right to assume and to subdelegate nuclear launch authority, an opinion which the Air Force's Judge Advocate General had officially published, based on esoteric Presidential 'alter-ego' and 'pre-delegation' doctrines.[2] This obscure publication had attracted no attention, but a paragraph in *Newsweek* (5 January 1987) reporting the Pentagon's lawsuit filing had irate and alarmed military officers around the world inundating the Pentagon to complain about the heresy.

The Pentagon strongly demanded that *Newsweek* formally retract and apologise for the publication, which *Newsweek* refused to do, because its report was simply true. However, a couple of weeks later *Newsweek* published a letter from the Pentagon vehemently affirming that only the President could order the launch of nuclear weapons, and drawing attention to a simultaneously filed affidavit of a Colonel Hope swearing so. But Hope was not enough. The filing of a retired admiral's testimony to the contrary, and a demand to interrogate Colonel Hope, resulted in the Pentagon (amazingly) *withdrawing* the affidavit. This epilogue was not reported in the press, and the suit was subsequently dismissed as beyond the court's jurisdiction to decide.

Thus the hoax of Presidential nuclear launch authority was sustained through the 1980s, until the issue of delegating nuclear launch to error-prone computers became redundant with the end of the Cold War – or did it?

1. *The Prince*, Niccolò Machiavelli, 1531 (Chapter 18).
2. See *OpJAGAF 1981/42*, Jul. 9: 'CINCSAC [Commander-In-Chief, Strategic Air Command] could, in our opinion, be legally authorized to command all strategic nuclear forces of the United States.' See also *OpJAGAF 1980/83*, Oct. 3.

PRICE, Harry (1891–1948) (*PARANORMAL HOAXES*)
A travelling salesman by trade, this English ghost-hunter became a prominent member of the Society for Psychical Research (SPR). Witty and imaginative, he was also competitive, ambitious for fame, and easily insulted. Such characteristics upset many of his more conservative colleagues, some of whom denounced him after his death as a fraud.

The claims originated in the 1920s when he and Austrian **medium** Rudi Schneider worked with one Baron von Schrenk-Nötzing, a character so dubious that he was widely known as 'Baron Shrink-at-Nothing'. Accused of faking spirit-photographs, Price's fury served to fuel later hostilities arising from his investigations of Borley Rectory. Located near Sudbury in Essex and built in 1863, after Price began investigating it in 1929 it soon acquired a reputation as 'The Most Haunted House in England' – and, by the time it burned down a decade later, Price had certainly done his best to prove the point. The phenomena he reported included a phantom coach, a headless monk, a ghostly nun, the spirit of a former vicar, plus eerie lights, bells that rang themselves, and water that turned into ink. 'The best authenticated case of haunting in the annals of psychical research,' Price called it – but after his death his claims were derided by three former SPR colleagues. In *The Borley Report* (1956) they alleged that he had faked evidence by burying bones, producing aural effects in the dark by crumpling cellophane, and so on. The affair got to a point where it had less to do with Borley Rectory than Price's integrity. Yet again in such cases the phenomena involved are so tricksy that it's easy to doubt the sanity and/or honesty of the investigators. Price was disliked not only for desiring fame, but for his social background, his over-eager imagination, and the Shrenk-Nötzing affair. There was a good deal of snobbery involved; and it remains hard to tell if Price's claims were fairly assessed. That there may have been bias is suggested by the fact that a later SPR report by Robert Hastings, *An examination of the 'Borley report'* (1969), which considered weaknesses in the arguments against Price, was never separately issued or widely publicised.[1,2]

1. *Search for Truth*, Harry Price, Collins, London 1942.
2. *Search for Harry Price*, Trevor H. Hall, Duckworth, London 1978.

PROPAGANDA (*See* **HOAXES IN WARFARE, MUSSOLINI**)

PROTOCOLS OF THE ELDERS OF ZION (*See* **ANTI-SEMITIC HOAXES**)

PSALMANAZAR, George (?1679–1763) (*LITERARY HOAXES*)
Arriving in London in 1701 with William Innes, a Scottish army chaplain, this strange individual claimed to be a native of Formosa, a land nobody in England knew anything about. Explaining that Formosans looked more European than oriental, he said Innes had converted him to **Christianity**. Introduced to the Bishop of London, he so impressed the reverend gentleman that the bishop became his patron, obtaining for him a sinecure at Christ Church, Oxford. Here he began training missionaries to be sent out to his heathen land, and translated the Church of England Catechism into what he claimed was Formosan. Though unlike any other known language, it was regular and grammatical, and impressed all who saw it, although of course nobody could read it. As for Psalmanazar, he too seemed impressively alien, existing as he did on a diet of raw flesh, roots and herbs while setting to work on his *magnum opus*.

This appeared in 1704 as *A Historical and Geographical Description of Formosa*. It was an instant bestseller. Explaining that most Formosans lived to be a hundred because they ate raw meat and drank snake's blood, he also admitted that every year 18,000 boys under the age of nine were ritually slaughtered to appease the gods. This led to a constant shortage of males, so that polygamy was necessarily practised.

The success of this spicy account led within a year to a second edition, but now Psalmanazar found himself in trouble. George Candidus, a Dutch Jesuit missionary who knew Formosa well, denounced his book as rubbish. Pointing out basic errors like placing Formosa in the Chinese rather than the Japanese sphere of influence, Candidus insisted that Formosan society, far from being bloodthirsty, was so lenient that there were virtually no laws at all. Robbers were hardly punished, and adultery was so disregarded that the gift of a few hogs was thought ample compensation by the affronted spouse. Not so, claimed Psalmanazar. Robbers and murderers were hanged head down then shot to death with arrows, while other offences were punished in ways that made medieval hanging, drawing, and quartering seem mild by comparison. And as the Jesuits were hated in Protestant England at the time, with the public much preferring Psalmanazar's account of the bloodthirsty, cruel, and heathen land which nonetheless was full of gold and silver, for a while longer he got away with it. Even so, doubts grew and, though the hoax lasted another twenty-five years, Psalmanazar found himself increasingly ridiculed. Taking work as clerk to an army regiment, in 1728 he fell ill and, fearing for his soul, confessed that he had invented the saga so as to lead a life: of 'shameless idleness, vanity, and extravagance'.

Thoroughly repentant, he spent his remaining thirty-five years atoning for his crime by contributing careful, thoroughly researched articles to reference books. His final years were not unhappy. Though given to opium 'in a pint of punch' each evening after his twelve-hour stint at the writing desk, he became famous for his piety. 'I would as soon have thought of contradicting a bishop,' his drinking companion Samuel Johnson said of him while, published posthumously, his *Memoirs* led Horace Walpole to remark that, as a literary impostor, Psalmanazar had more genius than **Chatterton**.

Speaking six languages and fluent in Latin, Psalmanazar's true name and origin never emerged, but he may originally have been from Avignon in France.

PSYCHIC SURGERY (*PARANORMAL HOAXES*)
One of the odder pseudo-medical fads of recent years concerns reports from Brazil and the Philippines that 'psychic surgeons' without medical education or facilities, often with only their bare hands, perform complex surgery with a high level of success and few failures. In Brazil in the 1950s the work of José de Freitas, nicknamed Arigó, attracted attention, but it was to Luzon in the Philippines in the 1970s that folk flocked to healers like Tony Agpaoa who, with their hands alone, seemingly pulled open the body to remove diseased tissue and organs.

Many belonged to the Union Espiritista Christiana de Filipinas, a network of rural Spiritist churches – a movement also popular in Brazil.

It seems incredible that anyone could believe such a scam and, sure enough, by the mid-1970s the 'psychic surgeons' were thoroughly debunked as sleight-of-hand tricksters by sceptics like James **Randi**. Where it comes to manufacturing evidence to support his own position, Randi's own record is not so good, but on this issue it's hard not to agree with him. Yet some were convinced by what they saw.

On three visits to the Philippines, author Lyall Watson watched over a thousand operations by twenty-two healers. One involved a middle-aged woman with stomach pains. He saw the healer apparently push his hands deep into her body. A tennis-ball-sized lump of flesh grew between the healer's first and second fingers. Lifting it clear with forceps, an assistant snipped a thread of tissue to free it from the body. Removing his hands, the 'healer' wiped blood from the body, leaving no visible wound. 'I rub my hand over her skin', writes Watson. 'It is hot, but there is nothing on it, not a mark of any kind.'[1]

Big surprise! But Watson didn't draw the obvious conclusion. Why no wound or mark? Because the body hadn't been opened! Yet, observing similar operations in 1973, Chicago journalist Tom Valentine dismissed sleight-of-hand, hypnosis or hoax. That same year and again in 1975 George Meek led two teams of 'experts' (in *what* is not said) to the Philippines. Deciding that some healers were fake, they nonetheless agreed that: 'the factual existence and daily practice of several types of psycho-energetic phenomena by several native healers was clearly established. The practice of materialising and dematerialising human blood tissue and organs as well as non-human objects was found.'[2]

One gets the point, just about – but what were the 'non-human objects'? Chicken guts? The 'experts' testified that, though no anaesthetic or sterile precautions were used, there was no infection or post-operative shock. Of course not. How can there be infection or post-operative shock without an operation? They were also unanimous that no fraud had taken place – save where they'd spotted it, which doesn't seem to have been often.

In Brazil, 'Arigó' became famous in his own land in the 1950s then internationally when author John J. Fuller published *Arigó: Surgeon of the Rusty Knife*.[3] An ex-miner and amateur doctor, it's said he performed thousands of operations with table knives or scissors in totally unsterile conditions. Allegedly in trance while diagnosing and treating the sick, he claimed he was advised by a voice in his right ear, and that it belonged to a Dr Fritz, who'd died in Estonia in 1918. Twice jailed for practising illegally, after his second sentence he turned exclusively to diagnosis. In 1968 a team of doctors led by New York neurologist Andrija Puharich saw him treat a thousand patients. Touching none, and taking under a minute per patient, he diagnosed and advised treatment for each. In verifiable cases, claimed Puharich:

'we did not find [one diagnosis] in which Arigó was at fault'.[4]

On an earlier trip Puharich had watched Arigó practise surgery: 'The people step up – they're all sick. One had a big goitre. Arigó just picked up the paring-knife, cut it open, popped the goitre out, slapped it in her hand, wiped the opening with a piece of dirty cotton, and off she went. It hardly bled at all.'[5]

Remember Puharich? He of the teleporting briefcases and metallic voices speaking from thin air in Uri **Geller**'s apartment? Again, it's hard to reject Randi's view that, even where trickery is *not* involved, observers like Fuller, Puharich and Watson want so much to see miracles that even simple operations like lancing boils are invoked as extraordinary.

As for the Filipino 'healers', Randi offers step-by-step demonstrations of how any competent stage-magician can fake such operations, even with witnesses at close quarters. He wonders why, when healer Tony Agpaoa (one of the wealthiest men in the Philippines) had his appendix removed, he flew to a hospital in San Francisco! Didn't he trust his colleagues? Did he know something those believing in his powers did not?

After all, it's serious. Thousands of sick people encouraged by such publicity went to Luzon for treatment. In a 1977 *World in Action* TV documentary aired by Granada in the UK, a group of hopeful sufferers was followed from Britain to Luzon, through their treatment, then back home again. The results were clear enough. Some who'd declared themselves cured suffered a relapse. Others just 'felt a little better'. Some were dead before the film was shown, others died subsequently. There were no cures. All tumours there when the patients flew out were still there when they returned. As for the Granada camera team, it was excluded from the operations after narrator Mike Scott grabbed a fake tumour. Returning to London, Scott submitted for analysis to Guy's Hospital other samples of tissue and blood his team had managed to snatch. The blood came from cows and pigs. A growth 'removed' from a little girl's neck turned out to be a biopsy sample from a grown woman's breast. Other growths turned out to be pieces of chicken. Enough said.[6]

1. *The Romeo Error*, Lyall Watson, Coronet, London 1976, pp.214–19.
2. *ibid.*, p.218.
3. *Arigó: Surgeon of the Rusty Knife*, John J. Fuller, Crowell, New York 1974.
4. *op. cit.* note 1, p.212.
5. 'Arigó: Surgeon Extraordinary', Roy Stemman, *The Unexplained*, Orbis partwork, London 1983, p.379.
6. Randi, *op. cit.*, pp.173–96.

PTOLEMY, Claudius (*c*.90–168) (*SCIENTIFIC SCAMS*)
Long revered as the greatest astronomer of antiquity, author of a

thirteen-volume work, the *Mathematike Syntaxis* ('Mathematical Composition'), Claudius Ptolemy worked in Alexandria in Egypt *c.*AD 30, and is probably the most successful scientist in history, at least insofar as his astronomical system ruled unchallenged for 1,500 years until Copernicus and Galileo came along. But not only was he wrong in claiming that the Earth is at the centre of the universe; he was also a fraud, plagiarising many of 'his' observations from a Greek astronomer, Hipparchus of Rhodes, and lying about his own data.

In the 1980s Dennis Rawlins, an astronomer at the University of California in San Diego, concluded that Ptolemy had looted Hipparchus by checking his original work and calculating back to the first century. The latitude of Ptolemy's star-references is consistent not with Alexandria but Rhodes, five degrees further north. As for Ptolemy's data in support of his theories about the Earth's position relative to other planets and the Sun, Robert Newton of John Hopkins University has shown how often his observations differed from what he should have observed. He cooked the data to suit his theory. 'All of his own observations that Ptolemy uses in the *Syntaxis* are fraudulent so far as we can test them. Many of the observations that he attributes to others are also frauds that he committed . . . Thus Ptolemy is not the greatest astronomer of antiquity, but he is something still more unusual: He is the most successful fraud in the history of science.'[1]

1. Goldberg, *op. cit.*, pp.47–9, quoting *The Crime of Claudius Ptolemy*, Robert Newton, John Hopkins University Press, 1977.

Q

'A liar should have a good memory.'

(attributed to Quintillian)

QUIZ SHOW HOAXES (*MEDIA HOAXES*)
Once there was a time, it seems, when most folk believed what they saw
on TV most of the time, at least when it was presented as fact. That was
back in the 1950s, the golden age of TV quiz shows, watched by millions
who believed the implicit promise that they too might win big money
and become national celebrities. But in 1959 it all crashed down when
the much-acclaimed winner Charles Van Doren was exposed as a fraud.
A thirty-three-year-old Ph.D who earned $5,500 a year as a teacher at
Columbia University, it emerged that he'd won $129,000 on NBC's
Twenty-One show having first been supplied by the producers with a
trumped-up script. Coaching him how to look perplexed and under
pressure as fake tension built along with the prize money, they had
persuaded him to go along with the charade because it would offer
encouragement: 'to the intellectual life, to teachers, and to education in
general'. After his big win he had gained a $50,000-a-year post with the
network, but once the scam was revealed he lost not only that but his
post at Columbia.

Investigating the scandal of the rigged shows, the Manhattan district
attorney's office called 150 people to testify before a grand jury. Of
these, said DA Frank Hogan, about a hundred lied under oath. During
the next three years, eighteen contestants who'd won anything up to
$220,500 on the now suspended quiz shows pleaded guilty to perjury and
were given suspended sentences, though they could have been jailed for
up to three years. The corporate sponsors, who had the power to decide
if contestants should win or be 'bumped' from the shows, got away
scot-free.

It also emerged that some panel shows periodically fixed answers to
heighten the entertainment level, and that celebrities would refuse to

appear on such shows unless guaranteed not to be made to look stupid by giving the wrong answers. Even so, the best-laid schemes of mice and men often go wrong, as when one retired boxing champ (or chump) was told that the correct answer to one of the questions during the show would be 'poison ivy'. With his brains fried by too many years in the ring he took to shouting 'poison ivory' in reply to every question, so that, when the poison ivy question did at last turn up, he just sat there in a bad temper and said nothing.[1]

The entire sleazy tale, which briefly brought America's naive faith in the idiot box to its knees, has recently been dramatised in Robert Redford's 1994 movie, *Quiz Show*.

1. *Hoaxes and Scams*, Carl Sifakis, Facts on File, New York 1993, pp.218–19.

QWERTY (*SCIENTIFIC SCAMS*)

The purpose of this entry is to explain a mystery that must have puzzled many a typist or anyone else using the standard English-language keyboard on all typewriters, computers, and typesetting equipment. Why, on it, is the alphabet distributed so oddly? Why, beginning from the top left of the keyboard, are the letters not in alphabetical sequence (i.e., ABCDEF), but in an apparently jumbled order that makes no sense at all (i.e., QWERTY, etc.)?

After all, when in 1873 Christopher Latham Sholes invented the world's first commercially produced typewriter, he placed the keys in perfect alphabetical order. So what made him turn to the QWERTY arrangement? The answer lies in the fact that soon he found that the keys jammed when struck by a typist of any speed. To overcome this difficulty, he turned to his brother-in-law, a mathematician, who found that the answer lay in separating on the keyboard those letters most frequently used together in English. This led to a slight but added delay in striking the letters, thus preventing jamming.

While accepting this solution, no matter how odd it looked, Sholes still had to find a way to persuade people that the QWERTY arrangement was best. This he did by means of a promotional gimmick that Wilfred A. Beeching, director of the British Typewriter Museum, has called: 'probably one of the biggest confidence tricks of all time'. For whatever reason, maybe because he didn't want to let on that such an arrangement was necessary to stop the keys jamming, Sholes announced that the QWERTY configuration had been scientifically determined as the fastest, most efficient way to type. This was a total fib. The truth is that, using QWERTY, a typist's fingers have to stray further across the board, not less, in order to type almost any word in English. As Beeching points out: 'any haphazard arrangement of letters would be mathematically better than the existing one'.[1]

But the fib stuck. Sholes's QWERTY keyboard caught on and was soon firmly established. Not even rival typewriter companies questioned his statement that QWERTY was the most scientific arrangement possible. Nobody knew about the jamming, or the brother-in-law's solution. Even odder, companies that tried to sell other arrangements rapidly went out of business, despite studies showing that much greater speeds can be attained on differently designed keyboards.

1. Goldberg, *op. cit.*, pp.11-13, quoting *Century of the Typewriter*, Wilfred A. Beeching, St Martin's Press, London 1974.

R

'I'm a charlatan, a liar, a thief and a fake
altogether. There's no question of it, but I'm
an actor playing a part, and I do it for
purposes of entertainment.'

(James 'The Amazing' Randi,
stage-magician and debunker of the
paranormal, 1982 TV interview)

RAJNEESH, Bhagwan (1931–90) (*FAKE MESSIAHS*)
One of the more sensational events in the recent history of New Age cults
occurred in Oregon in 1985 when, after long-growing tension between
the townsfolk of Antelope and the followers of Bhagwan Sri Rajneesh on
the nearby settlement of Rajneeshpuram, the cult's founder fell out with
his main disciple then fled, charged with immigration fraud. Arrested in
North Carolina, on 14 November Bhagwan confessed to two felonies,
paid a $40,000 fine, and left the USA, leaving behind him hundreds of
bewildered followers and a personal fortune that included a fleet of over
a hundred Rolls-Royces.

Born Rajneesh Chandra Mohan in the Indian state of Madya Pradesh
to a family of the strict Jain faith, Bhagwan attended the Universities of
Jabalpur and Saugar, obtaining his master's degree in philosophy from
the latter in 1957. Yet in 1953, while still a student at Saigur, he attained
samadhi, enlightenment. 'That night another reality opened its door,
another dimension became available . . . That night I became empty and
I became full. I became nonexistential and became existence. That night
I died and was reborn.' Or so he later claimed. Whatever the truth of it,
while still pursuing an academic career he began travelling and speaking
about his experience. Eloquently advocating radical new religious views,
in 1966 he resigned his university post to become a full-time spiritual
leader. Settling in Bombay with a small group of followers in 1969, about
a year later his first Western disciples found him there. Moving to Poona

in 1974, he bought land and set up the Rajneesh Foundation (later the Rajneesh Foundation International).

Synthesising all major religious traditions with new Western techniques of inner transformation and therapy, he centred his religion on himself as the Enlightened teacher or *Bhagwan* ('godman'), demanding total surrender from his disciples as the price of spiritual growth. Teaching them to affirm life in every aspect, especially sexual, he required those initiated as a *sannyasin* to dress in red or orange (colour of the sunrise); to wear a *mala* (a necklace of 108 beads) and a picture of Rajneesh in plain sight; to use the new name given when initiated; and to meditate regularly. He emphasised vegetarianism, moderation with alcohol, and renunciation of drugs.

So far so good. Yet traditionalists were enraged not only by his liberal ideas about *sannyas* (the renounced life) but by his emphasis on sexual freedom and the open displays of affection shown by his disciples. With many Westerners thus attracted and spreading the word, Rajneesh centres began opening in Europe, Australia and North America, to which in May 1981 he moved with his followers, just after a fire had swept through the ashram, thought by many to have been the work of arsonists instigated by his enemies.

Yet Indian hostility was minor compared to the hatred he evoked in Oregon. Two months after he arrived in New Jersey, his secretary Ma Anand Sheela announced the purchase of the 64,000-acre Big Muddy Ranch near Antelope. Soon over 200 followers were building Rajneesh-puram, a model community expected to house some 6,000 people by the end of the century. Already alarmed, Antelope residents became more so as first the town cafe was bought, turned into a vegetarian restaurant, and renamed 'Zorba the Buddha'; then when in July 1982 some 7,000 Rajneeshis gathered for a lengthy festival at Rajneeshpuram, now incorporated as a city. The alarm turned to hate when, in December's municipal election, disciples of Rajneesh won the mayor's office and a majority of seats on Antelope's city council. Who was this man? What was going on? There were attacks on Rajneesh and his followers as daily he was driven round Rajneeshpuram in one of the increasing fleet of Rolls-Royces gifted to him by wealthy devotees. Nobody charged that the *sannyasin* were being brainwashed, but the emphasis on sexuality scandalised many outsiders, especially with the spread of AIDS. Efforts were made to have him deported, but in February 1984 these failed: it turned out that in 1936 he'd been adopted by Swami Swarupananda (father of Ma Anand Sheela), who in 1973 had become a permanent resident of the United States.

By now claiming quarter of a million followers worldwide and with at least 20,000 US followers in over a hundred centres, the Rajneesh Foundation (publishing most of Bhagwan's several hundred books) had become a major force on the New Age cult scene. But cracks were showing. Rumours spread of criminal activity and of mounting hostility between the cult leaders. Suddenly in November 1985 Ma Anand Sheela resigned her position. Rajneesh denounced her, accusing her of crimes against himself and the movement. He also denounced 'Rajneeshism', which he said was her creation. She fled to Germany, later to be extradited on charges of attempted murder and under suspicion of having tried to organise the poisoning of Antelope's water supply.

Indicted for immigration fraud on 23 October, Rajneesh fled. Arrested by federal agents in North Carolina, he was fined and deported. Rajneeshpuram and the property, including the Rolls-Royces, were sold; then a court ruled that the settlement's incorporation was illegal, involving religious control of a municipal government. As for Rajneesh, thereafter he found himself *persona non grata* wherever he went. Enlightened 'godman' he may have been, but a scant few years after his downfall he died in Poona, perhaps of AIDS, perhaps poisoned by former disciples.[1]

1. *Encyclopedic Handbook of Cults*, J. Gordon Melton, Garland, New York 1986.

RAMPA, Lobsang (1911–?) (*IMPOSTORS, LITERARY HOAXES*) First published in 1956 and still in print, *The Third Eye* was an immediate bestseller. Purportedly the autobiography of a Tibetan lama, Lobsang Rampa, it tells how when he was seven the author, born into a prominent family, began training as a monk specialising in medicine. The pacy account of his life at the lamasery under his guru, Lama Mingyar Dondup, leads up to the operation to open his 'third eye'. Long associated in eastern tradition with the pineal gland (a tiny organ found in the limbic system of the brain), this is allegedly the centre of human psychic activity. In Rampa's case it was opened by drilling a hole in his head just above the bridge of his nose, then by inserting a sliver of wood treated by fire and with herbs. This caused a 'blinding flash' and 'spirals of colour'. His guru told him, 'You are now one of us, Lobsang'. Later Rampa describes his experience of clairvoyance, astral travel, telepathy, **levitation**, and a friendship with the Dalai Lama.

Published as fact despite the opinion of at least one expert on Tibet that it was clearly a fake, and ending with the promise of more marvels to come, by the end of 1957 *The Third Eye* was a bestseller in twelve countries. As for the sequels, by 1990 at least twenty-one had appeared, their writings or sales affected little if at all by the revelation in 1958 that 'Lobsang Rampa' was really Cyril Henry Hoskins, son of a plumber from Plympton in Devon, England. Unmasked by a detective hired by Tibetan scholars (including Heinrich Harrer, author of *Seven Years in Tibet*) who were unamused by the fraud, Hoskins turned out to be an unusual fellow who, early in the Second World War, had moved to Surrey, shaved his head, and grown a beard. Changing his name to 'Dr

Kuan', he told neighbours he'd been brought up in China, where he'd been a flying instructor with the Chinese air force. Captured by the Japanese, he'd been badly tortured as a prisoner of war.

Charged with fraud, Hoskins proved inventive. Agreeing in April 1958 that he had indeed been born Cyril Henry Hoskins, he asserted that nine years earlier he'd been bodily possessed by the lama, 'Lobsang Rampa'. This alarming event had occurred when, as he climbed a tree to photograph an owl, he'd fallen and concussed himself. Groggily coming back to his senses, he'd seen the saffron-robed lama floating towards him. Deftly cutting the future bestselling author's astral cord, the lama had then cut his own cord, sending it shooting back to Tibet. Connecting the loose end to the end emerging from Hoskins, he'd then taken possession of the Englishman's body. So there.

All this (and much, much more) is explained in *The Rampa Story*, the third book of the series. In it Hoskins also states that, in gratitude for the gift of his body, the Lama Lobsang Rampa had cancelled his karmic debt. It no longer mattered what anyone proved about his past. Obviously the tale was hooey, but who could prove it? Midway between claims by Theosophy's founder Madame Blavatsky and others to have been advised by similarly discarnate Tibetans, and **Castaneda**'s later claim to have been taught by the elusive Yaqui *brujo* Don Juan, it was as Lobsang Rampa that Hoskins went on churning out the tales of occult marvels that made him much wealthier than he could ever have been as plain Cyril Henry Hoskins.

RANDI, James (1928–) (*PARANORMAL HOAXES*)

Widely known as a stage-magician and escapologist, as a founder member of the Committee for the Scientific Investigation of Claims of the Paranormal (CSICOP), for some forty years James 'The Amazing' Randi has been active as a professional debunker of whatever he considers pseudoscientific nonsense. Maintaining that all seeming paranormal or occult events are explicable by 'normal' means or by fraud, much like **Houdini** before him Randi offers a cash prize ($10,000) to anyone who can prove paranormal powers. To date the prize remains unclaimed. Insisting that *all* psychics and **mediums** who do 'cold readings' (i.e., of clients they've never met before) operate fraudulently by producing general statements refined by client feedback, so telling people what they want to hear, Randi is probably best known for the ferocity of his attack in the 1970s on the Israeli psychic Uri **Geller**, and on the methodology used by those validating Geller's powers.

Yet while in particular accusing parapsychologists Harold Puthoff and Russell Targ of the Stanford Research Institute (SRI) on this issue, in turn he was accused by them of fraudulent distortion in his attack. They quoted twenty-four factual errors in the twenty-eight page account of the SRI tests on Geller as given in his *The Magic of Uri Geller*. They found that: 'in every instance Randi, in his efforts to fault the SRI experiments, was driven to hypothesise the existence of a loophole condition that did not, in fact, exist.' Even so, prominent scientists like Christopher Evans ('unarguably definitive') and Carl Sagan ('A healthy antidote to charlatanism on all levels') publicly supported Randi's conclusions.

Randi's well-publicised attacks on serious psychic research continue in books like *Flim-Flam!* – and, as noted elsewhere (*see* **Psychic Surgery**), as often as not his assaults on sloppy research, wishful thinking, fakery and humbuggery are not only witty but well-grounded. Yet in his desire to disprove all such phenomena entirely he has himself resorted to hoax, as in his Project Alpha, in which he planted two youths faking ESP powers on the McDonnell Laboratory, so conning the investigators into publishing spurious data which then triumphantly he exposed as such. 'If Mr Randi were a psychologist,' commented the *New York Times*, 'the hoax might have landed him in hot water.'[1]

Randi, of course, not only enjoys the publicity but remains unrepentant. Indeed, he admits he's a hoaxer. 'I'm a charlatan, a liar, a thief and a fake altogether,' he admitted with relish on TV in 1982. 'There's no question of it, but I'm an actor playing a part, and I do it for purposes of entertainment.'[2]

This assertion is at the least *faux-naïf*. His continuing war against Geller suggests that entertainment is not his sole purpose, and has legally embarrassed him. In 1993, in one case brought against him by the Israeli psychic, he was judged guilty of defamation of character (*see* Geller). At the time other cases brought by Geller were pending, including one to be heard in Washington D.C. 'Randi has claimed that I was convicted for the work I did in Israel,' says Geller. 'You can imagine how harmful that is to me and my family. I have never been arrested, let alone convicted, of anything, anywhere in the world.' He adds: 'The amount of the settlement is not important. It was my name and my vindication.'[3]

Randi publicly offers himself as the bluff, pragmatic entertainer, but maybe something else drives him. Why does he remain so persistently urgent in his desire to expose *all* unexplained phenomena as humbug?

1. *The Hidden Power*, Brian Inglis, Cape, London 1986, pp.252–8.
2. Randi, *op. cit.*.
3. 'Geller Gets Randi', *Fortean Times* No. 69, London June–July 1993.

RASPE, Rudolf Eric (1737–94) (*LITERARY HOAXES*)
The author of that enduring creation, *The Adventures of Baron Munchausen*, was versatile and talented but utterly feckless. The first German to champion **Macpherson**'s Ossianic poems and already in debt when he left university, while still in his twenties he wrote a geology text, the *Specimen Historiae Naturalis*, that later gained him membership of London's Royal Society. Inventing new mining techniques while also

writing widely on science and the arts, in 1767 he was appointed keeper of the collections of Frederick of Hesse-Cassel. He seemed set for a brilliant career but, unable to stop spending money he didn't have, was driven to start thieving gems from the collections to pay his debts. Even so, and despite marrying a Berlin banker's daughter in 1771, soon he was so besieged by creditors that he had to borrow from his father-in-law again and again. Worse still, when he was appointed elsewhere, the new keeper of Frederick's collections soon discovered the thefts, and the hue and cry began. Pursued by demands for the arrest of 'Councillor Raspe, a long-faced man, with small eyes, red hair under his stumpy periwig, and a jerky gait', he fled to England in 1775. There, though finding himself expelled from the Royal Society, he found work with the steam engine entrepreneur Matthew Boulton, who hired him as an assay officer at a tin mine near Camborne in Cornwall. Here, where some of his mining techniques had been adopted, he began writing the tall tales that made another man famous.

Born in 1720, Hieronymous Karl Friedrich, Freiherr von Münchhausen, had like many another German soldier served for years in the Russian army before in 1760 taking early retirement to marry a wife to whom he was devoted and to settle on his estates at Bodenwerder in north Germany. Here for years he enjoyed the pleasures of marriage, the hunt, and the dining table, meanwhile becoming locally famous for his habit of relating fantastic adventures with the dry precision of a man speaking the truth. Raspe, who was from the same region, may or may not have met him, but what is certain is that the scoundrelly author not only borrowed Münchhausen's persona but his name (save for a dropped 'h' and the umlaut), so making the garrulous ex-soldier's old age a complete misery.

Munchausen is unique. **Mandeville**'s *Travels* are tame by comparison. Yet, like Mandeville, in concocting the *Adventures* Raspe freely plundered old sources. Plutarch, Rabelais, and the Welsh tales later collected as the *Mabinogion* all went into the pot. Raspe invented only three or four stories himself.

The *Adventures* are so lunatic (literally, as in the Baron's journey to the Moon) that nobody could believe them for an instant, even though the blustering Baron insists that every word he says is true. Munchausen has a hound that literally runs itself off its feet; a horse which, cut in two, is sewn back together; and a servant who can run from Turkey to Italy and back in an hour. Living happily inside a giant fish after being swallowed by it, he also tells his disbelieving audience how a coachman tried on a cold winter night to blow his horn – but all the tunes were frozen, and only came out when they melted.

The first seventeen 'Munnikhousen' tales appeared in 1786, with five more, the Sea Adventures, being added in a third edition later that same year. The boastful Baron was an instant hit so that, by the century's end, with Raspe dropping out and other authors adding new stories, another eight editions followed. As for Raspe, he was his own worst enemy. Claiming to have found vast deposits of gold and silver in the north of Scotland, in 1791 he inveigled Sir John Sinclair into paying out a large development fee, then fled with the cash. Going to ground in Donegal in Ireland, he died of scarlet fever in 1794.

The fate of the real Münchhausen, through no fault of his own, was just as miserable. With the *Adventures* now translated into German, in his later years he was hounded by literary tourists turning up at his house to stare or to demand new tales. He couldn't get rid of them, and when his wife died he made a disastrous second marriage. Stared at from without, henpecked within, he lost his good humour entirely before he died. With only his faithful huntsman Rösemeyer to keep him company and keep the sightseers at bay, whatever he had to say about Raspe must have been unprintable.

REAVIS, James Addison (1840?–1908) (*FRAUD, IMPOSTORS*)
Queen Victoria was not amused when in January 1895 she learned that Don Jayme de Peralta-y-Cordoba, Baron de Arizonac and Caballero de los Colorados, had been jailed for six years in Santa Fe as a common swindler. It was only a few years since she – along with the German Kaiser, the King of Spain, the Pope, the Duke of Orléans, and various other European notables – had received that illustrious gentleman and his beautiful wife Carmelita. In fact, she now learned, 'Don Jayme' was really James Addison Reaves, a conman from the deep south of the USA who had just two talents – he was good at pretending to be who he wasn't, and he could forge other people's handwriting perfectly.

Joining the Confederate Army during the Civil War, he had practised this latter talent modestly by forging his commanding officer's signature on leave passes for himself and his friends. Going into real estate in St Louis after the war, he helped a client with questionable title to a piece of land by forging a quitclaim deed – the formal renunciation of a claim. Continuing west, the late 1860s found him in Santa Fé in New Mexico. Here, he encountered the government office for the investigation of Spanish land claims under the 'Gadsden Purchase' – a treaty concluded in 1846 at the end of the US-Mexican war. Involving the annexation by the Union of all southern Arizona and part of New Mexico, it required that the USA recognise all the old Spanish titles to lands in these territories.

Taking work as a clerk in the records room, Reavis now invented one of the boldest property swindles of all time. It demanded infinite patience. Not only did he have to learn Spanish, but legal Spanish of the eighteenth century. He had to make quill pens, acquire old parchment, and mix inks. He had to study documents whereby the Spanish Crown had rewarded its servants. These, drawn up by lawyers who'd never been near the New World, were geographically vague – which suited him (literally) down to the ground.

Choosing 'his' land with great care, first he invented the original grantee. In the mid-eighteenth century Ferdinand VI had awarded a vast tract of Arizona to Don Miguel de Peralta, Gentleman of the King's Bedchamber, knight of several orders, son of Don José Gaston Gomez de Sylva y Montux de Oca de la Cerda y de Caullo de Peralta de los Falces de la Vega. Recording the grant on magnificently forged documents, Reavis also invented life histories for the entire Peralta family, all similarly recorded.

For seven years he prepared. Leaving his job in Santa Fé in the early 1870s, with money from minor forgeries he travelled through Mexico, Portugal, and Spain, visiting archives, churches, and government offices. Good-looking and scholarly, soft-spoken and with excellent manners, he gained access to the records he wanted to read, steal, forge, or swap. Planting a forgery here, removing a genuine document there, his guile was immense and his patience as great. After another seven years of travel the documents were all in place – and Reavis, alias Don Jayme, was ready to claim nearly eleven million acres in the state of Arizona as his by right, and as guaranteed by the Gadsden Purchase.

Seeking a fellow conspirator, he found George Willing, a dissolute ex-doctor who signed statements that he'd bought, for just $1,000, the entire Peralta land grant from a poor Mexican, Miguel Peralta, descendant of Don Miguel, and that he, Dr Willing, had resold the grant to Reavis for $30,000. Whether Reavis paid him anything or only promised a share of the proceeds from the fraud is unknown: at any rate in 1881 Willing was found conveniently dead in his shack in Prescott, Arizona. Did Reavis kill him? More likely Willing had drunk himself to death. Hearing of his death, Reavis met his widow, who at first demanded half his future profit, but eventually agreed to take the $30,000 for which Willing had allegedly sold the Peralta grant. Of course the money wasn't there – yet.

In 1883 Reavis at last filed his claim. Fourteen years had passed. Certified copies of all relevant documents were submitted to the US Surveyor-General to prove that he was the legal owner of some 17,000 square miles of Arizona, including the state capital, Phoenix, He was not unreasonable. He would sell his claim to the government for a mere $50 million, and would also consider private offers from those who'd inadvertently been 'trespassing' on 'his' land and who were prepared to buy quitclaims from him.

The inhabitants of Arizona, and especially Phoenix, were stunned. With his claim still unacknowledged, Reavis moved into the best hotel in Phoenix, posting notices all over town saying those occupying land in the claim area had better get in touch with him or risk losing all that they had. His move was premature, but he needed cash. Soon it was rolling in. With lawyers saying the claim looked solid, the Southern Pacific Railway coughed up $50,000, and the Silver King Mining Company $25,000, so they could stay on 'his' land.

Though quick to pay Dr Willing's widow her $30,000, Reavis knew she might still spoil everything. He needed a 'Peralta heiress' to further substantiate his claim. With his usual patience he sought far and wide for a Mexican or Spanish orphan who knew nothing about her origins. He found her in Carmelita, a fourteen-year-old half-breed girl slaving for rancher John Slaughter in the mountains of eastern Arizona. Armed with his documents, cash, and a family tree, he proved to Slaughter that this girl who didn't even own a pair of shoes was, in fact, the last known descendant of the Peraltas, thus heiress to the Peralta grant. Yes, he was the legal owner, but he felt obliged to share the fortune, make her his ward, and in due course marry her. With his pockets bulging, Mr Slaughter had no objection to seeing the back of her. It would now be easy enough to find another.

In California Reavis became her legal guardian, then asked the nuns of a convent school to educate her to the condition befitting her future rank. With a new wardrobe and stimulated by journeys throughout the States, Carmelita blossomed. It seems Reavis fell in love with her. At any rate, as soon as she was sixteen, he married her. At the ceremony in Phoenix, she became Sofia Loreta Micaela ('traditional Peralta names'), while Reavis now styled himself 'Baron de Arizonac, Caballero de los Colorados'. Meanwhile, the money poured in. With legions of lawyers studying or contesting his claim, companies and small farmers kept paying up with quitclaims and rents, while businessmen fell over themselves to get the 'Red Baron' to invest in their projects. With an income of $300,000 a year, and with Carmelita-Sofia bearing twin sons, in 1890 he undertook his Grand Tour of Europe.

Riding a coach-and-four, Carmelita and Don Jayme and the twins (dressed in crimson velvet) created a sensation in Europe's capitals. In Madrid the twins played with Alfonso, the infant King of Spain. Life was good – very good! By now Reavis had a palace in Mexico City, a villa in Washington, and a mansion in St Louis. Luxury yachts and private trains bore him hither and thither. At last, he'd got it all.

But meanwhile in Florence, Arizona, sceptical newspaperman Tom Weedon had for years been questioning the still unproved claim in a series of articles, warning his readers not to give up their land rights. Homer H. McNeil of the Phoenix *Gazette* joined the fight and, when it became known that he too had bought a quitclaim deed, quickly withdrew it, begging his readers to understand that he too had been fooled. That had been in 1884. He and Weedon had continued the fight, supporting local citizens determined to resist Reavis. Even so, McNeil was never again trusted. Reavis had continued on his merry way. It was only in 1890 that Royal A. Johnson, Surveyor-General, completed his report. Questioning the authenticity of the Peralta documents and pointing out several historical incongruities, he advised the US government to reject the claim. Yet no action was taken until a year later when, with the establishment of the US Court of Private Land Grant Claims, Reavis came under renewed scrutiny. After all, a third of all such claims in the USA consisted of his individual claim alone. Appointed to investigate was Mallet Prevost, a linguist and historian who was about to prove himself as dogged and methodical as Reavis.

Testing the documents Reavis had submitted, he found that some had genuine top pages, but that pages following were written on parchment of more recent origin and with dogwood ink. The ink of the originals contained iron. Prevost then pursued the trail from Arizona and California to Mexico, Portugal, and Spain. In the church in San Bernardino, California, where Carmelita had supposedly been born, he found that in the births register Reavis had substituted an entire page, entering her birth. Paper and ink matched the original perfectly. But Reavis had slipped up. The local priest's private index denied such a birth. It mentioned only another child, missing from the forged page.

So Prevost tracked Reavis down, even as Reavis went on spending. He must have been shocked when, after all his years of obsessively careful preparation, the law pounced. Arrested and tried in Santa Fé in January 1895, he was so broke he couldn't even afford a lawyer. By then in his mid-fifties, with Carmelita bewildered in the public gallery (nobody wished to prosecute her: she'd been his dupe all along), he spent the next six years in Santa Fé penitentiary. Divorcing him, Carmelita moved to Denver: there is no subsequent record of her life. One of the twins served with distinction during the First World War, but no more is known of them. As for Convict No. 964-A, on release he returned to Phoenix, where for a time the State Capitol librarian saw him turning the pages of back issues in the newspaper room – until one day the 'Red Baron' returned no more.[1]

1. Larsen, *op. cit.*, pp.82–92.

REICHENBACH, Harry (1894–?) (*PRANKS*)

Leaving home at Frostbury in Maryland as soon as he could to join travelling circuses and medicine shows, this inventive hoaxer soon learned the tricks of the trade. Before the First World War he was making fairground money exhibiting a bowl of water that held 'The Only Living Brazilian Invisible Fish', while at the Mardi Gras celebrations in New Orleans he presented his celebrated dancing ducks. This involved three ducks on a frame of wire netting on a tin floor, elevated on a dry goods box. His spiel involved telling the punters how hard it was to train the ducks in the terpsichorean art; to teach them the proper mental and muscular co-ordination; and to make them acquire a sense of rhythm and an ear for music – at which point the ducks, formerly indifferent, would rise to their feet and start to dance. Why? Because an assistant had turned up the wick of a lamp under the tin floor. The unfortunate ducks raised one foot then the other in lively unison while a fiddler played *Turkey in the Straw*. 'The Dancing Ducks were the wonder of the Mardi Gras,' he later wrote. 'They grossed us over a thousand dollars on the week.'[1]

During the First World War, Reichenbach applied his talents to demoralising the enemy. Claiming to have projected silent films from Italian trenches on to snow-covered slopes for the benefit of Germans in opposing trenches, he also devised a diploma to be dropped over enemy lines. This qualified any German private to surrender himself unmolested and immediately receive promotion to officer's status, so gaining the rations and considerations due an officer. These benefits were listed on the back of the diploma – so many grams of bread per meal, so much meat a week, so many choices of vegetable, so many cigarettes. 'But the two items that proved to be the greatest inducements to surrender were the promise of 24 sheets of toilet paper per day and a delousing comb.'[2]

After the war he became a **Hollywood** publicity agent. Metro Pictures hadn't released one single film when he began his campaign for them based on the slogan: 'CAN THEY KEEP IT UP?' Persuading judges at the Los Angeles Exposition to award Metro a gold medal for Best Production when the film involved hadn't even been seen, for a decade he pulled some of Tinseltown's best stunts. To boost the career of his friend Francis X. Bushman, then a comparative unknown who'd been acting in Chicago for $250 a week, Reichenbach brought him to New York to sign a contract with Metro. Meeting Bushman off the train and walking him to the studio offices, at regular intervals he dropped fistfuls of pennies on to the street. Snatching them, first children began following, then curious adults began following the children. By the time Reichenbach and Bushman reached the Metro offices, the crowd was enormous. Impressed by Bushman's apparent fame, the Metro executives signed him up at $1,000 a week.

Perhaps his best-known hoax involved *September Morn*, the name of a painting by Paul Chabas, an early twentieth-century French artist. Depicting a nude young girl by the edge of the sea, reproductions of it reached the USA about 1902, but didn't sell. Left with hundreds, a Brooklyn shopkeeper offered Reichenbach $45 if he could find a market for them. Telling him to put a copy in his window, Reichenbach phoned Anthony Comstock, head of the New York Anti-Vice League, and complained about the public display of this indecent picture. Comstock refused to be drawn so, paying a group of children to leer and gawp at it, Reichenbach went to the office of the League and demanded action. Comstock went and had a look, and was suitably outraged.

The shopkeeper refused to remove the picture from his window, so

Comstock sued him. The resulting legal battle made *September Morn* famous. The reproductions sold like hot cakes, and years later the original fetched $70,000.

1. Yapp, *op. cit.*, quoting *Phantom Fame*, Harry Reichenbach, Noel Douglas, London 1932, p.68.
2. *ibid.*, p.246.

REIS, Arthur Virgilio Alves (*See* **COUNTERFEITERS**)

RICE, Boyd (contemporary) (*PRANKS*)
This American prankster tells the surreal tale of what happened when, in the meat section of a San Diego supermarket, he kept seeing bizarre items like pigs' snouts, skinned sheep's heads and so on, and couldn't imagine any tasteful use for them at all. He began experimenting with sheep's heads, using them in street theatre situations to put people on. One weekend, having paraded one of these gory items at an abortion rights demonstration, he drove downtown and saw a crowd blocking the street. Remembering that Betty Ford, the President's wife, was in town to visit the Senior Citizens Center, he got out to see what he could do. Realising by the way a line of people (many of them holding bouquets of flowers) was cordoned off from a door at the back of a building that Mrs Ford would exit there and work her way down the line, he decided to give her the sheep's head. Pressing into the crowd, he found the head so effective in making people get out of the way that soon he was right at the front. With Mrs Ford only about six feet away a Secret Service man appeared, asking: 'What is that?'
'It's a skinned sheep's head,' said Rice.
'What are you planning to do with that?'
'I was going to give it to the First Lady.'
'Would you mind coming with me,' said the agent – and so Rice shortly found himself handcuffed in a police car, the leaflets he had with him being studied by two cops.
'*Uh-oh*,' said one, 'this guy's handing out mass suicide literature. Looks like we got a *real nut* on our hands this time.' And they were searching him for weapons when a man ran out of the crowd shouting: 'He had a knife! I saw him earlier with a knife!'
'Huh?' said Rice. 'I didn't have a knife.'
'I saw him!' the man kept insisting. 'He had a knife!'
By now, with Mrs Ford gone, the crowd was swarming round the police car, with newsmen taking pictures, and little old ladies with Brownie cameras, all saying:
'That guy's crazy! They're going to lock him up!'
In the car one cop said: 'If I ever catch you in *my* city doing this again, I'm going to take a SHIT on you!'

At the police station cops stood around saying things like, 'We're thinking of not booking this guy, just taking him out to the middle of the desert, tying him up, and leaving him there three or four days to think about what he's done.' Eyeing the sheep's head with disgust as they removed it from the trunk, they took close-up photos of it. With Rice still handcuffed as he got out, one officer said: 'Now you better not stay more than two or three feet behind me, because if you get too far away I might have to *shoot* you!' Laughing, he started moving erratically, speeding up then slowing down, then suddenly cutting off in another direction, making it hard for Rice to stay on his heels.

'This guy thinks *I'm* a nut,' thought Rice, 'but *he's* completely psycho!'

In the station they made him sit so long he got scared, realising if he told them he'd done the sheep's head thing for *fun*, they'd probably throw him in a mental institution. He couldn't say: I did it because it was *fun*. He decided to say he was a vegetarian activist.

They questioned him all day. Someone had mailed death threats to the President from San Diego, so they made him write out phrases like 'Gerald Ford, President of the United States' over and over again. They asked: did he hate the President?

'No,' said Rice, 'I like Gerry Ford – I think he's a funny guy.'

Before they let him go one officer said: 'Listen, you're lucky the Secret Service was in charge of this, because if *I* were in charge, I'd throw you in County Mental Health for six months' observation, and if you aren't crazy now – which I think you are – you *would be* by the time you got out.' He added: 'We can get anything on you anytime we want – we could just follow you around for 24 hours and have enough on you to throw you in jail.'

The punchline? A week earlier he'd placed another sheep's head on a pedestal in a square downtown. A crowd grew, staring with sick fascination. Seeing some hippies over by the public phone booths, Rice had an idea. Getting the number of one booth, he went to another booth across the square and called the number. Someone answered.

'Hey!' whispered Rice. 'Is this the phone at Horton Plaza?'

'Yeah, it is,' said the voice from across the square.

'Listen, this is *real important*,' said Rice. 'Look around. Do you see what appears to be a skinned sheep's head sitting on a pedestal?'

'Yeah, I see it.'

'Listen, man, this is *real important*. Inside that head is $10,000 of uncut cocaine. I was supposed to pick it up but I can't get down and I don't want it to fall into the hands of *the man*. If you can get that head and take it away, the stuff is yours.'

'No shit!' From his booth Rice could see the guy in the booth across the square look around, then hang up. Sidling over to the pedestal, he'd grabbed the head and hared off down a side street. Now, as he was being questioned on the Betty Ford incident, the cops said: 'The Chief of Police is particularly concerned about this incident, because just recently somebody drove past the police parking lot and threw a head *exactly like this* in amongst the cars. Do you have *any* knowledge whatsoever of this?'

Rice didn't dare laugh. 'No,' he said, 'that's *completely* unconnected with me. I don't know *who* could have done that; that's *really weird*.'

You can say that again . . .[1]

1. Vale and Juno (eds), *op. cit.*, pp.18–20 (interview by the editors with Boyd Rice).

RICHARD III (1452–85) (*HISTORICAL HOAXES*)

Richard **Nixon** wasn't the only Tricky Dick in history – at least if Tudor propaganda and **Shakespeare** are to be believed. In 1485 a desperate villain, surrounded by enemies, shouted: 'A horse! A horse! My kingdom for a horse!' But too late. He was slain. His crown, found snagged on a bush, was placed reverently on the head of his conqueror. So died 'Crookback Dick', alias Richard III, the scheming hunchback who had murdered two innocent little children (the 'Princes in the Tower') to grab the crown. Now the Welshman Henry Tudor was king – King Henry VII. A new, more glorious era was about to begin, culminating in the reign of his granddaughter, Elizabeth.

Right had prevailed. Evil had been vanquished.

But it wasn't quite like that. Richard was the victim of one of the most successful posthumous smear campaigns ever mounted. Why? Because Henry had no real right to the throne at all. The Wars of the Roses had been raging for years; all England was in turmoil, and Henry had grabbed what wasn't his. How to justify his act and secure what he'd seized? How to persuade the English that a Welshman was their legitimate ruler?

For a start, by painting his predecessor as black as possible.

Thus Crookback Dick, hunchback and murderer!

There's no proof that Richard was either. On the contrary, he appears to have been an astute, capable ruler. But the Tudors, later aided by Shakespeare's dramatic skills, got away with it. The mud they threw has stuck ever since. Some historians and writers (like Josephine Tey in her novel *The Daughter of Time*) have tried to rehabilitate him – but, as usual, 'history is the lie commonly agreed upon'. In the popular imagination, Richard will always be an evil black-garbed hunchback stealing into the Tower to smother two little cherubs, before dying a coward's death in battle, defeated by the heroic Henry . . .

RILEY, Philip (1946–) (*CONMEN*)

Twenty-nine-year-old Philip Riley, formerly a Berkshire club owner, did not present himself as such on approaching Father Francis Garlick, a parish priest in Reading, England. Posing as a high-ranking agent in the British Secret Service who'd been sent on tough assignments against Communism, he swore the Roman Catholic priest to secrecy and conned £2,000 out of him before the imposture was discovered. Twice persuading the trusting father to say requiem masses for agents allegedly killed in action, once he turned up at the presbytery with faked gunshot wounds. Another time, insisting his cover had been blown, he said he was in dire danger and must get out of England, fast. He said he'd been ordered to go to Spain and that, because the father was involved, he must come too. Father Garlick gave Riley, his wife, and two children £1,000 to enjoy a fortnight's holiday in Spain. The priest went with them. Another time he put up £350 to get an agent out of jail. Understandably he had a nervous breakdown on learning how he'd been conned. Convicted at Reading Crown Court on 20 March 1975 of obtaining money by deception, Riley's reward was two years' free accommodation at Her Majesty's pleasure.[1]

1. McCormick, *op. cit.*, pp.206–7.

RODERICK, Ignatz (*See* **FOSSIL FORGERIES**)

ROSENFELD, Hans (*See* **END-OF-THE-WORLD SCAMS**)

ROSICRUCIANS (*HISTORICAL HOAXES*)
A huge European uproar began in 1614 with the publication of three anonymous pamphlets announcing the existence of the Rosicrucians, a secret society named after 'Rose Cross' and its alleged founder, 'Christian Rosencreutz'. The first pamphlet, the *Fama Fraternitatis*, published at Cassel in Germany in 1614, claimed that an ancient Fraternity founded by 'Father C.R.C.' had been revived to develop new wisdom opposed to old authority. It told how Christian Rosencreutz (1378–1444) had returned from eastern travels to his native Germany to initiate the Fraternity of the Rosy Cross, to aid the sick and spread knowledge.

Claiming to herald the growth of new learning via old **alchemical** lore and mechanical ('scientific') knowledge, the *Fama* was followed a year later by a sequel: the *Confessio Fraternitatis R.C.* Written in Latin and aimed at an educated audience, its thirty-seven declared aims included an end to sectarian and political strife; also an end to hunger, poverty, disease and old age. The furore caused by these pamphlets (the *Fama* was reprinted three times in 1615) increased in 1616 with the publication in Strasbourg of an alchemical romance, *The Chemical Wedding of Christian Rosencreutz*. Divided into seven days, this tale of a husband and wife in a magical castle described the mystic marriage of the soul via vision, theatrical performance, initiation rites, and the ritual of castle life.

It's hard to understand now, but this symbolic romance and the pamphlets had a vast effect. Europe's mood was turbulent and dangerous, especially after the outbreak in 1618 of the Thirty Years War. The Rosicrucians became as feared as Communists in 1950s America. Yet nobody knew who they were; nobody had met a Rosicrucian; nobody knew who'd written the pamphlets. The mysterious adepts were said to be here, there, everywhere. When in 1623 in Paris placards suddenly appeared announcing the presence of the Brotherhood RC and their Invisible College, incredible tales circulated. It was said that thirty-six of these dangerous magi had sworn before Satan to abjure **Christianity**, in return gaining magic powers of flight, invisibility, and an ever-full purse. Accused of being a Rosicrucian, the philosopher Descartes (1596–1650) had to deny it.

Now it seems they never existed. It was a joke, albeit a serious one. The pamphlets were probably written by a Württemburg theologian, Johann Valentin Andraeae. Born about 1586, he is known in about 1602 to have written a tract, *Chemical Wedding*, which he called a *ludibrium* (jest) of little worth. His refusal to own up to the pamphlets suggests common sense. In time the furore faded. Yet his jest of the Invisible College devoted to new learning had its effect. The foundation in England of the Royal Society by men like Boyle, Hooke, and **Newton** was one result. Men pursuing alchemical and occult studies privately while laying the basis of modern physics and chemistry in public, they so liked the idea of such a college that they created it. So there's little doubt about it – Andraeae's learned prank influenced the growth of modern science.[1]

1. *The Rosicrucian Enlightenment*, Francis A. Yates, Routledge & Kegan Paul, London 1972.

ROSWELL INCIDENT, The (*UFO HOAXES*)
With a major movie on the subject currently in production, the story of the Roswell Incident of 1947 refuses to go away. Among **UFO**logists 'Roswell' is synonymous with 'cover-up' or 'government secrecy'. Why? The tale is that in July 1947 an alien spacecraft crashed in the New Mexico desert near the USAF nuclear bomber air base at Roswell. Dead aliens were found and removed from the wreckage by the military; and the cover-up ('Operation Majestic') has lasted ever since.

But before the cover-up began, on 8 July Roswell Base Public Information Officer Walter Haut issued a press release confirming air force possession of a 'flying disc'. This release, published in the Roswell *Daily Record*, described the discovery of the 'disc' on 5 July by rancher William 'Mac' Brazel on his remote ranch. RAAF CAPTURES FLYING SAUCER ON RANCH IN ROSWELL REGION, was the headline. *No Details of Flying Disc Are Revealed*, ran the sub-head.

That was the first and last the public learned. A day later the Army Air Corps renotified the press that what had been found was merely the remains of a weather balloon with an attached radar device. With Mac Brazel illegally held in isolation for a week by the military, refusing to deny what he'd seen, the press bought it, and the story died – only to flare up again years later.

It appears that the crash took place on or about 2 July. With the base informed by Brazel, the debris had been retrieved by Major (later Colonel) Jesse Marcel, the base's intelligence officer, who was then ordered to fly it to Wright Field by way of Fort Worth Army Air Field. Marcel managed to show some of the debris to his wife and son before the cover-up began. Transferred to Washington D.C. to continue his intelligence career, he was furious at the cover-up. So were others. In the *New York Times* on 28 February 1960 Admiral Roscoe H. Hillenkoetter (the CIA's first director) declared that: 'Through official secrecy and ridicule, many citizens are led to believe that unidentified flying objects are nonsense. To hide the facts the Air Force has silenced its personnel.'[1]

Seven years before his death in 1986, Colonel Marcel refused to stay quiet any longer. In videotaped interviews he insisted that there *had* been a cover-up. He described finding beams at the crash site, about half an inch square: 'with some sort of hieroglyphics on them that nobody could decipher'. They resembled flexible, light balsa wood, but were hard, and would not burn. There was also a metal similar to but stronger than tin-foil; and a strong, brown, papery substance which Mac Brazel's daughter Bessie described as having flowers pressed into it. Today Dr Jesse Marcel Jr, the colonel's son, claims that he saw both this substance and the beams, which he describes as above.

Investigators Kevin Randle and Don Schmitt, in *The Truth About Roswell* (1994) have found 'about half a dozen' witnesses who were allegedly on the impact site and saw not only the debris of the spacecraft, but the dead bodies of ashen-skinned beings with humanoid faces and light-weight, almost bird-like, bone structure.[2] Over the years there have been many ancillary rumours concerning such bodies – that they are kept in secret Pentagon freezers for scientific study, and so on – even that one or more *living* aliens have been captured and remain alive. Yet, as the ever pragmatic Jacques Vallee points out, if the crash occurred on 2 July but debris and bodies were not retrieved until 9 July, then the bodies would have been exposed not only to the desert summer sun for an entire week, but to numerous predators.[3]

What happened at Roswell remains obscure.

1. *Majestic*, Whitley Strieber, Macdonald, London 1990.
2. 'Roswell Revisited', Vicki Cooper, *UFO Magazine*, March/April 1994, Vol. 9 No. 2, pp.26–8.
3. *Revelations*, Jacques Vallee, Ballantine, New York 1992, p.27.

ROY, William (1911–) (*PARANORMAL HOAXES*)

'Let no man or woman say smugly: "Roy would never have taken *me* in with that stuff",' wrote talented spiritual shyster William Roy in his confession, 'because I deceived the highest in the land, as well as the humblest. When I think of the big ones I completely bamboozled, I feel a little like a big-game hunter does when he looks at his trophies . . .'

Born William George Holroyd, later known as William Plowright, during the Second World War this raffish ex-telephone engineer became William Roy the **medium**. With many thousands of the bereaved longing to communicate with their dead, he was soon a brilliant success in his new career. SPIRIT VOICES SPOKE EVEN WHEN MEDIUM'S MOUTH WAS FILLED WITH DYED WATER, reported the *Psychic News* in 1948, explaining that the dyed water had been put in Roy's mouth by an investigator who knew all the tricks of the trade; and that it was still there after a seance at which many spirits had spoken.

Roy was never caught out. Even with his hands tied and sticking plaster put over his mouth, the 'spirit voices' that enlivened his seances were still heard, speaking not only in English but in Swedish, Spanish, French, Yiddish and even Malay. Thousands of people in Britain alone insisted that through Roy they'd heard the voices of their departed friends and relatives, speaking of things that no outsider could know.[1]

Yet his client did not simply walk into the bungalow in Hampstead, London, where Roy conducted his seances. Appointments were required, with Roy limiting each session to just twelve people, each paying £10 to £12. Thoroughly researching the backgrounds of his often wealthy clients first, Roy had them leave their coats and bags in his waiting room before the seance. Monitoring their talk, later his assistant went through their belongings and passed on to Roy whatever information he found. During this period his greatest triumph was to dupe the Canadian Prime Minister Mackenzie King into believing he had spoken with the voices of Queen Victoria and her Prime Minister William Ewart Gladstone.

All went well until 1952 when, after a quarrel with Roy, his assistant denounced him to the editor of *Psychic News*, displaying a complete set of the electrical apparatus Roy used to produce the 'spirits'. It included a background microphone connected to the earpiece Roy wore during the seance, and a miniature loudspeaker which, when telescopically extended, could plant 'spirit voices' or sounds (pre-recorded, or produced by Roy or his assistant) in any part of the room. These voices talked to individual clients; while direct messages from the dead came through Roy with the aid of a speaking trumpet which, luminously painted and held aloft, seemed to float in the dark room. Working with 'spirit guides' that included 'Tinka the Red Indian', Roy also used masks and an 'ectoplasm' of butter-muslin to suggest apparitions.

The assistant withdrew his charges but, with the editor of *Psychic*

News minded to press fraud charges, Roy undertook to leave England and go to South Africa. Three years later he was back, arranging new seances, so that in August 1955 spiritualist Maurice Barbanell, editor of the spiritualist journal *Two Worlds*, published a warning, naming Roy as one of four mediums: 'who had been exposed in fraud, yet still continue to give sittings'. Roy's wife Mrs Mary Plowright set about Barbanell with a riding crop, and was fined for so defending her husband's honour, while Roy himself started a lawsuit against Barbanell. This dragged on until February 1958, when Roy suddenly dropped the case and undertook to pay its costs, whereupon *Two Worlds* risked publishing its entire file. The London *Sunday Pictorial* sent a reporter to ask Roy what he had to say.

'Of course I am a phoney,' said Roy unexpectedly. 'So are other mediums. It is true that I have tricked women at seances, but I did no harm.' And there and then he made a lucrative deal with the paper to publish, in five instalments, 'A Shocking Confession of how William Roy Cheated his Way to Fame as a Spiritualist Medium'. In fact he'd cheated his way not only to fame, but to fortune as well: his bank account was fatter by £50,000 as a result of his deceptions.

Thereafter this most talented of fraudulent mediums dropped out of sight. Perhaps he continued his deceptions under another name – even though, in his opinion, he could have gone on using the name of William Roy. 'I know,' he wrote with assurance, 'that even after this confession I could fill the seance rooms again with people who find it a comfort to believe I am genuine.'

1. Larsen, *op. cit.*, pp.134–42.

ROYAL IMPOSTORS (*See* CONCORDANCE)

RUIZ, Rosie (*See* BRUSSELS MARATHON)

RUSSIAN FREE ENTERPRISE? (*CONMEN, FRAUD*)
Since the USSR's collapse, some Russians have eagerly embraced the shadier side of capitalism, not least in the USA. In 1992 a high-tech gang led by the elusive 'Serge' milked New York City corporations via a elaborate **telephone hoax**. Setting up two premium-rate '540' telephone numbers (as used by phone-sex lines) called 'Get Rich Fast' and 'Work For Yourself Inc.', the gang sent fake messengers to pick up packages from office reception desks. Told there was no parcel waiting, the 'messenger' would ask permission to 'call the office to see what is wrong'. Dialling a '540' number, he'd hold a long telephone conversation (in Russian) at $225 a minute. This charge would be automatically transferred from the victim company to the accounts of the front companies. The gang withdrew some $240,000 in cash before the scam

was detected. Only one 'messenger' was caught, the rest of the gang got away scot-free. Clearly, many nationals from the West's former chief opponent are learning fast![1]

Yet such scams are peanuts compared with the scale of some now running in Russia – not least the **Ponzi**-type pyramid schemes ruining thousands of citizens anxious to get rich quick, and the alarming growth in the theft and illegal sale from Russian nuclear facilities of weapons-grade plutonium and other radioactive materials like beryllium. With fully assembled nuclear warheads from SS-20 missiles available to all comers for a knockdown price of $70,000 making the nightmare threat of terrorist nuclear blackmail now realistic, and the growing breakdown of Russian society itself, one might even wonder if the end of the Cold War was such a blessing after all.

Such doubts are fortified by recent revelations of what has been called 'The Great Rouble Scam' – a tale so weird that, when it first came to light in Russia in 1991, few believed it, either in Russia or abroad. Are Russian government politicians really so desperate for dollars to buy Western goods that they make deals with the world's drug barons to launder dirty money?

Yes, it turns out, they are.

The story broke on 23 January 1991. Arrested at Moscow's Sherme-tyevo airport, British businessman Paul Pearson's briefcase contained a signed contract, endorsed by the government of the Russian republic, involving the swap, for $7.8 billion, of 140 *billion* roubles – the total of all Russian bank notes existing at the time. This turned out to be one of only several (undercover) Western propositions made to Yeltsin's government, to exchange (at absurd black market rates) roubles for dollars.

Why would anyone in the West want roubles? One,, colossal sums of narco-dollars have backed up round the world. Laundering them into 'clean' money becomes progressively more complex and exhausting. Two, the former Soviet republics possess not only the world's largest petrol reserves, and huge reserves of many other rare metals and minerals, but also what was once the world's largest standing army, with all its hardware, including missiles, planes, and nuclear warheads.

By buying up colossal amounts of cut-rate roubles, the global mafia (able to move money into Russia much faster than Western governments) not only safely launders its profits but can turn $1 billion into $5 billion or even more. How? By using the roubles thus purchased to buy, say, a ton of crude petroleum in Russia for the rouble equivalent of $5, and then sell it for $140 in western Europe. All such deals require is Russian compliance, either 'official' or criminal. So by 1990, 'the entire former Soviet bloc had become an enormous washing machine for dirty money – arguably the largest, safest, and most profitable ever invented.'[2]

Are Western governments and intelligence agencies ignorant of what's going on? Far from it. Evidence suggests that agencies like the CIA were, before the final collapse of the Soviet Union, happy to encourage this rape of the rouble, and equally happy to use the racketeers as their partners in 'patriotic' activity. As for the KGB, writer Claire Sterling suggests that the secret police chiefs of the former USSR were (and remain) quite as happy to downgrade the rouble. Why? To stimulate runaway inflation, cause popular unrest, force the Yeltsin government towards a repressive social policy, and thus further their own political ends . . . and perhaps to feather their own nests. Is this the triumph of capitalism?

1. *The European*, 8–11 Oct. 1992.
2. 'The Great Rouble Scam', Claire Sterling, London *Sunday Times*, 26 June 1994 (extracted from *Crime Without Frontiers*, Claire Sterling, Little, Brown & Co., London 1994).

S

'Gaiety is the most outstanding feature of
the Soviet Union.'

(Josef Stalin)

SAINT-GERMAIN, Comte de (1710?–84) (*PARANORMAL HOAXES*)

Some say this mysterious eighteenth-century adventurer and **alchemist** is still alive today, in the flesh or a more ethereal form. Either way, he lives on in legend, along with those other great contemporary conmen, Casanova and **Cagliostro**. First appearing in Viennese society *c.*1740, his origins remain a mystery. He may have been the son of a tax-collector born *c.*1710, and have picked up his jeweller's skill at the court of the Shah of Persia. A handsome ladies' man always dressed in black, he knew how to make an impression, with diamonds on his fingers and loose gems in his pockets in lieu of cash. Reputed to have distilled the Elixir of Life, he never ate in company, but sipped water while others gorged themselves. He was also said to be a healer . . . and to be immortal.

This legend began in Paris in a soirée given by Countess von Georgy, wife of the French ambassador to Venice in the 1670s. Hearing the name Saint-Germain, she said she recalled it. Had his father been in Venice? No, he said, *he* had; he remembered her as a lovely young girl. Impossible, she said, the man she remembered had been at least forty-five. 'Madame,' he declared, 'I am very old' – and recounted details of that meeting.

'You are a most extraordinary man!' cried the old lady. 'A devil!'

'No such names!' he exclaimed and, trembling with apparent terror, fled the room.

To feed his rapidly growing legend, he hinted that he'd known the Holy Family: had been at the marriage feast at Cana; and had: 'always known that Christ would meet a bad end'. It was he who at the Council of Nicaea in AD 325 had proposed the canonisation of Anne, mother of the Virgin. Of course he claimed no spiritual mission; only the good of humanity. Maybe this is why he began working as a spy for the French king Louis XV.

Moving to London in 1743, two years later (the year of the Jacobite uprising in Scotland) he was arrested for owning pro-Jacobite letters. Insisting they'd been planted on him, he was released. The English politician Horace Walpole wrote that: 'he will not tell us who he is or whence, but professes that he does not go by his right name. He sings and plays on the violin wonderfully, is mad and not very sensible.'

Hereafter openly working for Louis XV, in the Hague he met Casanova, who thought him a charlatan, but 'extraordinary'. Falling out of royal favour, he fled back to England, then back to Holland. Taking the name Count Surmont, he raised money to build dye factories, vanished with a fortune, then surfaced in Belgium as the Marquis de Montferrat. Appearing in Russia as General Welldone, for a time he was a high-ranking adviser at court. Unable to stop changing identity, in Nuremberg in 1774 he masqueraded as the Transylvanian Prince Rákóczy, but failed to persuade the Margrave of Brandenburg to fund new alchemical experiments. In 1776 he had a similar lack of success at the court of Frederick the Great. He died in Hesse in 1784 while setting up a new paint factory.

Or did he? Who was he? Over four decades, in many guises and pursuing many professions (healer, alchemist, jeweller, diplomat, dyer, musician, painter, linguist), he confused all who met him. Count Warnstadt called him, 'the completest charlatan, fool, rattlepate, windbag and swindler'. Count Alvensleben wrote that: 'Inordinate vanity is the mainspring driving his whole mechanism.' But Voltaire declared: 'C'est un homme qui ne meurt jamais et qui sait tout' ('*he's a man who never dies and who knows everything*'), and his last patron, Prince Charles of Hess-Cassel, called him, 'perhaps one of the greatest sages who ever lived'.

Parish registers record his death, but the myth of his immortality endured. Many reported seeing him in Wilhelmsbad in 1785, where it seems he warned Marie Antoinette of the coming French Revolution; and in 1789 he visited his friend Madame d'Adhémar, who noted that he looked like a man of forty-six. Apparently he told her he'd see her five times more; she claimed this happened, 'always to my unspeakable surprise', the last time being before the murder of the Duc de Berry in 1820. Sixty years later Madame Blavatsky annexed him as one of Theosophy's 'Hidden Masters'; while more recently in 1972 Parisian Richard Chanfray claimed on TV to be Saint-Germain. So too in the USA his myth has been annexed by the syncretic Church Universal and Triumphant. Its leader, Elizabeth Clare Prophet, claims him as 'Hierarch of the Aquarian Age' who, though now discarnate, channels dire messages of coming cataclysm and karmic evolution through her **medium**ship. It looks as if he's still going strong, in the imagination of some at least, and that those of us who believe he died back in 1784 will have to think again . . .

SCHRENK-NOTZING, Baron von (*See* **PRICE, Harry**)

SCIENTIFIC SCAMS (*See CONCORDANCE*)

SCIENTOLOGY (*See* **HUBBARD, L. Ron**)

SENOI, The (*SCIENTIFIC SCAMS*)
In his 1950 essay, 'Dream Theory in Malaya', American anthropologist Kilton Stewart described the culture of the Temiar branch of the Senoi tribe in the rainforest of the Malay Peninsula. Through daily analysis of their dreams, he claimed, this amazing tribe lived in such harmony that there had been no crime, murder, or intercommunal conflict among them for over 300 years. He said they believed that sexual dreams should move through to orgasm; that in falling dreams the dreamer should let himself fall, so rapidly contacting the spirit-world; and that in real life apology should be made to anyone the dreamer had insulted or injured while dreaming. For his description of this utopian culture, Stewart remains widely revered by followers of dream-based New Age therapies, and his widow, Clara Stewart Flagg, still leads Senoi dreamwork seminars in Los Angeles. Senoi dream therapy has also been promoted by influential New Age publications, such as Charles Tart's *Altered States of Consciousness* (1969); Richard Ornstein's *Psychology of Consciousness* (1972); Ann Faraday's *Dream Power* (1972); Marilyn Ferguson's *The Brain Revolution* (1973); and others.

The problem is that Stewart made it all up. In 1978 two British film makers went to Malaysia to make a documentary about the Senoi, and were staggered to hear them deny it all. There was no dream therapy. Back in Britain they went to a Senoi authority (as if the Senoi didn't know their own beliefs), Richard Benjamin of Cambridge University, who agreed with the Senoi. No dream therapy. Reading about this, author Kathryn Lindskoog contacted Stewart's sister, Ida Stewart Coppolino, a California education professor retired to Provo, Utah. Reminiscing about her brother, Dr Coppolino said he'd been a great raconteur, but not a writer, scientist, or anthropologist. What he *had* been (apart from a lapsed Mormon) was a skilled New York therapist with a degree in psychology from the University of Utah. Loaned Dr Coppolino's copy of her brother's 1947 thesis about the Senoi, Lindskoog realised that not only did it contradict the claims in the 1950 essay, but that the well-written 1950 essay had been authored by someone else, perhaps to interest people in Stewart's own dream techniques. The whole thing was a fable.

Stewart's one book, *Pygmies and Dream Giants*, fails to mention the Senoi or any dream theory. *In Search of the Dream People*, a posthumous book by Patrick Noone, the British anthropologist who was Stewart's host in Malaya, contradicts some of Stewart's claims while ignoring others. But why spoil a happy dream by exposing it as such? Stewart and/or his literary co-conspirator invented the Senoi dream culture much as **Castaneda** invented Don Juan – but who knows, maybe it really works – if you live in Los Angeles.[1]

1. Lindskoog, *op. cit.*, pp.202–4.

SERIOS, Ted (20th century) (*PARANORMAL HOAXES*)
Another psychic savaged by James 'The Amazing' **Randi**, this ex-Chicago bellhop became known after 1962 via the work of Pauline Oehler of the Illinois Society for psychic research, and later via investigations by Dr Jule Eisenbud of the University of Colorado Medical School at Denver. Claiming that in 1955 the spirit of Jean Lafitte, a French pirate of the early nineteenth century, had led him in search of buried treasure (with a few minor finds), later this odd individual convinced first Oehler then Eisenbud that he could produce 'thoughtographs'. By staring into the lens of a loaded Polaroid, Eisenbud asserted in *The World of Ted Serios* (1967), Serios produced identifiable images on film of whatever he was thinking about – a hotel with the name 'Stevens' across it; a picture of Westminster Abbey the day after he'd seen it in a travel magazine, and so on. Yet he was scarcely reliable. Drunk one day (intoxication being one of his required working conditions) before a committee of professors, he grabbed the camera, focused fiercely, and produced a photograph of a double-decker bus, telling the academics: 'Put that in your pipe and smoke it'. Another time, trying to 'get' the Chicago Hilton, he muttered: 'Missed, damn it', and came up with a colour shot of the Denver Hilton instead.[1] It seemed impressive – to some.

Yet, with Serios now gone from the psychic scene, it's hard not to agree with the scepticism of Randi and others, especially on learning that Serios routinely made use of what he called his 'gismo' – a small paper tube, one inch long, which he held before the camera while the 'thoughtograph' was taken. When photographers Charles Reynolds and David Eisendrath went to Denver with Persi Diaconis (an authority on conjuring at Stanford University), after one attempt Serios quickly put the hand holding the 'gismo' into his pocket. Diaconis reached out and tried to intercept the 'gismo', but Eisenbud threw himself between the two men and refused to let Diaconis grab it. Why?

Randi suspects that the tube held a small magnifying lens one end, and a colour transparency, cut in a circle, mounted at the other. With the Polaroid focused to infinity, and the tube held with the lens end towards the palm, when the shutter was snapped with the thoughtographer's hand held before it, an image resulted. If the tube was held off-centre, the resulting image was blurred – as were many of the 'thoughtographs'.

Just after Diaconis failed to grab the 'gismo', Serios produced it from his pocket for examination. The paper tube was empty. Big surprise. Randi does not consider Eisenbud party to the suspected fraud, but believes: 'His ego simply does not permit him to realise that he was duped' and that 'Dr Eisenbud is not rowing with both oars in the water.'[2]

A colourful phrase – almost as colourful as Ted Serios's language, not to say his 'thoughtographs'.

1. *The Occult*, Colin Wilson, Grafton, London 1979, pp.665–9.
2. Randi, *op. cit.*, pp.222–7.

SHAKESPEARE, William (1564–1616) (*LITERARY HOAXES*)

Four hundred years ago the man widely agreed to be the greatest dramatist in the English language was at work. Yet was William Shakespeare really the author of the plays ascribed to his name? For at least 200 years there have been rumours and theories that the Stratford actor was hired as the 'mask' for another, secret figure – the true author. Doubters still wonder if the genius who wrote *Macbeth, Hamlet, Othello, Henry V* and the rest of them could possibly have been the rural yeoman who, marrying Anne Hathaway in 1582, fled to London to avoid prosecution for poaching. They point out that nothing is known of his life between the late 1570s and his arrival in London a decade later; and that the true author was as versed in esoteric lore as in modern and classical languages yet that, according to Ben Jonson, Shakespeare had 'small Latin and less Greek'.

In Shakespeare's will nothing is said about disposal of a library or manuscripts. None of his heirs were involved in printing the *First Folio* or gained from it. No autograph manuscripts of his plays or sonnets were ever found. The six known examples (three in his will) of his handwriting are all uncertain signatures. All alleged portraits of the Bard differ in facial structure: the best-known, the *Droeshaut*, prefacing the *Great Folio* (1623), shows the head seemingly unattached to the body, which has half its coat on backwards.

All these anomalies plus the alleged appearance in the plays of cryptic clues planted to suggest the identity of another author have led some theorists, from Horace Walpole (the same man who decried **Chatterton**'s fakery in 1769) to Ignatius Donnelly (the Minnesota politician who almost made Atlantis respectable) and others, to conclude that the true author was Francis Bacon, Lord Verulam (1561– 1626?). A favourite of

Queen Elizabeth I and Lord High Chancellor of England under her successor, James I, Bacon certainly had the learning demonstrated in the plays, was an enthusiastic cryptographer, and was, all in all, a mysterious individual. Rumour long persisted that, after his downfall and disgrace, he faked his death in 1626 and went to Germany to promote **Rosicrucian** doctrines. It has also been said he was the secret son of Elizabeth and the Earl of Leicester[1], and that, due to the poor status of playwriting then, he attributed his work to Shakespeare while in it revealing his authorship via acrostics, ciphers, and other heavy hints.[2]

So in *Henry IV Part I* the name Francis appears thirty-three times on one page; while *The Tempest* (Act I, Scene 2) reads: '*B*egun to tell me what I am, but stopt/*A*nd left me to a bootelesse Inquisition,/ *Con*cluding, stay: not yet.' As Donnelly and followers of the Baconian thesis like Manly P. Hall indicate, the first letters of the first two lines and the first three of the third spell BACon. Baconians give many other examples and point out that, moreover, superimposition of Bacon's portrait as printed in the 1640 edition of his *The Advancement of Learning* upon the enigmatic Droeshaut portrait reveals an exact equivalence of the two faces in terms of bone structure and facial shape.

Donnelly's ideas as offered in *The Great Cryptogram* caused outrage among critics insisting that the Warwickshire yeoman's son wrote all that is claimed for him. But as 'there's no smoke without fire', and given the fallibility of 'experts', maybe the case remains slightly more open than orthodox opinion admits (*see also* **Collier** and **Ireland**).

1. *Francis Bacon's Personal Life Story*, Alfred Dodd, Rider, London 1949.
2. *The Secret Teachings of All Ages*, Manly P. Hall, Philosophical Research Society, Los Angeles 1989 (1926), pp.165–8.

SHAPIRA, Moses (1830–84) (*LITERARY HOAXES*)

A Slavic Jew converted to Christianity, in 1873 Jerusalem antique dealer Moses Wilhelm Shapira bought a set of Moabite pots offered to him as originating in the same area as an inscribed stone found in 1868 at Dhiban in Palestine, east of the Dead Sea (*see* **Christianity**). This had been a key find in a time when British, French, and German collectors vied with each other for relics from the Holy Land. A self-educated scholar, Shapira trusted his sources, and sold the pots to the German government. But when a French scholar, Clermont-Ganneau, exposed the pots as fakes, it turned out that Shapira's diggers had been fraudsters themselves, or were the victims of 'plants'.

Five years later Shapira bought fifteen strips of parchment recently found in caves along the Wadi Mujab gorge near the same Dead Sea area. On them was writing in a very early Hebrew script, containing Phoenician elements vanished from the language by the time of the Babylonian captivity of the Jews in the sixth century BC. Calling the contents biblical, Shapira sent them for study to Berlin where the expert, remembering the Moabite pots, refused to accept them as genuine and sent them back.

But, with advances in biblical discovery now made almost daily, it was now widely thought that the first five books of the Old Testament (the Pentateuch) had been written much later than the time of Moses, once considered their author. Turning again to his parchments, Shapira concluded that they contained most of the Book of Deuteronomy. If so, then his version was several centuries older than the Septuagint, the Greek translation of the scriptures dating from the third century BC. Preparing his own translation, Shapira persuaded the German consul in Beirut, Professor Schröder, that they were genuine, and at Easter 1883 Schröder took them to Berlin. When Berlin again refused them, Shapira took the parchments to London's British Museum, asking £1 million for them. The museum's Palestine expert, Christian Ginsburg, was asked to prepare a complete transcript.

Ginsburg soon saw that the text did indeed resemble Deuteronomy, though it was less abstract and more as if meant to be chanted aloud than in the Authorised Version of the Bible. Either it was an ancestor of the Authorised Version, with a pre-Exile date, or it was a forgery. In August 1883 the French expert Clermont-Ganneau visited the British Museum and, though denied a close inspection, swore that the parchments were forgeries. Shapira, he claimed, had taken recent parchment and aged it with chemicals. Indeed, the parchments were strips cut off a large biblical scroll that Shapira had sold to the British Museum some years earlier. Clermont-Ganneau published his verdict before Ginsburg was ready, so Ginsburg was perhaps influenced into revising his earlier conclusions. On 27 August 1883 he announced his verdict in *The Times*. Noting copyist errors indicating that an east European or Russian Jew had dictated them, he concluded that the text was a mish-mash, and its 'new' version of the Ten Commandments a 'spurious novelty'.

With debts mounting and faced by public derision, Shapira committed suicide in a Rotterdam hotel in March 1884. Like **Kammerer** after him, his suicide was taken as clear proof of his guilt. Yet following discovery in 1947 of the 'Dead Sea Scrolls', some scholars now suggest that his parchments – auctioned off after his death for a few pounds – were genuine. Like his, some of the scrolls mix Hebrew with Phoenician elements. Like his, some contain unusual variations of biblical themes. Like his, these Essene texts contain a pre-Christian emphasis on brotherly love. But unlike his, they were not viewed as frauds, and nobody had to commit suicide over them.[1]

1. Newnham, *op. cit.*, pp.117–21.

SHIPTON, Eric (*See* **YETI**)

SHIPTON, Mother (16th century) (*PARANORMAL HOAXES*)
In recent years commentators on ancient prophecies have referred not
just to the predictions of Nostradamus, the twelfth-century Malachy of
Armagh, or Scotland's Brahan Seer, but also to the foretellings of the
sixteenth-century Yorkshire prophetess, Mother Shipton. Apart from
predicting global disaster for 1991 (which we may now safely count as a
miss), her visions of the future included many fantastically insightful
glimpses of submarines, aircraft, and other marvels unknown to the
Elizabethan era. But, sad though it may seem, study of original editions
of her predictions as lodged in the British Museum led writer Alan
Vaughan to conclude that she never predicted anything beyond her
lifetime. Prophecies attributed to her by a nineteenth-century writer
were, he claims, revamped and updated in the 1960s, amid: 'an intricate
web of hoaxing for fun and profit'.[1]
  Oh dear. Whatever will idle hands get up to next?

1. *Patterns of Prophecy*, Alan Vaughan, Dell, New York 1976, p.20.

SHROUD OF TURIN, The (*HISTORICAL HOAXES*)
Long one of **Christianity**'s most venerated relics, and still claimed by
some as the winding-sheet in which Christ's body was laid after the
crucifixion, the *Santa Sindone*, or Holy Shroud of Turin, is a strip of
linen, 14 feet 3 inches long by 3 feet wide, on it impressed the faint image
of a tall man, front and back. This image shows what appear to be
bloodstains from wounds like those said to have been suffered by Christ
during his last agony. Though first appearing in the fourteenth century,
believers in the authenticity of the Shroud insist that no techniques
existed in the medieval era by which such a detailed image (which they
regard as miraculous) could have been produced. They point out that the
fibres of the thread from which the Shroud was woven were assembled
from linen and a species of cotton, *Gosypium herbaceum*, which is specific
to the Middle East; and also that in 1973 Swiss criminologist Dr Max
Frei determined that, of fifty-nine different pollens contaminating the
cloth, one was halophyte pollen, native to Palestine.[1]
  Yet doubts as to its authenticity have always persisted. Associated by
author Ian Wilson with the *Mandylion* (a wrapped cloth bearing the
image of Christ's face), it is first recorded in the West as belonging to
Geoffrey de Charny, a French nobleman whose Templar namesake and
ancestor had died at the stake in 1314. When de Charny himself died at
the Battle of Poitiers in 1356, his widow exhibited it for profit – and this
in a century when at least forty such images were in circulation. There is
no evidence that the Shroud existed before 1355, and de Charny's widow
was promptly accused of fraud. In 1389 it was described by one

apparently in the know as: 'cunningly painted, the truth being attested by the artist who had painted it'.[2]

Yet many people wanted to believe it was genuine. In 1578 reaching Turin, where ever since it has remained in the Cathedral of St John the Baptist, its fame grew to a point where scientists began to demand that it undergo modern tests to determine its authenticity. The ecclesiastical authorities reluctantly agreed, and so the recent controversy began.

Such tests since conducted on fragments of the Shroud prove that almost certainly it is a sophisticated medieval hoax. Geoffrey's hard-up widow hired an unknown artist to invent a relic so convincing that today it still leads to argument. But how was the image created? In his *Inquest on the Shroud of Turin*, American author Joe Nickell describes techniques known in the fourteenth century by which the image could have been created. These include making a statue, heating it, then placing linen about it, causing a scorch mark resembling the Shroud portrait. He also asserts that the 'blood' on the linen is nothing of the sort. Whatever stains the Shroud is only on the surface of the linen, and never entered the texture of the thread. Further, the portrait depicts a figure not in conformity with Judaic law (male genitalia exposed, hands folded over the chest), but agrees with medieval depictions of Christ's burial (hands folded modestly over the groin).[3]

Radio carbon dating by three different laboratories assigns a date of manufacture between 1260 and 1390. Believers assert that the samples used for the dating must have been contaminated, while some, like Ian Wilson (a Catholic convert) consider the Shroud a divine test for the faithful, as in Deuteronomy vi:16: 'You shall not put the Lord your God to the test' – a theory which, as he conceded to American author D. Scott Rogo in 1988, is a means by which he can continue to revere the Shroud whatever science says.[4,5]

1. *Miracles*, D. Scott Rogo, Aquarian Press, London 1991, p.138.
2. 'Heaven and Earth', Michael Hutchinson, *The Skeptic*, Vol. IV No. 4 (July/August 1990, p.21.
3. *Inquest on the Shroud of Turin*, Joe Nickell, Promethus Books, Buffalo, New York 1983.
4. *op. cit.*, note 1, p.xvi.
5. *The Turin Shroud*, Ian Wilson, Penguin, London 1979.

SIMNEL, Lambert (*See* **WARBECK, Perkin**)

SIMPSON, Edward (*See* **FOSSIL FORGERIES**)

SINATRA, Frank (*See* **HOLLYWOOD HOAXES**)

SIRIUS MYSTERY, The (*PARANORMAL HOAXES*)

Was American scholar Robert K.G. Temple deliberately pulling the other one in his 1976 bestseller *The Sirius Mystery* when he asserted that in their folklore and religious ritual the Dogon tribe of Mali in Africa retain memory of ancient landings on this planet by beings from a planet in the Sirius star system? Nobody has ever suggested that he was hoaxing – but maybe he was hoaxed.

Sirius (from Greek for 'sparkling' or 'scorching') was always a star of mystery. Called *Sothis* by the ancient Egyptians, its annual rising presaged fertilising Nile-flood and the enervating Dog Days of hot summer. Said to be the celestial home of the Egyptian goddess Isis, some modern occultists imaginatively claim it to be the home system of supernatural entities who anciently directed the development of terrestrial civilisation. Novelist Doris **Lessing** has ably exploited this belief in her recent, critically acclaimed *Shikasta* sequence of novels. Sirius has always stimulated human awe – and no wonder.

At 8.7 light years away in the constellation Canis Minor, this close stellar neighbour is the brightest star in our night sky. In fact it is not one star but two. Every fifty years, Sirius A is orbited by a white dwarf, its Companion, Sirius B. Sirius A is so much brighter than its Companion (a collapsed star so dense a cubic inch of its material weighs a ton) that, even when they're furthest apart, a telescope of 200mm aperture or more is needed to see Sirius B. Thus invisible to the naked eye, Sirius B was discovered in 1862 by American astronomer Alvin Clark. Or was it?

In 1950 French anthropologists Marcel Griaule and Germaine Dieterlen published the results of their twenty-year investigation into the cosmological lore of the Dogon. Few people paid any attention to their discoveries, until in 1976 Temple's book appeared.

Speaking of a secret star they call *po*, after the tiniest seed they know, the Dogon priests describe and draw in sand what appears to be their ancient knowledge of Sirius B. They know of its eccentric fifty-year orbit, and say it's made of a special material, *sagala* ('strong'), not found on earth but heavier than all the iron on earth. They also speak of a third, invisible sun in the system, the *emme ya* ('Sun of Women'), which orbits Sirius A also in fifty years and in the same direction as Sirius B, but at right angles to it. Also they tell of the landing on Earth, in an 'ark' and on the 'day of the fish', by the Nommo, a fish-tailed being from Sirius. You start to get the point?

Tracing the far-travelled Dogon and their cosmology back some two millennia, Temple concluded that their tale is the same as that told in surviving fragments of the *Babylonian History* by Berossus, a Chaldean priest writing *c.*300 BC. Berossus tells how the *Annedoti* ('repulsive ones') emerged from the sea to educate the ancient Sumerians, led by a being called Oannes, whose: 'whole body was like that of a fish . . . and had under a fish's head another head, and also feet below, subjoined to the fish's tail'.[1]

Well, maybe. Temple's thesis that Dogon folklore suggests alien intervention in human affairs long ago has been debunked by sceptics like astronomer Carl Sagan and author Ronald Story, who claims that the Dogon learned about Sirius B (also about the moons of Jupiter and Saturn's rings) from local French schools long before Griaule and Dieterlen began recording their folklore and beliefs in 1931. Already with an imaginative mythical system, they simply absorbed this new information and, when the anthropologists came along, offered what seemed to be proof that they'd known about Sirius B long before Alvin Clark's 1862 discovery. No deliberate hoaxing was involved, just the usual run of wishful thinking and conflation of mythic exuberance into historical fact.

Yet this case remains one of those where you believe what suits you. The description of Oannes ('under a fish's head another head') does suggest a primitive man's awe-struck description of an encounter with a space-suited alien being – doesn't it?

1. *The Sirius Mystery*, Robert K.G. Temple, Futura, London 1978.

'SIX S JOB', The (*FRAUD*)

Operated from a small Bangkok office where endlessly ringing telephones were never answered, in the 1970s this global con-trick netted over $4,000,000 – for someone. Known as the Siam, Singapore, Somali, Soviet Sugar Swindle ('Six S Job'), to this day Scotland Yard's Fraud Squad and other experienced policemen are baffled by how a small syndicate pulled off a coup involving the disappearance of 9,313 tons of sugar.

Amid a global sugar shortage the Somali Government ordered 10,000 tons of it and finalised the deal without checking on the cargo. To finance it they turned to Moscow. The Russians, taken in by a forged lading bill, arranged for the Narodny Bank to issue a cheque for $5,900,000. A company called the Crescent Impex of Singapore had told the Somalis that they could supply the sugar – but only after they'd negotiated the deal with Bangkok's Eastern Development Company, whose negotiater was a Mr Chern. Given the go-ahead with the Somalis to act as middle-man, Crescent Impex signed the deal with Eastern Development – but only after specifically requesting that the letter of credit be made out to a newly formed Singapore company. Established in May 1974, this company had a paid-up capital of just two dollars, and just two members on the company's board – the brother and wife of a Singapore consultant working for Crescent Impex.

Delivering the faked lading bill along with fake certificates of quantity and quality to Moscow's Narodny Bank, this company authorised the cashing of the letter of credit and said 10,000 tons of sugar had been loaded at the port of Ko Sichang, forty-five miles south of Bangkok. Delivery would be made to the Somali Trading Agency at Berbera.

The cargo was to have been put on a Liberian-registered ship owned by the Taiship Company, linked to the Consolidated Cosmopolitan Line. This unlisted Bangkok company not only had Mr Chern as a member, but had the same address as the Eastern Development Corporation. But in September 1974 a cable told the Somalis that the sugar would instead be loaded on the *Lord Byron*, owned by Valia Oceanica Armodara, a Greek company. With the *Lord Byron* just arrived in Bangkok, its master learned that the cargo would be loaded overnight before they sailed, but that the lading documents could not be filled out before sailing time. They would be sent on to the next port of call – Berbera in Somalia.

Sugar *was* loaded at Bangkok, but only 687 tons – not the 10,000 tons paid for by the Somalis with the Moscow loan. The *Lord Byron* reached Berbera and was impounded immediately by unhappy Somali officials. Inquiries led to a cable from Bangkok saying that the sugar was still in Bangkok, care of the We Hua Trading Company, agents of the Consolidated Cosmopolitan Line. Once again, the address for this company was the tiny back room office rented by the elusive Mr Chern. Yet, as nobody there admitted knowing anything about 'Mr Chern', the Siamese government was quick to inform the Somalis that the sugar deal they'd sought was illegal in Siam. The government allowed only two companies to export sugar and neither were associated with Mr Chern.

Nobody ever uncovered the ramifications or got the money back. As for 'Mr Chern', even James Bond in his heyday would have found him a master opponent.[1]

1. McCormick, *op. cit.*, pp.212–14.

SKAGGS, Joey (1945–) (*PRANKS*)

As prolific as Alan **Abel** and as socially committed as Abbie **Hoffman**, this New York-born conceptual artist and TV prankster may be the USA's most consistently *creative* hoaxer of recent times, deliberately stimulating people to question the role, impact, and morality of the media.

His imaginative put-ons like the 'cathouse for dogs', the 'radiation-proof cockroach hormone', and the Bad Guys Talent Management Agency have made news the world over ever since, in the late 1960s, as an art student claiming to have been stifled and infuriated by his harsh New York Italian family background, he concluded that: 'I as an individual . . . could strike out at what I perceived as hypocrisy and injustice *creatively*.'

As a typically rebellious and dropped-out child of the 1960s, this literally Angry Young Man's (he calls himself a: 'New York Italian cowboy') first public performance involved constructing a ten-foot-tall crucifix. On it hung a tortured Christ. The head consisted of a genuine American Indian skull with real human hair and a barbed-wire crown of thorns. The genitalia were not only exposed but enormous. On Easter Sunday 1966 he dragged this provocative monstrosity out to Tompkins Square Park in New York's Lower East Side, and there he set it up.

Unsurprisingly, it was attacked by a furious crowd – yet, though seized and detained by the police, Skaggs persisted with it until 1969. In that year (by then he was a long-haired, bearded, ragged, Christ-like figure), he dragged the heavy image along the Manhattan streets amid the Easter Day Parade to St Patrick's Cathedral, protesting what he saw as ecclesiastical hypocrisy. With the outraged crowd (his image of Jesus was not quite sweet or pink enough) howling 'Kill him!', on the steps of the cathedral he was kicked to the ground by the police, then made to drag the 250lb image to the paddy wagon. In this trial, like Christ by Simon of Cyrene, he was aided by a friend. At the last second, with his point well made, he ran for his life, abandoning the crucifix, which the police then smashed. In fact it was a copy of the original: he'd anticipated the conclusion.

Next, by now dedicated, and amid the Vietnamese war, he spent months constructing a life-size Vietnamese village that portrayed the Nativity. Trucking it up to Central Park one Christmas, with actors dressed as American soldiers he led an attack on it, having announced the event on radio. There were numerous arrests. Another time he filled a Greyhound sight-seeing bus with sixty hippies and toured them round Queens, a middle-class suburb. Horrified by this invasion, the suburbanites missed the point he was making: they thought it okay to go to hippy ghettoes to gawk and take snapshots of long-haired people; but *not* okay for long-haired people to gawk and take snapshots of them in their homes. This got him on the front pages and on to the chat shows; as did the time when, dressed as Jo-Jo, King of the New York Gypsies, he led a gypsy protest in front of the governor's office, shouting, 'Re-name the gypsy moth', and carrying a sign reading: 'GYPSIES AGAINST STEREOTYPICAL PROPAGANDA'.

Masquerading as Dr Joseph Gregor, a leading world entomologist, he persuaded United Press International that he'd developed a strain of nuclear-proof cockroaches. Their extracted hormones would cure arthritis, acne and anaemia, and also protect people from nuclear radiation. Inviting the media to a 'cockroach birthday party' in Dr Gregor's office-laboratory, with 'devotees' imbibing the miracle pills, he so fooled a UPI journalist that soon a headline flashed round the world: 'ROACH HORMONE HELD AS MIRACLE DRUG.' UPI were not pleased to learn it was a hoax.

Setting up the Bad Guys Talent Management Agency as a hoax, soon he found it a reality. Advertising himself as an agency for bad guys, bad girls, bad kids and bad dogs, and specialising in burly bouncers, slimy sleazes, and venomous vixens, he manufactured FBI WANTED posters for thuggish-looking friends and was soon getting calls from agents and managers wanting bad guys for their productions. With Bad Guys Inc. written up in *People* magazine, the TV channels started calling. At that point the agency didn't even exist. Gathering a group of his ugly friends, he had them pose for the media in leather, with whips, chains, and motorbikes. The news channels broadcast: 'If you're a mean-looking actor or model, here's the talent agency for *you*! Call Joey Skaggs at Bad Guys, Inc.' Hundreds of calls flooded in on his phone. 'I got creeps lined up all around the block, *real* bad guys – *real* bad girls wanting to be actors, 'cause they saw it on TV.'[1] So he got himself a *real* talent agency he didn't even want.

But his best-known prank remains the one he pulled in 1976. In New York's *Village Voice* he ran an advertisement that read:

CATHOUSE FOR DOGS
featuring a savoury selection of hot bitches. From pedigree
(Fifi, the French Poodle) to mutts (Lady the Tramp). Handler
and Vet on duty. Stud and photo service available. No weirdos,
please. Dogs only. By appointment. Call 254-7878.

To back this up he wrote a press release which explained that, as there already existed canine restaurants, cemeteries and clothing stores, he was now offering a new amenity, one a dog would enjoy the most. Now, for the first time, you could get your dog sexually gratified! Tongue-in-cheek, he told interviewer Andrea Juno: 'We had a wonderful bevy of bitches. We used a drug called Estro-dial to artificially induce a state of heat . . . And if we had a bitch who was in a natural state of heat we would administer a contraceptive called Ova-ban, so your dog would have no fear of being a father.'[2]

The response was unbelievable. People called not only willing to pay fifty dollars to have their dog sexually gratified, but wanting to have sex with dogs or to watch other people doing it. To lure the media, he assembled twenty-five actors and fifteen dogs, and staged *A Night In A Cathouse For Dogs*. The only people at the performance who weren't actors were media people: 'and they just took it hook, line and sinker'. Everyone believed it was real. Soon not only the ASPCA and The Bureau of Animal Affairs, but the vice squad, the Mayor's Office, and various religious and humane organisations were out to get him. With ABC TV doing a documentary on the Cathouse For Dogs, the ASPCA sent out armed investigators after him. A poster was put up offering $200 to anyone who'd turn him in for abusing animals. The police and other agencies kept ringing, trying to set up dates for their dogs, so as to entrap him. Saying he was about to franchise the idea and make bumper-stickers ('Get A Little Tail For Your Dog'), he cranked up the prank until it became international news. He didn't want *real* customers. 'To rip people off for money – no. To make them think – yes. An artist is much different from a con-man. I am a con-man, but I'm a con-fidence, con-ceptual, con-artist. That's different.'

With ABC's documentary nominated for an Emmy as the best news broadcast of the year, Skaggs was subpoenaed by the Attorney General for illegally running a cathouse for dogs. With an entourage of actors he appeared at the Attorney General's office and revealed it as a hoax – a 'conceptual performance'. There was shock, outrage, disbelief. Learning that it *was* a hoax, ABC wouldn't retract their story, thus highlighting the issue of the ethics and responsibility of investigative journalism. 'In the case of the Cathouse For Dogs,' Skaggs points out, 'they [ABC] did not want their credibility as an investigative news source questioned. They didn't have the integrity to tell their viewing audience that it didn't exist, because they didn't want to look bad.'[3]

In *The Total Dog Book*, published eight years later in 1984, the Cathouse For Dogs was still listed, again illustrating how disinformation is perpetuated. In this and his other pranks, Skaggs has made his point. 'Just doing the hoax is not the total performance; it's not . . . the finale or the objective. What's more important, and more difficult to do, is to get the media to come back and allow me to say why and what it means,' he explains.

1. Vale and Juno (eds.), *op. cit.*, interview with Joey Skaggs by Andrea Juno, p.47.
2. *ibid.*, p.39.
3. *ibid.*, p.40.

SMYTH-PIGOTT, Revd John (*See* **END-OF-THE-WORLD SCAMS**)

SOUTHCOTT, Joanna (*See* **END-OF-THE-WORLD SCAMS**)

SOUTH SEA BUBBLE (*FRAUD*)
People were always easily conned by the siren lure of easy money. Early eighteenth-century Europeans with cash to invest were more madly optimistic than most. With colonial expansion encouraging the dream of overseas profits, extravagant new joint-stock projects fought for subscribers to invest in what became known as 'bubbles' – enterprises selling what didn't yet exist to be sold and which usually collapsed, leaving despair in their wake. Of these, the most notorious was Britain's South Sea Bubble, promoted on the basis of a public fantasy that Peru's

gold mines were inexhaustible, and that Spain would concede to England trading ports on the Peruvian coast. It was a delusion that ruined thousands.

Founded in 1711 by Harley, Earl of Oxford and Queen Anne's Lord Treasurer, the 'South Sea Company' was initially intended to restore public credit. With the national debt soaring due to the War of the Spanish Succession, the Company of Merchants of Great Britain was granted exclusive trading rights on South America's east and west coasts, and ownership under the Crown of all lands found within 300 leagues of the shore. But, with the company soon known as the South Sea Company, it was already a fantasy. The scheme had nothing to do with the South Seas, and Philip V of Spain had no intention of letting the English trade freely in South America. Yet in 1714 the capital stock was increased to £10,000,000, and when in 1719 the company proposed to pay £7,567,000 to absorb the national debt, the scheme was already in trouble. Spain had agreed to just one trading ship a year, with a quarter of its profits going to King Philip. Harley's announcement that, in addition, two other ships would be allowed to trade in the first year was as much a fantasy as the published list of ports open to British shipping. The first annual trade ship didn't leave until 1717, and in 1718 trade was suppressed by a rupture with Spain. So, no actual trading was going on, but public enthusiasm was sustained by government support for the company and by the manipulations of financial con-men, ensuring that by August 1720 the stock had been carried up to £1,000 for every £100 subscribed.

The chief villain was company chairman Sir John Blunt, who took his cue from the dubious example of the Mississippi Plan, launched in 1719 by Edinburgh financier John Law. Fleeing to Paris after killing his opponent in a duel, in 1718 Law had induced the Regent of Orleans to let him set up a national bank via subscriptions. Out of this arose the Mississippi Plan, whereby Law's Louisiana Company acquired rights over all land drained by the Mississippi, Missouri, and Ohio rivers. Envisaging colonisation and investment on a huge scale, Law's plan was compromised when the Regent transferred the King's debt, all 1,500 million francs of it, on to the people. With the Louisiana Company effectively controlling France's currency and colonial trade, and its shares rising astronomically, in 1720 Law, now Controller-General of the national finances, tried to amalgamate it with the Banque Royale. But public confidence suddenly collapsed. Law's fortunes and those of thousands of French families collapsed with it. Scapegoated for the Regent's errors, Law fled France and died in Venice, penniless and hated.

Blunt, with none of the material prospects with which Law had tempted the French, had meanwhile embarked on one of history's biggest-ever cons. With even the name 'South Sea Company' untrue, he set out to manipulate both government and nation. With South Sea stock not rising as high as he wished, he faked reports that Gibraltar and Port

Mahon would be exchanged for lucrative trading sites in Peru. It worked. The company sought a subscription of one million pounds at the rate of £300 for every £100 offered. The Stock Exchange was stampeded. Anyone with money to invest rushed to buy shares in what was already called the 'South Sea Bubble'. New companies started up every day, all linked to the Bubble. Nearly a hundred such companies sought subscription, often on the most ludicrous pretexts. Asses were to be imported from Spain, horses insured, silver extracted from sea water, malt dried by hot air. One unknown trickster received a thousand two-guinea subscriptions in one afternoon: 'for carrying on an undertaking of great advantage, but nobody to know what it is'. That same night he shut up shop and left the country. Still the bubbles sprang up, despite government condemnation and the ridicule of the sane portion of the public. Print-shops teemed with caricatures, newspapers satirised bubbles like 'Puckle's Machine Company', which proposed to revolutionise warfare by manufacturing square cannonballs and bullets. This particular folly was among those satirised on a pack of 'South Sea' playing cards, being described as:

> A rare invention to destroy the crowd
> Of fools at home instead of fools abroad.
> Fear not, my friends, this terrible machine,
> They're only wounded who have shares therein.[1]

Such madness couldn't last. Rising throughout May, in four days from 28 May to 2 June the stock jumped from £550 to £890. Many, realising it could climb no higher, sold. Others, like the poet John Gay, believing their imaginary riches would continue growing, were soon to be ruined. On 3 June the price of the stock fell to £640. Ordered to buy, company agents restored confidence. By August the price had risen to a thousand per cent. Full-blown, the bubble was about to burst. By now it was known that Blunt and others had sold out. The unease grew. Again the price fell and this time nothing could restore it. By the end of September the crash had engulfed the nation.

There was panic everywhere. Knight, the treasurer of the South Sea Company, fled to the continent to escape arrest. The Chancellor of the Exchequer was jailed in the Tower of London. As for Blunt, his property was confiscated. His downfall and that of other eminent shysters was scant consolation: thousands had been ruined.

'I am tired of politics and lost in the South Sea,' wrote Matthew Prior a year before his death; 'the roaring of its waves and the madness of the people are justly put together.'[2]

1. *Extraordinary Popular Delusions and the Madness of Crowds*, Charles Mackay, Farrar, Straus and Giroux, New York 1932 (1841), p.63.

2.   McCormick, *op. cit.*, p.42.

SPAGHETTI HOAX (*See* APRIL FOOL'S DAY HOAXES)

SPIRITUALISM (*See* MEDIUMS)

STEIN, David (1935–) (*ART FORGERIES*)

Starting with a sketch which, attributed to Jean Cocteau, he sold for 600 francs, later in life this American art forger lectured on how to identify art forgeries. Disliking the expense and time involved in faking oil paintings, while on the wrong side of the fence he preferred to stick to sketches, drawings, water-colours and gouaches. Following his Grand Tour of Europe, paid for by his fakery, in the mid-1960s he set himself up in New York by producing (it's said) forty 'Cocteaus' and the inevitable 'Chagall' in a couple of days, thus improving his bank balance by some $8,000. This was just a start. In addition to specialising in 'Picassos' and 'Modiglianis', he went on to make an estimated $1 million, and with it opened a gallery where he hung his fakes alongside the real thing. But in time, suspicions were aroused. With the Certificates of Authenticity he'd faked to authenticate his fakes revealed as fake, he fled to San Francisco where, followed by a New York dealer, he was arrested and tried on ninety-seven counts of forgery. Eighteen months in a US jail led to another two years in a French prison, after which his fortunes improved. At a Sotheby auction of his fakes, in just quarter of an hour seventy Steins went for $11,000. Not as lucrative as Tom **Keating**'s two auctions at Christie's, but not bad.[1]

1.   Yapp, *op. cit.*, pp.131–2.

STEWART, Kilton (*See* SENOI)

STONE, Louis T. (d.1933) (*MEDIA HOAXES*)

As the journalistic perpetrators of the **Herschel** and **Ice Worm** hoaxes proved back in the nineteenth century, when there's no news, the solution is to invent some. After all, there's always a ready market for a tall tale – and nobody knew this better than Louis T. Stone of Winsted, Connecticut, whose newspaper career from 1895 to 1933 consisted of being paid for lying: so much so that he became famed as The Winsted Liar.

His career began when as a cub reporter he was hard up for cash and needed a story to sell to the big-city papers. As no such story existed, he invented one, filing an account of the Wild Man of Connecticut who roamed through the forests, uncaught and rarely seen. Though quickly spotted as a hoax, first it was printed by several New York papers – and Stone realised he'd found his *métier*. Every newspaper needs what are known in the trade as 'fillers' – brief, often deadpan items at the foot of a page – and Stone became expert at supplying them in the form of outrageous squibs that nobody really believed but everyone enjoyed. These typically took the form of claims made on behalf of the good folk of Winsted, and they went like this:

'I have seen with my own eyes a man in this town – name of Samuel – who had such trouble with the flies buzzing round his bald old head, he painted a spider up there and that sure did scare all them doggoned flies away.' Or: 'One of the chicken farmers round here always plucks his chickens humanely – with a vacuum cleaner.' Or: 'We have a cow that is so modest she only allows women to milk her. And another cow down Winsted way produces burning, hot milk, having been grazed on a horseradish patch.'

Other products of the Winsted Liar's imagination included a chicken that laid red, white, and blue eggs on Independence Day; a cat with a harelip whistling 'Yankee Doodle'; a tree that grew baked apples; and a deaf and dumb pig.

Everyone enjoyed these folksy, lighthearted lies, not least the citizens of Winsted. Visitors entering the town were greeted by billboards proclaiming: 'Winsted, Connecticut, founded in 1779, has been put on the map by the ingenious and queer stories that emanate from this town and which are printed all over the country, thanks to L.T. Stone.' Stone is also commemorated by a bridge named after him. It crosses Sucker Brook.[1]

1. *Heroic Hoaxes*, Andrew Mound, Macdonald, London 1983, p.75.

STONEHOUSE, John (1925–88) (*DISAPPEARANCES*)
Suspected of fraud, in November 1974 the British Labour MP and ex-minister John Stonehouse was reported drowned while swimming off the Miami coast. In fact nothing of the sort had happened. He was already in Australia under two other names.

Born in Southampton to parents dedicated to the co-operative and trade union movements, work as a clerk in the city's probation service led him into the RAF in 1944, and after the war to the London School of Economics. Intent on a political career in the Labour Party, after unsuccessfully contesting the 1950 and 1951 general elections he went to Africa where, working for the Federation of Uganda African farmers, his attempts to develop it into a politically active co-operative movement made him *persona non grata* with the still complacent Colonial Service. Back in England, in 1957 he entered the House of Commons as Labour MP for Wednesbury in the industrial West Midlands. In 1964, with Labour in power for the first time since 1951, as parliamentary secretary to the Minister of Aviation he set about imposing state controls on the aviation industry. In the process he not only got involved with arms dealer Geoffrey Edwardes and airline operator Freddie Laker, but with the Czech airline CSA. Visiting Prague, he also attended Czech Embassy cocktail parties, so maintaining risky Communist contacts. Yet his star continued to rise. In 1968 he became Britain's last Postmaster-General, and as such was required to reform the postal system. Openly hating the job, he also made no secret of his dislike of several powerful colleagues so that, when that year a defecting Czech intelligence officer falsely accused him of working for the Czech Secret Service, he had few friends. Grilled by counter-intelligence, he was cleared, but warned not to fraternise with eastern bloc officials – and when Labour lost the 1970 election and went into opposition, he was excluded from the shadow cabinet of ministers.

To supplement his reduced income and promote British exports, he now set up a limited liability company: Export Promotion and Consultancy Services (EPACS). With civil war then raging in East Pakistan and atrocities being committed by the Pakistanis, he was approached by British Bengalis with a view to creating a bank for Bengali immigrants. To explain the bank's objectives to these immigrants, a prospectus was prepared, describing the bank as a trust, and inviting investment. Amid considerable criticism, he got the project off the ground only by committing his personal and business resources, and by borrowing. With EPACS' accounts in a mess and only some £15,000-worth of Bengali share applications received, the Fraud Squad investigated rumours that £800,000 had gone missing from the Bangladesh fund. Suspected of fraud, and with his private life in a mess, Stonehouse had had enough. No prosecution ensued, but something in him now snapped.

In November 1974 he flew to Florida with two passports: one in his own name, the other in the name of Joe Markham. Queuing twice at Immigration in Miami International Airport, he was admitted to the USA as both Stonehouse and Markham. Soon on the beach, he went for a swim. Leaving his clothes on the hotel verandah, John Stonehouse vanished out to sea. Swimming back, 'Joe Markham' changed into a second set of clothes, then flew via San Francisco and Hawaii to Melbourne, Australia.

Transferring funds in Markham's name from the Bank of New South Wales to the Bank of New Zealand and an account opened in the name of Donald Clive Mildoon, Stonehouse rented an apartment, and prepared, he hoped, for a peaceful life at last. But he'd been too clever. Where one identity switch might have worked, two did not. With Mildoon recognised as Markham, and suspecting a banking fraud, the police arrested him when, as Mildoon, he arranged to pick up Markham's mail. Held as an illegal immigrant, in July 1975 he was returned to Britain in the care of Scotland Yard detectives.

At last the story broke. His disappearance in Florida had stimulated little interest in Britain, despite rumours of suicide or even that Mafia involvement had led to his murder. But now, with his crestfallen return, the true story of his imposture and flight had everything the media could want – a public figure disgraced, a scandalous misappropriation of funds, even an extra-marital affair with his secretary, Sheila Buckley.

His trial evoked huge interest. Claiming he was not responsible for his actions, and that the pressures of public life had led him to develop multiple personalities (Markham and Mildoon), he denied the unproven charge of stealing £800,000. The prosecution, asking why just before his disappearance he'd taken out £125,000 in life insurance to be paid to his wife in the event of his death, also drew attention to his creation of twenty-four different bank accounts in seventeen different banks, the sums involved finding their way to Switzerland, where they'd vanished from view. Multiple personalities or not, he'd shown considerable cunning in his efforts to vanish and create a new life for himself.

Sentenced to seven years in prison, on his release he lived on in obscurity until, sick and broken, in April 1988 he died.[1]

1. Clark, *op. cit.*

STRIEBER, Whitley (*See* **UFO ABDUCTIONS**)

SWAGGART, Jimmy (*See* **TELEVANGELISTS**)

T

'When a person cannot deceive himself the chances are against his being able to deceive other people.'

(Mark Twain)

TASADAY TRIBE, The (*EXPLORATION HOAXES*)
It seems there's always a market for the invention of exotically remote and primitive folk whose innocent, simple, natural lifestyle puts the rest of us to shame. Stewart's **Senoi** dreamers, and the fun-loving natives of the Filbert Isles discovered by the intrepid crew of the **Kawa** all spring to mind.

But perhaps most outrageous of all was the 'discovery' made in 1971 by Manda Elizalde, then Presidential Assistant for the Tribal Minorities in the Philippines. Working for President Marcos, and said to enjoy a harem of girls seized from tribes in his care, this notorious Harvard-educated playboy belonged to a millionaire family with interests in guns, gold, mining and timber – and it may have been greed for this latter commodity that lay behind his 'discovery' of the Tasaday, the 'world's only surviving Stone Age tribe', deep in the mahogany-rich rainforests of Mindanao.

It seems he invented the Tasaday by bribing and bullying members of two local tribes to go naked (save for a strategic orchid or two), and live in 'ancestral' caves, use stone axes, and eat roots and tadpoles. Swinging Tarzan-like through the jungle on vines, and ignorant of all arts, crafts, pottery, cloth, religion, agriculture and the outside world, they'd never even noticed the Moon, but proved quite happy to fly in helicopters. The famously humanitarian Marcos government found it so vital to protect them that (though they numbered only twenty-six) no less than 46,300 acres of mahogany-rich forest were reserved for their exclusive use.

Apart from profit from illegally logging the mahogany, another reason for creating such a large reserve was to make it difficult for outsiders to 'get at' the Tasaday and expose the lucrative fraud. For, with Elizalde revealing his sensational 'discovery', and the Western media clamouring for access, it was the Presidential Assistant's own helicopter that ferried in the journalists and camera crews – at a price.

Rhapsodising about the altruism of Marcos and Elizalde in its August and December issues in 1971, in August 1972 the *National Geographic* featured these noble savages in an article, by senior Editor Kenneth McLeish, that began: 'In naked innocence, a Tasaday boy toys with a bright bloom plucked from the wilds of a primeval Eden . . .'

Paying a million pesos to make a documentary called *Gentle Tasaday*, NBC TV declared these 'paleohippies' (as a Hawaiian sceptic termed them) to be: 'wholly unaggressive, with no words for weapons, hostility, or war'. Apparently the Tasaday word 'Chee' meant 'Wow! Oh boy!', while 'Oh-ho' meant 'Yessir'.

Next came the book: John Nance's *The Gentle Tasaday: A Stone Age People in the Philippine Rain Forest* (Harcourt, 1975). In the foreword, Charles A. Lindbergh roundly stated that: 'There is a wisdom of the past to which primitive man is close, and from which modern man can learn the requisites of his survival.' To which one might respond: 'Chee! Oh-ho!'

But by then, maybe realising that his 'leisure-intensive' primitives couldn't stand close inspection, Elizalde had first restricted access then in 1974 closed the reserve entirely. Meanwhile, as missionaries asserted government abuse of the tribes, Manila professor Zeus Salazar found himself harassed by threats of legal action for deriding Elizalde's claims. Even so, the hoax persisted until 1986, the year Marcos fell from power and fled to the USA. Elizalde also fled, with an estimated $55 million in loot. A 1988 documentary by the UK's Central TV, *Scandal*, showed the 'Tasaday' in a local village, in T-shirts and jeans, smoking cigarettes. One man, featured as the boy 'Lobo' on the cover of *National Geographic* and in NBC's *Gentle Tasaday* documentary, said 'Lobo' had never been his name.

'Elizalde promised us things,' he said bitterly, 'so we changed our names and did whatever we wanted. He sent ahead messengers to tell us to take off our clothes and go to the caves. We did as we were told, but just look at us. Look around and see if we got any help. We got nothing.'

Yet in 1988 Harcourt reissued *The Gentle Tasaday* as a $12.95 paperback, still sold as a true account. By 1993, not only had neither Harcourt nor the *National Geographic* retreated from their position but *The Lost Tribe*, a PBS TV documentary, asserted a revisionist position, claiming the Tasaday to be neither a hoax nor a 'lost Stone Age tribe', but the descendants of a group of people who a century ago belonged to a larger local tribe, one oppressed by slavers. They had fled deep into the then primeval jungle and (forgetting all their agriculture, arts and crafts) remained in hiding there . . . until recently rediscovered by the resourceful Elizalde . . .[1]

By then Elizalde was safely back in the Philippines. Is it cynical to assume that a hoax denounced may be reasserted in changed form – especially if there's enough money available to spin the yarn anew? After all, if the first Tasaday had fled slavers, why would their descendants have no words for weapons, hostility, or war?

'Chee! Oh-ho!' Even in the modern Stone Age, it seems, there's one born every minute.

1. Lindskoog, *op. cit.*, pp.206–8.

TAUSEND, Franz (1884–1939) (*FRAUD*, *see also* **ALCHEMY**)
With post-war Germany's rampant inflation at last curbed, by 1924 some measure of confidence returned with the introduction of a new currency. Reading an advertisement in a Munich newspaper offering several hundred thousand marks available for investment in a 'sound large-scale business, preferably chemical industry', Franz Tausend responded immediately. Born the son of a small-town Swabian plumber, he'd become apprenticed to a Hamburg chemist. Passing the war years in safe administrative jobs, in 1918 he'd put down the deposit on a farm near Ratisbon. With the farm failing, he and his young wife had moved to a Munich suburb, where in their new house he equipped one room as a chemical laboratory, hoping to discover or invent something lucrative. But, essentially untrained, in his mind chemistry and **alchemy**, science and magic, were all mixed up. In 1922 he published a booklet claiming that metals could be grown like plants if properly treated: the elements, each with its own 'frequency', strove for harmony like musical chords, and could be transmuted just as chords might be changed from one key to another.

It seems he actually believed in his theories. Attracting no backing, at home he continued his amateurish experiments, trying to produce morphium from salt, tin from clay, and so on. Moving into a cottage left to him by his brother, he was getting nowhere fast – until the day he read and answered the advertisement. To his surprise it was answered instantly by the advertiser, Rudolf Rienhardt, a twenty-one-year-old law student who'd just eloped with the wife of a rich Prussian landowner. She was so bowled over that she'd made him her financial manager; and Rienhardt, who had big ideas for her money, was impressed by Tausend's hints of modern alchemy. Meeting Tausend, he was even more impressed. The man was a genius! Forming a limited company, he handed over a large advance.

Making a down-payment on a castle in the Tyrol and registering it in his wife's name, Tausend continued to fail to turn clay into tin or salt into morphium. Fearing that Rienhardt would withdraw, early in 1925 he mentioned the possibility of achieving the old alchemical dream, of transmuting base metals into gold. With Rienhardt agog, jokingly he suggested that, if the first experiments worked, they might invite Hindenburg, the Reichs President, to patronise the undertaking. Completely hooked (as a reactionary nationalist the old general was his hero), Rienhardt went straight to Berlin, to the President's office, but was rebuffed. How could Hindenburg possibly sponsor an obscure alchemist! So, next, Rienhardt approached General Erich von Ludendorff, Hindenburg's right-hand man during the war. Despite involvement in various crazy schemes, Ludendorff was still respected in nationalist circles – and what the young man had to say made him prick up his ears.

Deep in personal debt and steeped in mystic notions, Ludendorff was immediately hooked. If Tausend could really make gold, what wealth and power was his! But he was no fool. Of course not! Before committing himself, he sent an 'expert' to check on the alchemist and his miracle laboratory. This expert was a would-be scientist named Kummer, an uneducated crackpot attracted by Ludendorff's absurd notions. And Kummer was no match for Tausend, who by now had worked out a 'gold-making' process elaborate enough to fool many a better man. Operating with two solutions which he heated and cooled then combined, at the end of the process Tausend removed from the bottom of the crucible a few pellets of what looked like gold. Kummer took one of the pellets to a jeweller – and it *was* gold! 'Your Excellency – it works!' Kummer reported enthusiastically to Ludendorff.

So began Tausend's success story. Ludendorff's name alone was enough to attract dozens of tycoons in German industry and finance. Banker Leopold Osthoff, steel manufacturer Alfred Mannesmann, and other visitors to the miracle laboratory reached for their chequebooks as soon as they'd seen the transmutation occur. The money came rolling in. Ludendorff, determined to get the lion's share, set up with Tausend in October 1925 a limited company called 'Society 164' (gold being element no. 164 in Tausend's 'harmonic periodic' system). With the general to receive 75 per cent of the profits from exploiting the process, Ludendorff also stipulated that Tausend move his laboratory to a remote house in the Upper Bavarian forests. Paying off his debts with the money invested by industrialists, Ludendorff also made further large advances to Tausend (who was to collect just 5 per cent of the ultimate profits).

Tausend enjoyed his forest exile. It was shared with young 'assistants' who, sent by Ludendorff to spy on him, soon became his admirers. Their girlfriends also doted on the miracle-worker, calling him 'master' and talking of his 'Christ-like eyes'. Amid this atmosphere of enthusiastic credulity, Tausend was sure that one day he could dispense with the trickery of slipping the little gold pellets down his sleeve into the solution in the crucible; he really *would* make gold.

But with 'Society 164' branching out, buying factories in Bremen and

Frankfurt, it became clear that only he could produce the goods. None of his 'assistants' had the knack. So where were the forty pounds of gold a day that he'd promised? His backers, who'd kept their involvement secret, grew worried – and the first blow came early in 1927, when Ludendorff withdrew. Perhaps not quite the old fool he seemed, he'd done well out of it. 'Society 164' was dissolved and immediately replaced by the 'Tausend Chemical Research Company', with shares held by most of the original backers plus some new ones. Continually alluring new money with ever more fantastic schemes, Tausend's luck held – for a while. With backers refusing to put up more money, he now issued 'gold vouchers' guaranteeing to investors that an appropriate amount of pure gold had been deposited for them in Tausend's safe – and this con-trick once again brought the cash rolling in. Most of it, looking to the future, Tausend invested in property. Living modestly and loyal to his wife (who never suspected his imposture), he now toured Germany, setting up production teams and new laboratories.

Yet he was nervous. He sensed it couldn't last. Visiting Berlin to negotiate more loans, he was questioned so sceptically by the director of the State Bank about the 'gold vouchers' that he left in a hurry. Turning up in Vienna, he visited his wife in the Tyrol, then in Saxony bought a castle and factory site without money to pay for either. Tearing everywhere at breakneck speed in his powerful Fiat, he was losing his head. He knew the end was near. And it was. Two retired industrialists, brothers named Meinhold, had bought 320,000-marks-worth of 'gold vouchers' a year earlier. Now suspicious, they went to the Munich police. Not finding Tausend, the police dropped their enquiries. But Tausend made a mistake. Crossing the Brenner Pass in spring 1929, he ran someone down, and drove on. Traced to his wife's castle and arrested for the hit-and-run, he was extradited to Munich. Here, the broader case against him took twenty months to prepare.

Of the victims of his imposture, only Herr Meinhold was prepared to testify. The others, all public men, preferred to avoid ridicule and the damage to their reputations. With the prosecutor concluding that Tausend must have pocketed nearly a million and a half marks from his fraud, one day before the trial Tausend was required to make gold in the Bavarian State Mint. Stripped and searched beforehand, and under strict supervision, the first attempt failed. But on the second run, on 3 October 1929, Tausend triumphantly fished out of the crucible a pellet of genuine gold!

'Mankind's ancient dream fulfilled', rhapsodised Munich's leading daily. The city seethed with excitement. But scientists refused to believe it and, as for the embarrassed director of the Mint, he was relieved when a policeman who'd watched the experiment told him of a fountain pen in Tausend's possession during the demonstration. He'd used the pen in a pretence of checking the quantities of his ingredients. It had since disappeared. The gold pellet must have been concealed in it.

When the trial opened in January 1931 there was sympathy for the sallow, pinched little man in the dock. He'd fleeced no pensioners or widows, his victims had been fat bankers and businessmen. Of the few witnesses willing to testify, all said Tausend was a simple, modest, sincere man. Even those who'd lost money spoke for him. But the prosecutor had an ace up his sleeve. Giving evidence, an Italian professor, Sistini, said that, watching Tausend 'make' gold in the Tyrol in October 1928, he'd seen him slip a pellet of gold into the crucible while adding more lead to the molten mass in it.

It was enough. Tausend was jailed, though for just three years. When he came out, Hitler ruled Germany and the nationalist cause was dead. Resorting to petty fraud, in 1938 he was jailed for a further three years in Stuttgart, and a year later died, behind bars.[1]

1. Larsen, *op. cit.*, pp.172–86.

TELEPHONE HOAXES (*PRANKS*)

The telephone is ubiquitous. Almost every household in the Western world has one. Most people use it for essential business or social communication of one sort or another – but some take advantage of the fact that you can't see who's behind the voice the other end of the line. To the prankster, the telephone can be invaluable. Reginald **Jones** would never have got his victim the other end of the line to dump the receiver into a bucket of water had they been face-to-face. Victor **Lewis-Smith**'s escapades as Sir Clint Rees-Bunce would have been impossible in person. The anonymity is essential.

Some telephone hoaxes are silly, like phoning a supermarket to report an escaped raccoon in the fresh food warehouse; or unpleasant, as in responding off-the-cuff to a wrong-number call of 'Is Jim there?' by answering 'Hang on. Who's calling?' – then, after a pause, 'I'm sorry. Jim's still angry with you and he doesn't want to talk.' Others are more elaborate, but still petty, as in phoning a random number and telling the call's receiver that the line needs repairs. On no account, the victim is told, use the phone in the next five minutes, or the repairman's life is at risk. The hoaxer then immediately dials the same number again. With the phone ringing and ringing, most victims soon give up and answer, to be met with a scream, as if the repairman's been electrocuted. Big deal.

Some spoofs display more wit. As part of his New York radio programme, host Don Imus once rang a McDonald's restaurant. Introducing himself as Sergeant Kirkland of the International Guard, he ordered some lunches to go – twelve hundred hamburgers for a scheduled troop movement. 'Twelve – pardon me, sir?' stuttered the assistant manager. 'Wait a minute please.' His boss came on the line, saying they didn't have that much food. 'So get it from other stores,' barked Imus. 'This is the *government*, you know!'

With the manager meekly agreeing, the fun started. Imus gave his rapid-fire order. It went something like: 'On 300 hamburgers hold the mustard but put on plenty of mayonnaise and lettuce and no onions. On 200 – sorry, 201, hold the mayo and lettuce, lay on the mustard, and make them medium-rare. On the first 300, make 275 rare with onions and mustard and mayo but no lettuce – and don't butter the buns on half of those. Butter 134 – no, 135, but no mustard or lettuce but plenty of mayo. Then 250 just plain, but with lettuce on three of those, cooked medium with no butter . . .'

And so on and on at high speed for the delight of the radio audience. But someone got their own back on Imus. Told he had won an award as air personality of the year, he turned up at the New Orleans hotel where the radio conference was allegedly being held, to find nothing but a telegram reading, 'Gotcha!'[1]

John Trubee, leader of the Los Angeles band The Ugly Janitors of America, has made prank calls for years, many available on his 'Calls to Idiots' cassettes. Mostly he calls businesses, pretending he wants to buy something bizarre and stringing his victims along until finally, asking for something they can't provide, he bursts out in hysterical laughter. 'I loved to call up businesses and make a farce out of the telephone ritual,' he told phone interviewer V. Vale. 'It was always so transparent that these people would lie just to sell you something. I always tried to keep a person on the phone as long as possible. The most satisfying reaction was getting the person on the phone so pissed off he was swearing at you. That was much more satisfying than someone just going *click*.'[2]

Working from San Diego (where in the 1970s he met Boyd **Rice**), media hoaxer and 'telephone research psychologist' Barry **Alfonso** sees words as tools. 'It doesn't matter whether you believe them or not,' he says; 'what matters is if *other people* believe them to be true.' Claiming that over the phone he's got women to beat their children, people break down and cry, or ready to buy an airline ticket and fly across the ocean, he says it works because they're playing by certain rules and he isn't. His technique on calling victims is to throw out odd bits of information and let them connect the dots. 'You say you've found some lost keys (that don't exist) – then mysteriously they *have* lost some keys – that's happened several times. They'll rack their brains to come up with some lost keys.' He adds: 'You could say that a meteor landed in your back yard, cracked open and you found their name and address inside, and they would sooner believe that than realise you picked their name out of the phone book. They can always find a way to take these bits of information and plug them into a scenario, and once that's done, they don't listen any more.'[3]

Such pranks may have little purpose beyond embarrassing their victims, but they aren't fraudulent or played for financial gain, as in the **Russian Free Enterprise** scam. Another similar con in the USA involves misusing the 900 numbers to offer credit. The victim, turned down by every other credit company, calls 907-EZ-CREDIT (or whatever) and hits a recording saying all lines are busy and please wait for the first available operator. Cheery music plays for a long time until an operator comes on the line and starts asking questions to fill out the application form – name, address, and so on. In due course, after many mistakes and giggles, with the operator explaining she's new on the job and can you spell that name again, the deal is made. The caller gets the credit card, good only if he puts up money to cover it. Only when he gets the phone bill does he realise why the call took so long – the meter was running at $15 a minute from the moment the call was answered, and guess who collected the cash from the phone company?[4]

1. Lindskoog, *op. cit.*, pp.41–2.
2. Vale and Juno (eds), *op. cit.*, p.199.
3. *ibid.*, pp.209–10.
4. Madison, *op. cit.*, pp.223–4.

TELEVANGELISTS (*FAKE MESSIAHS*)

In the USA as nowhere else, television and the hard sell of what purports to be **Christianity** go hand-in-hand. Appealing to a vast fundamentalist audience already well attuned to **end-of-the-world scams** of one sort or another, in every part of the land and twenty-four hours a day richly funded TV stations pump out an unending diet of hot gospel. Choirs croon while smartly dressed religious hucksters preach at high speed and full volume, alternately threatening, pleading, wheedling and promising while telephone numbers at the bottom of the screen tell you where to ring to pledge the donations that'll buy you salvation – supposedly. It's a new version of one of the oldest and most lucrative scams of all – playing on the superstitious fears of other people to gain personal power and wealth. In recent years vast organisations have been built and millions made through the charismatic, smooth-tongued rantings of televangelists like Jerry Falwell and Pat Robertson – and even if these two individuals remain relatively untainted, the much-publicised failings of many of their holier-than-thou brethren have thrown doubt on televangelism as a whole.

Thus, the claim by Oral Roberts that 'God would take him home' if an $8 million target for donations wasn't met by a certain date drew criticism from both religious and financial authorities. Carl Stevens of the Massachusetts-based Bible Speaks Church filed for bankruptcy when ordered by a federal judge to return several million dollars allegedly bilked from a naive parishioner. Donald Lowery and Pamala St Charles made a mint in the 1980s by luring lonely men to consort with their 'Love Angels' of the Church of Love (COL International). And as for the antics of shysters like Jim and Tammy Faye Bakker, or

Jimmy Swaggart, these caused horror or cynical hilarity, depending on your viewpoint.

For years, Jim and Tammy Faye were America's most successful duo in the field of religious scam-artistry. Presiding over *The PTL Club* TV show during the 1980s (PTL: Praise The Lord or People That Love), Jim's broad grin and clean-cut look and Tammy's off-key hymn-singing snared over $150 million from an estimated 150,000 devotees. They made no secret of their wealth, flaunting it openly, and apparently their congregation loved it. When Tammy Faye celebrated Jim's birthday live on the air during *The PTL Club* by presenting him with two live giraffes, the studio audience came to its feet and cheered.

But nobody cheered any more when it all fell apart and Jim was jailed for forty-five years. The fall began when Jessica Hahn, a former PTL secretary, claimed he'd raped her; whereupon John Fletcher, a defrocked and openly gay minister, admitted procuring Hahn for Bakker and to having an affair with Bakker himself. Suddenly the media was full of lurid tales: of Bakker and his young male workers romping naked in the steam-room; of the 'floozie jacuzzi' in Bakker's office in which he'd tried to seduce a Miss America; and, less licentiously but more to the point so far as the IRS was concerned, of the massive fraud in the operation. What had happened to that $150 million? Questioned, PTL staffers said that the contents of incoming mail had gone into two separate piles, cash and cheques, and that the unrecorded cash – tens of thousands of dollars of it – had gone out as petty cash.

Failing to bribe Jessica Hahn with some of this cash to keep quiet, Bakker did not display much faith in Christ when arrested. Sobbing, he fell to the floor and rolled up in a foetal position. Tammy Faye (her mascaraed false eyelashes described by one comedian as two tarantulas in heat) said he did this often. Wailing and pleading, he was dragged away. At his trial he again broke down and had to be carried from the courtroom. Adjudged sane, and found guilty of 125 counts of fraud and embezzlement, he was sentenced to forty-five years. This sentence was later reduced to eighteen years – but it'll still be after the turn of the millennium before he sees the outside world again.

Among those publicly admonishing the Bakkers for their many sins was the Baptist televangelist Jimmy Swaggart. From his TV pulpit he launched attack after attack on them, his holier-than-thou hypocrisy making many cringe as, his voice trembling in disbelief and scorn, he asked his nationwide audience how could they have been so duplicitous? How could they so defile their holy calling? How could they deceive their viewers so?

In fact he knew very well, and soon the world knew that he knew. Viewing one of this Man of God's more vicious assaults on the Bakkers, prostitute Debra Murphree was interested to recognise him as one of her regulars. Calling a press conference, she testified that he'd hired her to play with herself in front of him before having 'a little' sex, and asked that her pre-teen daughter join in the fun. An instant celebrity, she toured the talk-shows with Jessica Hahn. Now it was Swaggart's turn to wail. Sobbing crocodile tears, he prostrated himself before the nation in televisual apology, but nobody believed it. With the spotlight on televangelical sincerity, it even emerged that some Bible-thumpers, so as to squeeze more cash from their congregations, use handkerchiefs soaked with fresh onion juice to improve the flow of their tears.

May the Lord forgive them![1]

1. Madison, *op. cit.*, pp.67–87.

THOM, John Nichols (1799–1838) (*FAKE MESSIAHS, IMPOSTORS*)

Though now forgotten, the brief career of this impostor and fake messiah was extraordinary. Protestant by birth, after his mother died in a Cornish lunatic asylum his own madness led to the violent death of himself and nine followers. Handsome and imposing, styling himself Sir William Courtenay, heir to the Earldom of Devon, Thom first drew attention in 1832 when he got himself nominated as parliamentary candidate for Canterbury. Polling a fifth of the votes, and by now calling himself King of Jerusalem and Knight of Malta, in 1833 he began publishing (and writing) *The Lion*, a radical theological newspaper, in it declaring of all established Churches that: 'gold is their only aim'. After eight issues, in 1835 he was convicted of perjury against alleged smugglers, judged insane, and lodged in the Kentish asylum at Barming Heath. There his messianic dementia grew worse.

Released in 1838, he reassumed the identity of Sir William Courtenay, Knight of Malta, and began touring the land as a new messiah, the 'Saviour of the World'. Gaining many poor followers, he claimed to be invulnerable to steel or bullet, and said he: 'could slay ten thousand men by striking his right hand on the muscle of his left arm, and then vanish'.

Inciting communal revolt and by now with nearly a hundred followers, he insisted that, when the coronation of Queen Victoria occurred, he would be seated at her right hand. With the authorities now alarmed, he told his followers that they could not be shot, and that, even if he seemed to be dead, he would rise again on the third day and lead them on to victory.

On 31 May 1838 he shot dead a man named Mears sent to arrest him, then mutilated the body and declared himself to be Christ. An infantry regiment was sent to seize him. 'Courtenay' shot on sight their officer, Lieutenant Bennett. The soldiers opened fire. Thom and nine of his followers died, but not the insurrectionary fever he had stimulated. Even after his death many Kentish labourers believed he was truly the Messiah.

Attributing the madness to public ignorance, in Parliament the reformer Joseph Hume used it to demand the creation of a system of public education for all – yet many such fakers still prosper (*see* **End-of-the-World Scams**).[1]

1. *Surprising Mystics*, Herbert Thurston S.J., Burns & Oates, London 1954, pp.195–202.

TICHBORNE CLAIMANT, The (*IMPOSTORS*)

In a darkened room of a Paris hotel in January 1867 Henriette Félicité, the widowed dowager Lady Tichborne, grandmother of the infant owner of a Hampshire estate held in England by the family since the eleventh century, was desperate to believe that the man before her was her long-lost son. Her life had been unhappy, blighted by tragedy.

Forty years earlier, she'd married James, brother of the tenth baronet. Living in Paris they'd had four children – Roger in 1829, then two daughters who'd died young, then Alfred, who'd recently died aged twenty-seven. Roger, emotional and obstinate, had always been her favourite. She'd doted on him so obsessively that in 1845 her husband, on the excuse of a family funeral to be attended, had removed him to England and sent him to Stonyhurst, the famous Catholic boarding school. Four years after that James had secured him a commission in the Sixth Dragoon Guards. All had gone well enough until in 1852 the young man had fallen in love with Katherine Doughty, his eighteen-year-old first cousin. Her father Sir Edward Doughty, eleventh baronet of Tichborne, had ordered them not to see each other for three years. If then they still wanted to marry, he would seek Church dispensation. Resigning his commission, Roger had written her a letter which he'd left with his friend Vincent Gosport, then sailed to South America. From Rio de Janeiro he'd taken passage for New York on a small British trading ship, the *Bella*. Lost at sea, the only trace of the ship ever found had been its logbook, fished up four hundred miles from land. Pronounced dead in 1855, Roger had soon been followed by his father and brother. Now all alone, Henriette refused to believe he was dead. Clutching at straws, she had placed advertisements in papers from South America and Australia . . . and now at last she had met the man who claimed to be her Roger!

In fact his name was Arthur Orton (1834–98), also known as Thomas Castro, a ne'er-do-well from London's East End who'd ended up working as a butcher in Wagga Wagga in the middle of Australia. Here, deep in the Outback, he'd seen her advertisement. Though barely literate, he'd written to her claiming to be Roger. Her response had so encouraged him that in 1866, having raised about £20,000 on the strength of his 'expectations', with his wife and baby daughter he'd sailed to England and ventured into Hampshire to establish his claim. But there, nobody believed him. 'If you are [Sir Roger], you've changed from a racehorse to a carthorse!' the village blacksmith had jeered, pointing out that Sir Roger, weighing under nine stone, had a long sallow face with straight black hair. Orton, who had wavy hair and a large round face, weighed twenty-four stone.

Yet now at their first meeting in his darkened (he said he was ill) hotel room, the old lady uncritically accepted him as her son despite his blunders and the refusal of Henri Chatillon, Roger's old tutor, to buy his story. Emboldened by her allowance of £1,000 a year he began a legal action to claim the Tichborne estates. In his affidavit he said he'd been rescued from the *Bella* by another ship, the Australia-bound *Osprey*.

His case seemed absurd. Apart from the fact that he looked nothing like Roger and weighed almost three times as much, he couldn't speak French, or remember the names of boyhood friends or Stonyhurst teachers. Even so, reading all he could about the Tichborne family, and with the cool manner of the born con-man, he persuaded many people that he *was* the man he said he was. His dupes included the family solicitor, Robert Hopkin, and Roger's old friend Vincent Gosport was also convinced – until he asked Orton what was in the letter Roger had left for Katherine. When Orton said he didn't remember, Gosport concluded he was an impostor.

In 1871, four years after the preliminary examination, the full hearing took place. Though his case was weakened by Lady Tichborne's sudden death, Orton produced over a hundred witnesses, including many former officers of the Sixth Dragoons. On the other side, seventeen family members and friends denounced him as a fraud. They included Katherine Doughty, now Mrs Joseph Radcliffe, who'd kept a copy of Roger's letter. In it, he'd promised to build a chapel if ever they married. Orton knew nothing of this.

Lasting 102 days, the hearing cost the Tichbornes £90,000. Damned by his rough speech ('I would have won if only I could have kept my mouth shut,' he said later) and charged with perjury on twenty-three counts, the subsequent trial of Arthur Orton lasted 188 days: the longest criminal hearing in British legal history. Found guilty, Orton was jailed for fourteen years. Out after ten, he appeared as a music-hall turn and sold his 'confession' to *The People* for £3,000, but in 1898 died penniless at the age of sixty-four.

How had he fooled so many people? With Lady Tichborne it was a matter of wishful thinking, and no doubt some of his 'witnesses' were bribed – but others, it seems, were content to accept that, while in Australia over a ten-year period, the slender Sir Roger had blown up into a man almost three times as bulky and, in addition, had lost all his memory of the past. Some people will believe anything.

TOFT, Mary (18th century) (***FRAUD***)
In 1726 all England was bemused by the tale of Mary Toft, wife of a Godalming cloth-maker, who claimed to give birth to rabbits. Described as being of: 'a healthy strong constitution, small size, fair complexion, a very stupid and sullen temper, and unable to read or write', her amazing hoax or fantasy came to be believed by many simply because they could not imagine how anyone so dull-witted could deceive them. She explained this 'monstrous deviation from the laws of nature' by telling how, as she was weeding in a field (being then, she thought, five months pregnant), a rabbit sprang up near her, and after that she began longing for rabbits. Soon afterwards, another rabbit sprang up near her, in the same place. It too, says a contemporary account: 'she endeavoured to catch. The same night she dreamt that she was in a field with two rabbits in her lap, and awaked with a sick fit, which lasted till morning; from that time, for above three months, she had a constant and strong desire to eat rabbits, but being very poor and indigent could not procure any.'

Soon her story had supporters. The first was her doctor, Mr Howard, a man of sound reputation who'd practised medicine for over thirty years. It seems he truly believed that within a month he had personally helped her to deliver nearly twenty rabbits from her womb. With such professional support, the news reached Court. King George I was so fascinated that he sent his house surgeon, Dr Ahlers, to Godalming to investigate. Ahlers returned, convinced by 'ocular and tangible proof', that Mary indeed gave birth to rabbits and should be awarded a royal pension. So the King sent his anatomist, Mr St André, to Godalming. St André too returned convinced. Both these men brought some of Mary's progeny back to Court with them, and St André actually dissected one of them before the King. It was a regular rabbit.

Now the press got hold of it. A fierce controversy began to rage between believers and doubters. The King supported the believers, while the Queen led the doubters, and it was through her intervention that the absurd affair ended. She approached Sir Richard Manningham, Fellow of the Royal Society and of London's College of Physicians, who went to Godalming to examine the miracle. 'I presently took out what lay in the vagina,' he reported, 'and upon examining it, confess I was much surpris'd, it appearing to me so much like a piece of hog's bladder that I was not able to form any other judgement of it.'

Bringing Mary Toft to London, Manningham lodged her at 'Mr Lacy's bagnio in Leicester Fields', where for a few days she went on professing to have labour pains. Then Thomas Howard, a porter at the bagnio, made a statement on oath that with his assistance she had obtained a rabbit. Taken into custody and cross-examined, at last she broke down and confessed the fraud. The idea for it had come from a woman friend who had suggested it as a: 'way of getting a very good livelihood' without having to work. For a long time before beginning the deception Toft had often, 'by the assistance of that woman, [conveyed] parts of rabbits into her body till at last she could do it by herself, as she had an opportunity, and that she did continue so to do'.

So Mary Toft did not get her royal pension. With the reputation of the two Court doctors seriously impaired, and the public lapping up Manningham's *An Exact Diary of what was observ'd during a Close Attendance upon Mary Toft, the pretended Rabbit-Breeder of Godalming*, Mary herself was committed to Tothill Fields, Bridewell.[1]

1. McCormick, *op. cit.*, pp.28–32.

TOPLIS, Percy (1897–1920) (*IMPOSTORS*)

The career of this extraordinary military impostor, mutineer and outlaw began in Nottinghamshire, where even as a boy he was 'a bit of a tearaway'. Aged eleven he was birched by order of the Mansfield Petty Sessions Court for a con-trick that provided him with a new suit and five shillings. Soon in a jam again for selling newspapers and keeping the cash, with his parents' whereabouts unknown he was taken in by an aunt, Annie Webster, who kept him out of serious trouble until he left school. Ginger-haired, always smartly dressed, he was often caned but never cowed for japes that included drugging his classmates with laudanum (opium mixed with brandy). 'He had a weird magnetic quality to him, despite his roughness,' recalled classmate George Foulkes. Apprenticed to a blacksmith at the Blackwell colliery aged thirteen, he decamped to Scotland and lived by his wits. At fourteen he was jailed in Dumfries for ten days having not paid for rail tickets for himself and a girlfriend then, back in England in 1912, got two years hard labour in Lincoln Jail after trying to force himself on a young woman. He was just fifteen.

Volunteering for the army in 1915, his experience of trench warfare amid the carnage of Loos increased his contempt for authority. Contriving compassionate leave on the grounds that his non-existent wife had died in childbirth, he returned home in captain's uniform, the ribbon of the Distinguished Conduct Medal on his chest, a bandage rolled tight round his left knee to produce a noticeable limp. Mansfield hailed him as a hero.

Deciding that Mesopotamia sounded more interesting than France, he promoted himself to major and reached Malta, where news of British defeats by the Turks caused the troop ship to return to an England increasingly riven by social unrest. Perfecting his act as officer and gentleman, claiming to be the only son of a retired army general, Toplis enjoyed the bright lights of London's West End. By now absent without leave for weeks and not yet willing to risk a firing squad for desertion, he rejoined his detachment of the Royal Army Medical Corps. Posted to the notoriously harsh base camp of Étaples near Boulogne, he found the

20,000 troops there tense and angry. Morale was low. He heard of German and English soldiers in fox-holes agreeing to shoot away from each other; of communities of deserters in the woods nearby; and saw rampaging Australians insult the military police and openly free victims of field punishment who'd been tied to gun carriages.

With his eyes now opened, Toplis was about to challenge the entire British military establishment and to become the most wanted man in Britain.

In September 1917 the British army began its attack on Passchendaele, a ridge in Flanders. The weather was dire, with mud everywhere. Over the next two months over a quarter of a million men died to gain just three miles of German-held territory.

The battle nearly never took place.

Four months earlier seventy-eight French regiments, inflamed by Bolshevism, had mutinied. As for Private Toplis, RAMC, he'd already deserted. Sent to join the battle for Arras in April, he'd fled to join other deserters – French, English and German together – who survived amid the warren of trenches on the old battlefield of the Somme. With the French mutiny so widespread that only the British were left to fight, by autumn even the British were disillusioned. It wasn't just the front-line slaughter, but the violence and brutality of the regime at camps like Étaples.

And Toplis was there to take centre stage in a mutiny so severe it threatened the British war effort and the scheduled start of the battle for Passchendaele. Reaching Étaples early in June, he'd joined the Sanctuary – a community of deserters surviving in caves and pits round Camiers. Daily they mixed with regular troops, stole rations, and ran con-games to acquire money. Disguised as a captain or major, Toplis moved freely amid the confusion of the camp, where the military instructors were hated by all. Survivors of the Front despised the British officer corps, while the Australians, who respected nobody, encouraged mutiny among the Scottish regiments, particularly badly treated by the mostly English instructors. Nor did it help morale when the commandant, Brigadier Andrew Thomson, had the local brothels closed to the troops.

On 9 September 1917 Private Harry Reeve, a military policeman, shot Corporal Wood of the Gordon Highlanders dead for talking to a girl he knew from Aberdeen while he had his tunic unbuttoned. The Scots ran amok. Joined by the Australians, they fired the camp. Officers, Thomson among them, were told to get out or be burned alive. With the military police being hunted down, many mutineers joined the community of deserters.

Now Toplis took control, leading a column of deserters and mutineers back to camp to free prisoners held in the detention compound. With Thomson trapped in an open car, Toplis (dressed as the private he actually was) dictated terms for ending the mutiny. These included removal of the military police and better food and conditions. Meeting Horatio **Bottomley**, editor of *John Bull* and soldiers' champion (in Étaples by chance), he also demanded that army pay be improved. In time all these conditions were met.

With chaos raging, outside troops were sent in, but refused to fire on their fellow-countrymen. Extra food and pay were made available but after three days the mutiny still hadn't ended. Thomson gave in to every demand. The military police were dismissed; the town of Étaples was thrown open. The brothels did a roaring trade. Only after six days did the mutineers begin to return to their posts.

Thomson was sacked. Many of the ex-mutineers died at Passchendaele. But what about Toplis? The authorities, headed by Field-Marshal Haig, wanted revenge. British Secret Service agents infiltrated the Sanctuary. Agent Edwin Woodhall captured Toplis, who was wearing his monocle and a captain's uniform. He was impounded, but quickly escaped by tunnelling under sand and swimming a river. After that the trail went cold.

A year later, Armistice Day in Nottingham was a subdued affair. There was no beer in the pubs and the street lights were still shrouded. From the Flying Horse Hotel, Toplis watched the ambulances go by. Reaching England, he'd gone straight to the army recruiting centre in Nottingham to join the Royal Army Service Corps. Where better for a deserter to hide than in the army? But now, leaving the hotel in officer's uniform, he used a stolen cheque to pay for a gold watch. Arrested, he blamed the fraud on his war wounds. Unmoved, the magistrates gave him six months' hard labour – but they failed to penetrate his identity.

Discharged from Nottingham Jail in 1919, he promptly re-enlisted in the Service Corps – under his own name. His incredible effrontery now led him, from the Avonmouth depot near Bristol, to set up a black market in army petrol. Moved on to Bulford Camp on Salisbury Plain, he found almost everyone involved in rackets. He set about having fun. Ascot, the Savoy Hotel, the daughters of aristocrats – he enjoyed them all. One day he was a private, the next a colonel. He carried a revolver, and liked to show it. By now it was plain that the army knew who he was, but was scared to act. News of the mutiny had been buried, and the establishment wanted to keep it that way. So, it seemed, he could do as he pleased with impunity – forging and handing out leave passes, turning up to be paid then vanishing again. But one night he went too far. He absconded in an army car, a Sunbeam worth £100, to visit a mistress in Bath.

It was the last straw. The army sent the Red Caps (military police) after him. Almost trapped in a café, he ran for it, but was arrested on the Bristol train. Playing cards with his guards, he tricked them out of their guns, locked them in his cell, walked out – and enrolled in the RAF.

Again, amazingly, he used his own name, and again he got away with it. But four months later, when on 25 April Salisbury taxi-driver Sidney Spicer was found shot dead in Hampshire, Toplis (again absent without leave) was blamed.

The biggest manhunt in modern British criminal history began. Yet his nerve held. He turned up at Bulford as a sergeant-major, still carrying his Mark 6 Webley revolver. It was this that later led him to be declared guilty of Spicer's murder. With the newspapers full of rumours and the hue and cry on, over the next six weeks Toplis was reportedly seen in over a hundred places. Narrowly escaping pursuit in Monmouth then London (both times almost betrayed by the monocle), by the start of June he was in Scotland, bicycling from the highland village of Tomintoul up a high pass called the Lecht. Breaking into the Lecht Shooting Lodge, as the night grew cold he smashed furniture to make a fire. Seeing the smoke as he passed and knowing the lodge was meant to be empty, local farmer John Grant alerted the estate gamekeeper, John Mackenzie. In Tomintoul they roused Constable George Greig, the area's only policeman. Back at the lodge, they unlocked the front door. Taken by surprise, when Greig tried to arrest him for burning the furniture, Toplis shot Greig in the neck and Grant in the belly, then fled, singing. He knew it was almost over.

Next day, as the two wounded men reached a hospital in Aberdeen, Toplis was found hiding in the guard's van of the Carlisle train. Taking pity on the vagabond, the guard let him stay. In Carlisle, he went to the Border Regiment depot where, though the most wanted man in Britain, he was fed and lodged without question. Nobody would turn him in. Next day he began walking towards Penrith. Recognised by a local policeman, Alfred Fulton, he threatened to shoot, then fled on towards Penrith, making no attempt to hide himself. Now, with Whitehall orders, guns were issued to the police. Four miles short of Penrith, in the village of Plumpton, they caught up with him. On the evening of 6 June 1920, he was ambushed and shot dead outside Plumpton Church.

It was a national sensation, but the Penrith inquest exonerated the police. Toplis was posthumously found guilty of murdering Sidney Spicer. More than likely it was a frame-up – but at last the establishment, at which Toplis had thumbed his nose since 1917, could breathe again. The outlaw was secretly buried in a cemetery above Penrith – and with him, for over fifty years, was buried all memory of the Étaples Mutiny.[1]

1. *The Monocled Mutineer*, William Allison and John Fairley, Quartet, London 1978.

TRAVELLING STONES, The (*MEDIA HOAXES*)
In 1865 hoaxer Dan De Quille published in the *Virginia City Territorial*

Enterprise a studious report on the 'travelling stones' found in the Pahranagat mountains of Nevada. Magnetic, they attracted each other and huddled together in groups. The report was so well believed that scientists from the USA to Europe deluged him with inquiries. The letters poured in. P.T. Barnum allegedly offered him $10,000 for some of the stones. Hundreds of people wanted samples. One man wanted to become De Quille's partner in the deposit. The realism of his report rebounded on him so intensely that, after thirteen years, tired of people questioning him about it, he confessed in the paper that: 'we never saw or heard of any such diabolical cobbles as the travelling stones of Pahranagat – though we still think there ought to be something of the kind somewhere in the world'.

So, it seemed, that was the end of the travelling stones.

Yet in 1892, fourteen years later, De Quille reinvented them in his Salt Lake City *Daily Tribune* column. Describing his reasons for denouncing his own story as a fake, and telling how in the meantime the tale had travelled to the antipodes to become the 'Travelling Stones of Australia', he went on to admit, frankly and candidly, how:

> Shortly after I denied the existence of the traveling stones, I began to receive assurances that such stones had really been found in central Nevada. Among others who had found and owned such stones were Joseph E. Eckley, present State Printer of Nevada. M. Eckley has several times told me of his having owned a lot of such stones while he was a citizen of Austin, Lander County. He obtained them in Nye county on a hill that was filled and covered with geodes. Most of these geodes contained crystals of various colors. These are not the traveling kind. Those that appear to be endued with life are little nodules of iron.

And so on. He also reported a letter from a J.M. Woodworth, who'd seen many such stones in Humboldt County, California. These were: 'from the size of No. 4 shot to quail eggs'. Kept in a glass bottle they retained their magnetic quality indefinitely. Thrown on a table or a smooth floor 'they will all run together in less than thirty seconds, and the last one getting there jumping a foot or more and sticking to the pile wherever it strikes.'

De Quille's hoax must be one of the few where, retracting his confession that his hoax is a hoax, the hoaxer gets people to believe in it all over again.[1]

1. Lindskoog, *op. cit.*, pp.77–9.

TRICKSTER ENTITIES (*See* MYTHICAL HOAXES AND HOAXERS)

TROY, Hugh (d.1967) (*PRANKS*)

Working for the CIA until his death, Hugh Troy was also one of America's most successful and least malicious pranksters. Early on, he bet his sister he could get a poem of his printed in the *New York Times*. This he accomplished by writing to the paper asking for information about a poem he wished to trace: 'by an American, I believe, with some particularly moving stanzas about a gypsy maiden abandoned on the trail by her tribe'. Signing the letter 'Titus Grisby', he waited until the letter was published then, this time as 'G. Claude Fletcher', wrote a second letter to the paper, answering the first. 'Titus Grisby must be referring to the beautiful "Curse of the Gypsy Mandolin", written in 1870 by the celebrated Poet Laureate of Syracuse, New York – Hugh Troy.' This letter, quoting the entire poem, was also published. So Troy won his bet.

As a student at Cornell University, he borrowed a wastepaper basket reputedly made out of the foot of a rhinoceros, and with it made tracks in the snow down to a lake frozen but for a large hole in the middle, so fooling some into believing that a rhinoceros had blundered through the campus and drowned in the icy lake.

Attending a crowded exhibition of Van Gogh's paintings at New York's Museum of Modern Art in November 1935, he grew annoyed at the difficulty of seeing the paintings amid the throng. So, buying a piece of beef, he trimmed and modelled it to resemble a bloody human ear, then placed it in a velvet-lined box on a pedestal in the museum with a card that read: THIS IS THE EAR WHICH VINCENT VAN GOGH CUT OFF AND SENT TO HIS MISTRESS, A FRENCH PROSTI- TUTE – 24 DECEMBER 1888. Troy claimed he did this to draw the crowd away from the paintings, which he could then view at his ease. Apparently it worked.

As a spare-time writer – in 1947 he published a children's book called *Five Golden Wrens* – he was aware of the practice of ghost-writing, whereby a person claims authorship of a book written by someone else. Deciding to invent ghost-painting, he placed this ad in the *Washington Post*:

TOO BUSY TO PAINT?
CALL ON GHOST ARTISTS, 1426 33rd STREET, NW
WE PAINT IT – YOU SIGN IT!
PRIMITIVE (GRANDMA MOSES TYPE), IMPRESSIONIST
MODERN, CUBIST, ABSTRACT, SCULPTURE . . .
ALSO, WHY NOT GIVE AN EXHIBITION?

As Joey **Skaggs** was later to find with his Bad Guys Talent Manage- ment Agency, such hoaxes can work too well. The advertised address was so deluged with applications that ghost-painting became a reality.

What Troy had envisioned as a joke became a genuine profession still practised today.[1]

1. Yapp, *op. cit.*, pp.32–3.

TRUBEE, John (*See* **TELEPHONE HOAXES**)

U

'The Sudetenland is the last territorial claim
I have to make in Europe.'

(Adolf Hitler c.1936)

UFO ABDUCTIONS (*UFO HOAXES*)
Tales of people being abducted by supernatural, otherworldly, or
alien beings are as old as that of the prophet Enoch, who 'walked with
God and was not', or the Scots seer Thomas the Rhymer, lured into
Faerie for seven years by 'the queen of fair Elfland'. But never, it
seems, have so many people suffered the indignity and terror of being
suddenly uplifted from their everyday lives as today. Mostly in
America, but elsewhere too, the flood of reports of folk abducted by
sinister UFOnauts increases all the time. Typically the 'abductees'
recall the horrific event only later, under hypnosis. Typically, they're
snatched at night, alone, and conveyed (by means nightmarishly
vague) into circular UFOs by bald, grey-skinned, slit-mouthed,
pointy-chinned humanoids with mesmerising, slanted eyes. Typically,
they undergo incomprehensible, humiliating medical examinations, with
special attention paid to their genitalia; as if the aliens are trans-species
perverts interested in cross-breeding. Paradoxical sensations of horror,
yearning, familiarity and strangeness may be reported.

Abductees are not always clear if they're in a solid, nuts-and-bolts
spacecraft from another world, or in another dimension, or in a mental
realm. Nor is the nature and origin of the 'aliens' clear. 'They swarmed
at me, climbing up out of my unconscious', wrote Whitley Strieber of his
'visitors' in *Communion* (1988).[1]

Finally, just as typically, the shocked abductee is returned to earth
miles and hours from where and when he or she last remembers being.
Amnesia followed by nervous breakdown commonly lead to hypnosis, by
which the alleged event is allegedly recalled.

The prototypical abduction tale dates from fourteen years after the

UFO cult began with Kenneth Arnold seeing nine shining discs flying near Mount Rainier in Washington State; likewise fourteen years after **Roswell**. One night in September 1961, Betty and Barney Hill were driving through New Hampshire's White Mountains. Seeing a bright light descending, they stopped. Before them hovered a pancake-shaped object ringed with round windows. Through them, Barney saw humanoid figures in 'shiny black uniform'. Shocked, they drove on, reaching Portsmouth on the Atlantic coast near dawn. Soon Betty began dreaming that they'd been seized, taken on board the UFO, separated, and medically examined. Reporting the event to UFO investigators, they realised they'd 'lost' two hours – at the speed Barney drove they should have been home at least two hours earlier. With Barney exhausted and depressed, they submitted to hypnosis. Both told a tale matching Betty's dream-'memory'. Taken on board the UFO, they'd been put in separate rooms. Betty's dress had been removed; samples of her hair, skin, ear-wax and fingernails were taken; a 'pregnancy test' involved a needle being jabbed into her navel. She also drew from 'memory' a star-map showing the aliens' 'home port'. This was later tentatively identified as the stars zeta-1 and zeta-2 Reticuli, thirty-seven light-years from Earth.

Four years earlier, in October 1957, late one night Brazilian farmer Antonio Villas-Boas was ploughing alone in his tractor when a red star above grew into an egg-like object that landed softly. His tractor engine died (electrical failures are a common feature of such encounters); he was seized by four 'men', taken on board the UFO, stripped, washed, and left alone in a room. A small naked blonde blue-eyed thin-lipped woman came in. After they made love a man entered. Smiling, the woman indicated her belly then the sky, and followed the man out. Villas-Boas was taken to another room where crew members were 'growling' at each other. Failing to steal what looked like a clock, he was released with no evidence other than his own memory to substantiate the event.[2]

But the aliens didn't really get serious until the 1980s, nor was the public fully alert to this danger in our midst until Whitley Strieber published *Communion*, the bizarre tale of his recollection (under hypnosis, of course) of being abducted by 'visitors' in rural upstate New York in December 1985. Enticed out of the country home where lay his sleeping wife and son, in 'a black iron cot' he was dreamily levitated into a messy round room which reeked of Cheddar cheese. The aliens (smelling of cinnamon and cardboard) came in four types – the first, robot-like; the second, short and stocky beings in blue coveralls; the third, delicate beings with mesmerising black slanted eyes and vestigial mouth and nose; and the fourth also bald and small, but with round black button-like eyes. Supervised by a third-category female with leathery yellow-brown skin who exuded an air of ancient wisdom, Strieber now underwent the routine medical examination, which in his case meant buggery by a scaly proctoscope. Following this interesting experience, he awoke to find himself naked on his living-room couch, went upstairs, cleaned his teeth, and went to bed – and only later, due to panic attacks crippling his life, went to the inevitable hypnotist.

His book became a bestseller not just due to its narrative skill (Strieber being a pro writer of (guess what?) horror stories), but because of his ideas about the 'aliens', who told him this world 'is a school' and they 'recycle souls'. Implying that they're physically real yet also somehow rooted in the human unconscious, he concluded that they can enter the mind, affect perception, and even draw the soul from the body. Perhaps, he pondered, they seek to transform us; or perhaps, through them, we seek to transform ourselves. As for himself, it had been a shock to realise that such events had been affecting him since childhood, and that his fear had imposed amnesia on him, the events remaining hidden behind 'screen memories' – until hypnosis did the trick.

Was Strieber a hoaxer? Was all his talk of the unconscious an oblique admission of his uneasy knowledge that, at some level or another, he was making it all up? Or were aliens *genuinely* lurking in his unconscious? What if he's right, and *we*'re the aliens, tricking ourselves? Tricky question. At any rate, by the 1990s thousands of people had reported such encounters and millions of people believed them uncritically. Yet, taking a colder look at the problem, sceptics conclude that most accounts reek of paranoia, manic elaboration, and blatant fraud. As for hypnotic 'verification', the same problems arise as when using hypnosis to verify **past-life memories**: as often as not the 'memories' are nothing of the sort (*see* '**False Memory Syndrome**'). In addition, as Martin Orne (a professor of psychiatry at the University of Pennsylvania) has warned: 'if the hypnotist has beliefs about what actually occurred, it is exceedingly difficult for him to prevent himself from inadvertently guiding the subject's recall'[3] – meaning that eventually the hypnotised subject 'remembers' whatever the hypnotist, deliberately or otherwise, suggests.

As for the 'abductee' personality type, studies indicate a tendency towards high intelligence, high creativity, low self-esteem, emotional immaturity, confusion about sexual identity, egocentricity and paranoia. Reviewing the phenomenon in *Dark White* (1994), author Jim Schnabel concludes that abduction experiences are triggered in various ways – by stress, a desire for attention, hallucinogenic drugs, or hypnotic trance. Pointing out how people can produce information they don't remember receiving, he quotes female therapists treating Vietnam veterans who themselves start suffering flashbacks about their own 'combat experiences'. He also mentions a theory advanced by Princeton's Dr Julian Jaynes who, in *The Origin of Consciousness in the Breakdown of the Bicameral Mind* (1976), argues that until quite recent times, human introspection, evaluation, and decision-making were performed unconsciously by the right side of the brain, which then delivered commands in the form of hallucinated voices or visions to the obedient left lobe.

Such voices and visions were once interpreted as being those of gods – so (the theory goes) the 'aliens' doing the 'abducting' do literally exist: in the right lobe of our brains. They are part of our subconscious! A neat theory, though unproven and probably unprovable; but who knows, maybe Strieber's right after all, and the 'abductees' are not only hoaxing but *abducting* themselves![4]

1. *Communion*, Whitley Strieber, Arrow Books, London 1988, p.95.
2. *Dimensions*, Jacques Vallee, Sphere Books, London 1990, pp.139–40.
3. Quoted in 'Aliens stole my Virginity', Anthony Clare, *Sunday Times* Book Section, 6 March 1994, reviewing:
4. *Dark White: Aliens, Abductions, and the UFO Obsession*, Jim Schnabel, Hamilton, London 1994.

UNICORN HOAX, The (*PRANKS*)

Descended from Hungarian nobility, born in Burgenland in 1937, Antal Festetics enjoys high standing in Austria as a naturalist and conservationist, and many watching his TV wildlife documentary in April 1992 may have taken him at his word when he casually told his viewers that he'd both seen and photographed a unicorn in a Harz mountain forest.

An ancient region, the Harz is home to the Märchenwald, the original dark 'enchanted forest' of Germanic folklore – and also the legendary home of the mythical white horse-like beast with the horn that sprouts straight out from its forehead.

This wasn't the first time he'd made the claim. Interviewed by the weekly *Die Ganze Woche* for its December 1991 issue as part of the advance publicity for his three-part documentary *Wildtiere und wir* ('Wild Animals and us'), he'd told journalist Senta Ziegler how the unicorn had nearly knocked him off his horse. He had been deep in the woods in an area of the Harz Mountains which, sliced in two by the Cold War, for nearly forty years had been mined and fenced off, meaning that no hunting or toxic spraying had taken place there in all that time. With the Cold War now over and the area reopened it was an ideal opportunity, Festetics claimed, to study an untouched biotype of native animals such as roe deer, red deer, and various species of owl. One midnight he'd been filming small night creatures from horseback when: 'Suddenly, a unicorn came towards me at a gallop. There was a gleam of light around the animal. My horse reared and almost threw me – then, just as quickly, it was gone.'

Somehow, even while almost unhorsed, he'd kept filming with his video camera – and *Woche*, without comment or caption, printed with the article an atmospheric colour photograph of a unicorn in the forest at night. Writing up this tale for the magazine *Fortean Times*, editor Bob Rickard concluded that the photo was probably a still from the 1985

Ridley Scott fantasy movie *Legend*. Along with his German colleague Ulrich Magin, Rickard wrote to Festetics, asking specific questions about the encounter and the photo. The good professor replied courteously but vaguely that:

'The meeting with the animal near the Unicorn's Cave is logical and confirms the origin of its name.' He added: 'I can't explain how the unicorn was able to survive in the Harz into the present, and, naturally, I would like to see it again.'

Magin, also finding Festetics sticking to the tale, thought it not so much a hoax as a: 'metaphor, a poetic idea, to dramatise the appeal of the "fairy forest" by addressing "the child in every man". He wasn't really risking his reputation as a scientist, nor even acting strangely . . . I don't think anyone in Germany took it literally – it certainly didn't draw any newspaper discussion.' Magin added that, when he'd asked Festetics if he was using the sighting to 'enchant' his audience into greater awareness of the environment, the professor had invited him to Göttingen to view his Harz footage, and said he planned an expedition to film the second mysterious creature of the Harz – the deer with the Hubertus-cross. (This refers to the discovery by a young man who blasphemously went hunting in the forest on Good Friday, only to find that his quarry, a magnificent stag, carried a dazzling crucifix between its antlers. Converted on the spot, he became St Hubert (d.727).)

Festetics had also told Magin of his gloriously tongue-in-cheek ambition to harness genetic technology to reconstruct creatures from legend to delight the inner child. 'Instead of breeding monstrous rats for laboratory experiments,' he'd mused, 'it would be better to recreate the "lindworm" (Tatzelworm) for Carinthia, the basilisk for Vienna, and . . . a second unicorn for the Harz.'[1]

1.   'A Pointed Joke', Bob Rickard, *Fortean Times* No. 74, London 1994, pp.36–9.

V

'People's brains have adapted to TV; they're
ready for anything you say. Just as long as
it's said and summed up for them in a
second.'

(Jeffrey Vallance)

VALFIERNO, Eduardo de (*See* **MONA LISA**)

VALLANCE, Jeffrey (contemporary) (***PRANKS***)
Another modern American prankster, less wild and woolly than some,
his manner calm and soothing enough to camouflage his ironic efforts to
undermine authority and ritual via a host of somewhat unusual 'conceptual art' projects, Vallance is user-friendly.

Take the case of 'Blinky the Friendly Hen'. One day in 1978 Vallance
went to Ralph's supermarket in Canoga Park, the Los Angeles suburb
where he lived, and bought a Foster Farms fryer chicken wrapped in
plastic (in fact he knew fellow-prankster Boyd **Rice**, he of the sheep's
head jape). Back home, removing it from the plastic bag still bloody, he
put it on a sheet of paper to photograph it, and on lifting it up found it
had left a perfect impression of a chicken. He called it the *Shroud of
Blinky* (after the **Shroud of Turin**). Later, he says, he sold this sacred
item for a thousand dollars.

Calling up a pet cemetery, he said he had a dead bird to bury. With
Blinky now in a shoebox, he drove out to the cemetery. Playing it
straight with the lady at reception, he filled out all the forms and, having
already found out that all the other animals in the cemetery had names
like Fluffy, Biffy, Pinky and Winky, decided 'Blinky' would be just the
name for the dead hen, especially given the way hens look at things.
With a mortician going out to his car and carrying the boxed-up Blinky
into a back room, he was still filling out forms when a huge man with
dead-white skin like Lurch – the Frankenstein character in *The Addams*

Family TV show – emerged and asked in slow measured syllables, 'How – did – your – pet – die?' – because of course it was all plucked and cleaned. 'I'm not sure exactly how it died,' said Vallance truthfully. 'One day it just died.'

They asked no more questions, because by then he was flashing the cash to pay for the burial – $300, which he had in three one-hundred-dollar bills. So they were very cordial about burying the by-now defrosting Blinky. Vallance had ordered a powder-blue coffin with a pink lining, and they put a paper towel on the bottom, so as not to ruin the satin with moisture dripping from the thawing hen. There was also a little pillow, which they placed so that, if Blinky's head had still been on, it would have been on the pillow.

They went out to the grave, Blinky carried by silent pallbearers who looked to Vallance like illegal aliens. Their faces said they thought this was the craziest thing they'd ever seen. With astroturf all about to counteract any morbid sensation of real *earth*, the coffin was brought out. The name on it was not Blinky's, but Vallance's. He felt he was watching his own burial! After the ceremony was over, he went to a Howard Johnsons and ordered the 'Chicken Special'. Describing this prank as: 'sort of like a vegetarian piece', later he produced a booklet: 'Blinky the Friendly Hen, dedicated to the billions of hens sacrificed each year for our consumption'. He's nothing if not deadpan.

At Junior College he'd written to every senator in the USA and asked them to draw him a picture (he got replies from thirty-three), then sent neckties to the heads of state of every country in the world (cultural exchange = cultural tie = *necktie*), and got about thirty letters back, with ties. The Pope sent a medal, as he doesn't wear a tie, and the King of Saudi Arabia sent a royal head-dress.

As he says, marvelling, 'You can just sit there in your house writing letters that affect . . . world leaders, making them do weird things for you.'[1]

1. Vale and Juno (eds.), *op. cit.*, p.117.

VAN MEEGEREN, Han (1889–1947) (*ART FORGERIES*)

The twentieth-century's most famous art forger was a small man who thought big. Like other skilled fakers he despised the art critics, dealers, and experts. 'I don't think you'll find an honest man who is also a dealer,' said Eric **Hebborn**. 'They know more about fine words than fine art,' declared Elmyr **De Hory** of the experts. But Han van Meegeren was more to the point. He called the experts, 'arrogant scum' – and, to prove his paranoia not so crazy, took the art world for a ride that would probably never have been discovered if not for an amazing sequence of events after the fall of Nazi Germany in 1945.

Born in Deventer in the Netherlands, he had reason to be rebellious.

The second son of five children and in the middle of the family, his artistry came from his mother, a delicate woman fifteen years younger than his stern schoolteacher father, who regularly tore up all his drawings. Even so, he was a success as a student at Delft's Institute of Technology. Married in 1912, he failed his final exams but won the Institute's gold medal for the best painting by a student. In 1914 the couple moved to Scheveningen, then a little seaside town terrorised by seven-year-old Hugo **Baruch**, alias Jack Bilbo.

Here he produced his first fake, a copy of the watercolour which had won the gold medal. His wife Anna wouldn't let him pass it off as original: by 1917 the marriage had broken up, and in 1923 they were divorced. By then he was bitter not only at her but at the critics. The year 1922 had seen his first major exhibition, at the Hague. The critics, led by Dr Abraham Bredius, had slated it. Furious, over the next few years he had to design Christmas cards, restore paintings, and sell portraits to tourists to stay alive. His anger at the art world grew to the point where he decided to show them who really knew about art – who was the real genius! He'd forge paintings by the great seventeenth-century Dutch painter Jan Vermeer – the artist Dr Bredius admired most of all; and they'd never notice the difference!

This hoaxing mission kept him alive.

Already middle-aged, from a rented villa in France now he taught himself how to prepare canvases, mix paints, and artificially age his paintings. He devoted hours and huge effort to obtaining centuries-old canvases, scraping off most of the paint, and rediscovering the recipes for Vermeer's brilliant colours. For one shade of blue, he sent to England for powdered lapis lazuli. He mixed his paints with oil of lily and learned how to harden paint with phenol-formaldehyde. By baking completed canvases in a low oven he replicated Vermeer's enamel-like surfaces. After four years of technical preparation he was ready.

Between 1937 and 1943 he sold eight paintings to dealers, museums, and the Nazi Field-Marshal Hermann Göring for a total of about £2 million pounds (equivalent to £20 million today). The first to appear was the best, *Christ and his Disciples at Emmaus*. He put it on the market through a Paris lawyer, alleging it had been owned by a Dutch family in Paris who, falling on hard times, now had to sell it. The lawyer approached the acknowledged expert on Vermeer, Bredius – and Bredius was overwhelmed, declaring in an art magazine: 'It is a wonderful moment in the life of a lover of art when he finds himself suddenly confronted with a hitherto unknown painting of a great master . . . we have here a – I am inclined to say – *the* masterpiece of Johannes Vermeer of Delft.'

Game set and match to Van Meegeren. He could have exposed the fake. Bredius would have been a laughing stock; Van Meegeren would have proved his skills. But when a Rotterdam museum (urged by

Bredius) offered £50,000 for it, he thought again. The temptation was too much. He took the money, bought property, then went back to the easel. By 1943 five more Vermeers and two de Hooghs had emerged. By the end of the war Van Meegeren was rich, owning fifty houses, hotels, nightclubs, and many genuine works of art. To explain his wealth, he said he'd twice won the *gros lot* on the National Lottery. Yet he still had a bitter look, and the axe was about to fall.

After the Nazi collapse in 1945, Luftwaffe chief Hermann Göring's priceless art collection was uncovered at his Berchtesgaden mansion. Most of it had been looted from churches, galleries, and private collections as the Nazis overran Europe; but among the few honestly purchased was a Van Meegeren Vermeer, the *Woman Taken in Adultery*. Agents investigating soon learned that Göring's dealers had bought it for £150,000 from a dealer in Amsterdam. The dealer was Van Meegeren. A collaborator! The Dutch police arrested him. He was charged with treason for selling a national treasure to the enemy. If found guilty, he faced death. For three weeks he maintained his story; that he'd bought the painting from an Italian family then sold it in good faith. How was he to know it would fall into Nazi hands? The police were unimpressed. They kept on at him, until at last he cracked.

'Fools!' he yelled in court, 'You're like the rest of them. I sold no Vermeer to the Germans – only a Van Meegeren, painted to look like a Vermeer. I have not collaborated with the Germans, I have duped them.'

Threatened with ridicule and professional ruin, Bredius and other experts called him a liar. 'Paint *Emmaus* again!' they challenged. But Van Meegeren went one better. Placed under guard in his Amsterdam studio and under the unbending eye of a panel of witnesses, he painted his final Vermeer, *Young Christ Teaching in the Temple*. It was so impressive he didn't even need to finish it. The treason charges were dropped – but new charges of deception and forging signatures arose. After a one-day trial in 1947 he was found guilty and sentenced to one year in prison. Before he could serve it he had a heart attack. He died six weeks later. But maybe in his own way he had the last word.

'I had been so belittled by the critics that I could no longer exhibit my own work,' he declared after painting his *Young Christ*. 'I was systematically and maliciously damaged by the critics, who don't know the first thing about painting.'

Paranoid maybe, but then as now many agreed: he had proved his point.

VESPUCCI, Amerigo (1451–1512) (*EXPLORATION HOAXES*)

It is probably due to this Italian merchant-explorer's capacity to lie that not one but two continents – North and South America – are named after him. Claiming to have found the continent of America in 1497, he also claimed further voyages there in 1499, 1501 and 1503. Advertising his claims in a letter printed in 1503 or 1504 as *Mundus Novus* ('Our New World'), he declared that the information he offered about the South American coasts: 'will be a matter wholly new to all those who hear about them'. His self-advertisement was so efficient that when in 1507 a map-maker needed a name for the new continent of South America, he named it *America*, 'because Amerigo discovered it'.

Well, no. Almost certainly he didn't. Evidence for the 1497 voyage is tentative and unconvincing, while for the alleged South American trip in 1501 he gives two different accounts which disagree with each other on such minor matters as distances and dates. Nor, as he implies, did he take a leading role on the voyages he *was* on. He was not the captain, but only the astronomer, or pilot.

So why didn't **Columbus**, famously reaching the New World in 1492, object to the claims of this upstart braggart? Because Columbus never realised that the lands he had reached belonged to the Western Hemisphere. He thought the islands he found were part of the Indies. That's probably why we never got North and South Columbia instead.

'Strange,' wrote Ralph Waldo Emerson, 'that broad America must wear the name of a thief. Amerigo Vespucci, the pickle dealer at Seville, managed in this lying world to supplant Columbus and baptize half of the earth with his own dishonest name.'[1]

1. Goldberg, *op. cit.*, pp.45–7.

VIGLIOTTO, Giovanni (contemporary) (*FRAUD*)

Some men are unbelievably compulsive in their greed – and get away with it again and again, before someone puts a stop to it. Maybe that's what they sought to start with. This modern day Italian-American Don Juan got away with it 105 times. That's how many women he married (without divorcing any of the others) before he met one who went after him when he double-crossed her too.

As for the other 105, their ages varied, but all were lonely and easy prey for this lubricious Lothario, and every one got the same advice, that they move nearer his home, which just happened to be far out of state. The family would be so pleased to meet her, to see him settle down at last! He talked each starry-eyed new bride not only into selling her house but into loading all she owned on a U-Haul which he would drive to their new home while she stayed behind to wrap up her old life. Oh, and being a fragile woman alone, though only for a few days, of course, wouldn't it be a good idea if he looked after her money too – just in case?

Unbelievable? All of them, even the one-hundred-and-sixth, went along with it, waving a bravely smiling but tearful goodbye as her charming new man drove off into the sunset with everything she owned, having not even told her the exact location of their new home. He'd call and let her know. Tomorrow. Maybe two days. And when a day or two became three or four or even a week or two and still no word from Giovanni, most of them headed after him – only to find the trail cold. He'd taken everything and vanished. Most were too mortified even to call the police. The few who pressed charges got nowhere.

No. 106 was made of sterner stuff. When he did his flit and the light began to dawn, she got to thinking. She'd met him at a flea market where he had a lot of inviting *objets* for sale. They'd started to talk. He'd been so sympathetic! So lonely too – you could see that. Soon enough – now she'd kick herself if she could. Married in a week! He was probably at it again right now, the bastard! In a flea market in some other state. But she'd get the sonovabitch! So she got in her car and drove through several states, covering all the flea markets. And revenge she got. She found him in Florida, selling off her stuff, and called the law. So Vigliotto was slammed with what should have been 106 charges of theft, and 105 of bigamy – and was she surprised when most of those dumb broads not only refused to press charges but wanted him back?

The provenance of this tale isn't given in the source I take it from – no dates, places, and only one name given – but it sounds human, i.e., crazy.[1]

1. Madison, *op. cit.*, pp.162–4.

VOIGHT, Wilhelm (1849–1922) (*IMPOSTORS*)

Said to have spent twenty-seven of his first fifty-seven years in jail as a crook who couldn't do anything right, this cobbler who rarely practised his trade had seen tumultuous times. In his youth, Prussian militarism had stamped out the shape of the new Germany. There had been the Austro-Prussian War, then the Franco-Prussian War, and now there was an empire with possessions abroad, and here in Potsdam this autumn day of 1906 the blue-uniformed soldiers of Kaiser Wilhelm's army were everywhere – marching, saluting, clattering past on horseback, practising the goose-step on the parade ground. One in every three men in Potsdam was in the army.

But not Wilhelm Voight. Though bent and haggard, he'd got work here, as a shoe-machine operator, but there was nothing else left for him. His last attempt to get out of this Germany of endlessly barked orders by stealing a passport from a police court office had led to another long sentence. He was only just out of jail – but into what? Living in East Berlin with his married sister and commuting to Potsdam every day to earn a crust!

If only he'd been in the army. If only . . . one day in a second-hand clothes shop he saw the uniform of a Prussian Captain of the Guards. The idea hit him. He had nothing to lose. So that evening, with his monthly wages received, he stepped into the shop and, as clipped and stiff as any officer, said he was a captain in the reserve and needed to try on the uniform in the window. And the shopkeeper bowed before his rank!

It didn't fit, but he felt transformed. He bought it for half his monthly wages. His great plan began to take shape. He watched the changing of the guard at the Kaiser's palace, taking in every detail, memorising commands. He tested his new role as Captain Voight by attending a brewery exhibition in uniform. On his way to it, the passing soldiers gave automatic salutes that he acknowledged with bored condescension. At the exhibition he found he commanded automatic respect because of his uniform and the haughty officer's demeanour which, he was delighted to find, came naturally to him.

The cobbler made a perfect captain – and decided to have his day of glory. For his battleground he chose nearby Köpenick, a small town where one evening by rail he went in his uniform to familiarise himself with the territory. Two days later he woke up and put his plan into action. Putting on his working clothes, he breakfasted with his sister, then went out to catch the Potsdam train. Once in the station, he ducked into the toilet and donned his uniform. Out came Wilhelm Voight, Captain of the Guards.

He needed a squad of troops under his command to carry out his scheme, but they couldn't be from Köpenick. So he went to the other end of Berlin, to Plötzensee in the north-west. He'd spent years in the hard-labour prison there. He knew there was a military swimming pool used by small units of soldiers from local barracks. Leaving a closed cab, he steeled himself. As Captain Voight he marched round a corner – into a detachment of five soldiers under a corporal. 'Halt!' His alter ego took over. 'Where from? Where to?' He was in instant command. Four grenadiers swung round the corner. He commandeered them too. 'This unit is now under my command!' he snapped. 'Fix bayonets.'

And they obeyed. It was natural. Who'd question a uniform? He marched them to the railway station, bought tickets for Köpenik at the reduced military rate, and bought his men beer and sausages. So in mid-afternoon he reached Köpenick with his army. It was a quiet place, with few people about. Marching his column into the Town Hall Square, he gave his orders: one man to guard each of the three Town Hall doors, nobody to enter or leave. With the corporal and the other six men, he marched straight in and up to the office of the burgomaster, Dr Landerhans – and arrested him on the Kaiser's orders. He must prepare to leave for Berlin immediately. It was not permitted to say why.

Voight had to act fast. Leaving two men to guard the thunderstruck mayor, he marched down to the office of the Inspector of Police, shook the man awake, chided him for dozing on duty, then sent him down to the square to prevent disturbances. Next he led his squad to the town treasurer's office, and arrested this man too, telling him to balance his books immediately. The treasurer said he could do so only on the burgomaster's orders – so Voight explained the situation. The treasurer backed down.

By now there was a large crowd in the square below. He saw a mounted police officer arguing with one of 'his' guards, brush the bayonet aside, and force his way past. Voight went down to meet the officer on the staircase. The man was the deputy police chief of nearby Teltow, out exercising his horse. Explaining that his special mission involved irregularities in the management of Köpenick, Voight easily won him over.

'Will you help your incompetent Köpenick colleague keep that rabble quiet?'

'Sir!' The policeman clicked heels and marched out.

Returning to the treasurer's office, Voight found the books balanced at last. They were all neat and clean down to the last pfennig. There was the cash on the table – 4,002 marks and 37 pfennigs. 'Just put it in a bag, and make out a receipt,' he said. But he was disappointed. Not nearly as much as he'd hoped for. Yet all the same he took it, saluted the treasurer casually, then outside in the hall gave the corporal instructions as to what to do with the two villains when the military carriages came. There he left them.

Outside, the Teltow police officer cleared his way through the crowd. He scarcely acknowledged their curiosity, walked on, and reached the station just as the Berlin train pulled in. Recovering his civilian clothes from the left-luggage office in Berlin, he laid the captain's uniform to rest under floorboards in a deserted shed near his sister's home, and got back in time for supper. That night he slept well.

Meanwhile the burgomaster of Köpenick, his wife, and the treasurer had been brought to Berlin's *Neue Wache*, the military headquarters, where nobody had heard of them or knew what to do with them. Soon enough it became obvious that a uniformed impostor had duped an entire town. With Imperial Germany's reputation at stake, it was decided at the highest levels that the story could not be kept secret. The impostor must be arrested! The Kaiser himself followed the case. There was a reward of 2,500 marks.

Publication led to sardonic reaction. The radical press of Berlin made free play of how successfully the impostor had exposed the Teutonic obsession with obedience to rank and uniform. But who was he? For ten days the police sought. The uniform was found (the cockades on the peaked cap had been put the wrong way round, and nobody had even noticed!), 2,000 citizens were questioned – and at last the efficiency of the police led them to their man. With drawn pistols they burst into his room. The two thousand-mark notes were still in his pocket. Not resisting arrest, he said mildly that all he'd sought in Köpenick was a passport so he could leave this country where a uniform was everything and a man with a criminal record nothing.

The army couldn't gut him like it wanted. Meanwhile Europe roared. 'What an irresistible rogue he is,' said London's *Review of Reviews*, 'how simple, almost infantile his craft; how ludicrous his exploits! He kept the whole world laughing for a week – an exploit for which he deserves to be decorated and pensioned for life.' And another British journal (of course with pre-war tension building up, the British were specially delighted by this blow to Prussian military pride) suggested that Voigt should get the Nobel Prize: 'as a universal benefactor of humanity'.

Voight's trial opened in Berlin in December 1906. Again and again the tale of the passport he couldn't get came up. Here was a man who'd tried to break out of the vicious circle of his life in a thoroughly original way. Everybody sympathised. Sentencing him to four years, the judge shook Voight's hand and wished him luck. A model prisoner during his last jail sentence, Voight got the respect denied him all his life before. Released after just twenty months, on orders it was said from the Kaiser (who called him 'the lovable scoundrel'), he was endowed with a grant of a hundred marks a month for life by a wealthy Jewish lady of Berlin, while over a hundred women offered themselves as wives.

More interested in wearing his uniform again, Voight paraded his famous part on the music-hall stages of Germany. Everyone wanted to see him. Gaining his passport at last, his impresarios toured him over Europe then took him to America, where he played to the German population of New York and neighbouring areas. With his memoirs ghost-written as, 'How I became the Captain of Köpenick', he settled in Luxembourg just before the First World War, at last beyond reach of Prussian authority. There he died in 1922 – even as Harry **Domela**, another great impostor, was about to make Germany laugh all over again.[1]

1. Larsen, *op. cit.*, pp.93–106.

W

'An ambassador is an honest man sent
abroad to lie for his country.'

(Sir Henry Wotton (1568–1639))

WALKER, Thomas (20th century) (*LITERARY HOAXES*, *see also*
ZINOVIEV LETTER)
In 1934 the forger Thomas Walker nearly brought down a British
government. Claiming to be an American journalist who'd been investigating life in Soviet Russia, this suave, well-dressed con-man arrived in
England and set himself up at the American Club in Piccadilly in
London. With a passport showing he'd been in and out of Russia, and
gaining a letter of introduction from the American Trade Commissioner,
he had no difficulty interesting anti-Communist newspaper editors in his
articles, particularly those based on his experiences in famine-struck
Ukraine.

Whether he was paid, or worked just for himself, remains unclear. At
any rate, his con began when he hinted to the wife of a prominent British
politician that the then Prime Minister of Great Britain, Ramsay
MacDonald, had some years before been in 'treasonable communications
with the Russian government'.

Leader of the Labour Party, head of Britain's first two Labour
governments in the 1920s, now head of the 'National Government' (a
struggling coalition of Tories, Liberals, and some Labour MPs), Mac-
Donald had been a pacifist during the First World War (though no
coward: his visits to the front line were ignored by jingoists like Horatio
Bottomley when attacking him as such). Also he'd sympathised with
Russian revolutionary aspirations. Yet by the 1930s he was a moderate,
seen by opponents in his own party as more of a conservative than a
socialist. Now, with another general election approaching and the
National Government shaky, Walker had chosen a devastating time to
attack.

Contacting Lady Houston, a rich widow devoted to socialism's destruction, Walker told her of letters he had that 'proved' MacDonald's treachery. Rising to the bait, she paid him £5,000 for several of them. The first, typed on MacDonald's private writing paper from his home at Upper Frognal Lodge in North London, was to Grigori Sokolnikoff, Soviet Russia's first British ambassador. Dated 11 February 1926 and convincingly signed, it went as follows: 'The time does not seem ripe for the movement you suggest. Everything is to be gained by a few months' delay. You may count upon me to support you in your noble work.'

The second said: 'You must recognise that your Russian methods for serfdom and communism are not available for use here. Our British workman is more susceptable [sic] to worldly goods and material enticements. It is my wish that this country may follow in the same course that you have chosen, but we must have a more intelligent introduction.'

The third, dated 5 March 1926, the year of Britain's General Strike, was the real dynamite. Written by 'MacDonald' on House of Commons writing paper and addressed to Christian Rakovsky (a Soviet diplomatic agent in Britain between 1923 and 1925, then Ambassador to France), it said: 'Any change which is to readjust the reallocation of wealth in Great Britain and which is to establish a system of justice in settling the relation between services and rewards must be a sudden and violent change. I hope to see the day, not too far distant, when the King may follow the way of the Czar, but I do not feel optimistic about the results of the general action planned for May.'

Lady Houston excitedly showed her finds to one of MacDonald's main political opponents. Examining them more carefully, he decided the letters were brilliant forgeries. MacDonald's signature was especially well faked, but the content did not ring true. It was well known that the Prime Minister had a high regard for King George V. Scotland Yard began an inquiry which revealed that, while he'd been to Russia several times, Walker had a false passport, had escaped from New York's Sing Sing prison, and had paid none of his bills at the American Club.

Arrested, Walker denied that the letters were forgeries, but would not say how he'd got them, nor how he'd obtained MacDonald's personal writing paper. Imprisoned for a month for travelling on a false passport, he was deported back to New York, where the police awaited him. The story was suppressed. Persuaded not to publish, Lady Houston eventually turned the letters over to solicitors acting for MacDonald. None of it came out in open court and the newspapers never got hold of it. Yet Scotland Yard never did learn how Walker had got hold of MacDonald's writing paper – or if they did, they didn't say. The suspicion remains that it was an inside job, and that Walker had been paid by MacDonald's enemies to set it all up to end the career of the man Bottomley had called: 'the illegitimate son of a Scotch serving-girl.'[1]

1.   McCormick, *op. cit.*, pp.185–9.

WARBECK, Perkin (*c.*1474–99) (*IMPOSTORS*)

Having seized the English throne from **Richard III** in 1485, Henry VII – the first Tudor king – found himself plagued by bogus claimants to the crown. Perhaps he deserved it. He was a bit of a bogus claimant himself. Of these fakers, two stand out – Perkin Warbeck and Lambert Simnel (*c.*1477–1534).

Warbeck's imposture began when the Duchess of Burgundy, sister of Edward IV (king before Richard III), put out the rumour that her nephew, Richard Plantagenet, Duke of York, had escaped from the Tower of London. Of course Richard and his brother (the 'Princes in the Tower') were long dead, smothered in their sleep and secretly buried, but it wasn't hard to convince folk they might still be alive. With this rumour already circulating, her agents found a youth called Perkin Warbeck to play the part. Son of a Jew of Tournay who'd lived in London and been a favoured moneylender at court, Edward IV had stood as his godfather. There was even a rumour that Edward was Perkin's real father.

Groomed by the duchess, Warbeck was sent to Ireland to make his first showing as Duke Richard, and soon rallied support. The news reached the French king Charles who, about to declare war on Henry VII, invited Warbeck to Paris, where the impostor's bearing and personality impressed many. This success persuaded many English nobles and gentry to offer him their services against Henry, who immediately signed a treaty with Charles, one condition being that Warbeck leave French territory. Now protected by the Duchess of Burgundy at her own court, he had bestowed on him by her the honour of the White Rose of England. This persuaded many that his claim was genuine: how could the aunt mistake the identity of her nephew?

By now Henry was so alarmed that he created, for the first time in English history, a secret service, specifically to track down impostors and get evidence against them. With his spies infiltrating Warbeck's circle, many of the conspirators were caught, condemned, and executed. But Warbeck kept trying. A landing in Kent was repulsed, then back in Cork he found the Irish no longer enthusiastic, and so tried Scotland, where King James recognised him as 'the true Prince' and married him to a near relation, Lady Catherine Gordon. With two incursions into England both failing, Warbeck tried in vain to enlist the support of the Earl of Desmond in Cork, then landed in Cornwall, having heard of opposition to Henry there. With an army of 6,000 he marched to Exeter where, rejected by the citizenry with Henry's army nearing, his nerve broke and he fled. Promised a pardon, he gave himself up, but was betrayed and executed.

Luckier was Lambert Simnel, a baker's son with a striking personality who, about the year 1486, was groomed by an ambitious priest, Richard Simon, to play the role of another prince imprisoned in the tower, Edward, Earl of Warwick. Simnel not only had a remarkable resemblance to the prince, but was intelligent enough to play the part, while his detailed knowledge of the Earl's life and habits suggests coaching by members of the House of York, hostile to Henry. Simon was probably just their instrument. Like Warbeck later, Simnel went to Ireland to present himself to the Earl of Kildare and seek protection. With his story eagerly accepted by Yorkist supporters, he was lodged in Dublin Castle and publicly proclaimed King Edward VI. In London, Henry's reaction was to parade the real Earl of Warwick through the streets. This convinced the English (but not the Irish) that Simnel was a fake. And though he could have stayed secure in Ireland, Simnel decided to chance his luck. It was a bad idea. Crossing the Irish Sea with a small force, he was defeated and captured near Stoke-on-Trent. In this case, Henry proved magnanimous. Pardoning Simnel, he made him a scullion in the royal kitchen – and, knowing full well that one false move would finish him, Simnel caused no more trouble, later rising to the rank of a falconer in the king's service.[1]

1. McCormick, *op. cit.*, pp.7–11.

WARFARE (*See* **HOAXES IN WARFARE**)

WASHINGTON, George (1732–99) (*LITERARY HOAXES*)
'I cannot tell a lie', the first President of the USA is alleged to have said as a child, when asked by his father who'd damaged a valuable young English cherry tree in their garden; 'you know I cannot tell a lie. I did it with my hatchet.'

Washington never said anything of the sort nor even claimed that he had. This famous fable was invented for him after his death by Mason Locke Weems, an itinerant Bible salesman who knew how to please folk. Claiming in print to have been the rector of George Washington's Mount Vernon parish when the closest he'd got was to preach in a church eighteen miles away, when the great man died in December 1799 Weems seized his chance. 'Washington is gone!' he wrote to his publisher. 'Millions are gasping to read something about him. I am primed and cocked for 'em.'

So he was. His biographical sketch, *A History of the Life and Death, Virtues and Exploits of General George Washington*, soon appeared and sold like hot cakes. It said nothing of the hatchet and the cherry tree, of Washington's mother's dream presaging his success, or of his being found in prayer at Valley Forge. These tales first appeared in the fifth edition. By the ninth edition (1809), the 80-page pamphlet had grown into a 228-page book called *The Life of George Washington; with Curious Anecdotes Equally Honourable to Himself and Exemplary to his Young Countrymen.*

That they are *Curious* is undeniable. That they are *Honourable* is not. It only goes to show, yet again, that: 'History is the lie commonly agreed upon'. Of course, sometimes it takes men like Weems to invent the lie before History can agree on it.[1]

1. Lindskoog, *op. cit.*, pp.90–2.

WEILL, Joseph (1876–1976) (*CONMEN*)
One of the boldest of conmen, Joseph 'Yellow Kid' Weill (so called because he habitually wore yellow suits, ties, and canary yellow kid gloves) lived to be a centenarian before dying peacefully in a Chicago nursing home. Active in the trade for over half a century under such unlikely aliases as 'Sir John Ruskin Wellington', 'Count Ivan Ivarnoff', and even 'Prince Florizel of Bohemia', his scams earned him approximately $6 million dollars. This left enough for a comfortable retirement.

Inspiring the film *The Sting*, starring Robert Redford and Paul Newman, he preferred to bilk those as dishonest as himself. 'A truly honest man would never have fallen for any of my schemes,' he said, while reserving his most scathing comments for big businessmen and bankers. 'They are the biggest suckers in the world, because they are always looking for an easy way of making a quick dollar. Of all the people who can be conned, they are probably the easiest.'

Renting an abandoned bank, he hired billiards hall customers as tellers and filled money bags with lead discs. Convincing a soap manufacturer that he had established a bank, he conned the man into depositing a large sum of money at a high rate of interest. On another occasion he bought an abandoned quarry, then fired pellets of gold dust from a shot-gun into it. Spreading word that the land contained gold and that he meant to develop a mine, he sold shares to the greedy and gullible. The same tactic also succeeded on a stretch of the Chicago River. Most of his enterprises were short term, rarely lasting more than a week, though one of his bogus brokerage offices traded for nearly twenty years. Often caught, jailed forty-one times, he served only six years in all. Finally sentenced for twenty-six months in Atlanta for selling an oil well that gushed only water, on his release in 1941 he decided it was time to retire and enjoy the fruits of his labours . . . which he did, for the long last third of his life.[1]

1. McCormick, *op. cit.*, pp.189–91.

WELLES, George Orson (1915–85) (*MEDIA HOAXES*)

One of the most extraordinary mass panics of modern times occurred on 30 October 1938, when from New York the 'Mercury Theatre on the Air' broadcast a CBS radio adaptation of H.G. Wells' 1897 science fiction novel, *The War of the Worlds*. This chilling description of a Martian invasion of Earth was so realistic that millions believed it was actually happening. The man responsible was the amazing Orson Welles.

Born in Wisconsin as the second son of talented musical parents, Welles was a prodigy. Aged ten he'd delivered his first public lecture on art. At sixteen, on his own in Ireland, he'd joined the company of Dublin's famous Gate Theatre. In England he'd met George Bernard Shaw, then travelled in Spain and Morocco before, back in the USA at the ripe old age of eighteen, his *Everybody's Shakespeare* – a commentary on three of **Shakespeare**'s plays – made his name. Soon his orotund tones were popular on radio, both as *The Shadow* and as commentator on a news programme, *The March of Time*. Staging the first all-black production of *Macbeth* in New York's Harlem in 1935 and already famed as an actor, in 1937 he founded the Mercury Theatre – a classical repertory company for which he wrote, acted, designed, produced and directed. With the first production, *Julius Caesar*, a huge popular success, many other plays followed, on stage or on radio, the latter as the 'Mercury Theatre on the Air'. These included *A Tale of Two Cities*, *The Thirty-Nine Steps*, *Treasure Island* – and, of course, *The War of the Worlds*.

It nearly didn't happen. Originally scheduled for 30 October had been an adaptation of R.D. Blackmore's swashbuckling novel *Lorna Doone* – but a week before the broadcast Welles rejected the script as dull. He turned instead to another story to which the Mercury had rights – *The War of the Worlds*. Yet he disliked this script too. It used the novel's original date and locale – turn-of-the-century England. He decided to modernise the action and language, and set it in the USA. He wanted to air it on 30 October because that was Hallowe'en Eve – the ideal evening on which to spoof not only the radio public, but radio itself, which he regarded as far too serious for its own good.

But the spoof backfired.

For a month and more American radio had featured the ominous developments in Europe. The Nazis had annexed Austria; the English had been issued with gas-masks; the shadow of war loomed close. Few doubted that sooner or later the USA would become involved. People were nervous and on edge. Later, Welles denied meaning to cause a panic. Maybe his youth led him to misjudge the effect of presenting the drama via fake news bulletins, the names of real places and people, and terrified eyewitness accounts that might just be taken for real by listeners tuning in too late to hear the introductory disclaimer that what followed was a Mercury Theatre drama.

Few involved took the play seriously. Agreeing with scriptwriter Howard Koch that the play was unbelievable, Welles' secretary Augusta Weissberger told him that: 'It's all too silly. We're going to make absolute fools of ourselves'. Even so, when the script was submitted to the network, CBS disagreed. Changes had to be made, particularly in regard to the names of places and institutions. So up to the last moment Welles and Koch were rescripting the drama to make it less believable. They failed, even though programme listings in the Sunday papers had highlighted the fictional broadcast.

Exactly at 8 p.m. on Sunday, 30 October, announcer Dan Seymour went on the air. 'The Columbia Broadcasting System and its affiliated stations presents Orson Welles and "The Mercury Theatre on the Air" in *The War of the Worlds* by H.G. Wells,' he declared. Bernard Herrmann's Orchestra played twenty seconds of Tchaikovsky's First Piano Concerto, then Seymour introduced Welles, who delivered the sombre prologue. 'We know now,' said Welles in grave, scholarly tones, 'that in the early years of the twentieth century this world was being watched closely by intelligences greater than man's and yet as mortal as his own.'

This was followed by a weather report, then music, soon interrupted by a 'news' bulletin reporting gas explosions on the planet Mars. Played by Welles, 'Professor Pierson' of Princeton Observatory described what he saw through his telescope. Given the message of a seismograph registering a shock of 'almost earthquake intensity' within twenty miles of Princeton, Pierson assumed a large meteorite to be the cause. Following reports locating the 'huge, flaming' object at Grover's Mill near Trenton, New Jersey, a mobile broadcasting unit was sent to investigate. The programme, now eleven minutes old, cut back to dance music. A minute later on the rival *Charlie McCarthy Show* (with a third of the total radio audience), crooner Nelson Eddy began singing a light opera piece. Listeners began switching stations.

Later analysis suggested that twelve per cent of the McCarthy audience (about four million people) stopped at the CBS play in time to hear a seemingly authentic newscaster describe the scene at Grover's Mill. An odd object half-buried in a huge hole. A humming that came from it. The top unscrewing. The monster emerging! It had tentacles, a bear-sized body, black serpentine eyes, a V-shaped mouth from which saliva dripped! It sent out rays that made cars, barns, and people burst into flame! The newscaster's voice rose in terror – then, mysteriously, the report ceased, 'due to circumstances beyond our control'.

Six million people were listening. Many had switched too late to hear the initial disclaimer. The terror began when people heard that Martian poison gas was spreading over the East Coast. The CBS studio control room was phoned by a local police station already flooded by anxious calls. 'Of course it isn't real', the police were assured. But the calls continued. Forty-two minutes into the show, Dan Seymour broke into the broadcast to announce that it was only a show. But too late. Thousands of people, convinced that the Martians were coming, had already fled their homes. Some gathered in churches, others armed themselves. Everywhere, scared people were calling newspapers, radio stations, and the police, wanting to know how to escape the gas. The panic was worst in the Trenton area, barely twenty miles from Grover's Mill, with all highways gridlocked as people fled in their cars. A Rhode Island daily later reported how: 'weeping and hysterical women swamped the switchboard of the *Providence Journal* for details of the massacre and destruction at New York'. In Pittsburgh a man came home from work to find his wife about to poison herself. 'I'd rather die this way than like that!' she screamed. In the West Coast state of Washington, a power failure in the town of Concrete convinced many that the Martians were near. People who lived by the Hudson River, which the Martians were supposedly crossing, reported that they had actually seen the invading monsters. Staff at the *New York Herald Tribune* began donning gas-masks.

With the CBS studios now swamped by police, the show at last ended. Welles read a statement that the play was only: 'the Mercury Theatre's own radio version of dressing up in a sheet and jumping out of a bush and saying Boo! That grinning, globular invader of your living room is an inhabitant of the pumpkin patch, and if your doorbell rings and nobody's there, that was no Martian . . . it's Hallowe'en.' And at 9 p.m. on another network, commentator Walter Winchell also reassured several million listeners: 'Mr and Mrs America, there's no cause for alarm. America has *not* fallen; I repeat, America has *not* fallen.'

At midnight Welles saw, on the lighted bulletin circling the Times building in New York's Times Square, this message: 'ORSON WELLES CAUSES PANIC.' By next day he was an international celebrity. Called to a CBS press conference, he expressed his regret and bewilderment. There were rumours that he might be barred from radio and even face criminal charges. In England, the ageing H.G. Wells was furious at the changes made to his novel, and even more so at claims that he'd been involved in the production so as to create publicity for his new novel, *Apropos of Dolores*. Damage suits amounting to $750,000 were filed against Welles and CBS by listeners claiming injuries caused by their belief in the broadcast. These were settled out of court. For weeks, newspaper editorials held forth. As for the Princeton University study into the hysteria, it concluded that some two million people had believed in the broadcast, typically those badly educated and/or from the southern states. Published, the script as written by Welles and Koch sold half a million copies.

Welles assured CBS that no such jape would ever occur again. Now famous the world over, 'The Man from Mars' later refused to stage a production of *The War of the Worlds*. He'd had enough of science fiction.

Instead, he went to Hollywood to make *Citizen Kane*, which got him into more trouble for its irreverent depiction of the newspaper magnate William Randolph **Hearst**.[1]

The postscript? This one belongs to the believe-it-or-not category. A year later the production, in translation, was broadcast in Brazil.

The result? You guessed it. Mass hysteria and panic.

1. *Citizen Welles*, Frank Brady, Hodder & Stoughton, London 1990.

WEYMAN, Stanley (1891–?) (*IMPOSTORS*)
Aka Royal St Cyr, S. Clifford Weinberg, Ethan Allen Weinberg, Rodney S. Wyman, Sterling C. Wyman, and C. Sterling Weinberg, this quick-change artist with as many aliases as **Demara** was born Stanley Wein-burg in Brooklyn. A small man of poor immigrant background who rejected his drab clerk's life to ply the trade of conman and hoaxer, like **Voight** he loved masquerading in uniform and knew all about the inside of jails. Persuasive, witty and authoritative, whether as US consul delegate to Morocco, Serbian military attaché or Romanian consul general, he was never averse to running up bills in the best restaurants, nor to borrowing the hoaxes of others. In the latter role in 1915 he emulated **Cole**'s *Dreadnought* prank by being officially toured round the USS *Wyoming*. Donning the pale blue uniform of the 'Romanian Consul General', he was met at the quayside by a launch, inspected a guard of honour with the Romanian flag flying beside Old Glory, and was wined and dined in the officer's wardroom. Requiring that the world recognise his cleverness, he booked a room at New York's Astor Hotel having first publicly announced that the Navy's hospitality so pleased him that he wished to repay them with a slap-up banquet – for himself. Halfway through the entrée when arrested, and after time inside, he ran through a succession of identities before in 1921 pulling off his greatest hoax. This began when he learned that White House officials had refused to offer a presidential audience to Afghanistan's visiting Princess Fatima.

Posing as Lieutenant-Commander Rodney Sterling Wyman, the State Department Naval Liaison Officer (a non-existent post), Weyman called on the fabulously rich princess in her suite at the Waldorf Astoria. He was, he said, to arrange her visit to Washington and reception by President Harding. Phoning the State Department, who told him to get on with it, he told the Princess that of course in cases like this cash presents were customary, to buy 'gifts for high officials'. The princess understood perfectly and, for the privilege of meeting the president, shelled out over $10,000. And the fake protocol officer did his job. Finding hotel accommodation in Washington for the princess and her three sons, in spotless uniform he got them all the way into the Oval Office of the White House. With President in dress suit and Princess in white robes, snapshots were taken on the White House lawn. The princess got what she wanted, and so did Weyman.

His impostures varied. Hired as an assistant by renowned Viennese surgeon Dr Adolf Lorenz, the career of 'Dr Weyman' ended only when his lack of medical knowledge became too obvious. Next he was a popular, party-throwing medical consultant sent to Peru by an oil exploration company. Deciding Hollywood needed him, as Valentino's doctor he helped arrange the funeral of this idol of the silent screen, then became personal physician to the smouldering Pola Negri (*see* **Hollywood Hoaxes**). Trying his hand at being a lawyer, he was twice jailed for practising without a licence, leading him to conclude that it was easier and safer to find employment as a lecturer in medicine or law. During the Second World War, he was a 'selective service consultant', advising how to avoid being drafted into the military. He and nine of his clients were drafted into jail instead. After the war he became a journalist. This suited him down to the ground. In 1948, employed by a news agency as their United Nations correspondent, he became so well known at New York's UN headquarters that he was offered the post of press officer to the Thai delegation. But calling the State Department to ask if accepting the post would affect his rights as a US citizen was a mistake. The State Department found it had a fat file on Stanley Weyman, and was not amused. End of career in journalism. After that it was all downhill.[1]

But it's hard not to like him. He had his heart in the right place. Posing as a prison expert, at New York's Sing Sing jail he delivered a harangue against capital punishment, and at Middlesex University in England lectured on the topic: 'Insanity: its defence in crime'. During this lecture he suggested that all prison psychiatrists be 'subjected to a searching mental examination.'[2]

No doubt there was plenty of personal experience behind that remark.

1. Yapp, *op. cit.*, pp.57–8.
2. Madison, *op. cit.*, pp.115–17.

WHITE BROTHERHOOD OF KIEV (*FAKE MESSIAHS*)

The new post-Communist world east of what was once the Iron Curtain may not be so new after all. In Ukraine's capital Kiev in November 1993 erupted a religious panic of medieval intensity following the announcement by Maria Devi Khrystos, figurehead of the apocalyptic cult called the White Brotherhood, that the End was Nigh. Riot police flooded the streets, not least to stop thousands of hysterical, possibly brainwashed teenagers killing themselves in a central square, while their equally hysterical parents sought them.

A former journalist with the young Communist movement, Marina Tsvgun had met her Svengali-like mentor Yuri Krivonogov only a year earlier. Hearing that she'd seen God when close to death during an abortion, the hypnotic Krivonogov promptly married her then toured her through Russia and Ukraine. Posters depicted her as 'living god Maria Devi Khrystos'; leaflets proclaimed Kiev as the new Calvary, shifted thence from Palestine by the motion of tectonic plates. Gathering young followers everywhere (many fleeing their homes to make for Kiev), early in 1993 the hypnotic duo proclaimed that the world would end on 24 November. From points as far away as Murmansk and Sverdlovsk north of the Arctic Circle, desperate parents tracked their missing children as the cultists converged on Kiev. With the date for the end brought forward to 14 November, Krivonogov predicted soothingly that: 'There will be no explosions, only giant earthquakes and turmoil.'

Even with Krivonogov and his wife finally arrested for this enormous **end-of-the-world** scam; even with mass suicide prevented and the hour past without terminal convulsions, relatives of the missing children found little consolation. Horrific tales of brain-washing with drugs and of recruitment by handing out poisoned sweets abounded in Kiev. It was said Krivonogov (a scientific mystic variously called a cyberneticist, yoga teacher, and telepathist) had worked for the Soviet military, producing hypnotic drugs for use in psychological warfare. Whatever the real truth behind the panic and rumours, it was clear to many alarmed observers that the Soviet state had not destroyed but only suppressed a more ancient Slavic soul – passionately religious, given to austerity, superstition, even to extreme self-mutilation. As late as 1800 the *Khlysty* (flagellants) and *Skoptzy* (self-castrated) had roamed the land. Now, with former certainties all gone in the post-Communist world, millions of vulnerable people – especially the young – were suddenly wide open to hoaxers (or self-hoaxers) like Tsvygun and Krivonogov, leaders of the White Brotherhood of Kiev.[1]

1. 'Hold the front page – this could be our very last edition,' Matthew Campbell, *Sunday Times*, 14 November 1993.

WILD ANIMAL HOAX (*MEDIA HOAXES*)
As prominent as the **Herschel Hoax** and the inventions of Louis T. **Stone** in the annals of American newspaper hoaxes is the Wild Animal Hoax. This was perpetrated on 9 November 1874 when the *New York Herald* published a detailed eyewitness account of a disaster at the Central Park Zoo, where all the animals had escaped. Two hundred people had been injured, 60 seriously; and of the 49 dead the names of 27 were listed. Twelve dangerous animals were still at large when the paper went to press. The mayor warned people to stay inside until the beasts, in the area of Fifth and Broadway, were hunted down. With many readers panic-stricken, the owner of the *Herald* remained in bed all day, shocked by the news.

But those reading the article all the way through learned in the final paragraph that the *Herald*'s managing editor had asked for this fictitious piece to be written to highlight the need for improvements in the zoo's security.

WILKENING, David (contemporary) (*LITERARY HOAXES*)

Disgusted by the gory bestseller *American Psycho*, in 1991 Florida journalist David Wilkening tried an experiment. Taking Marjorie Kinan Rawlings' 1938 bestseller *The Yearling*, he typed out an outline and its first three chapters, and under his own name submitted it to twenty-two publishers. These included Scribner's, the original publisher of this much-loved, Pulitzer Prize-winning tale of a Florida boy and his pet fawn. Made into a 1946 movie starring Gregory Peck, it remains in wide library circulation – but apparently the editor at Scribner's who rejected Wilkening's proposal had never heard of it. Called by Associated Press after Wilkening had revealed the hoax, she said: 'We don't spend a lot of time on any one manuscript', and hung up when asked if she'd ever read *The Yearling*

Of the other twenty-one publishers, twelve rejected it outright and eight didn't even bother answering. The classic was recognised only once; by the owner of tiny Pineapple Press. 'We caught it in the first few pages because it was so obvious,' he remarked.[1]

1. Lindskoog, *op. cit.*, p.63.

WILLIAMS, Edward (*See* MORGANWG, Iolo)

WILLIAMSON GANG, The (*CONMEN*)

Arriving in Brooklyn from Scotland in 1895, to this day the Williamson family are America's most proficient 'con clan', swooping on towns and cities to fleece the gullible before quickly moving on. Comprising within their incestuous ranks the families Stewart, Gregg, Johnston, Keith, McMillan, McDonald and Reid, and keeping very much to themselves, this 250-strong gypsy-like tribe roams the land in luxury cars and RVs, and prefers to live in trailer parks where privacy is assured. Provoking fights and violence wherever they go, and using a number of basic but lucrative scams like faulty driveway or roof repair, or sloppy house-painting, they split all their loot among themselves, keeping back one share for the clan boss, who usually stays at home in Ohio.

How do they work it? Targeting one house, they do a good job with proper materials and for a reasonable fee, then tour neighbouring streets, telling potential victims that they have enough materials left over from the job they just did to do one more house for next to nothing. With dozens of suckers falling for the cut-rate offer, each thinking they're the only one to get it, the clan works the scam, but takes care to do so only in good weather. Why? Because rain washes away the 'asphalt' or paint thinned by crank-case oil. Also selling fake lightning rods and a whole range of bogus goods, the clan has been called the 'Terrible Williamsons' since 1938, when a law-abiding cousin exposed their activities to the Pittsburgh Better Business Bureau. Since then their tactics and pattern of movement have become so well known that when they turn up in large cities the police warn people through the media while trying to persuade the clan to move on. Avoiding New England, where they've been jailed for selling without a licence, their favoured Land of Opportunity has long been Southern California. Temporarily enrolling their children in public schools, they enjoy warm winter weather and drought conditions which ensure that for months few customers notice the shoddiness of the workmanship – and by the time the rains do come, the Williamsons are again long gone . . . [1]

1. Madison, *op. cit.*, pp.187–91.

WILSON, Sarah (1754–?) (*IMPOSTORS*)

Leaving her native Staffordshire village and arriving in London aged sixteen, this ambitious, nimble, quick-witted girl was lucky. Within weeks she was engaged as maid to Miss Caroline Vernon, a lady-in-waiting to the Queen, and so early in 1771 found herself in the 'Queen's House' (on the site of the present Buckingham Palace). Here she saw a lot of Queen Charlotte, wife of the Hanoverian king George III, heard all the gossip and scandals, and soon grew so used to her good fortune that envy began to replace admiration. These Court people enjoyed the good life without having to do a stroke of work, yet they were no better than her, not much better educated, and certainly no more intelligent.

Perhaps she acted on impulse when, finding herself alone in the Queen's closet, she went through the dressing-table drawers and removed jewels, earrings, a pendant, a gold ring, a miniature portrait of the Queen, even one of Her Majesty's many dresses. Maybe she thought that, as the Queen had so many jewels, the theft would go undetected. If so, she was wrong. The Queen noticed that items were missing and asked for a watch to be kept on the closet. A few days later Sarah was caught red-handed. Justice was swift. Charged with theft and violation of the royal privacy, the death sentence was commuted to deportation. So in July 1771, still only seventeen, a prison ship took her to Baltimore, Maryland. Put up for sale and bought by a Mr W. Devall of Bush Creek, Frederick County, she soon ran away.

Amazingly, in her bundle of personal belongings she still had some of the items stolen from the Queen, including a dress, a ring, and the miniature portrait. With these props she now proceeded to become 'Princess Susanna Caroline Matilda, sister of Queen Charlotte', who'd quarrelled with her family and gone into American exile following a scandal. The deception was naturally aided by her high-flown speech and behaviour, and by her intimate knowledge of what actually went on in the English Court.

The first to invite 'Princess Susanna' to stay was a Virginian land-owner named Smyth. Exciting notice with her pert beauty and her fund of gossip about the scandalous goings-on in upper class English society, soon there was competition for her presence. 'She travelled from one gentleman's house to another,' observed the *Annual Register*, 'and made astonishing impressions in many places, affecting the mode of royalty so inimitably, that many had the honour to kiss her hand.'

These, of course, were the years immediately before the War of Independence, yet the southern colonies were far less rebellious than those in the north, and there was little republican spirit in the gorgeous white mansions where 'Princess Susanna' held court. With all assuming that sooner or later she'd be restored to favour in London, many offered her money and gifts, which she graciously accepted, assuring the donors that she'd do all she could to grant their wishes. 'To some she promised governments, to others regiments, with promotions of all kinds in the treasury, Army, and Royal Navy. In short, she acted her part so plausibly, as to persuade the generality that she was no impostor.'

Some *were* suspicious. How was it that nobody had ever heard of the Queen's younger sister? And why, as she was German-born, did she refuse to speak German? For that matter, why was her English so good? It was widely known that even though they'd ruled in England for three generations, the Hanoverians still hadn't mastered the language. But she got away with it until her owner, Mr Devall, hearing that a girl answering her description was touring about posing as a princess, circulated an advertisement advising all who read it that 'Princess Susanna' was in fact his servant girl. Also he sent an employee, Michael Dalton, to track her down. Finding her on a plantation near Charles-town, at pistol-point he induced her to surrender and follow him back to slavery in Bush Creek.

'How distressing to behold a lady of these exalted pedigree preten-sions, thus surprised at the hands of her inexorable enemies!' exclaimed the editor of the *Annual Register*. But Sarah Wilson wasn't finished yet. For two years she worked quietly and patiently for Devall, but when the opportunity to escape arose, she grasped it. First came the coincidence that another slave girl named Sarah Wilson had arrived in Maryland; then Devall joined the militia and left to fight for American liberty. Somehow managing to substitute the new Sarah Wilson for herself, this time she got away for good, and made a good marriage, to William Talbot, a Cornet with the Light Dragoons. Following him through the campaigns, when the war was over she persuaded him to stay in the fledgling USA. Using the money from her royal career to set him up successfully in business, she bore him a large family. Settling in the

Bowery, then a respectable part of New York, by all accounts they lived happily ever after.[1]

1. Larsen, *op. cit.*, pp.52–7.

'WINEGATE' (*FRAUD*)

In 1973 eighteen of France's most distinguished wine merchants perpetrated an $800,000 swindle on the world's wine drinkers. Finding themselves that year with too little wine from the normally bountiful Bordeaux region, rather than take the loss they banded together (some say protected by the then Premier Chauban-Delmas) to ensure their interests. Led by Lionel Cruse, head of the shipping and bottling firm of Cruse et Fils, Frères, they blended cheap white wine with red, so producing an acceptable red, but failing to mention it was a blend (blends sell for a lower price than pure wines). Sadly for them, the scam didn't work. The news was leaked. The wine industry and France as a whole was shocked. The shame of it, in an industry where reputation and probity matter as much as content. The government seized 1.9 million bottles of tampered blended Bordeaux and also impounded 382,000 gallons of wine still in the vats. And that, after over a century in the business, was the end of Cruse et Fils, Frères.[1]

1. Madison, *op. cit.*, pp.185–7.

WINSTANLEY, Jenny (*See* LLOYD, Sophie)

WISE, Thomas James (1859–1937) (*LITERARY HOAXES*)

Starting his career as an office boy and later a partner in the same firm, and like **Ireland**'s father a keen book collector, this prolific forger made a name for himself as an expert on antique books and as a finder of rare first editions. After he died, his Ashley Library collection of these was bought for £60,000 by the British Museum.

The 1880s saw the emergence of many author-study groups. Carlyle, Dickens, Ruskin, Shelley, Swinburne, Thackeray and Tennyson all had a society devoted to their work. Such groups sponsored the publication of facsimile reprints of first editions at affordable prices. Sometimes these were 'type facsimiles', editions mirroring every detail of the original's typography; and Wise had already experience of these when the Shelley Society put him in charge of its reprints. Spending three-quarters of the Society's funds on reprinting thirty-three books during the year 1887–8, he soon realised the potential for exploiting his knowledge to his own advantage.

Starting by pirating some Shelley poems for a non-existent American society, his technique was simple: he reproduced facsimiles of first editions, which was legal enough, but left out his own name and imprint and any mention that the product was a facsimile. So he could pass it off as a genuine 'first edition'. Specialising in early nineteenth-century works, he duped even his printer, Richard Clay & Sons, who had no way of knowing, when instructed to print a genuine early year on the title page, that this was to support a forgery. With the books in hand, it was then just a matter of treating them to suggest age.

Working with Harry Buxton Forman (1842–1917), for years Wise kept up his output of bogus first editions. From first editions of dead authors like Wordsworth, Tennyson, and Dickens, he went on to forge those of the living – Kipling, Morris, Ruskin, Stevenson, Swinburne. He was never suspected until in his seventies, when at last the truth emerged about his 'discovery' of a small volume of poems by Elizabeth Barratt Browning, entitled *Sonnets by E.B.B. Reading [Not for Publication.] 1847*. These had ostensibly been published by her friend, Mary Mitford, dead by the time that Wise first claimed to have obtained copies from a Dr Bennett, who'd died soon after. Backing up this tale with invented 'evidence' based on his study of the Brownings, he had sold one copy in New York for £250. The exposure began in 1932, when two booksellers, John Carter and Graham Pollard, noted that some apparently rare works kept turning up far too often. Starting with the *Sonnets*, they subjected the volume to a battery of tests, showing that the paper contained esparto grass, only in use in England since 1861, and also chemical wood made by a process unknown before 1874. The printed text was traced to a fount dating from 1876.

They approached Wise, but his only reply was to give a muddled account of how he'd found the *Sonnets*. When a full explanation was demanded, his wife shielded him, pleading that he was ill. Soon afterwards, he was dead. It remains unknown how many such forgeries he perpetrated, though at least another fifty faked first editions have since been attributed to Forman and Wise.[1]

1. Newnham, *op. cit.*, pp.124–6.

WOODS, Dorothy Mae (contemporary) (*FRAUD*)
Antonio Jiminez **Moreno**'s success as a welfare cheat in France in the 1960s was equalled in the 1970s by the flamboyant career of a young black woman, since dubbed the 'US Welfare Queen'. A sharecropper's daughter from Hermanville, Mississippi, aged sixteen Dorothy Mae had married a Chicago numbers runner and alleged drug dealer. Soon his income brought them and their eight children a Spanish-style mansion in Pasadena, California; three luxury cars; and all the designer clothes she could wear. It wasn't enough. Not even her many trips to Las Vegas satiated her desire for excitement. It's unclear when she first turned to crime, but around 1970 the city of Chicago came after her for fraudulent use of stolen credit cards. Suspecting that she and a confederate had

charged over $500,000 in merchandise, the district attorney's office went for prosecution on under $250,000, none of it ever recovered. Serving six months of a two-year sentence, and paroled on condition that she leave Illinois immediately and never return to Chicago, she was glad to return to her mansion in Pasadena – but then her husband deserted her, leaving her with the children but no income.

She needed cash, fast. But rather than sell any of her possessions, she turned to welfare fraud on a huge scale. 'It never occurred to me to liquidate instead of perpetuate, and my need became a greed,' she told the media later when her audacity became headline news. 'Besides, there was no way I could let go of my fancy lifestyle. That would have been too embarrassing.' So, refusing to sell mansion, Rolls-Royce, Cadillac, or Mercedes, she filed for state and county welfare, claiming the servants' quarters in a shack behind the mansion as her only residence. Because of her eight children, the pay-out was substantial. After all, she looked the part – a plump black woman in rags and a cheap wig, ashamed at being forced to beg for public money.

Of course it wasn't enough. Reasoning that as most welfare workers were white or Hispanic they couldn't tell one black woman from another, and posing as Dorothy Palmer, she filed a second claim at a different county office, giving an address in one of the low-rent Los Angeles slum apartment buildings she owned. This worked so well that soon she was claiming for herself and her children on a total of six fake identities. Pausing only to remarry in 1974 to real estate executive John Woods, she added another six aliases and a total of forty-nine children to her welfare portfolio. Blank birth certificates for herself and her non-existent children were created by Xeroxing the originals and erasing the names and dates. She then typed in new data as required. She had driver's licences, Social Security cards, and other necessary identification under all twelve aliases, each with a different caseworker. Not one of these aliases was ever questioned. When faced with a visit by a welfare officer at one of her slum apartment addresses, she'd 'borrow' neighbourhood children to augment her own. Spending the money as fast as it came in, weekend trips to Las Vegas became a commonplace. Her new husband, who claimed he had nothing to do with the actual fraud, was happy to help her spend the loot – and for years they enjoyed themselves even as she had another five children of her own – making thirteen real children to augment the forty-nine fictitious ones.

It all fell apart in 1980, when a friend visiting the mansion saw welfare cheques lying on a desk and tried to blackmail the couple. When they refused to pay up, she turned them in. But by the time the police turned up, Dorothy Mae had vanished with the children, leaving husband John to carry the can. Fleeing to Jamaica, she installed eight of her kids in a $12,000-a-month apartment, and enrolled them in a private school. For a year, while accumulating evidence for a grand jury indictment, nobody could find her – until, yet again, there was an anonymous tip-off. When she refused to return to California voluntarily, the Jamaican government had her forcibly put on a Miami-bound plane. Greeted at the airport with a federal warrant, she was extradited to California and sentenced to eight years in jail. Her husband received a lesser sentence. The Wood's fortune, estimated at $2.4 million, was confiscated. During her nine-year imposture, from 1971 to 1980, Dorothy Mae Woods had received $377,458 in welfare cash and an unknown amount in food stamps and free medical aid. When her assets were seized, the authorities found $14,000 of uncashed welfare cheques and $100,000 in food stamps and medical benefits. Nobody else had ever taken the US welfare system for such a ride.[1]

1. Madison, *op. cit.*, pp.107–15.

WOODWARD, Arthur Smith (*See* **FOSSIL FORGERIES**)

X

'Almost all people of all eras are hypnotics.
Their beliefs are induced beliefs.'

(Charles Hoy Fort)

X-RAY-PROOF UNDERWEAR HOAX (*SCIENTIFIC SCAMS*)
Never let anyone tell you that the Victorians didn't have sex on the
brain. No sooner in 1895 had the German physicist Wilhelm Konrad
Roentgen discovered the existence of X-rays than a rumour began to
spread among prim and proper English ladies that a company planned to
manufacture X-ray glasses that would let dirty old (and young) men see
right through their clothes! Naturally they were so scandalised by this
prospect that, when another manufacturer marketed 'X-ray-proof'
underwear to thwart the awful threat, they rushed to buy. The underwear manufacturer (and a leading department store) both made a fortune
before the myth was exploded. As for the X-ray glasses, they never
appeared, and, though it was never proved, the common belief was that
– guess who? – the underwear manufacturer had originated the rumour.[1]

1. *Hoaxes and Scams*, Carl Sifakis, Facts on File, New York 1993,
   p.290.

Y

'Most writers regard the truth as their most
valuable possession, and are therefore most
economical in its use.'

(Mark Twain)

YAZOO LAND FRAUDS (*FRAUD*)

Late in the eighteenth century the Yazoo territories in west Georgia
extended to the Mississippi River and comprised the present states of
Alabama and Mississippi. In 1789 members of the Georgia legislature
permitted the sale of over twenty-five million acres of rich Yazoo lands to
three land companies for just $273,580, and six years later sold another
thirty-five million acres to four other companies for only half a million
dollars. The cost per acre was thus barely over one cent. Though
claiming to be thus enriching the dirt-poor state treasury before being
forced to cede the land to the US government, in fact (big surprise!) the
politicians were enriching themselves. How? Because the land companies in turn sold shares for next to nothing back to the legislators, who
thus made big profits when tracts were sold to cotton farmers and
northern investors. Also, it later emerged, they had even bribed each
other to make sure the bills went through, and had approved the sale of
warrants to much more land than actually existed.

When this all came out, the politicians involved were lucky to escape
lynching. In 1796 a new legislature revoked the original deals but, with
property deeds now utterly confused, greedy agents went on selling
tracts to suckers in New England and elsewhere. Many purchasers were
ruined, and, when in 1802 Georgia ceded the disputed territories to the
USA, the state stipulated that the federal government take responsibility
for all claims arising from the initial sales. Yet the Virginia Representa-
tive John Randolph fought tooth and nail to stop Congress granting relief
to those who held the lands (many of whom were innocent parties known
locally as 'widows' and 'orphans'); so that in 1810 the Supreme Court

unanimously decided that the original grants were valid, and that the Georgia legislature's later efforts to rescind the deals violated constitutional obligations on contracts. Thus when in 1814 Congress awarded the shareholders $4.7 million in relief for losing their lands, the original swindle was officially validated by the highest court in the land.

YETI (*ALIEN ANIMALS*)

Also known as the 'Abominable Snowman', this best known of various hairy man-apes unknown to science is said to survive in remote high regions in the Himalayas. As with the **Loch Ness Monster**, the sole evidence for the existence of such a creature comes from sightings by local folk or mountaineers – leading many a sceptic to suspect that the yeti exists only in the imagination of hoaxers or those suffering from altitude sickness.

Yet the Nepalese say there are three kinds of yeti: the small *yeh-teh*, the large *meh-teh*, and the giant *dzu-teh*. Local reports are legion. The abbot of Thyangboche monastery under Mount Everest matter-of-factly tells of yeti often visiting the monastery gardens.[1] In 1974 a Sherpa girl, Lakhpa Domani, allegedly met a yeti while tending yaks at Pheriche in Nepal. It was a big apelike creature with black and red-brown hair, prominent cheekbones and large eyes. It carried her off, but dropped her when she struggled, then attacked the yaks, killing two before making off. Again, in January 1987, a youth in northern Kashmir is said to have been attacked by a two-legged, hairy creature about four foot tall. It ran off, squealing, after he hit it with his fire-pot. Two other villagers witnessing its flight said it jumped a ditch in a manlike way.[2]

In 1832 the Resident British Officer in Nepal described how his porters had fled a hairy beast they called the *rakshas*, 'demon'. Later they told him that similar wild men had been known and feared for centuries.[3] Westerners saw footprints in 1887, as did a British army officer 21,000 feet up Everest in 1921. F.S. Smythe's 1937 photographs of yeti prints were taken at 16,500 feet, and in 1951, crossing the Melung glacier, British climber Eric Shipton found and photographed tracks in the snow. His photos showed a footprint as long as his ice-axe, with definite toe-formation – *too* definite, claim sceptics. It may be that his account began as a joke but that he maintained it when he found it taken seriously. Even so, his partner, surgeon Michael Ward, insisted that the spoor was authentic (though it may be remembered that another surgeon was involved in the 1934 Loch Ness hoax).

Still the reports came in. On Annapurna in 1970, climber Don Whillans saw prints in the snow. Later in bright moonlight he looked out of his tent and through binoculars saw a black ape-like beast, then: 'quite suddenly . . . as if it realised it was being watched it shot across the whole slope of the mountain'.[4] In 1972 an American expedition found prints so clear they made plaster-casts. A year later Lord Hunt, leader of the 1953 British Everest expedition, found footprints; photos he took in 1978 show prints fourteen inches long and seven inches wide. He believes in: 'an unidentified creature still to be discovered'.

No yeti bodies have been found. The 'yeti scalps' found in some Himalayan monasteries are probably made from goatskin, created to represent the yeti in ritual dances. But whether lack of yeti bodies proves non-existence of yeti is problematic. Gorillas and orang-utans are not regarded as mythical, because they have been shot, captured, and so on. If it exists, the yeti is a shy creature living in a wilderness at great height – and for its own sake it's probably best that it stays there, beyond reach of *homo sapiens*.

1. *Arthur Clarke's Mysterious World*, Simon Welfare and John Fairley, Fontana, London 1982, p.19.
2. *Modern Mysteries of the World*, Janet and Colin Bord, Grafton, London 1989.
3. *The Directory of Possibilities*, eds Colin Wilson and John Grant, Corgi, London 1982.
4. *op. cit.*, note 2, p.199.

Z

'Peace is at hand.'

(Henry Kissinger, during the Vietnam War)

ZINOVIEV LETTER (*FRAUD*)

In 1934 the literary forger Thomas **Walker** nearly brought down a British government by making out Prime Minister Ramsay MacDonald to be a Soviet agent. But ten years earlier, the so-called 'Zinoviev Letter' actually had destroyed MacDonald and his Labour Government, the first ever to be elected. Appearing just four days before the 1924 General Election, which in any case the Tories were expected to win, the fraud effectively sank Labour, which had already recognised Soviet Russia and had been seeking commercial treaties with the USSR. Allegedly written by Gregory Zinoviev, president of the Third Communist International, it incited the British Communist Party to violence, sedition, and subversion of the British armed forces. Published in the *Daily Mail* on 25 October 1924, it appeared too late for adequate disclaimers, and unleashed a 'red scare' throughout the land. On printing the forgery, the *Mail*'s editorial declared:

> That such a document should have been held back until
> the very last moment of the election campaign is another
> sign that the government has a bad conscience in the
> matter. And well it might have! The country now knows
> that Moscow issues orders to the British Communists and
> they are obeyed by the Communists here. British
> Communists, in turn, give orders to the Socialist govern-
> ment, which it [*sic*] tamely and humbly obeys.

Obviously the *Mail*'s editorial writer was no stronger on logic than grammar, but it mattered not: the damage was done, and the Conservatives were elected. And though for years leaders of the Labour Party and the Soviet government both continued to insist that the letter was a fake, it was not until 1966 that the *Sunday Times* effectively established that a group of White Russian émigrés were behind the forgery. It also emerged, forty years too late, that, though many Tory voters and party officials had honestly been taken in, some Tory leaders had known all along that the letter was a fake – and had kept quiet.

Concordance of Themes

Entries are listed under the following categories:

Alien Animals
Art Forgeries
Conmen and Fraud
Conmen, Counterfeiters, Fraud, Fraud in Sport, Political Fraud, Sexual Cons, Super-Salesmen
Disappearances
Exploration Hoaxes
Fake Messiahs (*see also* **Religions and Cults**)
Historical Hoaxes
Hoaxes in Warfare
Imaginary Lands and Make-Believe
Impostors
20th Century, 19th Century, 18th Century and before, Fake Professors, Literary Impostors, Royal Impostors, Sexual Impostors
Literary Hoaxes
Modern, 19th Century, Pre-1800, Medieval and Ancient
Media Hoaxes and Pranks
Hoaxes in Journalism, On Radio and TV, Pranks, Telephone Hoaxes, Theatre
Paranormal Hoaxes
Religions and Cults (*see also* **Fake Messiahs**)
Scientific Scams
20th Century, 1900 and before, Ancient
UFO Hoaxes

NOTE: All following entries in brackets refer to cross-references within the text to other entries. All other entries are given in full.

ALIEN ANIMALS
Giant Penguin Hoax, the Hampstead Seal, Loch Ness Monster, (Eric Shipton), Yeti.

ART FORGERIES
Michael Bidlo, Elmyr de Hory, Dietrich Fey and Lothar Malskat, Eric Hebborn, Tom Keating, Mona Lisa, David Stein, (Eduardo de Valfierno), Han Van Meegeren.

CONMEN and FRAUD
Conmen: Clarence Adams, Arnold and Slack, Hugo Baruch ('Jack Bilbo'), Arthur Furguson, Maundy Gregory, Oscar Merril Hartzell, Victor Lustig, Gaston Bullock Means, James Addison Reavis, J. Bam Morrison, Philip Riley, Joseph Weill, Williamson Gang. **Counterfeiters**: José Beraha, William Brockway, 'Russian Free Enterprise?'. **Fraud**: Sir Edmund Backhouse, Jabez Balfour, David Begelman, Horatio Bottomley, ('Mr Chern'), Computer Fraud, Counterfeiters, Marthe Hanau, Thérèse Humbert, Gregor MacGregor, Antonio Jiminez Moreno, Carlo Ponzi, (Arthur Virgilio Alves Reis), Six S Job, South Sea Bubble, Franz Tausend, 'Winegate', Dorothy Mae Woods, Yazoo Land Frauds. **Fraud in Sport**: Brussels Marathon, (Rosie Ruiz). **Political Fraud**: William Randolph Hearst, Richard Nixon, Zinoviev Letter. **Sexual Cons**: Celestial Bed, Mary Toft, Giovanni Vigliotto. (*See also* **Sexual Impostors**.) **Super-Salesmen**: Arthur Furguson, Victor Lustig, Solun Osmun.

DISAPPEARANCES
Donald Crowhurst, David Lang, Glenn Miller, John Stonehouse.

EXPLORATION HOAXES
James Bruce, Richard E. Byrd, Sebastian Cabot, Christopher Columbus, Frederick E. Cook, Donald Crowhurst, Greenland, (Iceland), Cesare Maestri, Robert E. Peary, Senoi, (Kilton Stewart), Tasaday Tribe, Amerigo Vespucci.

FAKE MESSIAHS
David Berg, End-of-the-World Scams, L. Ron Hubbard, 'Billy' Meier, Rajneesh, (Hans Rosenfeld), (John Smyth-Pigott), (Joanna Southcott), Televangelists, John Thom, White Brotherhood of Kiev. (*See also* **Religions and Cults**.)

HISTORICAL HOAXES
Alchemy, Anti-Semitic Hoaxes, Arthur's Grave, Christianity, Donation of Constantine, Pope Joan, Richard III, Rosicrucians, Shroud of Turin.

HOAXES IN WARFARE
Ievno Azeff, (Black radio), (D-Day Landings), Rudolf Hess, Hoaxes in Warfare, Reginald Jones, (*Maletta*), ('Major William Martin'), Benito Mussolini, Lord Norwich, Presidential Nuclear Launch Authority, Harry Reichenbach, Percy Toplis, Thomas Walker.

IMAGINARY LANDS and MAKE-BELIEVE
Kawa, Sir John Mandeville, Senoi, Tasaday Tribe, Unicorn Hoax.

IMPOSTORS
20th century: Frank Abnagale, Anna Anderson, Ievno Azeff, Archibald Belaney, John Blay-Miezeh, Harry Domela, David Hampton, Rudolf Hess, Percy Toplis, Wilhelm Voight, Stanley Weyman. **19th century**: James Barry, Caraboo, Revd Wilfred Ellis, Gregor MacGregor, Maria Monk, James Addison Reavis, John Thom, Tichborne Claimant. **1800 and before**: Cagliostro, Martin Guerre, Saint-Germain. **Fake Professors**: Ferdinand Waldo Demara, Marvin Hewitt. **Literary Impostors**: Archibald Belaney (Grey Owl), (Asa Carter), Linda Davison, George Dupre, Will James, Lobsang Rampa. **Royal Impostors**: Anna Anderson, Stella Chiappini, Horace Cole, Harry Domela, Jim Moran, Karl Wilhelm Naundorff, Otrefief, (Lambert Simnel), Perkin Warbeck, Sarah Wilson. **Sexual Impostors**: James Barry, D'Eon de Beaumont, Concepción Jurado, Hadju Karoly, Jerry Dean Michael. (*See also* **Sexual Cons**.)

LITERARY HOAXES
Modern: Rutherford Aris, Hugo Baruch (Jack Bilbo), Archibald Belaney (Grey Owl), Carlos Castaneda, Janet Cooke, Linda Davison, George Dupre, Graham Greene, Lillian Hellman, *Hitler Diaries*, Mark Hofman, Clifford Irving, *Kawa* (*The Cruise of the*), Will James, (Konrad Kujau), Doris Lessing, Lobsang Rampa, Thomas Walker, David Wilkening. **19th century**: John Payne Collier, Jacob and Wilhelm Grimm, Maria Monk, Moses Shapira, Thomas James Wise. **Pre-1800**: Thomas Chatterton, William Henry Ireland, James Macpherson, Iolo Morganwg, Bishop Thomas Percy, George Psalmanazar, Rudolf Eric Raspe, William Shakespeare, George Washington, (Edward Williams). **Medieval and Ancient**: Aesop, Sir John Mandeville.

MEDIA HOAXES and PRANKS
Alan Abel, Humphry Berkeley, Horace Cole, 'Disgruntled Employee' Scams, Edward VII Coronation Hoax, Hollywood Hoaxes, Theodore Edward Hook, Reginald Jones, Sophie Lloyd, Jim Moran, Rawson Pickard, Hugh Troy, Stanley Weyman. **In Journalism**: Bathtub Hoax, Cathouse Ranch, William Randolph Hearst, Herschel Hoax, Ice Worm Festival, Mike McGrady, H.L. Mencken, Morris Newburger, Harry Reichenbach, Louis T. Stone ('The Winsted Liar'), Travelling Stones, Wild Animal Hoax. **On Radio and TV**: April Fool's Day Hoaxes, Muriel Gray, (Frank Sinatra), (Spaghetti Hoax), Orson Welles, Quiz Show Hoaxes. **Pranks**: Alan Abel, April Fool's Day Hoaxes, Michael Bidlo, Monte Cazazza, Abbie Hoffman, Theodore Edward Hook, Boyd Rice, Joey Skaggs, Unicorn Hoax, Jeffrey Vallance.

Telephone Hoaxes: Barry Alfonso, Reginald Jones, Victor Lewis-Smith, Telephone Hoaxes. **Theatre**: Ken Campbell.

PARANORMAL HOAXES
Aetherius Society, Amityville Ghost Scam, Bermuda Triangle, (Arnall Bloxham), (Channelling), (Sir Arthur Conan Doyle), Cosmic Joker, Cottingley Fairies, Gerard Croiset, Crop Circles, 'False Memory Syndrome', Uri Geller, (Daniel Dunglass Home), Harry Houdini, Peter Hurkos, Levitation, Mediums, Carlos Mirabelli, (Bridey Murphy), (Eusapia Palladino), Past-Life Memories, Harry Price, Psychic Surgery, James 'The Amazing' Randi, William Roy, Saint-Germain, Ted Serios, Mother Shipton, Sirius Mystery, (Spiritualism). (*See also* **UFO Hoaxes**.)

RELIGIONS and CULTS
Anti-Semitic Hoaxes, Christianity, Cosmic Joker, Donation of Constantine, Hell, Hell under Siberia Hoax, L. Ron Hubbard, (Jim Jones), (David Koresh), Rosicrucians, Mythical Hoaxes and Hoaxers, (Protocols of the Elders of Zion), (Scientology), Shroud of Turin, Sirius Mystery. (*See also* **Fake Messiahs**.)

SCIENTIFIC SCAMS
20th century: Bruno Bettelheim, 'Doc' Brinkley, Sir Cyril Burt, Sir Arthur Conan Doyle, 'False Memory Syndrome', Fossil Forgeries, Sigmund Freud, (Glozel Mystery), Paul Kammerer, Trofim Lysenko, (Piltdown Man), Senoi, Franz Tausend, (Arthur Smith Woodward). **1900 and before**: Cardiff Giant, Celestial Bed, Anton Mesmer, Sir Isaac Newton, Ptolemy, QWERTY, (Ignatz Roderick), (Edward Simpson), X-ray-proof Underwear Hoax. **Ancient**: Alchemy.

UFO HOAXES
George Adamski, Aetherius Society, 'False Memory Syndrome', Gulf Breeze Mystery, Hamilton's Airship Hoax, the Martian Head, 'Billy' Meier, Roswell Incident, (Whitley Strieber), UFO Abductions.